Experiencing Difference

Experiencing Difference

EDITED BY CARL E. JAMES

Fernwood Publishing • Halifax

Editing: Douglas Beall
Cover image: Judith Baldwin
Design and production: Beverley Rach
Printed and bound in Canada by: Hignell Printing Limited

A publication of:
Fernwood Publishing
Box 9409, Station A
Halifax, Nova Scotia
B3K 5S3

Fernwood Publishing Company Limited gratefully acknowledges the financial support of the Ministry of Canadian Heritage and the Canada Council for the Arts for our publishing program.

Canadian Cataloguing in Publication Data

Main entry under title:

Experiencing difference
ISBN 1-55266-023-0

1. Differentiation (Sociology) 2. Social perception. I. James, Carl, 1952-

HM1041.E96 2000 305 C00-950044-8

Contents

Acknowledgements

I owe a tremendous debt to all the contributors—my colleagues, friends and family—who have so willingly participated in this project. I have been inspired by their enthusiasm, support, belief in this project and, of course, their dedication to social justice and activism. I am encouraged by their perceptions of this project as an opportunity to advance their activist work and challenge well-entrenched oppressive attitudes and practices. I am very grateful to all of the contributors, not only for their essays with their personal stories, but also for their stimulating conversations and challenges that helped me to stretch my understanding of difference. I remain convinced that our individual and collective contributions will certainly further the debates and discussions of difference, diversity and identities.

A very special thanks goes to Celia Haig-Brown for her support and insights in helping me with this project, and for her encouragement during the moments when I questioned the worthiness of this endeavour. Celia gave generously of her time and energy during a particularly demanding period of her professional life. For me, our conversation which forms the concluding chapter represents the high point of this project and tangible evidence of rewarding work together.

To Gordon Pon, Leanne Taylor, Maxine Bramble, Kai James and Toni Chahley I express my sincere gratitude for their contributions, their ideas, research assistance, and help in reading various iterations of the manuscript. To Elma Thomas who, as on many other projects, has been consistent with administrative support and computer know-how, I say thanks. Because of her reliable support during important moments, I was able to complete tasks and meet deadlines. Thanks also to Hannah Wilson and Belawati Husain, whose word-processing skills and general assistance were also valuable in the completion of this project. And to Junya Ho and Liat Jacob, I say thanks; their computer expertise was very helpful at a crucial time in the production of the manuscript.

I acknowledge with gratitude the superb editorial work of Douglas Beall. The care with which he worked with our prose, and the detailed revisions he provided, have certainly helped to strengthen the ways we have communicated our ideas. I am grateful for the cooperative way in which publisher Errol Sharpe and his staff of Fernwood Publishing facilitated this final publication process. Errol's enthusiasm, support, confidence in this project, and counsel have been essential in bringing this project to fruition.

Finally, I acknowledge my friends, relatives and son, Kai, who have been consistent supporters and have played a critical role in my work with the complexities of difference. Through your conversations, challenges and understandings you have contributed to this book, and I thank you; and with you, I look forward to a Canada that is truly respectful and accepting of difference.

Contributors

Carl E. James teaches in the Faculty of Education and in the School of Social Work at York University, Toronto. A former youth worker with an education in sociology, he teaches courses in foundations of education, urban education and practitioner research. He has published in the areas of race and identity, anti-racism, multiculturalism, and sports socialization.

Kathryn Alexander was born and raised in North Vancouver, British Columbia, across the water from where her grandparents settled in the early 1900s. Kathryn's interests have taken her to Simon Fraser University, where she is completing doctoral studies in the curriculum program in the Faculty of Education. She also teaches socio-cultural theories of language and writing in the English Department of Simon Fraser University. Robert, Kathryn's twin brother, is interested in, among other things, the mystical and technical. He is a self-taught computer whiz, and still wants to become a mad scientist when he grows up. Kathryn's research interests include exploring curriculum as genre; feminist textual discourse theory; and qualitative research methodologies.

Maxine Bramble is a doctoral candidate in education at York University. Her doctoral research looks at the relationship between biography and pedagogy in the awork of second-generation, Black, Caribbean-Canadian teachers with students of Caribbean heritage. Her broader research interests include Caribbean sayings and proverbs, languages, and diasporic identity.

Kevin G. Davison is a Ph.D. candidate with the Faculty of Education at the University of South Australia in Adelaide. His doctoral research interest is in the area of masculinities and bodies in schools. He is currently a part-time faculty member with the Department of Education at Mount Saint Vincent University in Halifax, Nova Scotia, and a research assistant on a major project on masculinity and schooling. He has taught graduate courses on masculinities and literacies, research literacies, and courses in educational foundations.

Carolyn Ewoldt is a professor in the Faculty of Education at York University in Toronto. She previously worked as a research specialist at Gallaudet University in Washington, D.C., for ten years.

Tara Goldstein is an associate professor at the Ontario Institute for Studies in Education at the University of Toronto, where she works in both the pre-service teacher education and graduate education programs. She teaches courses on anti-discrimination education and critical ethnography. Her research interests include the education of immigrant adolescents, schooling in multilingual communities, playwriting as critical ethnography, and applied theatre research. These interests have come together in a play she has written called "Hong Kong, Canada" (1999).

Fyre Jean Graveline, Ph.D., is a Metis (Cree) Traditionalist, feminist, anti-racist, scholar, teacher, healer, activist and mother. She has worked in the fields of education and social work for more than twenty-five years, consistently challenging individuals and organizations to examine their oppressive, Eurocentric, patriarchal, homophobic attitudes and practices. In her book, *Circle Works: Transforming Eurocentric Consciousness,* Dr. Graveline combines Aboriginal teachings with feminist and anti-racist theory and practice to document her daily lived experience as a teacher/healer/activist. She is the director of the First Nations and Aboriginal Counseling Degree Program in the school of Health Studies at Brandon University, Manitoba.

Celia Haig-Brown teaches in the Faculty of Education at York University. She is the author of three books, including *Resistance and Renewal: Surviving the Indian Residential School.* In 1996, she moved from her home province of British Columbia to Toronto.

Denny Hunte was born in the Caribbean and immigrated to Toronto with his siblings and parents in 1967. He holds a degree in Social Work and has worked as a youth worker and social service worker. He is currently employed by the City of Toronto in the Community Services Department.

Judy Iseke-Barnes is a faculty member at the Ontario Institute for Studies in Education at the University of Toronto in the Department of Sociology and Equity Studies in Education. Her research focuses on Aboriginal educator issues. Dr. Iseke-Barnes' teaching and activism focuses on Aboriginal and Indigenous knowledge, culture and technology and on creating awareness of equity issues in both teacher and graduate education.

Kai James currently attends high school and has been a member of the basketball team. He is completing his OAC (Ontario Academic Credit) year and plans to attend university. In addition to basketball, his interests include engineering science, chess, creative writing, and surfing the Net.

Didi Khayatt is an associate professor at the Faculty of Education of York University and the director of the York Centre for Feminist Research. In the past she was a co-ordinator of the bilingual Women's Studies Programme at Glendon College, York University, and a secondary school teacher. She holds a Ph.D. in Sociology of Education and has published works dealing with gender, race, sexuality and social class.

David G. Mason, Ph.D., was born in Lloydminster, Saskatchewan, and calls Edmonton, Alberta, home. He was educated at the Mackay School for the Deaf in Montreal; Canadian Union College, Lacombe, Alberta; Gallaudet University; Western Maryland College; and University of Alberta. He has worked as a teacher at the Alberta School for the Deaf, as an adjunct professor at the University of Alberta, and he currently works as an assistant professor at York University. He is actively involved in both the Deaf and hearing communities.

Elizabeth McGibbon is a nurse with over twenty years of clinical practice experience in community and institutional settings. Most recently, she designed and implemented Atlantic Canada's first health service for homeless young people. She completed her Master of Nursing at Dalhousie University in 1999, concentrating on issues of oppression in theory and practice. She also started doctoral studies at the University of Toronto in 1999, with a focus on the fields of mental health and traumatic stress. She lives in Halifax, Nova Scotia, with her partner Patrick Gardner and their two daughters, Emily and Sophie.

Bina Mehta is a Gujarati-speaking South Asian Canadian woman who immigrated to Canada from East Africa. She is interested in issues of identity, race and place and teaches at Trent University and in local high schools in Peterborough, Ontario. Currently, she is developing a bibliography of anti-racist training materials for the Canadian Race Relations Foundation, in a continuing effort to combine academia and community-based education.

Karen Meyer is the director of the Centre for the Study of Curriculum and Instruction at the University of British Columbia. She holds a M.S. degree in the interdisciplinary study of Cognitive Psychology and Natural Science. Her Ph.D. is in Curriculum and Instruction, with a focus on Science Education. Her interests lie in curriculum theory and pedagogy;

in her research and teaching, she explores alternative ways of making curriculum relevant and accessible to students. She is particularly interested in the connection between the body and mind as they relate to learning.

Gordon Pon is pursuing his doctorate in Education at York University. He is interested in the areas of anti-racism education, globalization, identity, and the schooling of the Chinese in the diaspora. He has a master's degree in Social Work from Carleton University and is currently working with homeless youth and ESL students.

Lorna Renooy has worked in the area of body image and appearance-related issues for more than ten years. In 1995, she received her Master of Education from the Ontario Institute in Education, University of Toronto. She currently lives in Toronto.

Belle Richardson, the daughter of Boyce and Shirley Richardson, is a proprietor of a shop in Hermosa Beach, California, where she resides.

Boyce Richardson is a writer and filmmaker who has specialized for fifty years in human rights issues. He lives in Ottawa.

Robert Richardson, son of Boyce and Shirley Richardson, is a renovation carpenter, social activist and part-time community college instructor teaching courses that cover social issues. He lives in Toronto.

Sandra Schecter is a member of the Faculty of Education, York University, where she teaches courses in language pedagogy and research methodology. An ethnolinguist, she has published on language planning, language education, and language socialization.

Kevin Spooner is an Anglo-Canadian who was raised in a working-class family in the small Ontario town of Collingwood. He is a Ph.D. candidate at Carleton University in the Department of History and teaches part-time with the Canadian Studies Department at Trent University. His research interests include issues related to Canada's global, national and individual identities.

Leanne E. Taylor grew up in Eastern Ontario. She has studied at both Queen's University and York University and presently resides in Toronto, where she recently completed her master's degree in Sociology. In her graduate work, she explores the complexities of mixed-race identity, race and racial classification, and the paradox of racelessness. She is currently pursuing her Ph.D. in Sociology.

Susan A. Tilley was born and bred in Newfoundland. She grew up in St. John's, the capital, but reminds others that her mother and father were from "around the bay." She began work in education as a high school teacher in Labrador. After completing a doctoral program at Simon Fraser University, Susan began work as an assistant professor in the graduate and undergraduate departments of the Faculty of Education at Brock University. She teaches courses in Curriculum Studies. Her research interests include curriculum theory, feminist and cultural studies, teacher education, and qualitative research/critical ethnography.

Cathy van Ingen is completing her Ph.D. in Physical Education at the University of Alberta. Her research draws from cultural geography and explores how the spatial and the sexual constitute one another, specifically how sexual minorities create spaces and how these spaces become sites of resistance. Her work focuses on the Toronto Frontrunners, a running club for gay, lesbian, bisexual, and transgendered runners.

Kevin Wilson is an autoworker and union activist who lives in Windsor, Ontario. He has been employed at DaimlerChrysler's Windsor Assembly Plant since 1993. He is a regular contributor to Toronto's *NOW* magazine, is currently the labour columnist for CBC Radio Windsor Morningwatch, has contributed to *Canadian Forum* and has appeared on CBC Newsworld's "Counterspin."

Introduction
Grappling with Differences

> There is no better point of entry into a critique or reflection than one's own experience. It is not the end point, but the beginning of the exploration of the relationship between the personal and the social and therefore the political. And this connecting process, which is also a discovery, is the real pedagogic process, the "science" of social science. (Bannerji 1991: 67)

Questions regarding difference have long dominated the interactions of Canadians, particularly given the multicultural character of our society. Canada's multicultural ideology has often framed the discourse of difference in a way that views some people as "Canadians" and others as foreigners. The inference is that only "others" have ethnicity, race and different cultures, while "Canadians" (read Whites) do not.

Within the past decade, the questions have become more open, persistent, disturbing and even hostile, as individuals positioning themselves as the moral and cultural leaders and guardians of our society attempt to impose their version of the values and norms that constitute what it means to be a Canadian. Others, opposing marginalization, negation and degradation, have challenged normative assertions that contribute to their being viewed as "different" and to a reading of their bodies as foreign, deviant, fragile or limited. Related to these challenges are calls for recognition of the diversity, complexity and variance that are part of every society, neighbourhood and group, and hence an acceptance, and not mere tolerance, of differences that are to be found in any group of people.

In attempts to show acceptance and/or tolerance, at times we tend to talk about "sameness." We have all heard the comments: "We are all the same" and "We are all human beings." This notion of sameness is an attempt to obliterate difference, which ironically reimposes difference. For if difference were not an issue, why would there be a need to assert sameness? Often, this claim of the sameness of human beings is related to individuals' efforts to avoid charges of racism, sexism, ableism, heterosexism, homophobia, xenophobia, classism and other such characterizations, usually informed by the very "isms" and phobias that individuals are trying to avoid. What might be considered non-racist comments in fact reflect racism, as represented by the failure to acknowledge the racism which underlies the construction of difference that prompts the original statement.

Conversely, in our liberalism and bid to embrace difference, we may say, "Everyone is different," in other words, that experiences of difference are common among people. Asserting such commonality implies that there is nothing unique about the experiences of a particular individual or group, and that one person's experience with difference is the same as another's. It is assumed that in understanding the dynamics of our own or another person's differences (be they ethnicity, gender, sexuality, dis/ability, race and so forth), we are able to understand those of others. In our interactions or communications, we tend to borrow from our experience and understanding of difference and apply it to others. (In the same way, we borrow from our sameness, thinking that, because we share backgrounds related to ethnicity, immigrant status, occupational position etc., our experiences are likely to be similar.) On this basis, we might hear one person say to another, "I get treated the same way," or "I have been asked the same questions by police," without giving attention to differences in social class, gender, race, ethnicity or occupational status. Nor is context considered; that is why it is not surprising to hear comments such as this from a dominant-group Canadian: "I know what it's like to be a minority because when I was in Jamaica...." Inherent in this statement is the idea that being a minority-group member in the Canadian context is the same as being one in the Jamaican context, and that in both contexts minority status is interpreted in the same way. In making such comparisons, no attention is given to the historical, social, structural or cultural realities of the societies in question.

Difference, with all its variances, ambiguities and discrepancies, is a fundamental aspect of our human existence. It is a reality that cannot be avoided; neither can we avoid the messy, complicated, unpredictable and contentious realities of human interactions. Seeing everyone as the same, not acknowledging difference, is to deny the diversity, complexity and contradictions within society, groups and, correspondingly, the multifaceted identities of individuals. Hence, experience of another's difference is likely to occasion ambivalence, uncertainties, tensions and inconsistencies—a "messy swamp," to borrow a metaphor from Loughran and Northfield (1996) in reference to the teaching and learning situation. They describe this swamp as "an array of interconnected sets of events, personalities, social and intellectual abilities, individuals and groups, all of which are seen differently depending on the time and perspective of viewing. So to the casual observer it may appear to be a swamp, but to the skilled pedagogue it is a kaleidoscope from which different possibilities emerge" (1996: 51). And should there be any debate as to whether the swamp is an appropriate metaphor, the authors add, quoting a colleague, "The swamp is a wonderfully rich and diverse biosystem. Lots happening, lots growing, but only very slowly evolving" (1996: 53).

This anthology emerges from my attempts to navigate this messy swamp—the complex, variable and unpredictable materiality of difference—in my own interactions, particularly in teaching situations dealing with issues of equity, access and merit. Quite often in such situations, I can expect to facilitate discussions in which students' articulation of difference is premised on some form of ranking, and on assertions about their own group's position in the social structure in relation to others, based on race, gender, class, sexuality, dis/ability, geography and so forth. Understandably, the identities mentioned are usually ones with which participants are familiar—their own and/or those of others they know. The challenge then is how to facilitate discussions about identities and differences without privileging some over others, collapsing differences, essentializing people, or denigrating individuals' stories. But more to the point, the question is: How do we navigate and negotiate the messy terrain of difference?

I am not convinced that an anthology can or should provide such answers. Only the source or questioner can appropriately provide the answer, since it necessarily relates to her or his experience. My hope is that the essays in this anthology will help stimulate discussion, elucidate individuals' struggles and experiences with difference and provide insights into living with differences so that our interactions, communications and relationships with each other are enhanced by acceptance of differences. If we accept the view that diversity is a reality in any group, and that freedom of choice is not a privilege but a right and entitlement of everyone, then we can expect individuals to have opportunities to experience themselves and participate in society without fear of reprisal because of look, dress, physical appearance, ability and so on. It is this desire and wish for a healthy existence that Audrey James (1999) craves when she laments the fact that her "light skin colour" contributed to the "imposed difference" she experienced in our society. She writes:

> It seems as if I am always bombarded with questions about my racial composition. I am still amazed when complete strangers meet me and ask me the question, "What are you?" as if I were some kind of alien, an aberration. In addition to being rude, jarring and out of place, the question, repeated often, scars the soul, injures the psyche, and ignites feelings of inadequacy and alienation, and further contributes to feelings of being different.... Being asked this inevitable question has become part of

> my very being and it continues to evoke a sense of despair and ambivalence that unleashes a floodgate of emotions, and opens up my entire soul to debate and scrutiny. Interactions with individuals and my relations with people always seem to be dominated by questions of race.... My identity, then, is constantly being mediated and negotiated by the identity others assign to me (both mistaken and supposedly correct).... This hypersensitivity to things racial makes me painfully aware of the complexities of growing up "different" as often experienced by individuals whose racial composition is not always homogeneous and which often crosses racial and ethnic lines. (1999: 1)

As James points out, the painful experiences of growing up with difference and living with difference as an adult fosters hypersensitivity to how one's difference is viewed and presented. Given my own experience of living with racial difference in a society where Black bodies are read in troublesome ways, one would think I would pride myself in having a sensitivity to difference and a willingness to learn about and understand other people's experiences with difference. But we can never think of ourselves as being fully prepared for the responses we might receive when we ask individuals to tell us about their differences. And while I was convinced of the worthiness of this anthology, there were times when I wondered if the project was such a good idea after all.

My communications with Lorna Renooy was one of the most revealing. I first contacted Lorna at the office of Aboutface, a support and information network concerned with facial difference. My attention was drawn to this organization through an article in its monthly magazine, *Aboutface*, in which singer Ani Aubin talked with Lorna about what it was like growing up feeling "different a lot of the time because of my birthmark" (Renooy 1999). In my initial conversation with Lorna, I asked about the organization and requested additional information. A week later, I received a package with a number of magazines and photocopies of articles (mostly by Americans) about living with facial difference. I looked for something that could be included in this anthology but found nothing I thought suitable. I contacted Lorna again and asked whether she had any essays written by Canadians that might be appropriate for my project. Within two days, Lorna sent me by e-mail an essay she had written. I read the essay and asked her permission to publish it, and at the same time I requested that she elaborate on some points. She agreed and promised to send me the revised essay later that week. Soon after, I received and responded to the following e-mail.

Friday, August 13, 1999 1:23:34 PM
From: Aboutface
Subject: Essay for book (Lorna Renooy)
To: Carl James
Dear Carl:
I think that incorporating a range of diversity issues in one book is an exciting endeavour, and one that is long overdue. I would like to participate in this effort and understand that you are working under time constraints; however, I have concerns that need to be addressed before I can feel comfortable and give further consideration to contributing to your book.

You are interested in the experience of "growing up different." Through my experience in this regard, I care a great deal about how my story and the stories of other people with differences are told. Too often people with physical differences or disabilities have been portrayed as "heroes who have overcome great challenges" or "victims who suffer because of their disfigurements." With all due respect, I don't know what you are going to say about me or this issue that I live with and care so much about. I need to see your introduction to, and writing about, these issues, to better understand how and in what context my essay will be used.

I have also come to understand that one of the issues for people with physical differences is that others are fascinated by these differences. Social norms change when you have an unusual appearance; the boundaries of privacy become blurred. Some people have expressed this as strangers "feel you owe them an explanation." Issues arise as to how people are included/used by others in the world. In order to ensure that the integrity of my writing is honoured, I want an opportunity to review any editorial changes that will be made, and the option to withdraw my entry.

I want to reiterate how wonderful I feel it is that you want to give voice to these issues. I also want you to understand that because I don't know you (or your writing), I am not comfortable with the manner in which this issue of contributing has proceeded. I feel I need a written agreement before I can allow a piece of very personal writing to be published.

This agreement would outline:

1. Context and structure of the book (including the introduction to the book and the introduction to the chapter);
2. An opportunity for me to review any editorial changes;
3. The right to withdraw my essay;

4. In the event the essay is published, the right to reproduce and distribute it as I choose.

I look forward to hearing from you.

Lorna Renooy

Friday, August 13, 1999 4:58:28 PM
From: Carl James
Subject: Essay for book (Lorna Renooy)
To: Lorna Renooy

Hi Lorna:

Thanks very much for your e-mail and for sharing your concerns. You are correct, there is the tendency to see "difference" in the ways you have identified, but I have no interest in reproducing this way of seeing "difference." I respect very much your position, and it is in that vein that I am trying to produce this book on difference. I have not written the introduction as yet, but I have attached the prospectus and the table of contents in order to show you the essays and the authors.

I am very interested in honouring your integrity and representing your work in a way that respects you and represents your political position. I see this book as an opportunity to place before readers how their/our perceptions and understandings of difference need to be critically evaluated taking into account the ways in which we have been socialized to see others and how we "other" people. Contributors are encouraged to be as political as they wish in presenting their positions. In this regard, this could also be considered a political project which aims to bring about acceptance and social change.

As I said, the introduction has not yet been written, but these are my thoughts, and the Introduction will be written after I have received all of the essays. Then I will read all of the essays and develop the introduction from there. So your input will be taken from your essay; and I have no problem in picking up the points you have made in your e-mail as a way of contextualizing the book. In fact, I quite like your challenge and feel that I am being responsible in that direction.

I should state that my interest in difference comes from my own identity regarding race and how I am classed as different, but I know that difference is more complicated and complex than that.

Certainly, authors retain the right to review editorial changes and can withdraw their pieces at any time.

I look forward to your response.

Carl

Lorna's essay in this volume further reveals the challenges of growing up different which, in turn, inform her caution and politics which I had to negotiate in soliciting her essay.

As Lorna's concerns illustrate, asking someone to publicly share personal experiences and politics is likely to be met with reservations or resistance—reservations with respect to, not only their personal, but also their professional life. As David Mason, a contributor who writes about being deaf, said to me, "I do not know if I can write something personal." Concerned about implications, some contributors debated the merits of submitting an essay that would "expose" them. Most likely, individuals' comfort with recounting their experiences and disclosing their politics is related to their perceptions of the readiness of others to listen, hear or deal with their experiences with difference, and with the professional consequences of their stories. One contributor bluntly said: "What do you want? Do you want me to come out in your book?" Thus the personal nature of these essays varies widely.

I take the view that inviting individuals to talk about difference based on their own experiences means that we have to be prepared to accept their starting points. And it is very likely that some people's view of difference will be one about which we have given little consideration. Kathryn Alexander, for example, wrote me an e-mail asking if I would accept her essay about growing up as a twin—not a commonly addressed topic—in terms of dealing with the issues twins confront, and not a topic I had considered when I was thinking of what might be presented in this volume. I later told my colleague Celia Haig-Brown that I myself have aunts and first cousins who are twins, and since they are fraternal twins, occasionally when we were together, I was asked I if were one of the twins. But that was when I was growing up, so it is not something that I have thought about in recent years; neither have I thought much of how the idea of twin-ness contributed to the construction of my cousins' identities and sense of self, even among family members. Nevertheless, I was always conscious of the fact that twin-ness runs in my family and there are twins in my generation of cousins. Kathryn Alexander's contribution, then, and the "scars" she writes about, should remind us of the variations in difference and the unique ways in which people treat issues of difference.

Generally speaking, this anthology tries to present the various ways in which difference is experienced, interpreted and articulated and not to say that all these differences can co-exist comfortably. Contributors tell of when and how they are named and/or recognized as different by others, and of their own naming and recognition of themselves as different. The essays show that gender, social class, ethnicity, race, region, appearance, dis/ability, sexuality, twin-ness, age, religion and occupational status are experienced and lived in multiple, complicated and contradictory ways. How the writers and others make sense of their differences is related to context, space and interaction. Difference, then, as the essays demonstrate, is relational, fluid, multiple and contextual, and therefore must be thought of in complex ways.

In referring to their personal and sometimes very difficult experiences, the contributors advocate a politics of difference that invites us to question and reflect on our perceptions, understandings and articulations of difference, and the extent to which we are implicated in the process of how difference gets taken up and perpetuated. This book is an attempt to frame the diverse ways in which identity, location, status and other factors are identified as differences, and how structures and conditions serve to maintain privilege for some and negation and marginalization for others.

Contributors have written in different styles and genres, which represent their respective voices and preferences. Through essays—written in narrative, journalistic and academic forms, short stories, letters, conversations and dialogues—contributors thoughtfully communicate their stories in ways that I hope will maintain interest and attention, as well as facilitate an appreciation of "layered complexities" of difference (Schuster and van Pelt 1992). Conversations with contributors sometimes served as triggers for the styles and genres they chose. Kevin Spooner and Bina Mehta's dialogue, for example, grew out of a conversation with them during my visit to a class they were co-teaching. I heard them mention their dialogue about interracial marriage, and this unique presentation turned out to be the basis of their contribution to the book. A conversation with my colleague Celia Haig-Brown, which concludes the volume, was a valuable opportunity for me to reflect on the value and implications of this book.

Obviously, while some stories provide moments to celebrate the progress that our society has made toward acceptance of differences, others may prompt us to question that progress. Any such debates is healthy; I believe that discussions about equity, inclusivity and identities, however controversial, must be engaged in if we are to move toward accepting rather than merely tolerating difference.

The essays are organized around six themes that emerged as I read them. Grouping essays of people's personal experiences around any one theme is always problematic, for the ideas communicated in the essays are diverse, but grouping them gives focus to some of the ideas and messages.

Appropriately, we start with the early experiences of contributors. Kathryn Alexander discusses the impact of the gendered lessons she and her twin brother received in school and from their peers. The theme of gendered lessons is also taken up in Kevin Davison's essay, which explores the difficulties he had—as do today's male students—"in negotiating and resisting hegemonic masculinity." He contends that bodies should be read in ways that take into account the complexities and contradictions of identities. Similarly, in their contributions, Kai James and Leanne Taylor, with reference to their Black racial identities, reinforce the point about the multiple complexities, fluidity and contradictions of identities. Both Kai and Leanne articulate the need to critically reflect on our assumptions about physical appearance. This idea is also echoed in the essay "Looking Back While Facing Forward," by Lorna Renooy.

In the section "Schooling and Difference," contributors explore how educators have responded to issues of gender, race, religion and ethnicity. With reference to her experiences as a female science student, teacher, professor and researcher, Karen Meyers examines the gendered ways in which science at the secondary school level and beyond is presented, making it inaccessible to and problematic for females. In my essay on the question of role models, I assert that it is unrealistic and limiting to expect that Black and other racialized teachers and educators will be role models. Educators, I contend, have a responsibility to be informed about the diversity of their student population and to be responsive to their needs and concerns. One of the needs that teachers should be addressing today is that of religious difference, but as Tara Goldstein indicates, educators are still a long way from dealing appropriately with this difference, and celebration of the Christian holiday of Christmas continues to be illustrative of the tensions that result from educators' limited knowledge of and inability to deal with difference. Along the same lines, Sandra Schecter illustrates how diversity has been co-opted as a rationale for schools' ineffectiveness and absence of social justice. This was evident when her son's teacher suggested he was having trouble in school because he was "not used to being in school with so much diversity"—the diversity being racial and ethnic minority students. It seems that when in doubt, blame diversity.

In modern times, the composition of the family reflects more openly the heterogeneity, complexity and unpredictability that is evident in all other institutions. And as the essays and conversations in the section on family and difference illustrate, family life is one in which members are constantly negotiating and navigating not only the expectations of society, but also the differences within the family. As the family experiences of Boyce, Robert and Belle Richardson reveal, adaptation and racial difference contributes to differences in experiences and hence the ways each family member understands and articulates his or her issues and concerns. Kevin Spooner and Bina Mehta provide insight into how one interracial couple negotiate their concerns and issues. Also using a conversational approach, Tara Goldstein talked with Chris and Chris about experiences as parents raising their son Zak in a lesbian family. For them, as Chris said, difference in family composition creates "new ways of thinking about family." That parents expect good and easy lives for their children—lives free of barriers and hurdles—is well articulated in the contributions. But most pointed is Kevin Wilson's story about the fact that his father cried when he finished university and went to work at Chrysler.

How and when difference is identified is explored in many of the contributions. But in the section entitled "Naming Difference," contributors focus on many of the specific ways in which their differences are engaged. For Judy Iseke-Barnes, it was having to respond to questions such as "Where are you from?" and "What nationality are you?" These questions indicate the desire of questioners to have Judy assist them in reading what to them appears to be an ambiguous body. Interestingly, this was not the case for Denny Hunte. But while there was no mistaking that he was a Black man, he was a member of that group of people whose identity is difficult to differentiate from one another—"they all look alike." In both cases, therefore, while differences are acknowledged, they are engaged in ways that negate the complexity and variations that are to be found among individual group members. Negation is also a theme that David Mason explores in his essay about difference as applied to deaf people. This negation is a manifestation of "audism" which, similar to racism, represents the hegemony of hearing people and the oppressive consequences for deaf people. David challenges us to think more broadly of difference, and not only of that related to race, ethnicity or language. Taking this inclusive approach, particularly when you are invested in other differences, is quite difficult, as Elizabeth McGibbon informs us in her essay exploring the learning involved in integrating social class, gender and race. She points out that unpacking previously held knowledge and becoming an advocate is pretty risky and conflicting.

The construction of differences is related to the extent to which individuals' characteristics coincide with the constructed norms of a society, community, organization or group. This, therefore, speaks to the complexity, fluidity and relational aspects of difference. Accordingly, physical (or geographic) and social contexts play a significant role in the identification of difference, and the possibility of movement within difference. This theme, "Moving into and through Difference," a phrase used by Celia Haig-Brown, informs her essay and those of Gordon Pon and Susan Tilley. For Gordon, moving through geographic spaces such as his hometown neighbourhood of Ottawa, Chinatown in downtown

Toronto and Chinatown in Markham, Ontario, revealed the complexities of being Chinese. Celia's essay brings into focus the question of who we become when we travel. She suggests that once we change contexts, we lose some part of ourselves, because we interact with different people, who through their history and experience will construct our identity in relation to theirs—hence our acquisition of difference. For instance, Susan Tilley acquired her difference as a Newfoundlander by living outside Newfoundland. While in Newfoundland, that identity never drew attention, but in other parts of the country, it prompted comments such as "You don't sound like a Newfoundlander." The essay by Carolyn Ewoldt is indicative of someone whose difference of gender was not something she had contemplated as a hurdle or barrier. However, her move into her difference of blindness, as she puts it, becoming "an other," uncovered a whole new world. Cathy van Ingen tells of confronting her difference as a lesbian and in the process confronting her own homophobia and that of others around her.

Arguably, education is vital to the process of accepting difference. But as Cole (1989: 13) contends, education is a meaningless process unless it is concerned with struggle against all forms of oppression and tyranny, whether based on ignorance, oppression, inequality or explorations. The contributors to this book echo this view and articulate the issues and concerns related to difference that must be addressed.

In the concluding section, whose theme is equity and inclusivity, Didi Khayatt advocates the teaching of equity in the classroom and contends that, in doing so, educators must understand, acknowledge and address "the power relations and the politics of the classroom." Maxine Bramble, talking about her experience in university, maintains that university educators must acknowledge difference and the diversity of experiences that students bring to their post-secondary schooling. And Fyre Jean Graveline argues for a transformation of educational curriculum that will enable educators who resist the current educational process to have hope, develop the ability to bring about change and have the power to survive.

My concluding conversation with Celia Haig-Brown pulls together themes that emerge from the essays, and we conclude that differences cannot be lumped together, but must be understood as socially constructed, relational, shifting, contextual and complex. In this conversation, we reflect on some of the themes of the essays: individuals' denial of differences, the tendency to collapse differences, how differences tend to be named and acknowledged, the ranking of difference, the refusal to categorize people based on identities, the question of privilege, the borrowing and uses of terms that might be considered exclusive to a group, the responsibility to work with and through differences, and the need for political action.

Growing Up Different

1

On Being More than One/Less than One
Exploring Twin-ness

Kathryn Alexander

My bother and I are fraternal twins. We are double eggs easy over, "dizygotic," two-egg twins born from separate but simultaneously fertilized eggs. My brother and I have been accompanied by the presence of another since before our birth. My identity and personhood have been shaped by the implacable presence of my twin. Of course, braided into this experience is the dyadic sharing of gender difference. As a boy / girl, girl / boy dyad, biological gender was the primary category of difference that we experienced throughout our childhood.

This prompts me to wonder whether, having been shaped within a multiple-birth dyad, we experience connection, similitude and multiplicity differently than "singletons" or single-birth people. In a world that values "the autonomous individual," I question whether twins experience self differently than single-birth children. I call this blur of self and salient memory of fusion "twin-ness." I wonder as well at the ways our gender awareness has been blurred or hardened at the boundaries of our twin-ness. In this chapter I explore the experience of "being a twin" with my twin brother, Rob. Later on, I consider the impact and consequences of gender difference on twin-ness, and how this difference constructed our experience of schooling and identity.

The following conversation with my family took place at a Sunday-night dinner in North Vancouver, British Columbia. I was pleased that my father, Gordon, participated, as over the years he provided a crucial and wonderful perspective as both parent and friendly observer.

Kathy: What has being a twin been like for you? I don't think we have ever really talked about it all that much.

Rob: Well, put it this way—you could always call on your most dependable friend, and if you ever wanted to play, there was always someone there. That was an integral part of our existence—just playing together.

But first a qualifier. It seems strange for me to write about "being a twin" under the rubric of identity and difference, because it seems so inconsequential in the scheme of things. Twins happen everywhere. It should be just one accidental part of a whole set of markers, such as a family's history, immigrant, class or ethnic status. Perhaps it is telling that being a twin felt significant because we were raised in such a thoroughly middle-class, White and homogenous fifties/sixties suburban western community that for a long time, being a twin was the only identifiable characteristic that distinguished us from the stifling, milky swarm of all the other kids.

A few years ago, my brother shared an early memory with me. When we reconstructed the time frame, we figured we were probably under a year old. Rob recalls the sensation of lying on a blanket in the dappled shade of a tree. We were lying head to head. This was our mother's strategy, because we would distract one another if we could see each other, and she desperately wanted us to nap. He said he remembers having an awareness of his being extending out from the top of his head to engulf me, so that we were linked. In our conversation, he related this memory to my father:

Kathy: Robbie has this memory of being an infant and it's quite powerful.

Gordon: Is it a dream?

Rob: It's more than that. Sometimes I feel that it is prebirth, the way it feels. I remember feeling this other presence next to me.

Gordon: Maybe it was in the womb.

Rob: Possibly. What I feel is this total sense of oneness. Yet I sense also—it's like we are the same, yet it's not just my body. It is like an extension of myself. We're the same; it's hard to describe. There is a certain unity that I sense from way back. I guess there are two hearts beating, or something, is the only way I could tell it was different. Other than that we are the same. There was such a sense of peace and harmony existing between the two of us, that—we were one, and it was a oneness.... Even after birth. I guess some of it comes from just lying around together, but I remember coldness though, I remember coldness.

When I mentioned to a friend that I was going to write about being a twin, she lent me Arundhati Roy's remarkable novel *The God of Small Things*. I was startled at how accurately it depicted the physical and emotional qualities of some of our earliest memories. The book is written from the perspective of the female fraternal twin, Rahel, and I was fascinated at how well it captured the complexity of the "beyond-the-skin" connection of twins and articulated my personal "feeling thoughts" (Flax 1993) of being more than one/less than one. In the opening chapter, Roy writes:

> The confusion lay in a deeper, more secret place. In those early amorphous years when memory had only just begun, life was full of Beginnings and no Ends, and Everything was Forever. Esthappen and Rahel thought of themselves together as Me, and separately, individually, as We or Us. As though they were a rare breed of Siamese twins, physically separate, but with joint identities. Now, these years later, Rahel has a memory of waking up one night giggling at Estha's funny dream. (1997: 4)

I too have been woken by my brother's dreams, and we took it for granted that we shared our dreams. We loved the flying dreams the most. In the morning we would compare details of our travels. During the day we'd practise jumping down the stairs of our hallway, opening the outside door in case we got a good flying jump started. Most of our play was based on imaginary scenarios with well-rehearsed plots and villains. Perhaps twins develop better memories than single-birth children, because they are constantly provided with opportunities to remember, replay and rehearse.

Throughout my childhood, I never knew a time without Robbie; we ate, played, shared childhood diseases, fought, bathed and dreamed together. We negotiated the streets as a team: he was the explorer, I was the communicator. He chased garter snakes and I chased fairies. Mom and Dad used to fill up the bathtub to the brim and let us scoot back and forth like little pink torpedoes. Our father lost many watches those first years, dashing into lakes to grab us at the last minute. As toddlers, we'd wade up to our pug noses, happily hand-in-hand and oblivious to danger. This suggests that from the parents' perspective, raising twins is perhaps exponentially more demanding than raising two separate birth children.

My mother was well into her pregnancy when her doctor first realized that she was carrying twins. She told me often about that moment, when he paused, listened again to his stethoscope, then held up two fingers and said, "There are two heartbeats."

I have learned recently, on the World Wide Web and in newspaper articles, that the likelihood of having twins is on the rise; the word "epidemic" has been used. Gene Hayden (1998) reports that twin births have increased by 35 percent during the last fifteen years, due to fertility drugs and older baby-boomer parents. Soon there may be new sociological categories worth studying—"parents of twins," "twin attachment theory," "twin genetics."

A few years ago, I wrote a creative piece for a retreat on the experience of being a twin. It was after I had heard my brother's earliest memory, that I first considered the possibility there might be something tangible about twin energy or twin identity. In my taped conversations with my brother, I have tried not to put words in our mouths that are overly adult-theorized, and I have tried to listen to the unspoken languages of our child bodies that lived alongside one another and the dialogue between our adult bodies that now live apart.

I almost cannot tell a story about my childhood without using the pronoun "we." And, writing down stories about "us" feels peculiar, because in these retold and remembered stories, I recognize that we have become familiar archetypal characters in a childhood landscape of Kathy-and-Robbie, Robbie-and-Kathy. Perhaps it is no coincidence that one of our favourite fairy stories was Hansel and Gretel, which raised some anxiety among our cousins. The only time in my entire childhood when I was not with my brother was during early adolescence when I was hospitalized for a ruptured appendix.

Since I began thinking about writing this, I have been playing with the expression "more than one/less than one" in order to try and articulate the contradiction of having been in a relationship with another person since before birth, yet obviously separate and unique as individuals. I sometimes wonder if a single member of a pair of twins is more, or less, than the combined unit. I have wondered when thinking about our twin identity if (I/we) are more than the exterior extensions of the limits of (my/our) bodies. Where does the we/me boundary begin when we take into account the importance of autobiography, language, memory and physical embodiment in the development of self? Roy writes of Estha and Rahel's birth and the connection of the "Siamese souls":

> They emerged without much fuss, within eighteen minutes of each other. Two little ones, instead of one big one. Twin seals, slick with their mother's juices. Wrinkled with the effort of being born. Ammu checked them for deformities before she closed her eyes and slept. She counted four eyes, four ears, two mouths, two noses, twenty fingers and twenty perfect toe-nails. She didn't notice the single Siamese soul. (1997: 49)

My brother and I are together in all of our pictures as blobby infants and roly-poly toddlers; apart from the length of my hair, we are indistinguishable unless dressed up "for good," usually in the similar uniform of T-shirts and overalls, shorts hanging under our rounded tummies, or baggy-bummed in our footed sleepers. And at birthday parties—one cake, same number of candles, "to Kathie and Robbie." We always shared "that special day." When I put a ten-year stockpile of photographs into albums last spring, I noticed that they were an indistinguishable series of summer birthday celebrations or Christmases. We had never spent a birthday apart—until our fortieth birthday, when I committed the ultimate sin and left town. I escaped my middle-age benchmark and flew to L.A. to spend "our" birthday with my dearest woman friend and her family. When I called to tell my twin that I did not intend to be in town, I was really asking for absolution and forgiveness. It hurt—and a week later when we had dinner together, I realized that perhaps I had made the wrong choice. I remember waking up in L.A. and momentarily wondering, "Did I do the right thing?" No, but it wasn't the wrong thing either, it was just differentiation, a painful effect of being "more than one / less than one."

I wonder how important the lifelong dynamic of differentiation is in the lives of twins. What I call "differentiation" is the constant tension between a life lived alongside another and the mapping of genetic, familial and sociocultural characteristics that constantly point out one's simultaneous sameness and difference. Certainly differentiation is more dramatic for identical twins, but it is also present more subtly in fraternal dyads. It is interesting to consider how profoundly the accident of "gender" has played out in the dynamic of our twin-ness. Our parents worked hard at not favouring one child over the other, but they could not buffer the effects of the larger world.

I was the first born, by seventeen minutes, so I was able to seize the lifelong advantage of being the eldest child. Robbie, however, was the first male offspring in our generation of the extended family. This fact of birth order and gender was vividly brought home in 1973, when on an officially certified family genealogy, my brother was named as the first-born male issue and I was absent, as were my two older female cousins. It was the first time in our lives I had faced the reality that girls really do not count, or, in this case, were not counted. While growing up, I reluctantly accepted certain inequities in the distribution of what girls and boys could or could not do, but it is this particular, curious erasure that still resonates almost twenty-five years later when I stand and read the careful calligraphy that tells the partial tale of a family history.

As to other facts of differentiation, I recall how Rob was encouraged to explore and I was protected; how his toys were technical, mechanical and scientific, and mine seemed to be dolls, dolls and more dolls. I pull out an old Christmas photo where we look like poster children for the

1950s. Robbie is wearing a cowboy hat and sitting inside a brilliant red roadster. I am triumphantly clutching a Betsy Wetsy doll. Now I am embarrassed by the exaggerated pink and blue evidence of our gendered shaping. However, from the inside of memory and feelings, I re-echo Roy's characters Rahel and Estha, who thought of themselves together as Me, and separately as We or Us. I wonder whether this juncture of fusion and separation circulates more around fraternal or gender differences. I wonder how it intrudes now into our adult lives. I have experienced the sensation that my own successes and journey into academe are transgressions, because it was my brother who was the "scientist," while I was the dreamer and talker, the girl who would be a mommy.

In truth, my brother and I are in many ways quite different from each other, but how to tease out which are nature versus nurture differences I cannot determine. I can catalogue our physical differences quite easily—which I think comes as second nature to twins and their families. I was born head first, he was breech; I am right-handed, he is a lefty; I take after the plumpish Aberdeen aunties on my father's side, Rob takes after the wiry, peat-house Hebridean grandfather on my mother's side. Rob has the curly auburn hair and deep hazel-brown eyes of my mother; I carry my father's face, the chestnut hair and grey hazel eyes. When I say I have a twin brother, most people reply immediately: "Are you identical?" It was Robbie who developed our now-standard reply, "Yes, but *she* shaves the moustache!"

I can most certainly say that my world view has a peculiar girl/boy aspect. When I was quite little, perhaps three years old, I decided all families were composed of sets of twin girls and boys raised together, who then got married and had their own set of twins; a little boy and girl. After a particularly long day with my brother, I went to my mother demanding, "Do I have to marry Robbie when I grow up?" One more anxious moment for my mother; one very confusing but definite answer for me. I knew I didn't have to marry my brother when I grew up, but the alarm in my mother's voice indicated that I would have to marry someone else's brother. Confusing. I probably still sort all people I meet into two categories: like/not like Robbie. From there the rest of the details sort themselves out.

A few years ago we participated in a twin study conducted at the University of British Columbia. I believe the study was exploring genetic markers for personality and addiction patterns. My brother and I were sent a thick wad of survey questions, which we were instructed to fill out separately. We dutifully answered hundreds of questions about our lives, personalities and preferences; all the while, this question of twin-ness hovered in the background. By the time I finished my questionnaires, I was aware of how profoundly my childhood twin experiences still resonated in and influenced my adult life. In particular, I realized that our first experiences of separation and difference were linked to schooling and reading. I remembered that my first separation from my brother occurred in the classroom. This separation was further reinforced on the playground by the "boys against girls" rules. In grade two I learned how to read silently and for the first time in my life I entered a realm where my brother could not physically join me. I recall my mother telling me that when I began to read, I entered the world of books with such passion and absorption that I completely tuned out the world and my brother. The world of reading was the one place where he could not accompany (or bother) me. I left Robbie completely and utterly alone, and this was a hurtful experience for him. He began to tease me about being a bookworm, and I retorted that he was just a smelly puppy-dog-tail boy. He took to the backwoods to play with the other boys, and I settled into the escape of my stories. Our "alienation" was more or less complete by grade four, the first time we stopped being in classes together.

Rob: I guess the twin-ness kind of left around grade three.

Kathy: So okay, so return to that thing about reading, because that was a big thing, about me being the librarian and reading books. Because I retreated into the world of books.

Rob: What happened then was, I guess, you were a little detached with the social thing, how the girls were treating you then. I couldn't read it that much but didn't really see you interacting so much with your roles, because I was just doing my own thing. But I noticed that you talked more, and you just grabbed books, and I remember YOU talking to me and you saying "Books, books are what I like." You'd say that to me. "Why don't you come out to play?" and you'd just say, "No, I've got my books." And I used to kind of bug you about that. And I used to say, "Bookworm, bookworm."

In the years that followed, I remember us as living under the same roof as strangers or, worse, guerrilla snipers, competing, quarrelling and enduring the conflict until we left the stifling constraints of elementary school and "remet" in our adolescence and once more became best friends as allies against our parents. Years later, at my wedding, Rob raised the toast to the bride. He claimed the privilege as the person who had known the bride since *before* she was born. Rob spoke of books, of how they had always been there—more and more of them—and of how that was really scary and had made all the difference between us. I felt the tears and realized that I had never known how profoundly I had abandoned him when I began to read. I realized also that I had carried the burden of doing well in school while my brother struggled. However, Rob puts it differently:

Rob: School for me was not satisfying, because it never really touched on anything that was meaningful for me. A couple of times, but I was mostly brushed off....

Kathy: So what was it like for you? I seemed to do a bit better in school. I succeeded, I fitted in a little bit better once I got into high school.

Rob: Women generally do.

Kathy: Women generally do?

Rob: For me, [men] are still kind of scattered; I mean I was scattered then too.

When I first thought about writing this, I looked around my community to talk to other twins. I discovered that we were everywhere. There were at least two sets in my housing co-op alone. I spoke with a colleague who is married to a twin, has identical twin sons and has written a book on the topic. I talked to another graduate student, Janet, who has a fraternal twin brother and discussed her school experiences with me. I sent her an e-mail with some of the questions I was wrestling with, and her replies seemed like a form of validation—at least around the issue of fraternal gender relations. I realize, from my framing of questions and Janet's reply, that twins may share an additional burden in school—which centres around the tensions of constant comparison and a closer proximity to the effects of those comparisons than for other children. School can be a place where girls' early successes are "rationalized"—"girls generally do better than boys at this age"—but they are later muted or penalized. Yet boys who struggle in elementary or middle school may altogether lose their appetite for school success.

> Dear Janet,
> I am writing that piece on being a twin, having a twin brother and looking at how school may have contributed to some separation and identity issues. Do you have anything to say, I wonder? I don't know many other fraternal boy/girl dyads. I am

> wondering at this notion of dominance, of valuing the autonomous self over the connected self, how the playground enforces gender issues for fraternal twins that contribute to separation, or the guilt when one thrives and the other struggles in school. But, if I recall, you were a disgustingly well-adjusted kid (me, I was a wimp).

Janet replied, saying, "Yes, school did indeed reinforce the gender conflicts" and introduce tensions for her twin and herself. Perhaps what makes this so revealing about the similarities of our experiences is that her schooling took place in a remote mining community in the Northwest Territories, while our dramas occurred in the southern suburbs of the lower mainland of B.C. She wrote me:

> Yes, yes and yes. The schoolyard really enforced those gender differences. My brother did not have a real friend in school for a long time, but I was "not allowed" to play with him. I played with the girls, and the girls I played with played with the boys, but my brother was not part of that boy crowd, and I usually abandoned the girls when they played with the boys because I didn't understand the game. The girls were wild horses (I liked that part of it, I like the idea of being a wild horse) and the boys tried to catch them and put them in corrals, and I wondered why all those girls used to get caught. I was really good at escaping and it wasn't that difficult to out-run and out-hide the boys.
>
> It wasn't until I was in my thirties and telling my kids about those other silly girls always getting caught that I realized that that was the point of the game for them. Grant used to play at some solitary game. He was not that much into groups. But the schoolyard and home play groups were an interesting split. At the mining camp we lived in, my best friend was two years younger than me and went to the Catholic school. I wonder if I would have been allowed to associate with her if we attended the same school?
>
> School was very different than home, and many of the kids were the same. I wonder what made the difference? Perhaps the balance of dare-to-be-different girls was greater at home, and perhaps the interference of parents vs. the "benign neglect" (not so benign when you consider the consequences) of the teachers. And the guilt as I did well at school, and Grant was always in trouble for not getting his homework done, and I felt I had to defend him to our peers and the teachers, and Grant told me he

> didn't want to hear anymore that he was really smart. (He had his IQ taken. I was not exceptional in any way, so hadn't had it taken. So I really thought that I was not that bright, just did well because I tried hard). But I did have to take care of him. High school was worse in some ways, but at least in high school, I could openly invite him to join me and my friends, and we had a number of misfit boys who were part of our crowd (McVittie 1998).

My quest for twin stories also led me to my next-door neighbour Karen. Karen and Jackie are identicals in their early fifties, and lifelong best friends. Over the summer, while her sister was visiting, I talked with Karen and Jackie about their experiences. They told me that they had worn the same outfits to school every day of their lives, with the exception of one day in grade eleven. They both laughed and admitted that on that unique occasion they'd gone home at lunch and changed back into the same clothes because dressing differently felt miserable. They had even participated in a television documentary about identicals. As we talked and joked about twin energy, I was impressed by the give and take of their verbal exchanges, their lively mutuality and their fierce sense of individuality and self.

Of course there is a fierce side to twin life. My brother and I have shaped each other through our struggles and we each bear the physical and emotional scars that are testimony to a lifelong rivalry. For instance, Rob wears a tiny white ring on one finger that masks my three-year-old teeth marks. And he can wound me in a mini-second with a word or a retrieved memory. We have shaped our psyches together—this provides insight into the darker side of twin life: the binaries. I have discovered that being a twin means supporting certain mythic binaries in our cultures. I often notice references in films and on television to the "evil" twin, which assumes that one will always be dominant or better, as if similitude, cooperation or connection were abnormal. This belief seems to have biblical origins. In Social Studies and English classes, I learned that if we had been born in Sparta I—the girl twin—would have been left to die in the hills or left at the gate of an orphanage. It seems we have taken for granted the roles we played, but I see here the assumptions that one would lead and the other follow:

Kathy: What did you notice about us as little people, Dad?

Rob: Wasn't I the explorer?

Kathy: You were the explorer.

Gordon: Yes, as little people, Robbie did everything first. He walked first, he talked first.... Those little things [cots] that fitted into the car, your mother had put them on the floor in the kitchen, and she worked around you. And you would be laying around in them, and Robbie would lean over and "Aaahhh!" you would cry. [We all laugh.] And that's all he had to do, and you would cry and cry. And he got a great delight from that, and you were a sucker for it.

Kathy: Still am. Whaahah! I am sure Robbie really got a kick from that. So as a father watching us, what can you say about our temperament or our character? Robbie was sort of the leader in some ways.

Gordon: In some ways. I thought he was going to be the leader, but you snuck up on him. Eventually, everytime somebody spoke to Rob, or asked him a question, you answered for him.

Kathy: How old was I when it started happening?

Gordon: Very young, you were three.

Rob: I was quite content with her saying whatever she said, so she was like my spokesperson. That was what was actually happening.

Gordon: I'd say she was your mouthpiece.

Rob: My mouthpiece, yeah. She loved me, you know. I guess that's why she was speaking up. I felt quite content to sit back and look at them and smile. I didn't even think of the difference between us. If Kathy wanted to speak for me, that was the way it was, because she knew me as much as I knew myself, and vice versa. So Kathy knew what I was thinking. I never said, no, that is not the way it is. That was the way it was.

My brother says I knew what he was thinking. Tales of togetherness like this prompt questions about twin identity. I find that whenever I mention that I am a twin, I encounter beliefs about twin telepathy and twin secret languages, which are perhaps less threatening than the more ordinary virtues of empathy, connection and mutuality. I know that most people confuse being a twin with being a clone, a mirrored self, and that the impulse to catalogue and compare erupts immediately.

Being a twin invites a certain public intrusiveness on the part of strangers who might normally be more reserved about making verbal comparisons. I found that as a child, being a twin produced both wanted and unwanted attention, and we were not even identical.

When I was young, I thought we were second-rate twins because we were not identical. As small children we looked as similar as most dumpling-like siblings, and by school age, we still had not separated. I understand this now, perhaps more profoundly than before. Perhaps differentiation is a lifelong project for all families and siblings. My brother and I recall that school was the first place where we tangibly experienced separation, where we were physically, psychically and emotionally separated.

Kathy: How has being a twin really affected you, especially as a child, and what you remember from our schooling experiences?

Rob: Well, the earliest, biggest thing was actually just being separated, I'd say.

Before school age, Robbie and I had evolved an unspoken and well-honed repertoire, a way of negotiating our world: he scouted and I talked. Robbie was fairly quiet and I was timid. As Arundhati Roy (1977: 5) has said, "And these were only the small things." I have always wondered if one reason twins are often separated in school is so they do not remain "dependent" upon each other. Upon reflection, I find it very strange that sharing and cooperative support would be considered developmentally detrimental for a young child. This fetish for independence and autonomy is especially contradictory since human social life has evolved for millennia from the sinews of interrelation, interdependence and community sharing. Ironically, by adolescence and young adulthood, just at the stage of a person's life when they are seeking to differentiate and become independent from family life, the school curriculum begins to work very hard to develop "cooperative" learning strategies and teamwork.

When we entered grade one in the autumn of 1961, we had just turned six a few weeks before. My father reminds us that we left for school holding hands, and I recall that we came home embarrassed and separated. Like all other six-year-olds in the 1960s, we entered the first day of school unique and special, and exited resorted, numbered and averaged out in the group of many. The older grades were segregated by gender. There was a boys' side and a girls' side of the playground and the gym class. At the primary school level, they let the playground rules take care of socialization. In our first-grade class, we were not permitted to talk with one another (or any other child, for that matter). We learned very quickly that boys and girls do not play together, unless it is "boys against girls" games. Brothers and sisters never play together. There could be nothing more disgraceful than playing with a boy who was also a brother. Our interview reminded me that this ironclad rule was even more ruthlessly enforced for boys.

Kathy: Okay, Dad, do you remember much about our earliest school years?

Gordon: No, not really, I don't. All I remember is watching you going off in the first years of school, walking down the road hand-in-hand.

Kathy: How did we come home? Did we come home hand-in-hand?

Gordon: I wouldn't know, I was at work! [We laugh.]

Rob: Most of the time we did, for two years in a row, each day after school. We'd come home, and I'd remember walking Kathy home after school—unless I was chasing after Fay, my first girlfriend, but that was after, when we were separated—I think it was kind of during grade one. Kathy wasn't sitting beside me—we tried to, but we were separated, we were moved. And Kathy actually left home a couple of times before, so I found a surrogate twin sister named Fay.

In the following conversation, my father recalls how primary playground politics provided the first terrible crisis in our sibling bond together.

Gordon: Say that thing, Rob, when you were at school … and they made you say derogatory remarks about Kathy and then you came home and you said you were sorry. [I was startled, because I had forgotten about this incident.]

Kathy: Oh! Do you remember that?

Rob: Yeah, as a matter of fact, it was like the boys against the girls, and I had to say something or else I would probably be beat up or ostracized as a male in the young male society of eight years old.

Gordon: I think it was about six or seven. You were quite young.

Rob: Either grade one or two—. It was already happening, the segregation of the males and the females, the boys and girls. I think we were the only fraternal twins happening at the time.

Kathy: So tell me about that. Do you remember that incident at all?

Rob: Yeah, I do actually. I didn't say too much. Actually, I didn't say too much through the whole thing.... I couldn't say anything. I think I was prodded on to say something about the girls. But afterward I came home and said, "I didn't mean to say that, you are my sister!" Oh yeah, for sure I didn't mean that.

Kathy: What do you remember?

Gordon: He came home, and he said to you after he went to his room, "I am sorry, Kathy, I am sorry."

Kathy: Oh, is that right? That must have been really painful, that must have been really tough.

Rob: Yeah!

At this point, my brother was overwhelmed and had to stop talking for a moment. Later we returned again to this theme of gendered separation at school. I realized that I must have accepted the inevitable bullying of boys at school and so had pushed this incident from my conscious memory.

Kathy: One of the things I explored in my writing is the first day of school and arriving there and the separation. It was the first time that we were ever truly separated.

Rob: Well, as I said, I had to really protect myself in a sense, because if I really associated closely with you, in the eyes of the (boys) at school, I probably would have got my ass kicked every day, because there was by then a traditional girl-hater league throughout grade three to grade six.

Kathy: That was really painful because I remember we brought that home with us.

Rob: Yes, unfortunately, that's right.

Kathy: [I explain to my father.] It was this intense rivalry where Robbie wasn't my friend or brother anymore; he was this enemy and we tormented each other.

Rob: Even at home, Kathy and I would do this "boy germs, girl germs" thing, when we were here in this house. Right? So it really segregated us.

Kathy: It was really segregating. We lost each other's friendship and it was very painful. I remember being really uncomfortable; we were so policed, it seemed, by school.

Rob: But then suddenly there would be birthdays and summer holidays—forget it, we were back together again.

Kathy: And then school would start all over again.

Rob: But we didn't even question the segregation back then. It seemed to be part of the whole thing. I guess, like sheep, we just tolerated it, just fell into the status quo of it for kids.

I was a confirmed bookworm by grade two, a dreadful identity for a girl. And Robbie belonged to the bona fide "girl-hater's league" of grade three. On the school playground, we learned not to play together, because boys and girls just did not do that and, although we walked to and from home together, it was no longer hand-in-hand as we had dne on the first days. Boys and girls had to do different things, and so we were divided by the unspoken but heavily policed rules of the schoolyard. I remember looking longingly over at the huddle of boys on the marble pit, my plastic skipping rope (pink handles, green and white peppermint striping) limply in hand. I was only allowed to watch. Robbie had to fake an avid interest in trucks. No catching caterpillars in the trees together, no huddling under some table to whisper made-up games; brothers and sisters did not spend recess or lunch hour together.

Having twins in the classroom sometimes evoked unconscious responses from teachers. In grade one, our first two report cards were identical in every category, until our mother realized from our assignments that we had quite different strengths and called the teacher. Our teacher explained that she didn't want to create feelings of competition. She didn't know how to treat us—the same or differently. Yet in the next school year she put me in the coveted "Elves" reading group and put

Rob in the "Brownies." Rob came home crushed and dejected, moped around the house, announcing that he was "dumb." Mom rushed up to the school for a second emergency meeting with the teacher. This time, the teacher explained that she had run out of room in the first group, and so had slipped Robbie into the "slow" group, thinking we wouldn't notice. But notice we did, and that event seemed to colour the rest of our school experience.

Kathy: We were in the same class.

Rob: But we kind of separated.

Kathy: We got separated in that class.

Rob: It was like you were the fast learner and I was the slow learner.

Kathy: But that was a mistake, do you remember?

Rob: Oh, I know, it was terrible!

Kathy: Do you remember when that happened, Dad, in grade two?

Gordon: No.

Kathy: Mom noticed that Robbie was coming home feeling really upset.

Gordon: Oh?

Kathy: And it turned out that the teacher had put me in the "Elves" and had put you in the" Gnomes" or the" Brownies," or whatever.

Rob: No, I wasn't a Gnome; that was the bottom of the list. I was second from below. But it was because of my writing habits, right? Because I was left-handed.

Kathy: Yes, Mom went to the teacher and said, "Robbie is a good reader. Why is he in the slower group?" And the teacher said, "There wasn't enough room in that top group and so I put him in the lower group, but he won't notice. Those kids don't care." But we did, we cared terribly.

Rob: Yeah, but halfway through the school grade that year I did get up into the same level as you.

Our father mentioned later that I seemed to blossom once I went to high school. It seems from his observations that, once I lost the connection or resource of my brother, I found it difficult to locate friendships where I could fit in as a whole person. I found that I didn't have the knack for "just being a girl" or enjoying games that required extreme competition or conflict. It was as Roy (1997: 18) describes in her novel: "It was, they whispered to each other, *as though she didn't know how to be a girl.*" As a child, I did not know how to be a girl, and having lost the familiar resource of my constant playmate, a fraternal twin boy, I retreated into reading, a place where identity and selfhood can be somewhat fluid. This escape provided me with solitude and solace, a space where my brother could not follow. The activity of reading and the world of books provided a resource where "I" could be renewed and reimagined, a buffer from the "girl-haters league" and a temporary respite from the now-embattled, unbearable environment of "girls against boys."

As I retreated into the solitude of reading, Robbie met a whole network of male friends from grade one onwards. He can name them still. He describes how their interests drew him out into the world, away from the confines of family life and his twin sibling, into different areas of interest—exploring, chemistry, marbles, frog collecting and, of course, the "girl-hater's league." Yet, I wonder what parts of my brother's imagination and personality were suppressed by this separation from his female side, for I am sure he was as heavily policed by the watchful "girl-hater's league" as were the girls. The effects of schooling intruded into our home lives, not only through the development of skills such as literacy and reasoning, but also the manner in which the gendered classroom and schoolyard's hierarchies and values influenced our family and interpersonal dynamics.

I had always talked for both of us, so my repositioning far from my brother disrupted our usual mode of communication. In class, I put up my hand in order to tell the teacher what my brother meant to say, but she wouldn't let me speak. Robbie was a quiet little guy, and though I suspect he breathed a sigh of relief to be able to "talk for himself," he now had to speak up and bark like the rest of us. There is never much room in school for naturally quiet, independent kids.

As I remember our lives together as children, I am overcome by the knowledge of how gender relations regulated our connections as siblings and produced antagonism and estrangement in our home life. I am struck by the powerful effects of the school's hidden curriculum of gender norms. It shaped us, both in the classroom and in our private and intensely experiential world of play.

I am also reminded of the rich and separate world that children create and dwell in, amongst the coming and goings of the larger family and social structures. My brother and I have reminisced about experiences of family, school and neighbourhood events that my father knew nothing about. Reviewing these memories centres my faith in the power of children's rich and creative inner lives, and encourages new ways of sustaining and nurturing those qualities.

As we talked and tried to remember some of our lives together as young children, we reactivated our memories and questions around what it has meant to share our lifelong relationship. We quickly noticed that the most significant influence on the shaping of our awareness of differences took place outside of family life and was most powerfully enacted once we entered school. Perhaps my most significant finding of this brief exploration of my twin identity is how powerfully schooling regulates the sibling/gender dynamics of children. Ironically, at a time when it seems that schools work so hard to keep family life from "disrupting" the classroom, it may be the family that is at greatest risk. It seems this may occur despite the best intentions of children, parents and teachers. In particular, I am struck by the sense of helplessness that children can experience in questioning or interrupting these effects. My brother and I learned our most difficult lessons about gender difference in the schoolyard and classroom. We carried those lessons home and they intruded upon our relationship well into adulthood.

Finally, I offer this observation: that twins may provide a window on the resilience and fragility of sibling relations. A venture into twinness is a means to explore lifelong connections and support systems between siblings. Exploring twin-ness can teach us something about the normative values that school life imposes upon sibling dynamics. I think that as a society we are both careless and fearful of the deep love and intimacy that many siblings and twins can share, most likely because we have demonized the passionate and playful embodiment of the physical connections and intimacy of those bonds. Perhaps twins are given permission to sustain those bonds a little more because we are expected to be close, and because we travel together "more than one/less than one" through all of our life's passages.

Writing this chapter has renewed my connections with my brother in ways that I could not have predicted. It gave us the opportunity to revisit the pair of children who live within us still, who remain playmates, albeit a little more mature in our squabbling. I appreciate that the scars remain on the finger of my brother, who at heart is my "most dependable friend" if I "ever want to play."

2

Masculinities, Sexualities and the Student Body

"Sorting" Gender Identities in School

KEVIN DAVISON

Between the ages of twelve and seventeen, I remember many gendered lessons in school and the difficulty I had in negotiating and resisting hegemonic masculinity. Robert Connell (1989: 291) has argued that schooling has the strongest influence on the construction of masculinity, yet few researchers have examined the intersection of masculinities and schools. The high school "tweenage" years are particularly ripe for the exploration of gender identity negotiation and construction, for "not only does the body change, but bodymeanings and the image-repertoire of bodies become, in contradictory ways, 'available'" (Corrigan 1991: 206). Complexities and contradictions of masculine identities and sexualities are learned by the body in school and, in turn, shape the physical body (Butler 1997; McLaren 1991). Ursula Kelly argues that the "regulation of bodies has historically been a primary focus of the project of education" (1997: 31). This chapter, based in my own experiences, will attempt to illustrate points where inquiry into the individual masculine articulation process in schools is possible. Further, it will strive to deconstruct the binary sorting of gender relations that structures the everyday and night schooling environment for students.

Good Gender/Bad Gender and the Unavailable In-Between

> *"Who's got the new boy gender?"*
> —Culture Club, "I'll Tumble 4 Ya"

Gendered behaviour in popular media during the mid-1980s was hegemonically stereotypical and contradictory. On the one hand, there were hyper-masculine images of masculinity, such as Sylvester Stallone as *Rocky* and *Rambo* and the "muscle" films of Arnold Schwartzenegger. And on the other, there were counterhegemonic images of masculinity and femininity in popular music, such as Boy George and Culture Club, "androgynous" Annie Lennox and Grace Jones, the boys of Duran

Duran who had pink hair and wore lipstick, Jimmy Sommersville, k.d. lang, and Lorraine Segatto and the Parachute Club who sang queer-friendly or feminist lyrics. The *image* of pop stars became increasingly important in the 1980s with the advent of music videos. Their alternative images of gender were quite appealing to me, because they represented a way to opt out of the rigid gender expectations to which I was supposed to conform. However, I learned quickly that unconventional gender behaviour was not acceptable among my peers at my suburban high school. Hegemonic masculinity was carefully policed there.

Like many schools reflected in ethnographic research on institutional education (Wexler 1992; Willis 1977), the suburban high school I attended included predictable hierarchical social groupings, such as: Jocks, Preppies, Rockers and Mods. Of course, not all students fit neatly into these peer categories, but there was heightened pressure to conform to a particular identity group; most important was the need to be acceptably gendered.

I was often reminded through the verbal and physical taunting by my peers that I did not fit the masculine stereotype. I was slim and not very athletic; I was not interested in sports or the internal workings of automobiles. I consciously knew that my body could not live up to the standards of hegemonic masculinity, nor did I want it to. I did not have dreams of being the star football quarterback or champion wrestler. I consciously chose not to go to the gym and lift weights and strive for an acceptably masculine body. I did not actively participate in the reproduction of the dominant image of masculinity. Therefore, my struggle was not how to achieve the ideal but how to safely rework it. Hence, I desired the attributes of pop-stars who offered an alternative to rigid masculinity.

The "genderfuck" (Bornstein 1998) of the pop stars allowed me a particular language of resistance through bodily transgressions. Of course, the discourse of resistance is not a simple act in which one rejects and reconstructs. The reconstruction of gender and sexuality is far too complex to explain simply by illustrating my own process of resistance to hegemonic masculinity. What is interesting about the way I challenged dominant expectations is that I manipulated gender through bodily performance. The performative "act" of gender not only constructs the dominant illusion of acceptable gender (Butler 1990) but may also act as a means of counterhegemonic gender subversion. It is not surprising that this particular bodily resistance occurred in school, which Corrigan refers to as a "theatre of regulated performances" (1991: 207) and, I would argue, is also a theatre of *unregulated* performances. That is to say, while gender performances are policed by peers in schools, there is still room for subversive performances. The very fact that there is peer policing illustrates that unregulated performances occur within the school. Fashion, as Wienke (1998) notes can be a strategy to deflect perceived gender deficiencies as well as a reworking of gender performance.

My re-embodiment of masculinity consisted of a particular style of dress that was seen as "less masculine." I grew my fingernails long, I purposefully dragged my feet slightly when I walked and I grew my hair long in front so it covered my eyes. As a result of my physical challenges to hegemonic masculinity, I remember being often asked by my peers to identify myself. I was asked: "Are you a Mod?" "Are you a New Waver?" "Are you a fag?" I really did not have an answer to these questions.

The days I spent in school seemed to last forever, not because I disliked learning but because of my fear of other students. My embodied performative challenges to acceptable masculinity also had a bodily result. I always felt vulnerable. I felt I always had to be on guard. I always felt unsafe. The longing for gender flexibility required further work, for in a Lacanian light, "desire arises out of the lack of satisfaction and it pushes you to another demand" (Sarup, quoted in McLaren 1991: 158). To counter these feelings, I spent many hours planning my safety, avoiding the bully's locker, avoiding contact sports, avoiding hot spots of humiliation like a crowded cafeteria.

I learned that masculinity was a very rigid, complex and contradictory equation. Consider the following: *long hair + fancy shirt + slim build = fag;* however, *long hair + girlfriend + athletic ability = acceptable masculinity.* While these two examples may seem like pieces of a simple stereotype, the many possibilities that make up identity and gender performance are sorted and slotted into binary categories (good / bad, masculine / feminine) on a daily basis. Thus high school becomes a strong filter for hegemonic gender patterns (Frank 1994; Mac an Ghaill 1994).

Sexuality/Reality

He learned the rules as a normal boy
She learned them too, but they weren't quite the same
He learned how to fight, he learned how to win
She learned how to smile and to stand there by him
They called it common sense
They grew up so different
They were the typical children
Livin' in a myth—Parachute Club, "Sexual Intelligence"

Those who challenge hegemonic gender are not only viewed as inappropriately masculine or feminine, but also become suspiciously unheterosexual. When I went to school, girls who didn't conform to feminine expectations were called tomboys, dogs, bitches, sluts etc. When boys stepped outside "acceptable" masculine behaviour, they were simply girls, sissies or fags. For young men, it seemed that if you were not masculine, you were left outside the definition of "man" altogether. It followed, then, that if you didn't look or act straight (read: masculine), the only other possible explanation seemed to be that you must be gay. This construction of the Other is inherent to hegemonic masculinity, and thus heterosexuality. Each aspect of binaries is defined by its opposites. Therefore, much rests on "sorting out" the gender equation; specifically, how the dominant hetero-masculinity is constructed, understood and performed.

In high school there were plenty of hints to guide boys to the "proper" gender answer. To begin with, there is social terrorism by peers. Sissies are alienated, ostracized, humiliated and verbally and physically abused (Rofes 1995). "Everyday practices of 'fag-baiting,' such as poking fun, teasing, name calling, scrawling graffiti on lockers, insulting and harassing someone, produce the 'fag' as social object" (Smith 1998: 309).

If we start from the belief that gender is a performance (Butler 1990), we come to see how hegemonic heterosexuality becomes naturalized through everyday actions within the institution (Frank 1993). Marilyn Frye points out clearly how we take for granted the naturalness of heterosexual performance:

> Heterosexual critics of queers' "role-playing" ought to look at themselves in the mirror on their way out for a night on the town to see who's in drag. The answer is, everybody is. Perhaps the main difference between heterosexuals and queers is that when queers go forth in drag, they know they are engaged in theater—they are playing and they know they are playing. Heterosexuals are usually taking it all perfectly seriously, thinking they are in the real world, thinking they *are* the real world. (1983: 29)

As Mary Bryson and Suzanne deCastell point out, "being any gender is a drag" (1995: 24). Thus, from the perspective of heterosexual hegemony, it is important to consider how Others are defined, named and sorted as an everyday feature of school life. Hegemonic heterosexual masculinity is enforced through the discrimination of sissies and gay youth (Kinsman 1996; Rofes 1995). The stigmatization of being named the hated

Other, whether it's "girlish," "fag" or "sissy," weighs heavy on these students. The history "of being called an injurious name is embodied ... the words enter the limbs, craft the gesture, bend the spine" (Butler 1997: 159). Name-calling, which is often dismissed with the phrase "boys will be boys," is not so simple. "If we understand the force of the name to be an effect of its historicity, then that force is not the mere casual effect of an inflicted blow, but works in part through an encoded memory or a trauma, one that lives in language and is carried in language" (Butler 1997: 36). The act of naming, sorting and creating Others through binary concepts may result in heavy psychological and emotional baggage for young men. Thus bodies not only perform gender but also are shaped by the punishments of gender-inappropriate behaviour.

Bodily Performances

I remember intensely disliking Physical Education class because it was the most blatant arena for the sorting of masculine bodies. Salisbury and Jackson suggest that "the playing field, the changing room and the gym are some of the most important institutional sites where boys masculinize their bodies" (1996: 4). In my high school, P.E. instructors evaluated students on how well they could demonstrate a particular masculine performance. Muscles and bodies were displayed publicly and measured routinely; for example, peers chose teams from a line-up and then divided them between those with shirts on and those without. I remember fearing the change room and gang shower, where masculinity was highly contradictory and unstable in the raw nakedness of young men. As Marilyn Frye points out, "being physically 'normal' for one's assigned sex is not enough. One must *be* female or male actively"(1983: 26). In such an overtly homosocial/homoerotic environment, young men would often manipulate their bodies in a way that would reinforce hegemonic heterosexual masculinity, either with sexist or homophobic gestures or by a forced avoidance of displaying admiration for their own or each other's bodies.

Boys are often told by P.E. instructors that they are "playing like a bunch of girls" or that they are "pansies" (Davison 1996; Frank 1992), illustrating the use of sexism and homophobia to reinforce hegemonic masculinity. Physical Education class plays an important role in teaching boys and their bodies how to *be* masculine. Salisbury and Jackson conclude that:

> those boys who can't measure up against the traditional stand-

> ards of the dominant body-culture begin to perceive themselves as inadequate, failed boys and, as a result, are often put down and marginalized. A great deal of personal unhappiness and psychological damage result from this marginalization. (1996: 190)

Thus, P.E. acts to reinforce the belief that boys should assume the patriarchal role of dominance, and boys who do not, cannot, or will not do this become traumatized by the taint of being a failed man. As a result of not being able to measure up to the ideal masculine body type in P.E. class, I developed a great dislike of my body, and little appreciation of health and fitness. I developed what George Yúdice (1995: 275) refers to as toxic shame, "an unhealthy and self-disempowering indulgence in self-blame." I remember feeling shamed for not *appearing* masculine. Feelings of shame require an internalized understanding "that I *am* … what I am *seen* to be" (Bartky 1996: 227). Thus, shame works to uphold the dominant gender regime. It lends "legitimacy to the structure of authority that occasions it, for the majesty of judgment is affirmed in its very capacity to injure" (Bartky 1996: 237). The masculine failure here is rooted, psychologically and physically, in the body and its inability to replicate a dominant masculine standard.

Selling A Contradiction

> *"I'm a man who doesn't know how to sell a contradiction"*—Culture Club, "Karma Chameleon"

How do you sell a contradiction? I found it quite difficult to convince my peers that I was heterosexual when I did not act heterosexual or embody heterosexual performances. I did not conform to hegemonic hetero-masculinity partly because I did not feel I could meet the rigid demands and partly because I did not desire to meet manly expectations. I found a certain excitement in the possibilities of gender offered by pop icons such as Boy George. The excitement of difference was stronger than the tempting privileges of masculinity or the punishments of not conforming.

Those who do not conform to the narrow definitions of masculinity and femininity are punished "severely for their failure to be the 'facts' which would verify the doctrine of the two sexes"(Frye 1983: 25). On and off the school grounds, I was a target for gay-bashing. I was chased, punched and kicked. I had things thrown at me from passing cars, along with homophobic taunts. There seemed little recourse at the time other than *acting* masculine or *acting* heterosexual, neither of which was a choice I felt I could make or take. I was a person who was more willing to suffer wrong than to commit wrong (McLaren 1991: 169).

Laurie Anderson explains clearly the limitations of the binary system that overwhelmingly structures our social world:

> Now, I'm no mathematician, but I'd like to talk to you about just a couple of numbers that have really been bothering me lately, and they are zero and one. Now first, let's take a look at zero. Now nobody wants to be a zero. To be a zero means to be a nothing, a nobody, a has-been, a ziltch.
>
> On the other hand, just about everybody wants to be number one. To be number one means to be a winner, top of the heap, the acme. And there seems to be a strange kind of national obsession with this particular number. Now, in my opinion, the problem with these numbers is that they are just too close—leaves very little room for everybody else. Just not enough range.
>
> So first, I think we should get rid of the value judgments attached to these two numbers and recognize that to be a zero is no better, no worse, than to be number one.
>
> Because what we are actually looking at here are the building blocks of the Modern Computer Age. (1994)

My non-masculine position outside of the tight zero-sum definition of hegemonic masculinity left my peers with only one binary place to identify me: if not acting straight, then assumed gay. However, aside from my performance outside dominant masculinity, as a White male student I was still able to occupy a position of privilege in relation to others at the school. Having been attacked physically and verbally for my gender transgressions in high school, I related more to those on the margins than to my privileged potential. Thus I had little interest in replicating the sexism and homophobia inherent to hetero-masculinity. From what I recall, I was not the only person in my school whose understanding of identity and identity performance was a complex and complicated matter. High school offered me many lessons about gender and sexuality that contributed to and constricted my understanding and manipulation of masculinity performance.

Silences and Dangers

In conducting research for my master's thesis, I interviewed men, women and a transgendered person and asked them about their memories of masculinities in school (Davison 1996). Those I spoke to recounted many stories of brutality in Physical Education class at the hands of both their peers and the teachers. Some spoke of their fear of the change room, group showers and the lack of privacy in these spaces during a pubescent time when bodies were changing at different rates and in different ways. Difference was dangerous in these raw homosocial spaces. To be differently masculine or less masculine was a trigger for discrimination.

Men I interviewed spoke of bullying to such an extent that it became social terrorism—they dreaded every day. One of the men spoke about how he shut down by isolating himself within himself in order to cope with daily harassment. Another man spoke about how he chose to join a gang to deal with the pressures of violent bullying at school. Bullying operates by means of humiliation and shame, which often destroy self-esteem. As a result there is a great amount of silence around bullying. Further, masculinity is also measured by the degree to which boys can "take it like a man" (Askew and Ross 1988), thus also requiring silence about verbal and physical violence.

As part of the research process, I recycled the data back to the participants. All of them expressed amazement and interest in reading the experiences of the other people in my study. Some were surprised, and others could identify similar experiences with masculinity and schooling. What I found most interesting about the memories of the people I interviewed was the silence and danger surrounding men and boys discussing the way masculinity operates and how it shapes bodies.

In my doctoral research on masculinity, body image and schooling, I have found it very difficult to overcome the silence around, and the danger of discussing, the everyday practices of masculinity and boys' bodies in schools. Since the rise of the second-wave feminist movement, feminists have often used women's bodies as a starting point to theorize about women's historic and contemporary oppression and inequality. However, theorizing about masculinity by using the body is a difficult task, due to the silences ingrained in the definition and practice of hegemonic masculinity. To talk about boys' bodies and the differences between them is a highly political action. As Frye points out, "the appearance of the naturalness of the dominance of men and the subordination of women is supported by anything which supports the appearance that men are very *like* other men and very *unlike* women" (1983: 34). To expose differences between men is to question the assumed naturalness of men's dominance in everyday relations.

Conclusion

This essay has attempted to illustrate, through my own experience, the complex bodily performances and practices of masculinity in school. The interplay between bodily performance of masculinity and sexuality within educational institutions may play a significant role in shaping our social understandings and interactions with each other. Gendered lessons in school shape young men into adult men; therefore, explorations into how young men sort out gender in school are necessary if gender inequities, sexism and homophobia are to be addressed in educational institutions and in the greater society. These multiple intersections and tensions are ripe for use in an exploration of new approaches to the interplay of gender and education. If, to paraphrase Frye (1992: 66), it is the articulation and the differentiation of experiences that gives rise to meaning, then perhaps future academic inquiry should focus on the differences in the way masculinities are constructed and actively performed by boys in school.

3

A Letter to a Friend

Kai James

Alex,

I am writing this letter as a follow-up to our conversation last week. You expressed an envy of some Black athletes' apparent natural prowess in certain sports, which I am not convinced is inherent. I understand that as a White basketball player, who plays well, it would seem that you have to spend considerably more time proving yourself on the court. You also said Blacks appear to have an advantage in getting basketball scholarships, and again I'm not convinced. But could you imagine having basketball as the only option? The image of the Black student as a superior athlete extends beyond the basketball court and into the classroom, where Blacks are seen as incapable of performing at the level of their White counterparts. Statistics would show that neither you nor any other basketball player from our school will make it to the NBA and few will even receive scholarships—a dream shared by you and just about all the other players in high school. So when that dream falls through, who will really have the advantage? Darcy Frey talks about this in his book *The Last Shot* (1994).

You also asked why so many Black athletes waste their talent by putting forth little effort in their classes. The points you brought up are valid observations, and I want to remind you of some of the issues faced by Blacks and other marginalized students in school. In this letter, I do not speak for all Black students, nor do I wish to act as an advocate for those I am discussing. But I do wish to talk about some of the factors which help to determine the achievements of some students in school and over which we as students have little or no control.

The social barriers presently encountered by youth from minority groups takes different forms for each group. In order to succeed, members of each minority group must overcome the ethnocentricity of the curriculum as well as the stereotypes, which contrast greatly from one group to another and are manifested in the culture of the high school community. In particular, the socially constructed image of the Black student as primarily an athlete contrasts greatly with that of the White student, who is most often seen as one who can and should excel academically.

In many instances, Black students are disadvantaged even before entering a high school classroom. They are often lured into taking general-level courses by guidance counsellors who have little knowledge of the student's actual capabilities but make their assessment based heavily on skin colour or perceived social class. Conversely, White students constitute an overly representative portion of gifted and enriched programs. These programs are set up in such a way that White and middle-class students are detached from the rest of the school population and placed in an elitist environment. Here they are rewarded for creativity and encouraged to go on to university and pursue careers. For them, the sky's the limit, while a large number of Black students are relegated to general- and basic-level courses where they are less often exposed to the types of standards, that would allow them to set goals that include university and open doors to a wide range of career opportunities. This is a shame because Black students have a variety of interests going into high school and have a variety of experiences other than basketball; however, these interests are suppressed and these experiences receive little attention amidst all the stereotypes.

From the moment a Black student walks into the school, or his grade nine teacher reads his or her African name on her class list for the first time, an image is conceived in that teacher's mind. These images are based on the teacher's past experiences with students of the same race or the experience of another teacher who gossips or complains about his or her students. They are also based on media images and even images in the curriculum. These preconceived notions make it difficult for teachers and students to form a good working relationship, and a student may spend an entire semester or high school career trying to prove himself as one who doesn't fit the stereotype. This is a marginalizing factor limiting the student's academic achievement.

Gym teachers are perhaps the most overt in their interpretations of the stereotypes. I remember the track coach coming into my grade nine gym class and asking all the Black students if they would be participating in the track meet. I know you, like myself, were recruited for basketball, but for a totally different reason. If your brother hadn't played for the school before you arrived, and if you hadn't already built your reputation in spring leagues, most coaches would have overlooked you in their recruiting rounds. I, on the other hand, was recruited by a coach who had no knowledge of my athletic ability or my interests. At the same time, an Asian friend of mine was being encouraged by the math department to write the math contests.

I recall an incident a friend told me about last year. He is a tall Black youth who has little interest in basketball. On the first day of school, his social studies teacher, a complete stranger to the student, greeted him as follows: "I hope you are not one of those basketball players that's gonna show up for class once a week, because if you are, you can just leave right now." I experienced an equally discouraging encounter when my grade nine Latin class played host to a substitute teacher. The students were working quietly on individual assignments when the student sitting beside me asked me for some assistance on one of the questions. I began to explain the answer but was rudely interrupted by the teacher who asked, "Why are you guys talking?" The student, Ted, of Greek descent, explained that I was simply helping with a question that he was having trouble with. The teacher, a White woman, removed her glasses and looked confused. She paused for a second and then said, "Wait a minute, which one of you guys really needs the help here?"

I was somewhat surprised but said nothing, as I had no real evidence to suggest this occurred because of the colour of my or Ted's skin. Based on my experience, these incidents take place regularly but are almost always overlooked by those involved. The teacher was probably surprised to see that I did not appear to fit the description of a typical Black youth as categorized by many high school teachers. That categorization holds that Black are athletes, Asians excel in math and computer courses, and White students have the ability to excel in all high school endeavours and hence their possibilities are limitless. Naturally, the various student populations within the school are also likely to have their own agendas, and most Black students' agendas differ only slightly from those of the teachers. According to many of the Black students with whom I talk, especially those who participate in sports, Asians have a monopoly on math and computer courses, Whites can't play basketball but will always be the teachers' favourites, and the role of Black students is to uphold the school's athletic reputation through stellar performances in basketball, soccer, football, and track and field, as dictated by the coaches.

Coaches' favourite Black athletes are those who just play the game and have little to say about the systemic oppression that takes place in the school and in the basketball program in particular. If you're Black and failing classes, it's no problem as long as you are performing on the court, field or track. Strings are always pulled so a good athlete never has to miss games.

Black basketball players sit in the back of the coach's van on the way to games listening to them mutter racially motivated jokes. I've heard coaches gossip about or ostracize players, and refer to them in their absence with nicknames such as "mudface," while their Black teammates laugh as if oblivious to the forces at work against them, confirming the coach's stereotypes with their apparent lack of intelligence and social consciousness. Ironically, it is those students who will be given the most playing time and for whom the coach will talk a teacher into overlooking a failing grade on a test. The whole system is part of a culture that rewards students for fulfilling stereotypes.

Students are no better than teachers when it comes to allowing our actions to fall victim to the stereotypes in our minds. For example, last year on the first day of the chess club, I had gone in for a friendly game against my chemistry teacher when a White girl, whose accent told me she had just recently come from Europe, said, "You don't look like a chess player." I felt no need to respond to her comment, which later proved to be a good decision as it became obvious that I was a much better chess player than she was anyway. But it is not just Whites who operate on these kinds of stereotypes. I am sure a Black student would have been just as surprised to see me in the chess club. It often seems as if playing basketball and getting into the occasional scuffle is the criterion for being Black. Those who can't play ball, who get good grades in school and don't hang out with other Black people are seen as nerds. In this way we play a significant role in our own oppression.

Stereotypes are also learned by students through the curriculum. I've been in high school for three years now, and in my studies I have yet to be introduced to an African person who has made a significant contribution to science or English literature, which is not to say that there aren't any. There are people like George Washington Carver, Elijah McCoy, Patricia E. Bath, Richard Wright, Dionne Brand, Toni Morrison, Austin Clarke, Cecil Foster and Chinua Achebe, to name a few. Instead we are bombarded with the likes of Ernest Rutherford, Charles Dalton, Shakespeare and William Golding. But there is a whole world of experiences within our own school community which are not addressed in *To Kill a Mockingbird* and *Lord of the Flies*. As a result, all students, and Whites in particular, are denied an understanding of the rich and diverse history that has shaped and characterized this country. In order to fill the void created by this under-representation, an overwhelming number of Black students build their aspirations around the achievements of the Blacks most frequently discussed at school. Whether in the cafeteria or in gym class, it is most often athletes like Michael Jordan who are given to us as role models. Teachers and coaches are of no help in providing some sort of context for the glamour of professional sports that is portrayed on television.

Through books and documentaries, I've come to realize that there are many reasons not to pursue basketball as a career—basketball players can become injured or drop out of school and fail to complete their education. We are not told that professional athletes' careers last less than ten years on average, or even that only one in a million actually makes it to the pros. Neither do teachers insist that athletes, like everyone else, need good grades so that we can get into university and college, and to think seriously about university studies as something for them to fall back on. Three of four New York City basketball players profiled in Frey's *The Last Shot* who received scholarships didn't complete their degrees and had little to fall back on after dropping out. It is generally assumed that Black athletes who receive scholarships are not in school to get an education but to play basketball—and they are still very far from realizing their dreams of playing in the NBA. Some students stay in high school for up to seven years playing ball and hoping to be offered a scholarship, all the while struggling to pick up their last few credits to graduate.

You have argued that Black students take on a "victim mentality" whenever something bad happens, and in this way set themselves up for failure. I agree that might be true of some Black students, and many are more responsible for their own lack of success than they would have you believe. But at the same time, I must point out that there are many factors out of our control. The issues some Black students must deal with in and around school are vastly different from the issues faced by Whites and are much more complex than they appear. There is definitely overt discrimination, but also there is systemic discrimination that is evident in sports programs, many of which are simply setting students up for failure. And the fact that students are streamed into various levels of educational programs helps to segregate the school community, largely on the grounds of race and social class under the disguise of perceived intelligence. Another form of systemic discrimination toward Blacks and minorities is the Eurocentric curriculum, the unquestioning acceptance of which could lead the unaware person to believe that Whites were the people primarily—if not entirely—responsible for building our nation. Many textbooks simply do not acknowledge the fact that African-Canadians, like Aboriginal people, have been active participants in the shaping of Canada's history. These are marginalizing factors which play a role in how a student forms his or her own self-image, self-esteem and career aspirations.

When I pointed out this misrepresentation in my grade nine geography class, I was attacked by an angry group of White and Asian students whose reasoning was: "That's because White people are the ones who did all the important stuff. If it was Black people, we'd learn about them too!" I knew this was far from the truth, but like many Black students, most of my formal education comes from the same source as the White students—school—so I was unequipped with information to refute this argument, which I knew in my heart was wrong. Facing this me-against-you relationship with peers and teachers can spark hostility in some Black students, which, in my opinion, is part of the reason why many are often labelled as aggressive. And the ethnocentric school curriculum is less likely to attract the interest of Black students, many of whom are frequent skippers. Violence and truancy are the main grounds for suspension, so it seems logical that marginalized students are more likely to be suspended. Suspension has a number of purposes, one of which is to academically suppress students with a history of violence or truancy. While suspended, students stay at home and receive a mark of zero on all tests and assignments. The whole system seems like nothing short of a trap.

From this and other discussions we have had, you would probably agree with me—but you might not—that there is enough evidence to suggest that the behaviour and performance of Black students in school is not only of their own making. It is much more than a matter of finding God, or a lack of morals and values, and it is definitely not a matter of coming up with excuses. It is a matter of stereotyping, discrimination and systemic barriers. It is about principals, superintendents, teachers, coaches and others who are well aware of the problem but do little to help the situation. This is why some of us struggle to succeed and why others don't even try.

I expect that we will have many more of these discussions, and I appreciate the fact that you are able to share with me such controversial opinions, which many White students would be afraid to say out loud or even mention to most Black students. I have learned from our conversations and quite enjoyed them.

Peace out,
Kai

4

Black, White, Beige, Other?
Memories of Growing Up Different

LEANNE E. TAYLOR

My brother, Greg, and I grew up in a small, predominantly White town in Eastern Ontario. We are the only son and daughter of a Black Jamaican-born father and a White Canadian-born mother who is of Irish and Scottish descent. Despite the gender difference and the fact that I am the eldest by two-and-a-half years, on the surface our similarities are eerie. Not only do we look incredibly alike, sharing roughly the same complexion of "tanned beige," the same prominent jawline, and strikingly similar facial features, but also we have frequently been mistaken as twins. Even when we ask our parents whom they think we most resemble in the family, they always respond, "You look like each other." We both attended the same schools (with the exception that Greg completed grades twelve and thirteen at a nearby boarding school) and were involved in many of the same clubs and school organizations. We share the same warped sense of humour and a similar sense of style and, surprisingly enough, we even graduated from high school with exactly the same grade average. But perhaps most notably, we both grew up with all-White friends, as we were the only people of colour in our classes and small community.

Perhaps it was because I had just finished my master's degree, focusing on mixed-race identity, and was filled with that kind of harmless intellectual arrogance that follows most academic achievements, that I assumed I was informed on the nuances of multiraciality. As part of my research, I had spent countless hours exploring how our physical appearances, races, looks, colours and ethnicities are significant in mediating our encounters with others and in shaping the identities we choose. However, for some reason I foolishly assumed that my brother—being a product of virtually the same social environment—would naturally share my current perspectives and opinions on mixed race and, accordingly, have similar memories of growing up. I was so confident that our memories were the same that I was shocked and embarrassed, yet intrigued, when I learned otherwise. This realization spurred me to look again at my formative years, and in doing so I was reminded that each of our identities and experiences fluctuate from context to context and are differently gendered, sexualized, classed and racialized. What is more, beneath each experience, encounter and perception are underlying influences we must not take for granted. I had overlooked how these variables shaped my own life differently than my brother's.

Race

Initially an e-mail discussion between Greg and myself alerted me to some of the differences in our memories. As a tangent to another point he was making, he said, "Leanne, you know as well as I do that growing up as a minority in a small town means everybody knows who you are, because you stick out like a sore thumb—a racial blip on an otherwise all-White screen." Surely many would assume this to be the case in most small, racially homogeneous towns, where any presence of visible racial difference would be all the more noticeable. This does not fit my memory, however. We both remember people recognizing us at the mall, the bank and at grocery store checkouts. But (and I may have been naive at the time) I had always assumed that people would be more likely to know each other in such situations, regardless of race, simply by virtue of being in a small town. My dentist was a close friend of the family, the lady at the post office was the mother of a classmate and so on. No matter where we went, people were for the most part "small-town friendly." In fact, race was seldom a negative factor in my life and, looking back, I see that I was as racially unaware as a member of a minority could be in such surroundings. Race was never even mentioned in my classes, with the exception of the odd lesson on Native American history, something I had assumed to be obligatory material because we lived adjacent to a Mohawk reserve.

I do not remember experiencing overt racism of any kind, although I was conscious that racism existed in the world. My father told many stories, from before we moved to our small town, showing that my parents' interracial marriage was not only seen as unacceptable, but also was seen as an issue of moral importance. Most comments took the form of "real concern"—"What about the children?" or "Who, me? I'm not against mixed marriages, but you have to think about the society in which we live." In any case, I always felt a sense of pride that in the face of such lack of acceptance, my parents raised their children—at least as it seemed to me at the time—as well adjusted and invulnerable to experiences of prejudice and racism. Again, I transferred this assumption to my brother's experience, assuming that he was similarly spared.

But Greg told me that he, quite unlike myself, can rhyme off several incidents in which he found himself at the brunt of racist jokes or slurs, being frequently forced to deal with insults like "Chocolate bar," "Blackball," "Blackie," "Nigger" and even "Slave." In an e-mail (March 23, 1999), he described one incident that really stands out in his mind:

> I was playing a soccer game at a local high school in grade ten or eleven and developed what I thought was a friendly competitive rivalry between myself and the guy on their team I was always paired up against. This happens a lot and generally isn't much of a big deal. Anyway, this other guy decides to increase the competition by elbowing me. I (because I hate conflict) started walking away. To my back he says to me: "Why don't you go back to your own fucking country, you fucking nigger." I turned around and replied, "Why don't you go back to the sixties?" He didn't have an answer, but he didn't really need one because he was standing there looking for a fight. Anyway, I always thought it was interesting that he told me to go back to my own country. Where would that be, exactly, if not Canada? This is my country and I belong here as much as he does. It's not like we snuck in here and are secretly leeching off the system.

This is only one of many such experiences for Greg. But, I remember only one incident when, in grade four, an older boy (and known troublemaker among classmates) approached me in the schoolyard and called me a nigger. Actually, he was quite nonchalant and matter of fact about it and said it just like that: "Hey, Nigger." His comment seemed so effortless that he may as well have been passing by, whistling and saying, "How do you do?" However, the comment didn't provoke any response from me, not because I was trying to ignore him, but simply because I immediately attributed his comment to a case of mistaken identity. I remember looking behind me and thinking, "Surely he wasn't talking to me? I must have misheard him because isn't that a bad word reserved for insulting Black people? But I'm not Black, so he must be confused. Yes, that's it, he's just confused."

Growing up, I never saw myself as Black or White but, conversely, I did not claim an identity of mixed race either. Sure, I realized that my parents were of different races and that my hair was curlier than that of most of my friends, but for the most part I just felt neutral and generally avoided situations in which I might be forced to define myself racially. So, although I understood this boy's comment in grade four to be offensive, it did not offend me. If anything, I felt it was an insult to my father, but the boy hadn't called my father a nigger, so there didn't seem to be a problem.

Only once do I remember actively asserting any sort of "racial" identity. When I was four or five years old, I would parade around the house, chanting: "My daddy is Black, my mommy is White and I'm *beige*." This new identity, however, quickly gave birth to uneasy racial sentiments from people on the Black side of my family who, cringing over this ambiguous and inappropriate identity, started insisting that I call myself Black. I was also faced with the other side, as White friends would say: "Don't worry, Leanne, I don't see you as Black. I see you as White." But, I think it was in large part my father's denial of racial classification and his insistence that we call ourselves *human*—actually writing this word under the category of race on my brother's birth certificate—that forced me to abandon, at least for the duration of my childhood and teenage years, all labels entirely—Black, White, beige or other. Interestingly, my dad is still of the mind that with hard work and perseverance, as well as limited emphasis on potential racial barriers, one can conquer all obstacles. His optimistic world view—one I have more recently criticized and debated with him—no doubt stems from the fact that through hard work, he moved from an impoverished life in Jamaica to become a successful and prominent ophthalmologist, a position he has held all of our lives. But growing up, my father's particular "racial work ethic" undeniably held some appeal for me at the time and shaped my racially neutral position.

Nevertheless, the kind of neutrality I felt was not a factor in my brother's experience and identity at the time, and I now understand that for many reasons it could not be, not only because of his encounters with racism, but also because of how his friends saw and treated him differently. We mustn't forget the powerful role of others in helping us to define and shape our own identities. For example, although my friends all insisted on seeing and understanding me as White, all of Greg's friends saw him as Black. Greg and I chuckled over the time in grade ten when he and his friends asked a new boy at an adjacent locker what his name was. The boy had answered, "My name is Greg Black." My brother's friends all laughed and said, "Oh, really? There's only one Black Greg in this school!" On other occasions, Greg has told me that friends easily accepted him as Black and were rarely curious or doubtful about his Black identity, in many ways displaying pride in having a friend who was of colour or different. Yet, instead of rejecting a confining identity, as I had, Greg took on the Black identity applied to him, acknowledging that Blackness was a solid point of identification that helped him negotiate many of the feelings he endured of in-betweenness and non-belonging. Although he admits that he has now moved away from this label as the one definition of who he is, Greg maintains that "growing up, I eventually started calling myself Black simply because most people viewed me that way and it was easier. But on another level, using the word 'Black' to describe myself was also a way of fighting for my own identity—for my own name."

As the discussions between Greg and I intensified, his memories seemed more and more out of the realm of my experience. For instance, any racially motivated comments I received occurred only much later, at university. These comments were not phrased along the lines of the aggressive "Go back to where you came from," but were more like an inquisitive and annoying "Where are you from?"—a completely differently intentioned remark. I cannot help wondering why Greg's looks provoked aggression, while mine instilled, if anything, a strong sense of curiosity and ethnic intrigue. I see one possible explanation: that certain ethnic appearances such as those embodied by Greg and myself (namely, non-White) are interpreted as either exotic, offensive or curious, depending on the context and with whom we interact, as well as on the degree of visible difference in colour and shade. We must understand that ethnicity is socially constructed, varied and complex. Therefore, how we understand ethnic appearances is significant in terms of what those looks can and do mean for those who see them and for those who display them. Also, as Julien and Mercer (1996) remind us, ethnicity is often associated with being from somewhere else and not here. For example, ethnic looks are frequently associated with being not only different, but as being inherently non-Canadian, as what it means to be "Canadian" is often associated with assumptions of Whiteness (Frankenberg 1997). Several authors have alluded to this internalization of Whiteness as neutral or normal, reminding us of how society commonly uses "White" as a measuring stick against which all "non-White" others are gauged (Frankenburg 1997; Julien and Mercer 1996). So, how our ethnic looks were differently perceived is partly related to our small-town environment and the fact that its White homogeneity presented a microcosm of "true" Canadianness, sustained through the lives of the town's inhabitants.

Small-town life for a racial minority person reveals another interesting question characteristic of the perceived racial neutrality and normality of Whiteness. The maintenance and acceptance of White neutrality helps us understand how our friends' interest in seeing us as one thing (Black or White) also helped them to reaffirm their own sense of who they were. For example, over the past year I conducted tutorials for a third-year race and ethnic relations course and noticed this kind of tendency in many of my White students, who, eager to show me how they were free of racist sentiment or bias, referred to their Black friends or partners in all discussions, no doubt hoping to prevent any accusations of being racist. Similarly, the memories I have of growing up, including any feelings of difference I may have experienced, are part and parcel of the politics of inclusion and exclusion. As such, how we come to understand ourselves, as many scholars such as Lawrence Grossberg (1996) and Stuart Hall (1996) argue, is in relation to what we are *not,* and through perceived notions of privilege and dis-privilege. I believe that in many ways it was easier for my girlfriends to see me as "White" because it facilitated a certain inclusion into their group and made my fitting in that much easier. Perhaps the difference with my brother's friends and the fact that they saw him as "Black" is related to the fact that many of his racist encounters occurred in male-focused activities, such as sports. His friends were more directly involved in witnessing Greg's experiences of racism, more likely to defend him and hence continually reminded of his racial difference.

The presence of difference in any community presents two interesting scenarios. When differences are made visible—differences of any kind—we find an immediate need for others to label, classify and minimize them by somehow incorporating them into the known social world; or those differences may be accentuated, put down, rejected or excluded. But, interestingly, my experience suggests that whether or not differences are perceived as intrusive depends on a combination of other variables—not only race and ethnicity, but also location, class, gender and so on.

While addressing the possible reasons for his feelings of difference, Greg said, "In a small town there's no middle ground, you're either Black or White." In this sense, if it is true that identity is contextual and formed through our experiences, as I believe it is, then a town without much first-hand experience with people of colour—let alone with mixed race—would likely follow the notorious "one-drop" rule and classify all racial others according to these restricting racial categories. (The "one-drop" rule refers to the view that one drop of black blood designates a person as Black [Harris 1993]; it has also been interpreted as the "inheritance of the lowest status category of one's ancestors" [Zack 1995: xvii].) But this still doesn't explain why Greg was seen as Black and I was seen as White. Moreover, to what extent did the fact that I wasn't seen as Black contribute to my ambiguous or neutral perception of self, as it was clear to me that I certainly wasn't White? And how did that identity influence others' interpretations of me?

I asked my brother if he felt that people need to minimize the threat of the unknown, which could help explain why we were labelled as we were, regardless of how we individually saw ourselves. He said his experiences suggest that the acknowledgement and identification of his race and ethnicity was not necessarily threatening to others, but was only potentially threatening for *him,* if and when others crossed the line and used racial slurs. He told me he understands "labels [as] a method of knowing a person, and to know how to act" around that difference and not offend that racial other. "It is hard enough," he says, "to learn how to interact with the social scenario of a racial / ethnic other, let alone negotiate all the grey areas of mixed race, newer to those in a small town."

Race and ethnicity, and other differences, are extremely important reference points for negotiating how we all get on in the world. Discriminating differences of race, gender, sexual orientation or class help us maintain order in an otherwise "chaotic" world, and the understanding that there are differences in the world allows many to determine how they should act according to those perceived differences. Indeed, as Patricia Williams has eloquently reminded us: "We derive a sense of security from knowing who is on what side of the great racial divide" (1997: 54). Just because I didn't feel exceptionally racially awkward or racially alienated while growing up doesn't mean that my race, colour and ethnic looks were not factors in how others interacted with me and how that further shaped my identity.

Class

Recognition of the differences in our personal experiences extends beyond race, ethnicity and colour, as these experiences were also influenced by other factors. That being said, I was most aware of my class difference and the fact that I was a doctor's daughter. For instance, Greg and I realized that one of the methods our friends may have used in their efforts to deal with our differences was to create several myths about our family's social position. These myths included that we lived in a mansion, that our dad was the best ophthalmologist not only in our town but in the world and that we had our own private jet. True, we lived in a house considerably larger than those of many of our friends, but it was certainly no mansion. And true, my dad is a reputable surgeon who frequently travels, performing volunteer surgery in countries overseas, but it is quite a stretch to claim that he is the best in the world. (And to this day, I have no idea where the myth of the private jet comes from.) In any event, emphasis on our class status was frequent, overshadowing—for me anyway—large feelings of racial exclusion. But I believe it also blinded me from sensing cases of racism or feelings of racial awkwardness among my peers.

A few years ago, my father reminded me of a question he had asked me when I was eleven or twelve—whether I thought he was rich. The question was no doubt fostered by a concern about the potential social consequences of his children having an economic advantage and position of privilege in a largely low-income community. I think part of this concern was a fear that this could be a new source of alienation on top of our different racial and ethnic backgrounds. My answer was, "No, I don't think you're rich, but my friends think you are." So although I never really saw our family as wealthy and certainly didn't feel Greg and I were spoiled (my parents went to great lengths to ensure that we weren't), I knew others believed we were, and it was therefore easier for us to pretend we were the same as our friends where money was concerned.

Many of my memories revolve around what I understood as differences in wealth. I recall sitting around a cafeteria lunch table in high school where my friends and I were filling out university application forms. A few of them aggressively commented that I musn't apply for OSAP or any other scholarships—since I was rich, they believed, and my application might reduce others' chances of receiving assistance. The fact that I might win a scholarship based on academic merit never came into the picture. In terms of class difference, Greg and I had similar experiences. He recalls "playing down his class" and defending himself by saying, "No, my *dad* has money, I don't." But this is where the similarities seem to end.

Thus it seems that the various myths created about our wealth sheltered me, at least, from recognizing that others may have felt uncomfortable around my racial and ethnic difference. I tended to attribute any feeling of alienation to other forms of difference such as class. On another level these myths may also have conveniently served as "justification" for my father's social position and his success as a Black man and immigrant to Canada. In other words, it is easier for others to accept racial difference when that difference is coupled with success, erasing many of the stereotypes that present racial minorities as unsuccessful, impoverished or criminal. On the other hand, I believe that my father's success and Blackness also fostered racist sentiments, including frustration, jealousy and even disgust among those who resented the fact that an immigrant had succeeded where "real Canadians" had not. In a stratified society, skin colour and race have currency in that the closer one appears to be culturally White, the more likely one will appear to be sharing the interests of the White class. But whether or not such a perceived attachment to the dominant White class is seen as acceptable or legitimate varies according to context, individual histories and personality.

Gender

What I now realize is that the feelings of alienation associated with my class position were not unconnected to my particular race and ethnicity, regardless of whether I acknowledged or established a racial identity. This is also particularly noticeable in the area of dating and relationships, where we can see that differences between us are mediated not just by class and race but also by gender. In this respect, how Greg and I were perceived in our hometown was very much dependent upon the stereotypes and assumptions typical in a society with strong undercurrents of sexism, classism and racism. Looking back, I realize that growing up as a mixed-race female and a doctor's daughter also exposed me to different experiences—as well as different social prejudices and privileges—than my brother faced.

For example, I suffered from the "liked by all, dated by none" syndrome. I had plenty of friends, many of them guys, but none of these males approached me with "extra-friendly" motives until I had almost graduated, and even then such experiences were few and far between. Interestingly, I learned much later that my lack of romantic involvements was not due to a lack of interest on their part. Several of my friends and my brother's friends had in fact admitted that they considered me to be "gorgeous," "hot" and sexually attractive to many guys in school, but for some reason I was also seen as unapproachable. I attribute part of this to the fact that many boys were intimidated by my father, the tall, Black, wealthy eye surgeon. In fact, several of Greg's friends would joke about his image, nicknaming him Garth Vader, a play on his first name and the dark and powerful Star Wars character. However, my father was not the only deterrent to potential dates. I believe another explanation is the negative stigma attached to so-called rich girls, namely, that a wealthy female poses a certain threat to males who are less economically secure. This would make sense in our society, which still values a strong element of male dominance and chivalry. In Greg's case, however, his label of "rich kid" may have held more appeal to girls who were looking for a partner who represented the image of the wealthy male who is also tall, dark and handsome. Greg even told me that his popularity with girls during high school sometimes made him question to what extent his image as a "rich guy" made him a more desirable dating option.

However, my feelings of rejection by boys and Greg's popularity with girls go back to my younger years, even before my peers could have significantly understood our class position and used it to structure their interactions with us. Consider, for example, Greg's experience in grade three, when several girls chased him around the schoolyard, obsessed that he was Michael Jackson. Others, he says, continued to be openly attracted to his ethnic difference, commenting on his skin colour as a major element of his good looks. Interestingly, when I was in the same grade, just three years earlier, in that same schoolyard, I was told I couldn't play kissing tag with my friends because I supposedly ran too fast. Kissing tag (a game that involves boys chasing girls around the schoolyard, catching and then kissing them) is a popular juvenile pastime in which children may be for the first time exploring their sexual feelings and actively seeking out those whom they find attractive. A closer inspection of who is seen as most attractive, even at this young age, reveals what I understand now as an entrenched racial stereotype. At the time and long afterwards, I assumed that my exclusion from the game was because I actually *did* run too fast and that my actions somehow contradicted the purpose of the game, which was to get caught and be kissed. But, looking back, I realize that I cannot ignore the power of dominant notions of ideal beauty that are perpetuated in the media and continually reinforced in our families and community. Such assumptions, I believe, are rooted in that still-potent image of the White, blonde bombshell or brunette beauty. Is it any coincidence that not only were all the kissing-tag participants White, but many of them also represented a particular look conducive to that ideal—blonde or light-eyed?

To me, this indicates that the mould of North American beauty is internalized even at a young age, and that the ideal is gendered, with different standards for males than females. Even Greg has admitted he was attracted to White women who had the Cindy Crawford look—the image of the ideal woman among his friends. Conversely, I would suggest that my curly hair, slightly darker skin, Jamaican heritage and ethnic difference (combined, of course, with the perceptions of my wealth and possibly my strange, ambiguous identity) was, particularly as we got older, outside the dating norm. In other words, I think I was in many ways seen as too exotic and too different from the ideal, whereas my brother's looks were seen as "tall, dark and handsome." I am reminded here of bell hooks' (1992) work on desire and the male gaze. She argues that the act of looking carries with it a certain power, accompanied by objectification and stereotyping. For example, she writes that because ethnic looks are now popular in entertainment, fashion and international modelling, society seeks out ethnicity. But not all ethnic looks, she argues, are equally desirable. Greg's looks may have been more acceptable because there is a somewhat less rigid emphasis on dominant models in the conception of male attractiveness. Accordingly, my rarer relationships with boys in high school shows that I represented a difference that others were less able to understand because they were unable to locate my skin colour and ethnicity within the dominant standard. So, it seems to me that Greg and I were differently affected by certain ways of looking and seeing the world, perceptions that are built on internalized stereotypical, supremacist and sexist values and assumptions—perceptions we must not ignore.

I have recently been very interested in why we choose the partners we do and how our choices are influenced by racial and ethnic standards and stereotypes. For instance, is the fact that we tend to see more interracial couples involving a White female and a male of colour indicative of a particular racialized preference? If so, this may explain why I have been consistently most attracted to Black men, whereas my brother tells me that he finds White women to be most attractive. However, it may also result from growing up in a household where this was the particular mixture we saw and understood as acceptable. Or perhaps part of this preference is indicative of how we were seen and how we saw ourselves in our youth. Because Greg never experienced significant rejection by White girls, he may not have seen any reason to later modify his preferences. My memories of being rejected may have consciously or subconsciously influenced my later choices of potential partners, steering me away from Whiteness, as I associated it with that rejection.

A Mixed Racial Identity

Looking back on our youths reveals the complexity of the "mixed-race experience," if there can be such a thing. Mixed-race authors have started to discuss the variations and differences in experiences of racially mixed individuals and are acknowledging that it is important to understand these variations and where they come from (see Root 1997). Indeed, there cannot be any one mixed-race position, experience or memory. I was naive to assume that my memories would be the same as Greg's. Instead, how we lived within the interlocking forces of race, gender and class continually changed and affected how we negotiated who and what we were at that time.

Over the past year or so, I have become painfully aware of the transforming and contradictory nature of identity formation. Hall (1996), among others, is right in arguing that our identities do have a history and come from somewhere but are also constantly changing and shifting as we are individually subjected to the forces of culture, power and history. Our identities are not just waiting out there for us to find and slap onto ourselves forever, but how we see and name ourselves is directly related to how we are positioned within structures and past narratives.

Today, Greg and I see ourselves differently than we did in the past. We now both proudly claim mixed racial identities, but not for the same reasons. Although we both see ourselves as racially mixed, *how* we understand what it means to be mixed is still different. For instance, our understanding of the term "mulatto" is a perfect example of this difference and highlights the nebulousness of semantics. Personally, I have always found the term to be highly offensive, implying the union of two "unmixable" beings producing a somehow volatile, unstable and abnormal offspring not unrelated to the notion of the sterile, hybrid mule, (and a stereotype rooted in slavery) (see Zack 1993, on why people of mixed race have little documented history—because this subject was regarded as undesirable or taboo). Greg, on the other hand, sees the label in quite a positive sense because it helped him to eliminate many feelings of in-betweenness and ambiguity as he gradually moved away from a monolithic and monological Black identity. He claims that "it [mulatto] is an identity to cling to and the fact that there is a name for what I am means that I am not the only one out there, and that it is okay."

In fact, the whole issue of labelling presents an interesting challenge. Terminology is now taking centre stage in discussions of mixed racial identity, as we continue to struggle over what we can or should call ourselves and to what extent we can step away from old labels and create new ones. For instance, debate over whether there should be a new category on census forms for people with racially mixed heritages has cultivated the use of new terms such as "interracial," "transracial," "biracial" or "multiracial." But questions remain: What importance should we place on such labels? Should we criticize those who find comfort in labels we may personally find to be offensive, such as "mulatto"?

For Greg and I, claiming a mixed racial identity is not always easy. Sometimes it's easier for us to do so, because sometimes we're taking advantage of the privileges that such a characterization entails—the ability to cross boundaries and remain anonymous while at the same time presenting a challenge to racial classification. Sometimes being of mixed race frees us from boundaries; sometimes it only imposes new ones, which we must struggle to break through. However, our memories of growing up, though different, are still fundamental to the identities we have presently chosen. Each time I sit down and talk with my brother about the past, we are both enlightened by new experiences and encounters. How we interpret and understand the past shifts and takes new forms. Memories are wonderful, but hindsight also presents a clarity shaped by our current positions and world views.

5

Looking Back while Facing Forward

LORNA RENOOY

The first ten years of my life I lived in a three-bedroom apartment above my parents' bakery with my four older siblings, Mum, Dad and various family pets. I remember chilly winter mornings downstairs in the shop. On any given weekday, the warm air was filled with the clatter and clink of dishes, and the smell of cigarette smoke intermingled with the aroma of coffee and fresh baked cinnamon buns. It was a friendly, comfortable atmosphere where I felt a lot of freedom, as long as I didn't get underfoot.

This was the time before school filled my days. The bakery and the familiar faces within it were of infinite interest for me. I could watch all the activity and go practically unnoticed. My strongest memory is a feeling of ease—moving comfortably, freely, in this safe and accepting environment. I never worried about how others would react to my appearance.

I remember standing on stage as a sixth grader—slim, straight and tall in a new blue gingham dress that my Mum had sewn for me. Before the music festival audience, I recited Robert Frost's "On a Snowy Evening." That year, my best friend and I tied for first place.

Many spring days, and on into the fall, I raced my bike down the side streets with the other kids. In winter, almost every Saturday afternoon was spent at the skating rink. Back home, a friend and I would rub our feet warm again, sip hot chocolate and enjoy the bakery's delicious buns. I spent hours playing and going for walks with our various family pets. I was thrilled when my big brother took me for a ride in his new convertible, my long hair flowing with the wind as it rushed past my face.

I was active in community youth groups, served on the student council and yearbook committee and played various sports. I always did well at school, had a group of good friends and was encouraged to explore and develop my interests in photography, drawing and reading. All this helped build a strong foundation for my positive self-image.

Like many of my peers, I also liked to go shopping or to see a movie in the city. But unlike most other girls my age, I received a lot of negative attention from strangers. Surrounded by people who didn't know me, I had experiences very different from those in my home town. Whenever

I ventured beyond the scope of my village, I tried to ignore the stares, the teasing, the pointing fingers, but these things did have an impact.

I was born with craniometaphyseal dysplasia, a condition that caused the bones in my head and face to grow unusually large and thick. Over time, as I grew bigger, my face became longer and wider. My eyes grew very far apart and the bridge of my nose became more broad and heavy. The bone on my gums was so thick I could hardly close my lips together, and I always wore bangs to cover my prominent forehead.

I also have other clear, distinct memories from my childhood the ones that dwell in dark corners and forgotten places. I endured a lot of tests and underwent a few unsuccessful surgeries to change my appearance. I learned how to cope with a different face, with feeling misunderstood and sometimes feeling alone, that it was just me against the world.

I learned to avert my face when I met strangers on the sidewalk; I would take a sudden interest in whatever happened to be in the shop window. I learned that kids can be cruel. One Halloween an older boy sneered, "Hey kid, where'd you get that mask?" And I wasn't wearing one. I learned to be strong and not complain, so that I could shield my parents— who were helpless to change my circumstances—from hurt and frustration. I felt I had to be tough and resilient, and I never cried. I was afraid that if I allowed the tears to come, all the pain, anger and injustice I felt deep, deep inside of me would flow up and out and that then the tears would never stop.

Although my family and I never talked about my face or the challenges I experienced because I looked so different, my parents and siblings were a source of unconditional love, acceptance and support. They, and the people in the community where I grew up, helped me to believe in myself.

I had many ideas about what I would do when I finished school. At first I wanted to be a veterinarian. Then, later, I decided to pursue a career in graphic arts. I wanted to travel to Europe. I plotted a course of action, including all that I'd do and see. I embraced the future with open arms.

On a November day in 1979, when I was seventeen years old, my father took me aside to tell me about a surgeon in Toronto who "may be able to help." At first I was surprised and confused, then I felt angry and indignant. "Why did I need to change?" I asked myself. "Why did I have to have a face that looked like everybody else's?" After I had a traumatic experience with surgical failure when I was fourteen, I had ruled out medical intervention as a viable option. "And besides," I reasoned to myself, "I've gone ahead with my life; I'm determined to make it rich and rewarding."

Throughout my childhood and teens, as far back as I can remember, actually, I was very adept at minimizing the impact that my appearance had on my life. I didn't think of myself as being "different," and in many ways I was more like other kids than unlike them. Some might say this was denial, but it was my way of coping and it served me well in some ways. I felt that it made those around me more comfortable, but it also meant that any difficulties related to my experience of facial difference became my personal, private problem, rather than one shared openly with family and friends.

By the age of twelve, I became painfully aware that my physical difference did matter, more than it ever had before. Before, I might have been teased by kids who didn't know me, or stared at by strangers, but I always felt a part of my peer group. But things began to change, starting with my body. I was glad to reach puberty, since many of my girlfriends already wore bras and had their periods. But it was clear that while I was friends with many boys, I was definitely not dating material. It was a ridiculous contradiction; I was maturing sexually but was regarded as asexual by my peers (the males anyway). I was invited to parties but never sat in dark corners with anyone. I went to the school dances hoping that for one night, for one dance, things would be different.

Through this subtle rejection, I concluded that I would never marry. I believed, to my very core, that no man could ever accept my appearance enough to love me. No one would or could look past my face to see the person I was. I resolved to pursue a life of world travel and an exciting career.

Now, in my last year of high school, the spectre of surgery was once again intruding upon my future. I felt the enormous weight of uncertainty upon me. Once the option was raised again, I couldn't help but think long and hard about it. Questions—"What if I did? What if I didn't?"—crept into my mind when I least expected them. No one knew the conflicts I struggled with. I had sworn my father to secrecy. Although Dad knew I was corresponding with the surgeon, I didn't talk to him about it.

After several weeks, after I had really considered what it meant for me to look the way I did in a society that emphasizes conformity to a particular idealized beauty standard, I wondered if my hopes and dreams for the future were enough to see me through. I felt a bit defeated, but I also felt determined to meet this new challenge head-on.

In January, I flew out east to meet with the craniofacial surgeon and other specialists. I learned more about my options. The surgeon was very frank. "You can never expect to look normal," he said, "but I can give you a 70 percent improvement." The risks—blindness, brain injury, death—terrified me. After speaking with him, I hastily made my way down the hall to the nearest bathroom. Sitting on the toilet seat, hidden from sight, I muffled my sobs into my coat. My body shook with tears of sadness and fear; what I had kept buried inside me I couldn't hold back any longer. It just didn't seem fair. Why couldn't society simply accept me and my face the way I was?

After a long, emotionally draining week, I went home. At Sunday dinner, I shared what I had learned. One of my sisters-in-law said to me, "You don't have to do this, you know. You don't have to have this surgery. It's other people's problem, not yours."

"Yes," I countered, "it may be their problem, but I have to deal with it."

So I decided to take my chances; even a 70 percent improvement would make dealing with the negative reactions—the stares of strangers, the unkind comments and inappropriate questions—a little easier.

Leaving home to have radical surgery in a different part of the country was the first tenuous step in a journey that would change my perspective on life. It took a couple of years to complete the reconstructive process and a couple more years to adjust to the physical changes. I would look at old pictures and think, "That's not me." But I would look in the mirror and think, "Well, that's not my face, either." I couldn't close my eyes and picture my face as it now appeared. My "new" face felt like a mask, something I'd been given to wear, but not something that was part of me.

After many painful procedures and long recovery periods that were physically and emotionally demanding, I felt saturated with surgery. Any additional improvements just didn't seem worth the risks.

I decided it was time to pursue my dream of travel. I applied to a student exchange program in New Zealand and Australia. On the other side of the world, and for the first time in my life, I was entirely on my own. No one knew me or anything about my history, and I relished what I saw as a chance for anonymity, obscurity. But I discovered that because I still looked different, there was nowhere that I could be just another face in the crowd.

While my appearance was more acceptable—or, to put it another way, elicited fewer visceral reactions from strangers—some people still asked me, "What happened to your face?" I had to learn to deal with people's curiosity; there was no getting away from it. So I developed a short, simple explanation that seemed to satisfy most people.

People are by nature inquisitive, and particularly about appearance. Coming into contact with a person who has an unusual appearance is for many a new experience, and this can cause social norms to change. Strangers feel they can ask you personal, intrusive questions.

They may have many misconceptions or false beliefs about what it means to live with a physical difference, and they tend to make a preconceived, negative judgement about the quality of our lives.

The face—particularly the eyes, nose and mouth—is considered to be the centre of communication. This is the area of primary focus when we speak with another person. It is where we look for emotional cues to connect and engage. If something is different or unusual about the face, then people who are not familar with such situations may feel uncomfortable and awkward (Cole 1998; Partridge 1990).

While reconstructive surgery may offer improvements, there are often residual differences that cannot be eradicated. My experience of plastic surgery is not that portrayed by mainstream media, which spreads the notion that any difference can be completely "fixed" (Bull and Rumsey 1988).

There are abundant examples in folklore and mythology of negative stereotyping of physical differences or disability (Cooke-MacGregor 1974). In our society, we learn as children that "What is beautiful is good" (Dion and Berscheid 1972). As adults, we find ourselves surrounded by images of perfection that are all too often equated with narrow definitions of success, health and ability. In these ways, appearance contributes to the ways in which we are defined. This can make it difficult to go about our ordinary, everyday lives.

Looking different has given me so much. I have found that identity is something to be actively negotiated, rather than a matter of fate to be passively accepted. At an early age, I was determined that I would not be written off because of my face. Through my experiences I've gained a lot of insight into human interactions. While I was growing up, I faced situations in which I could sense a person's discomfort with my appearance, and I learned how to put that person at ease. I looked them in the eye and engaged them in conversation. I sometimes used humour to break the ice. I learned how to get them to see me as a whole person, and not only as someone with an unusual appearance.

Over time I have learned that I don't have to be strong all the time. I have learned that sharing my difficulties doesn't necessarily mean that I'm complaining. Sometimes, I can laugh with my partner or friends over an encounter that, if left to fester in isolation, could have been more hurtful. I can share my frustration when I feel injustice in the world. I have developed a respect for other people's differences and a passion to try to make the world a better place to live in.

Most significantly, I have come to value and appreciate all my experiences because they've shaped the person I am. Ultimately, my facial difference is an integral part of my identity. It is not all that I am, but it is a large part of me. I don't want to change my face now; I only want to change attitudes. I wonder why we, as a society, can't appreciate and value our physical differences instead of thinking that we can or should control, perfect or transcend our bodies.

It has been years since I left the small village where I grew up. I have travelled to many parts of the world and I have a rewarding and satisfying career—not despite my facial difference but because of it.

Schooling and Difference

6

Looking for Science in All the Wrong Places

KAREN MEYER

This chapter addresses the estrangement of females from science soon after they cross the threshold of the school laboratory. My stories on this subject come from my experiences as a laboratory debutante, as a teacher and interpreter of seminal science textbooks, and as an educational researcher looking for pedagogical transgressions and solutions. I wish to offer an alternative science pedagogy that engages our bodies, memories and imaginations as co-participants in the phenomenal world. I assume that knowing is rooted in our experience and relived in our stories. For many of the women education students I have taught, this (re)incarnation of science subverts the legacy of "school science and the deficient female." Inspired by our presence in the living world, we look for a sensuous science in what we hear, see and touch that will create connection and intuitive understanding. The following stories and voices (of women students of mine as they were interviewed in a doctoral study by Lynn Fels) point towards an engaged pedagogy (hooks 1994) with alternative methods for teaching science.

What's Wrong with This Picture?

What I recall about growing up in science classrooms resonates with stories I hear from women education students in my science methods courses. Dispirited yarns spin in and out of our collective stories, weaving the stigma of an engendered antipathy:

> As rookie science student in the 1960s, my privileged adolescent self was a compliant wallflower, Cinderella without the mother-mentor, without the vitreous slipper, without the alluring ball. The clock high on the wall reads 12:01, and the glum puerile belle wears a stained lab coat and sits in a technical room with noxious smells and the dull dreariness of a dungeon. A fairy tale goes wrong. As I saw it, any serious sabotage of my scientific learning was an inside job, my fault. And not knowing was a crime punishable by peer humiliation. All considered, my sedulous silence was strategic, and avoidance was a logical

> long-term plan. The world can be rose coloured when your eyes are shut. Un-credible school counseling soon slated me along with other grateful girls to more humane subjects where I belonged and genuinely longed to be. (Meyer 1998: 464)

What happens to girls en route from elementary to secondary school science? My own feelings of alienation did not come from elementary school experience. On the contrary, I have comfortable, even euphoric memories of language-arts science, where I happily wrote about fish, birds, ants and my grandmother's cataract, which I brought to school in a tiny glass bottle—a piece of my grandmother's eye. Back then most of my knowledge of the living world was set in motion by curiosity and wonder. There isn't much opposition in this carefree world; friction is simply overcome with a downhill slide at a playground or by a rusty pair of training wheels attached to an elder brother's bike. Wheels can keep a little girl going over the bumpiest of times and surfaces. Karen's got new skates. See her roll. What I learned about the physical world was the result of my participation in it, my way of being present and aware of it. These are the observations natural laws are made of.

In elementary school, science is not bound to the textbook but follows a child-centred approach. Is there any other choice? It happens that young children of the blackboard jungle simply will not tolerate any other kind of teaching. If a science professor arrived at a primary classroom with one too many overheads and with jargon-laden lecture notes, chaos would quickly ensue. What does work there are learning centres that have: water tables with water wheels and pouring devices; balance blocks and building apparatus that leave standing structures behind; magnifying glasses that transform our perception (or "magic-finding glasses," as I once heard a child call them); a world-class collection of rocks gathered from all over the playground; and long, stringy bean plants potted in Styrofoam cups lining the window with one unfortunate control plant under a box. The world becomes meaningful when it is treasured.

Secondary school science, on the other hand, is the unannounced jolt; the snapping rope of a whim; the critical time when we lose the interest of girls. In this period of science there is an abrupt turn of the desk from a student-centred to a teacher-directed approach. Open-ended activities become recipes or demonstrations out of students' hands. Without the slide and the training wheels she stops. Karen's skates don't fit anymore. I think they're in the basement somewhere. And there she will sit, another adolescent belle in the same stained lab coat, sitting in a row of desks, staring out the window, with the dry-as-dust lecture about inertia hitting her body as sound waves. She longs to be connected to the living world, but by now inert scientific laws from heavy textbooks displace experience and rank above embodied knowing. Everyday language is unheard of and playful patois has no place.

> I just remember sitting at the desk, taking notes off the board. That's how I remember my science class. Like learning about the tree or plants and stuff, there'd be a hand-out, we'd label it and take notes on it. I don't remember very much other than that (Maria).

> When I got to junior high school we had science, but again it was taught by a man in a lab coat who did all the experiments at the front of the classroom, and we simply watched and wrote down the results of the experiment without asking why. It was like a recipe, a formula. We just wrote down the results, and we remembered those results for the exam and that was our science (Annie).

> I never enjoyed science in high school, because there was no connection to my experiences or my world, me, my background. No, high school chemistry, it was just ... we learned all about the periodical table and then learned how to do all these different diagrams; but how did that apply to my life? (Teresa)

Most fundamental to secondary school science are textbook explanations that describe distilled descriptions of phenomena as final truths, as completed maps. As such, these decontextualized explanations are extrinsic to a girl's perception, experience and fantasy. The curious questions they answered long ago have been forfeited to an over-structured and overcrowded curriculum. Within the instructional broadcast of these preserved explanations comes a barrage of jargon, and silence is the recourse for many girls. In the end, the passwords are the glossary at the back of the textbook or the parroting of definitions as if they were lines from a travel phrase book. Science as a second language is a liability to participation and communication, making access and inclusion problematic.

> The reason I probably got turned off science was the textbook. Let's just do it this way; and all that scientific jargon, and you're going, "What's going on?" (Maria)

> The one thing I had the toughest time with when I was growing up with science was that I was asked to memorize.... I was

> asked to sit there and memorize.... I just didn't get science. It was such a mystery. It was such a mystery to me. I just didn't understand. It was so abstract. Little light bulbs were going off everywhere, but not mine.... With me ... it seemed like I missed the first step and everyone was way ahead of me. (Christina)
>
> It didn't feel like I had access. (Pam)

My own teaching struggles to break the routine, the status quo, the guise of school science, from which story, body and passion are erased (hooks 1994). What has worked for me and for the girls and women I teach is the integration of knowing, doing and creating with inquiry, enacted methodologically through storytelling, participation with physical phenomena and creative interpretation. The world becomes meaningful when we engage with it.

The remainder of this chapter shares my experiences of using these interrelated themes in my learning and teaching of science.

Storytelling and Embodied Knowing

> I am charged with translating decontextualized, analytic explanations into phenomenological meaning for my students. In doing so I become midwife. My voice slips from Physics 101 jargon to mother tongue. I nurture, I hold hands, I push. I encourage primal screaming so I know *when and where physics hurts.* (Meyer 1998: 464)

My first goal as teacher is to interrupt the sounds of silence in science class. To begin, we tell our stories related (sometimes figuratively) to the science topic at hand. For example, within my introduction to buoyancy, I have listened to students' anecdotes about first learning to swim, about what it felt like to be in the deep end for the first time, about playing Marco Polo, about sitting at the bottom of the swimming pool for as long as possible. These stories act as memory triggers, bringing forth experiential ways of knowing and revealing how that knowing came to be. From these stories we realize what we already know about the physical world (e.g., movement through different mediums, displacement and force, sinking and floating). In an elementary classroom, twenty hands go up in the air making offers immediately after the first story. In the secondary science classroom, or in my university classes, students are initially reluctant to share their stories, but, even so, their reminiscing eyes speak. Surely, somewhere in students' educational experience, stories seemed to stop mattering. In any case, I take the first risk.

It was nighttime and late, when a little girl should be asleep inside the house. Nevertheless, on this hot summer night, I was cozy laying on a cot in the corner of our patio. I pretended to be asleep as the adults on the patio visited, mostly Grandpa's poker buddies. I heard bits of their stories and the clacking sound of plastic chips on the long redwood picnic table. I saw only faint silhouettes sitting there, backlit by lanterns and ghostly cigarette smoke. Over in my corner was a dimly lit lantern sitting on the cement floor. I had insisted it be there so I could open my eyes at any time and find the light. But tonight, as my sleepy eyes circled the patio, they were caught by a dark shape moving along the wall across from me. This foreshadowing of peril alerted my eyes to focus. There I saw the sharp outline of a spider at least as big as I, moving as tarantulas do, one leg at a time slowly feeling its way forward. I pulled myself deeper into my cocoon-like sleeping bag. So this is what it's like to be a small bug on the ground. *Just before I was about to leap from the cot, I noticed the lantern beside me. On the glass was a small spider, just pea-size, moving synchronously with the shadow on the wall. Realizing what this special effect was about, my panic passed away. But my imagination kept the portentous shadow alive, as I safely fantasized my own shadow defeating it.*

Apparent in this story is a little girl's knowledge about shadows candidly cued by the relative positions of light, spider, shadow and herself as perceiver. How did I understand, as a young child, such variables related to shadow formation and size? Perhaps I had experimented with my own shadow, watching it grow as my body moved closer to a light. The body, with its various sensory and motor capabilities, is the way we are present in the world, the way we perceive, interact and, as learners, create meaning.

In the elementary classroom I spoke of earlier, interaction with objects is encouraged. However, in too many secondary science classes, students only read about their properties and behaviour. "A shadow is an absence of light," says the textbook—rather than the presence of "something that follows me around in the light, as I once heard a child describe one." As such, embodied knowing (from touching, listening and observing) appears insignificant in the classroom and in due time becomes dormant. I find that reviving knowing based intuitively on our bodily experience prompts students to think profoundly about complex phenomena. We begin inquiry with knowing.

We pulled ourselves and our chairs into a circle, which isn't an easy task in a lab where most everything is stationary and set up to face the lectern. Today the circle was about sharing memories to find out what we know about the complex phenomenon of swinging. We had explored the oscillating motion of pendulums, but now it was time to integrate our bodies into the source of its motions. "Can I go all the way around the top bar?" "When is the best time to jump out of a swing to fly over to the sandbox?" "Can my swinging motion tip over the backyard swing set not cemented in the ground?" As children, we wondered; our bodies enacted possibilities. But today our task was to describe in words the mechanics of swinging. I asked for a brave volunteer to sit in the middle of the circle, mime the movements of swinging on a lab stool and narrate the steps, as a playground parody, choreographed without feet touching the floor. She leaned back and stretched out her legs, then shifted forward and bent her legs back to the rhythm of an invisible swing. Strangely enough, we in the circle became participant observers as we swayed in our seats while thinking hard about whether or not the description we were hearing was accurate. For me, it was not possible to listen without visualizing my own memory of swinging. A mind/body resonance compelled me to move back and forth rhythmically on my seat. Clearly, I was thinking with my body. Our next lab would be held at the nearby park. By now, we were all anxious to swing.

Becoming Participants

Beginning understandings of the living world require engagement with phenomena in the moment or in retrospect, both inherently tied to experience and language as situated meaning. Qualitative understanding requires the moment of relevance that experience brings forth. But the requisite for prepackaged school science is vicariousness: how (usually male) scientists do it, how (usually male) progenitors did it, how the textbooks (often written by males) explain it. No part of the program feels feminine or in any way relevant.

Today our science class happily abandoned the lab to undertake an academic adventure I dubbed "laboratory on ice." This act of heresy (to the traditions of science courses and the doctrine of scientism) lead us to the university rink, equipped with skates hanging from shoulders, and personal memories of junior hockey and spinning axels atop frozen ponds. From this chatter, it was clear that many of these students learned to skate soon after they had learned to walk. But today's lab wasn't about skating particularly, it was about experiencing and thinking about sliding friction. Today the icy surface held our attention to movement and our intention to think deeply about it. Of course, I, a neophyte to the slippery sport, had the most to lose to friction. That is, my downfall was about to come. The first glide brought the sensation of imperfections in the ice and in my manoeuvres. While hugging the boards, I marvelled at a woman skater who was spinning in the centre of the rink, enacting the moment of inertia as a moment of grace. At the same time, a former hockey jock raced around the periphery, breezing by me, chasing an imaginary puck with an imaginary stick. Upon meeting at the centre of the rink, these two quite different skaters planned their experiment. They switched hockey skates for figure skates. And neither had tried the other skates before. As we watched for the consequences of the provisional trade, we observed an extraordinary metamorphosis as they each began to skate. Our hockey performer transformed into an ice dancer moving across a frozen Swan Lake; our once graceful figure skater transformed into a hockey enforcer moving in a rather aggressive manner. Those of us who watched huddled and conferred about the differences between the two types of skates in relation to the ice, to particular movements and to social contingencies. Skate or identity? Science is never quite that simple.

Creative Interpretation

The culture of science includes the art of description and interpretation. In science, descriptions of phenomena begin with the dynamic conditions of an event but proceed further to descriptions of underlying mechanisms. Initial episodic descriptions attempt to conserve a process of relations and contingencies that can lead to explanatory meaning. What does this event mean in a bigger picture? Like the relation of parts to a circular whole, phenomenological descriptions are imagery for an explanation; yet the explanation can bring a sense of coherence (Aha!) to the event.

Omitted from conventional science teaching is an exposure of students to the first level of description, which requires their participation with the phenomenon, and storying the possibilities and dependencies; that is, playing with variable relations and interpreting what happens. Dynamic description arises from mindful engagement and questions such as, "What matters?" and "What if?" These qualitative questions necessarily precede formal explanations and the question of explanatory relevance: "So what?"

> If you allow more than one venue, more than one way of expressing it, you open that up, there's no longer a gatekeeper, the gate's wide open. All you have to do is walk through it and try. (Pam)

Needless to say, there are as many ways to describe the living world as there are participants. Let's not forget that such diversity is fundamental to creative expression. While descriptive words themselves are neither transparent nor opaque, they are chosen from our existing repertoires to situate and strike meaning retrospectively for ourselves and others. But the correspondence of phenomenon with language is variable, full with possibilities, like a landscape reflected in a rippled pond on a windy day. Particular words, analogies, metaphors and stories indigenous to contexts and cultural circles provide bands of meaning. At best the mirror image blurs and resembles an impressionist painting.

Descriptive forms I encourage in my teaching and learning of science include poetry. I wrote the following poem after observing some interesting wave patterns on a long and wide beach on the Washington coast. As a sort of deconstruction, I thought about what mattered to the phenomenon, including my feet in the water.

Waves of Time
Tide leaves his lover as the sands run out
Evermore pulled back by the whim of a celestial goddess
Restless Sea responds with calculated beauty
the wind at her back cradled in patterns
She chants kindred lullabies of chaos in recursive breath
while her wetness paints sensuous graffiti on the sand
imprinting the transient shore forever. Come back.

Another form of expression that brings out the best in science is drama. I had the good fortune to co-teach physical science with a drama educator in a teacher education program. In this mix of drama and science, we called our participation with physical phenomena "performative inquiry" (Fels and Meyer 1997). In our three years of teaching together, the students produced a variety of expositions, including portfolios, scripts, videos, readers' theatre, improvisation, soundscapes, as well as a play (written and performed). Drama offered us an opportunity to explore alternative ways to teach and learn science that sanctioned doing, knowing, talking and creating. We brought to the stage our knowing as language embodied in performance.

> What drama does is offer more than one way of expressing a discovery, more than one way of expressing how something works, more than one way of expressing a principle, a theory, a hypothesis. (Pam)

> I guess drama just brought the different situations that we encounter in our everyday lives ... and just made the connection between science and real life. It allowed us to express ourselves. (Teresa)

The highlight of these three years of co-teaching was the production of a play written and performed by our university students for several hundred children in a theatre on campus. Beforehand, during the semester, we had explored light, colour, sound and motion in the lab.

> And the the idea of the play emerged. The blockage of light from a chair with clothes thrown on top became the shadow monster in a little girl's room. The journey from idea to stage involved the creative and practical application of the students' knowledge of shadows and light, sound and silence, motion and stillness.... Wendy is our play's heroine. The stage is a bedroom at nightfall cluttered with scientific textbooks, a (six-foot) stuffed bunny named Einstein, and an unexplained monster in her room. Intrigued, she abandons her textbooks and seeks out the monster through her closet door, a journey that unfolds in the surreal lands of light, sound and motion. With a reluctant Einstein in tow, she unravels the mysteries of coloured shadows, survives exploding carrots, jive-dances on musical stairs, and rescues her long-eared companion from shark-infested waters (all choreographed according to physics).... The play came to be the integration and interpretation of what the students had learned, imagined and created during the course. Through the writing and producing of the play, students applied phenomena and "special effects" explored earlier in class investigations. (Fels and Meyer 1997: 78, 79)

Annie, the director of the play and a student in the class, later reflected.

> The science was pervasive in this course. In problem-solving the lighting, there was not one area of light that we did not actively discuss during our preparation for the play. I now know intimately how to make large and small shadows and create any colour shadow on demand. And don't even get me started on spotlighting.... There is nothing we can't do now.

Final Thoughts

As difficult as it may be to believe, physical science provides a most creative context for integrating knowing and doing into learning. After all, we move, we see, we hear, we touch. We enact our presence in the living world, and it gestures back for our attention. Yet somewhere along our life in school, we became disenchanted with our natural surroundings and our curious awareness of it was left dormant. In secondary school science, girls in particular are estranged from the language of science, from the lack of connections to themselves. Access and inclusion are, to say the least, problematic. Their stories, their bodies and their passions are forfeited to a prescribed and decontextualized curriculum. Stories I hear from women all play back the regrettable drama of being an outsider. Generally, school science has lost the most valid purpose for teaching it: to engage students into an appreciation of the living world. This is surely an important point, because only a small fraction of our students will become scientists. Still they memorize.

There is, I believe, an urgency to these points I raise. In the teacher-education program in which I teach, countless numbers of the women students show their discomfort with science and recount their unfortunate experiences with the subject in high school. They will be teachers soon, possibly teaching science to girls during that critical dropping-out time. They may be in charge of translating decontextualized, analytic textbook explanations into meaningful experiences for their students. I am truly empathetic, given my own legacy of learning science. At the same time, my response has been to intervene, to experiment with pedagogy that includes women's voices, participation and creativity. Such a procedure includes working with resistance and confronting obstacles in myself. To this end, I have been captivated by bell hooks' holistic proposal of engaged pedagogy which commits to self-actualization and well-being for students and teacher. She emphasizes risktaking participation, intellectual and spiritual growth, making connections to life experiences and healing.

Several years ago, I had the honour to teach with a former education student of mine. She was teaching grade seven science in a school rich in cultural diversity and poor in resources. She paid particular attention to the girls in the class during our pedagogical experimentation. Density was the topic for the week, and most of the time was spent in a generative space for explaining some curious questions about why some large heavy objects float and some small light objects sink. There was much discussion during these science periods, but the teacher warned me in the beginning that many girls still remained silent. That meant us going back to the drawing board for more inclusive strategies. Fortunately, in the end, most of the girls became engaged in class discussions, offering their ideas. At the end of this week I talked with a small group of girls about how they felt about the week of science. One of the girls reached inside her desk and pulled out her wallet. She opened it and pulled out a carefully folded piece of lined paper. As she showed it to me, I recognized it as her explanation of buoyancy which she generated today in class. She told me it was the best explanation she had thought of, ever written. Her eloquent statement printed so carefully on the paper, spoke with no jargon, yet matched any explanation I've read in textbooks. I pulled my wallet out from my pocket, opened it and shared some of my own treasures I keep there. A fairy tale goes right for this adolescent belle. The world can be rose coloured when your eyes are opened.

7

"You're doing it for the students"

On the Question of Role Models

Carl E. James

At a meeting with some high school teachers in the fall, I was approached by a Mr. Sosa (a pseudonym), a teacher at a Catholic high school in suburban Toronto, who asked if I would come to his school to talk to his media class. He said they would be discussing racism in the media, and he felt that the students would benefit from hearing me talk about how minorities, and Blacks in particular, were represented there. I said I would get back to him. However, I was unable to do so before we met again at another meeting in early spring of the following year, when Mr. Sosa again reminded me about my standing invitation to talk to his class. He said he thought the students, especially the Black students who made up nearly a third of his class, would benefit from "meeting someone who holds a position in a university." He wanted me, someone he thought of as a "a successful Black male who has also experienced systemic racism," to give some advice to the students about how they too could become successful by focusing on their academic work. He ended by saying, "You're not doing it for me. You're doing it for the students."

This conversation with Mr. Sosa raised a number of questions for me. Yet again, I was asked to advise students about how they too could "overcome" racism and become a "successful" Black person. I was seen as someone whom the teacher could present to the students as a role model who could, as Mr. Sosa said, help to "empower" them, as in me they would see the possibilities and power of education. I was expected to encourage these students to apply themselves to their school work (their "academic work," as opposed to sports, which seemed to be the primary interest of some young men), so they might someday attain a university position or some similar professional position—indeed, I was expected to provide a testimony to the fact that meritocracy exists. As a role model, I was expected to, as Deborah Britzman (1993: 38) puts it, "do the work of education" as informed by the liberal multicultural approach.

I am sure many young people are quite familiar with the kinds of presentations in which they are told that "you can achieve like me only if you apply yourselves." As Warren Crichlow (1999: 3) argues, based on a "dubious economy of likeness, students are blithely provided role models whom they resemble or whom they are assumed to intrinsically share a collective interest [with] and will therefore automatically 'be like.'" This "role model" message is highly problematic, for, as Britzman says (1993: 25), it "fails to address the disruptive question of whether it is even possible to imitate a role." She continues: "This status is thought to produce rightness, clarity, completeness, and stability. Role models arrive preassembled. They are not only larger than life; they are rolled out precisely because they have rolled over all that stood in their way" (1993: 25). Isn't there an inherent contradiction in this liberal, linear conceptualization of the role model? Is it really true that so-called role models have overcome barriers to success (however "success" is conceptualized) because we are found in organizations and institutions that hitherto excluded people like us? Or do we manage to attain certain positions precisely because we can be held up as role models for those who might become despondent with their possibilities in the society and become "social problems"? It is instructive that Mr. Sosa was more concerned about the Black males. This concern might be a reflection of the social image of Black males as potential problems if they are not properly socialized, managed and policed (see James 1998).

My role, then, as a role model would be to help in that socializing process[1]—to work with the teacher in *managing* these youth, and the young men in particular, and participate in the use of my body as curriculum. Was this something that I should be doing? Did I want to? What about the "proper" social values and morals that I was expected to represent and communicate as a role model? How does Mr. Sosa know that the ideas he wishes me to communicate to the students reside within me simply because of skin colour? After all, as far as I could discern, he did not know me. He had met me for the first time and was making the assumption that I would be an appropriate person to talk with his students. Should I accept his invitation or decline? I always question this "multicultural" curricular approach, which is premised on the notion that I not only represent and understand the purportedly monolithic group of Other Canadians, but also I am able to talk to them so that they understand and become convinced that there are exciting possibilities for them in the future.

Indeed, I am one of those who argue that Black students need to see people who look like them in schools, people with whom they might be able to identify, or whom they think will understand where they are coming from in their ideas, values, aspirations and behaviour. It is not merely skin colour, social class or similar experience that are the basis of this argument, but giving students opportunities to connect with a diversity of individuals from whom they can choose their own role models. But there are times when Black "role models" are invited to schools to talk about "Black things" such as racism or "the Black experience," because it is perceived that these are the areas in which we can best be fitted into the curriculum, or in which we have some expertise. Black History Month is a time when this is particularly evident.[2]

Then there are special events, such as career days, when "successful Black role models," particularly those identified as the first to hold a job in an institution or field, are invited to talk about their success. The problem comes when the motive is based on skin-colour representation, that is, when the physicist, nurse, physician, professor or engineer is invited to events more because he or she is Black than because of their professional expertise. In many cases educators are not only identified by others as good role models but present themselves as such. For example, in research I conducted some years ago, candidates asserted that they were motivated to become teachers because they wished to "become role models" or, as one person said, to "prepare young brothers and sisters to get a job." They seemed to believe that as teachers they would be able to counteract the negative influences and expectations students were receiving, not only from school but also from the media.

In one candidate's first meeting with the classroom teacher in the school in which he was to practise-teach, the teacher (a non-Black woman) said to him and another Black male in front of the whole group of teacher candidates: "It is important for you two Black gentlemen to be here. You should go out of your way to help a lot of the Black kids along and make it known to them that you are available. You guys are going to be role models whether you like it or not, and it's very important that you realize what being a role model is" (James 1997a: 167). The message was clear: The Black male students needed role models and these Black male teacher candidates were to fill this void. A possible reading of the teacher's remark is that she considered the individuals whom the students presently viewed as role models to be deficient, which could include the students' parents and/or relatives. The assumptions that the teacher and teacher candidates in this case were making are not unlike those of Mr. Sosa. They seem to think that part of their job as teachers is to identify role models for students, and often race, nationality and gender are chosen to establish a match between the role model and the youth over things such as experiences, aspirations and expectations in life. I am familiar with the school where the teacher candidate had this experience. I often went there in the course of my duties as faculty liaison with the school, and I too have been told that it is good for me to be there because I am a role model for students. Similarly, in another school, I facilitated for about two years what was called the Empowerment Committee, whose objective was to help reverse high absenteeism and dropout rates and the "low academic participation and performance" of Black students. Both of these schools are located in working-class, ethnically and racially diverse areas of Toronto.[3] Many of the students' parents are immigrants, a significant proportion of the students were being raised by single women.

By participating in these schools' socialization programs and fulfilling their expectations of us, we reinforce the notion that Black youth in general, and males in particular, are "diseased"[4] and need to be fixed. Hence, as role models, we are perceived as those best able to respond to students' needs. Interestingly, factors such as middle-class status, educational experiences, past and present family situation, migration history and neighbourhood experiences are given little or no consideration. Those individuals from like neighbourhoods are assumed to be the best role models, for they symbolize how, despite the odds, high achievement is possible for students from the area. For this reason, educators and community members encourage students to become teachers and return to their neighbourhood school to help others. But is it true that these former students and (probably former) residents of the area will be able to transcend generational, historical and contextual differences and help students to "make it," or, as one youth termed it, "ghetto out"?[5]

Let me be candid: I am not against the idea of role models. Rather, I find the linear way in which the idea of role model is conceptualized and used in practice highly unproductive. The issues and questions I identify here illustrate the problematic, contradictory and ambivalent positions in which I and many others often find ourselves. I contend that the conceptualization and practices of role modelling are part of a hegemonic system in which educators inadvertently participate that encourages young people to conform to prevailing values, role expectations and beliefs about the educational system.[6] Role models are expected to collude with the educational system to produce uncritical students who have no sense of the complexity and contradiction of the racial construction of identities, their relationship to the histories of colonialism and social structures, and "their own proximity to the histories and experiences of racism and sexism" (Britzman 1993: 39). This conceptualization of role modelling reinscribes difference in terms of "otherness" while purporting to preserve difference, and it obliterates the liberal notion of the individual's uniqueness by presenting some groups of individuals as the same, simply based on physical characteristics.

How then to reconceptualize role models? I believe that role models are people who are chosen and created by individuals based on their conscious and unconscious motivations, aspirations and expectations, which are constructed within a particular political, social, economic, cultural and historical context. As Celia Haig-Brown (1998) explains, role models are people from whom students derive inspiration, with whom they choose to identify, and from whom they believe they can learn specific things. So identification of a role model rests with the individual or student who, in pursuing a particular life or occupational / career goal, "sees another person who has achieved that place as a site / sign of hope" (Haig-Brown 1998: 108). In this way, we are able to acknowledge and respect that students come to school with contradictory expectations, aspirations, and understandings of themselves and their places in their communities and society as a whole. Therefore, in leaving it up to students to choose their own role models, rather than just presenting or imposing them, we acknowledge that students have the capacity to make decisions that correspond to their own reading of their needs and realities. In doing so, we avoid the risk of them dismissing us as role models—and our message—because they see us as a party to the school's process of conformity socialization. More importantly, we will be working with where individuals really are at.

Nevertheless, whether imposed or chosen, role models, particularly Black role models, embody contradictions, in that the success that we are presented as exemplifying—and the belief that "if I can do it, you can also"—could be viewed as masking the claim that inequality, racism and discrimination are barriers to the achievement of aspirations. Recognizing these barriers, would it not be ironic and contradictory if I presented myself to Mr. Sosa's students as one who has overcome the barriers of racism and therefore can empower them along a path toward the successful attainment of their life's goals? Equally problematic is the notion of presenting ourselves as role models when we might represent for some students a contradiction—suspects, "sell-outs"—individuals who are working within the system. It is this aspect of our role as role models that I wish to consider in the remainder of this essay. Specifically, I contend that the expectation that we can help to empower students is misguided; empowerment can only be gained through an individuals' own efforts, and the contribution that role models can make to such efforts will not come from those presented to students, but rather from those whom students themselves identify as role models. My role, therefore, and the way Mr. Sosa should think of it, is to make connections with the students. It is up to them to decide how they wish to relate to me. In this way, the relationship is less likely to be fraught with problems and dilemmas.

Black Teachers and Black Students

In an essay, "I've Never Had a Black Teacher Before," which appears in the book *Talking about Difference* (1998), I described my relationship with Black students as paradoxical, ambivalent and antagonistic. I indicated that there were tensions that both White and Black students tended to attribute to the fact that I was their first Black teacher. The idea was that I was different and they were unfamiliar with a Black teacher/student relationship, so, as they said, they were "unsure" of how to relate or what to expect. On the basis of my constructed difference (as well as my perceived similarity), there were particular expectations they had of me and thought I had of them. Contrary to my thinking, some of the Black students felt that I had higher expectations of them than I had of their White peers, and that they had to work harder to satisfy my expectations. (Some likened the expectations to those of their parents).

Some Black students felt that having a Black teacher would validate their experiences and give them a voice in the class. I was expected to "go easy on them," something they did not expect of their White teachers. In cases where I might, in their view, make "extra" demands of them or give them lower grades (especially if they have been "succeeding" before with White teachers), I was perceived as ignoring or not affirming their experiences, imposing "harsher standards" and having unreasonable expectations. Moreover, sometimes I was seen as no different than their White teachers—equally given to assimilating them into Eurocentric values and ideas.

The expectations of students are informed by their racialized experiences in an educational system from which they have felt alienated, and in schooling contexts in which having a Black teacher meant that they would be noticed more, so their relationship with me was often scrutinized. Particularly illustrative were occasions when they felt they had to prove to their peers that the grades they received on assignments were well deserved and not due to bias grading or favouritism. Thus constructed differences and similarities between Black teachers and Black students contribute to tensions in their mutual relationships. As a result, students often seek to create a distance between themselves and Black teachers, the very people considered to be "good role models." In the process of distancing, students might claim a dislike for Black teachers or, alternately, a preference for White teachers.

Black teachers are not uncritically accepted as an alternative to White teachers, nor are we automatically regarded as role models. We are scrutinized, tested and evaluated according to the extent to which we meet students' expectations and conform to the social standards and conventions of our role as educators, which, as Crichlow (1999: 6) notes, are "authored by the dominant group of society." All of this leads to antagonistic, stultifying and difficult relationships,[7] and to situations where "role models are trapped, and often trap themselves in role performance defined outside of the self" (Crichlow 1999: 6).

While it is very important for Black teachers to be part of the educational experience of Black students, we cannot expect to be accepted as teachers and role models without questioning or ambivalence, for, like us, students understand the paradox of our power and privilege in the hegemonic structure of the school and society. Within this context, we are either seen as individuals who have been able to navigate the constraints of the social structures, have "made it" and therefore have ideas to pass on, or we are dismissed by those cynics who find it difficult to believe that someone can work within the educational system and still remain committed to social change. Therefore, race and the assumption that educators share similar histories and racial experiences as Black students do not guarantee that we will be trusted allies. We must be prepared to deal with students' ambivalence, expectations, conditional support and doubts. Given all this, we can expect that our relationships with Black students will often be filled with tension and conflict.

The Myth of Empowerment

Mr. Sosa wanted me to "empower" the students. I was expected to make the students believe, if not through my words then through my presence, that they have the power within to attain the goals they aspire to. This notion of empowerment is part of a cultural system that would have those without means and access to power believe that empowerment can be given and role models can facilitate the process. However, as Martena Taliaferro (1991: 1) writes in her essay, "The Myth of Empowerment":

> True power (empowerment) cannot be beneficiently bestowed upon a group by another.... Moreover, those who propose to "give" power often return to monitor, supervise, or redefine that gift to keep it within their control or in their own image. Empowerment is a conscious self-inducement controlled by an individual. It comes from within; it cannot be "given" to students.

Hence, it is not for me to seek to empower the students but rather to ensure that Mr. Sosa's pedagogy and course content, and the school environment, are responsive to the needs, aspirations and expectations of students. Do they nurture, promote and even demand that consciousness from the students that will enable them to become and feel empowered? Before inviting me to the school, did Mr. Sosa find out from the students if they wanted me to visit? What was their input into inviting me to the school? Were they likely to find that I model judgements and critical actions that also can apply to their lives and aspirations?

In fact, Mr. Sosa did discuss my visit with the students beforehand. And the students were attentive, had questions, and participated in the discussion. But I understood from them that very little was done by their teachers to address their needs and issues. Some reported that school was "a bore," and the young men in the group felt that their only way to become successful was by winning a basketball scholarship. We devoted quite a bit of time to the subject of athletics and the possibilities they hold for Black young men. In a conversation after my talk, Mr. Sosa expressed his concern about this interest among the male students in his class. He was hoping that, as a role model, I would dissuade them from their interest in athletics and turn them on to education instead. How can I, in one visit to a school, do what that school and the school system in general have been unable to do for years?

I found out that the school was about 20 percent Black, and while Blacks were well represented, and even significantly overrepresented, in winning athletic awards, this was not the case for academic awards. How can I empower students when, evidently, there are systemic issues that the school needs to address? Recently, referring to the situation in another school, a student pointed out to me that she had heard a social worker in the area, which she describes as "inner city," say that one of the main problems in the area is that there are not enough role models. This social worker contended that "all of the role models, particularly for Black youth, are athletes or recording artists. In this way, Black youth in particular do not feel that they can make a contribution to the world of science and technology." The student further pointed out that "when you walk around in the hallways of the school, you come across the Hall of Fame with pictures of Black students excelling in athletics, but they are not equally represented in the Academic Hall of Fame." It is in cases like this that individuals are brought in as role models to do the work of the teachers. But it is unlikely that role models can help students empower themselves when educational structures limit their possibilities.

Creating an atmosphere that enables students to empower themselves requires trust and mutual respect which, in part, are learned through interactions with teachers, including Black teachers. In Mr. Sosa's school, where the students with whom I spoke had very little experience with Black teachers,[8] it was possible, and understandably so, that they would be suspicious of me and what I had to say, since their schooling had not given them the opportunity to respect and build trust and confidence in someone like me. Given this lack of experience and familiarity, my credibility was likely to be influenced by, among other things, how they understood and viewed Mr. Sosa. Did they respect and trust him? Did he seem to understand their issues of alienation and disempowerment? After all, the students did not know me, so how could they understand any commitment I had to their concerns?

I do not think we can effectively connect with students unless they are schooled in an environment that promotes and nurtures empowerment and gives them the opportunity to build trust, respect and confidence through questioning and active participation in their schooling. Until that happens I will be merely another Black adult, sponsored by the school, who comes in to talk with them.

Role Models Are Chosen and Constructed

Being a role model is a challenge. It is a dynamic role, but also one that can be problematic, full of paradox and ambivalence, and at times, contradictory. It is not a role for which a person nominates herself or himself or is nominated by their peers. It is a role created by those who identify with us as individuals who represent the possibilities in particular aspects of life, not necessarily related only to race, gender or professional status. The middle-class, liberal notion upon which role modelling is largely premised and practised is contrary to the fact that individuals' desires and aspirations move them to create their role models. It is a role constructed within social and political contexts.

Marginalized young people who make connections with and eventually choose role models arguably do so conscious of the contradictions that they represent. Their choice of role models will not be based on success as defined by Canada's multicultural and meritocratic assumptions. Their choices will be informed by their perceptions of how the role model has been able to *manage* and live with the contradictory and complicated issues that he or she faces within institutions and society. A student will want information about how role models have been able to navigate the social, economic and political systems, and negotiate the paths to their respective positions without losing sight of their goals or compromising their politics.

This understanding of what it takes to make connections with students was brought out clearly when I went to talk with Mr. Sosa's students some six months after the invitation was first issued. I went not because I agreed with the idea that I was a potential role model, but because I believe, like Crichlow (1999: 18), that inequality in material conditions and social justice within and across communities makes access to role models and other kinds of supportive relationships relatively difficult for racialized students. As I had expected, the fact that I was an educator who worked at a university seemed unimportant to the students, and my race or colour did not create an instant connection. They were less interested in what I had to say about the benefits of schooling and the idea of educational outcomes, but more interested in hearing about how I understood the educational system and their possibilities within it. They articulated their desire for me to understand their experiences, situations and challenges from their perspectives. In time they can be expected to identify their role models based on their own needs, aspirations and expectations, as well as on what they know and with whom they have connected. My visit to their school supported this process.

In concluding, let me point out that I am well aware that raising critical questions about role models is a dangerous business. This has been clearly communicated to me in the many fora in which I have discussed these ideas. But as Crichlow (1999: 19, agreeing with Anita L. Allen) and others have correctly argued, raising critical questions about role models is not meant to cripple activist work for equity. Nor is it meant to invalidate the work of those who seek to model or identify possibilities for marginalized people. Indeed, it is important to actively address inequalities and barriers to opportunities. Nonetheless, it is also politically important to question the assumptions upon which role modelling continue to be based and practised.

8

Classroom Doors at Christmas
Negotiating Religious Difference in Public School

TARA GOLDSTEIN

This is a story about being Jewish and going to a Canadian public school in the 1960s. It is also a story about being Jewish and teaching in a Canadian public school in the 1990s. It is about what it means to be Jewish during the month of December when the upcoming celebration of Christmas weaves its way into the everyday life in classrooms across the country. It is also about the legacy of institutionalized Christianity in Canadian public schools and what it means to negotiate religious difference in them at Christmastime.

In telling this personal story of schooling and Christmas, I hope to make connections between institutionalized Christianity and the difficulty of respecting religious pluralism in public schools. Because this is a personal story, I ask that you read it with care. You may or may not like what you read, but I hope you read my story with the goal of trying to understand my experience as a Jewish student and teacher in public school. When you have finished reading my story, I hope that you will ask yourself what you have learned about schooling, Christianity and religious difference, rather than if you agree or disagree with me. If you are a teacher in the public school system, I also hope that you ask yourself how you might work with others in your school towards respecting religious difference. In keeping with the story's theme of decorated classroom doors at Christmastime, you might ask yourselves: What will go up on my classroom doors? And what will go on behind them?

Jewish Students, Christian Schooling

I grew up in Montreal in a neighbourhood called Snowdon. It was a working-class and middle-class neighbourhood with many young families who lived in apartments, duplexes and houses. My family lived on the bottom floor of a duplex, the advantage being that we had a basement. When my brothers got older, my parents turned the basement into their bedroom and turned their former bedroom beside the kitchen into a dining room.

Many of the young families in Snowdon were Jewish, and I grew up surrounded by other Jewish people. The family upstairs, who owned the duplex, was named Cutler, and the Hefezt and Lewis families lived in the duplex attached to ours.

The shopping district in Snowdon was on Queen Mary Road. We did our grocery shopping at Steinberg's or Grostern's, bought Jewish bread and baked goods from Pinky's and had kosher meat delivered from the NDG Meat Market. Our family didn't keep kosher, but everyone knew that kosher meat from the NDG Meat Market tasted better than the unkosher meat they sold elsewhere. My father was a pharmacist and owned one of three pharmacies on Queen Mary Road. I worked in the post office located in his pharmacy for two summers while I was in high school. There was also a Jewish bookstore that sold books in Hebrew, Yiddish and English, Caplan's gift shop, a Jewish cleaner's right beside my father's pharmacy, a Jewish variety store named Black and White, or Blackie's, and a Jewish delicatessen known by everyone as Snowdon Del or Snowdon Deli. Snowdon Deli was so popular that they opened up a second restaurant in Thornhill, a Jewish community north of Toronto, a number of years ago to serve all the Jewish families who had moved to Toronto from Montreal in the seventies and eighties.

My family lived in Snowdon from the time I was four years old until I was sixteen. I attended elementary school at Iona Avenue School from grades one to six. Only one of my teachers, my grade five teacher Miss Ostrum, was not Jewish. Most of my classmates were Jewish. On Jewish high holidays in September and October, only a handful of non-Jewish students would be in class and they would most likely have a substitute teacher because their Jewish teacher was also not at school. Yet, every morning from grades one through six we began the day by saluting the Canadian flag, reciting the Lord's Prayer and singing a Christian hymn. While I know very few Hebrew prayers (though I can light the candles at Hanukkah and Passover and bless the wine), I can still recite every word of the Lord's Prayer.

Our grade two teacher, Mrs. Schneider, allowed us to take turns choosing which hymn from the hymn book to sing, and I always chose "Onward Christian Soldiers" because I liked its tempo and energy and drama. My favourite line was "Christ, the loyal Master/Leads against the foe/Forward into battle/See his banner flow." It was many years later that I actually understood what the hymn was about and learned that throughout history Jewish people like myself were killed by Christian soldiers for being the foe. I wonder what it was like for Mrs. Schneider, a young woman in her twenties in 1964–65, to have to sing that hymn with us over and over again knowing that, just twenty years before, nearly six million Jews (approximately one-half of the Jews in the world) had perished in the European Jewish holocaust; and knowing that Hitler's "Final Solution" to the "Jewish Problem"—the extermination of all of Europe's Jews—was buttressed by ideas that can be traced back to Christian religious anti-Semitism that began at the beginning of the Common Era (100–600 CE).[1]

My favourite month of the year in elementary school was December, because we got to go to the back of our hymn books and sing Christmas carols. I know the words to many of them: "O Come All Ye Faithful," "Away in a Manger," "Hark the Herald Angels Sing," "O Little Town of Bethlehem." In grade five, I was a member of a school choir asked to sing Christmas carols at a new indoor shopping mall located near the train station. It was Miss Ostrum and our music teacher, Mrs. Frieberg, who accompanied the choir to Place Bonaventure. I remember that my mother and grandmother came to watch the performance. My favourite carol at the performance was a Calypso hymn with the line "Mary boy-child, Jesus Christ, was born on Christmas day." I remember swinging my shoulders in rhythm to the Calypso beat and my grandmother saying that she loved watching me move to the music. (My grandmother and my mother were big Harry Belafonte fans and I grew up listening to lots of his music. My favourite line?: "That's right, the woman is smarter.")

In Miss Ostrum's class, we decorated our classroom door every month. I was assigned to be in charge of December's decorations, so the next time I went shopping at Steinberg's with my mother, I bought a bag of lollipops and a package of Christmas paper cups. Steinberg's, a large supermarket chain, not only sold Jewish products, but they also sold items for Christmas. Then I went to Blackie's and bought a piece of white bristol board. At home, I created a lollipop Christmas tree by gluing the plastic-covered lollipops to the bristol board in the shape of a pyramid. I also glued one of the Christmas paper cups to the bottom of the tree to make it look like the tree had a pot. After hanging the lollipop poster on the classroom door, I put the rest of the lollipops in the cup. Miss Ostrum really liked the Christmas lollipop poster, and so did I. I liked it so much that I created a lollipop menorah poster for the first night of Hanukkah at home. But it never occurred to me to decorate the classroom door with a menorah. The classroom door of the public school was for posters of Christmas trees; menorah posters were for our private celebrations at home.

Despite the fact that I sang Christmas carols throughout December, performed in a Christmas concert at Place Bonaventure and created a Christmas poster for our classroom door, if you had asked me, "How do you celebrate Christmas?," I would have replied, "I don't celebrate Christmas, I'm Jewish." Being Jewish meant that we didn't have a

Christmas tree at home, that we didn't receive presents from our family on December 25th, that we didn't go to church on Christmas Eve or Christmas Day and that my mother didn't cook a big turkey dinner like the mothers on television did. I did not feel left out because we did not celebrate Christmas; we had Hanukkah, which was celebrated with the retelling of its own story from the past, its own prayers and rituals, its own sharing of gifts, its own playing of games and its own special food.

I don't remember experiencing any conflict around Christmas in elementary school and I don't remember feeling it was difficult being Jewish at school. Perhaps it's because Mrs. Schneider and about twenty other Jewish children sang "Onward Christian Soldiers" with me. Perhaps it is because I could buy the lollipops for the Christmas tree poster at Steinberg's and the bristol board at Blackie's. Perhaps it's because both my mother and my grandmother came to hear me sing Christmas carols at Place Bonaventure and made me feel good about the way I sang the Calypso carol. I was lucky.

Two decades earlier, when my father had attended high school in Montreal, there were only three Jews in the whole school and he remembers getting beat up for being Jewish. A decade later, my mother graduated from MacDonald College in Ste. Anne de Bellevue with an elementary school teaching certificate and was told that, being Jewish, she would only be allowed to teach in schools with large numbers of (immigrant) Jewish students—schools, like Devonshire, which were located in the working-class Jewish neighbourhood in Montreal.

Teaching as a Jew

While I lived through my own experiences of anti-Semitism in high school and at the military base in St. Jean, Quebec, where I held my first teaching position, the first time I ever experienced conflict around Christmas was as a teacher in a public school in Toronto. By the time I joined the school, students in public schools in Toronto were no longer reciting the Lord's Prayer or singing hymns every morning. Public schooling had become a mostly secular experience. In an attempt to acknowledge the increasing religious diversity in their schools, many teachers and principals were replacing or supplementing traditional Christmas celebrations with festivities celebrating a variety of winter-season religious holidays.

Having grown up designing a lollipop Christmas tree for the door of my grade five classroom, I personally felt comfortable celebrating Hanukkah, my non-Christian holiday, at home, and Christmas in public. But I realized that not all non-Christians felt the same way.[2] And I supported the efforts of teachers and principals who were creating a more inclusive curriculum around holidays in December. So when the planning of Christmas celebrations started in November, I raised the issue of religious diversity at a staff meeting. I made what I thought was a relatively uncontroversial suggestion: instead of holding a Christmas door decorating contest, we could hold a "holiday" door decorating contest in which we would decorate doors with a variety of holiday themes, not just Christmas themes. I didn't mean no Christmas themes; I meant other holiday themes in addition to Christmas themes.

The suggestion was greeted with a silence that I remember as being icy, embarrassed and tense. Nobody told me they didn't like my suggestion. Nobody explained that the Christmas door decorating contest was a cherished tradition amongst the almost entirely Christian staff. Nobody told me that many of staff had been working together and decorating doors together for almost two decades. Nobody said anything—until mid-December when I casually asked one of my colleagues why no one was decorating their doors for the holidays. Well, it turned out that no one knew how to decorate a "holiday" door; they only knew how to decorate a Christmas door. And they felt resentful that they couldn't decorate their doors with a Christmas theme after my remarks about diversity and inclusion at the staff meeting. In fact, my colleague told me, people were saying that I had stolen Christmas from them and that the only reason I was so interested in "holiday" doors was because I was Jewish and I wanted everyone to celebrate Hanukkah instead of Christmas. I had had no idea that people were so angry with me.

At the Christmas party later that month, I was the first person to gather around the piano to sing Christmas carols. I knew the words to all of them and I sang with frenzied energy to show everyone that I had nothing against Christmas and, in fact, liked Christmas even though I didn't celebrate it. My energetic singing didn't help me. People still avoided me at the party, averted their eyes when I tried to make contact, walked away when I approached them. I had stolen Christmas.

While teachers and principals in other schools working with families from a variety of religious backgrounds had learned to accommodate the diversity in their schools and develop new traditions like the annual winter "Festival of Light," my colleagues had had the privilege of keeping their Christmas traditions intact. Almost all of my colleagues were Christian (the year I joined the school only three of approximately one hundred teachers were not Christian). As well, most of their students were Christian and those who were not had been educated, as I had been, to accept the public celebration of Christmas, to the exclusion of everything else, as normal. What could be wrong with singing about the birth of Christ when Mrs. Schneider taught you the words? Nothing, until you grew up and learned that some of your ancestors had been killed or harmed by people acting in the name of the baby whose birthday is observed on December 25th. Nothing, until you grew up and realized that by including holidays other than Christmas during December celebrations at schools, teachers have the opportunity to teach children something about religious tolerance and freedom so future generations of Jewish and other non-Christian people do not have to fear that their lives are in danger because they don't celebrate Christmas.

What I underestimated in my request for a holiday door contest, and what had caused the extraordinary anger and the feeling that I had stolen Christmas, was the sense of loss my Christian colleagues felt at being asked to modify a set of traditions that had brought them much pleasure and comfort and, perhaps most importantly, a common bond.[3] "But Christmas is for everyone," they tried to explain to me at the staff meeting. "No, it isn't," I tried to explain back.

My insistence for inclusivity at Christmas and my insistence that Christmas was not a holiday for everyone not only brought a loss of pleasure and commonalty, it brought a loss of innocence: it's hard to acknowledge that not everyone shares your joy at Christmas. It is even harder to acknowledge that throughout history millions of Jewish people have been massacred simply because they were Jewish and not Christian.[4]

Promoting Religious Tolerance and Freedom in Public School

The tradition of decorating Christmas doors at the school never resumed. Nor did a new tradition of decorating holiday doors begin. We continued to have Christmas/holiday parties just before the Christmas holidays/winter break. These days, as teacher educator, I promote religious tolerance and freedom behind my own classroom door through readings and discussions about religious oppression and accommodating religious diversity at school. I also light my menorah after—not during—class on the first night of Hanukkah. Students who are interested in the ceremony come to my classroom on their own time. I realize that my promotion of religious freedom at Christmastime has become somewhat private, limited to the students in my own classroom, rather than fully public or institutional—just like the work of the eleven-year-old who designed a lollipop tree for school and a lollipop menorah for home. The difference, though, is that this private space is a space within a public school, that the people who share this space with me are going to be teachers of their own classrooms very soon, and they will bring their sensitivity and understanding around religious oppression to bear on their work with a new generation of Christian and non-Christian children. In this small way, I hope that we all can work towards the kind of education and schooling that will ensure that religious tolerance and freedom prevail.

9

Diversity as the Fall Guy
When Adaptations Go Awry

Sandra R. Schecter

I was ecstatic returning to my homeland, Canada, in 1996 with my two young sons following a prolonged exile in the United States. Personal circumstances had carried me to a distant land—to the lotus fields of northern California—but I had never fully intended to remain there permanently, notwithstanding the incomprehensions of the many who thought I must be mad to yearn for the land of galoshes and rear defog. To those sufficiently emboldened to question my judgement, I responded that I was allergic to lotus flowers and the public schools were better in Canada.

The quality of public schooling has been a major issue for me for a long time, on both a personal and professional level. A healthy state of affairs was clearly nowhere in evidence close to where I lived in the State of California, arguably the result of successive years of retrograde educational policymaking on the part of the legislature which, over a fifteen-year period, had caused the state to plummet from second highest ranking on standardized national measures of academic performance to second lowest. This situation had not been of central concern to me in my children's early years, because I was content to have them start their formal education in a private, denominational school where I would receive assistance in providing my children with a base in Jewish theology and observances. But I couldn't rationalize a private-school lifestyle for my children over an extended period (and couldn't afford one either). I was determined to reside in a linguistically and ethnically diverse setting and that my children would benefit from an intelligent public-school education. When I accepted a position at a university in the vicinity of metropolitan Toronto, I based my decision largely on my judgement of the city's ability to present the socio-demographic factors I was seeking in conjunction with reputable public schools.

I have spent most of my adult life in university environments, and I am in the education business. Hence, as a parent making decisions about formal schooling for my children, I had considerable cultural capital. I was knowledgeable about the reputations of the various school boards within the broad vicinity of my workplace and used this information to identify potential neighbourhoods for living. Although pickings were slim, and rents prohibitive, I managed to find an airy flat in a diverse community not far from my workplace, within a catchment administered by a board with a reputation for considered schooling.

Two years later, I have some good news and some not so good news to report. The good news has to do with the school's academic strengths, a reflection, in my view, of the parent board's enlightened, inquiry-based policies with regard to curriculum. The school receives a steady influx of non-native-English-speaking immigrants who are placed in grades appropriate to their developmental levels, as opposed to their language proficiencies. School personnel follow through on these placements by devoting generous resources to facilitating the learning of groups with diverse educational needs and, specifically, to preparing non-native-English-speaking learners for academic literacy. They manage to do all this despite the provincial government's disparaging stance towards the quality of teachers' work, and despite their overseers' patronizing admonitions to teachers regarding their roles as gatekeepers of high academic standards.

In my children's early months in grades two and three, respectively, I received a letter from the school which I especially appreciated. Addressed to parents of grade three students, it invited me to consider whether my child might be better served by one of the board's special education programs, and suggested a number of strategies I could pursue should I conclude that this scenario might be worth looking into. My instinct was to respond defensively. I felt my muscles tighten at the very suggestion that my son Jacob, for whom academic learning can be a struggle, was being counselled into a stream that would limit his abilities to engage critically with his surroundings and, ultimately, his life opportunities. Reading further, however, I learned that in this schooling culture "Special Education" referred to programs designed to enrich individual children's educational experiences by focusing on either a special need or a special talent. If a child's abilities and interests warranted, they would have the option of attending a school with an intensive fine arts program, for example, or the resources to allow a focus on the development of musical intelligence. Under the umbrella of "Special Education," my child could be enrolled in a class with resources devoted to fostering children's literary imaginations, or to the cognitive activity involved in the pursuit of mathematical knowledge. Of course, several of the scenarios addressed the pedagogic needs of children who were performing below grade level in their primary subjects, but in this "inclusive" context, all of these scenarios were palatable.

Engaging that letter in the solace of a partly furnished flat that was acquiring the characteristics of home, I experienced a response similar to a religious epiphany. The same response was evoked by a simple notice I received several weeks later, requesting that I arrange an appointment for my first parent-teacher conferences at my sons' new school. Following the lines on which I was to list my preferred dates and times, I read the following: "Please indicate if you will require an interpreter for the conference and in which language." My God, I thought, I have finally crossed over from the darkness into the light.

Now for the not so good news. I should first mention that the events and circumstances that stimulated my thinking related to the central premise of this essay concern mostly my younger son, Zachary, at the time in grade two. From the outset, my older son, Jacob, appeared comfortable in his new social surroundings (although academically he was and continues to be not nearly as driven as his achievement-oriented parents would like). For Zachary the adjustment was decidedly more difficult. I initially chose to attribute this condition to the more obvious causal factors involved with displacement (missing one's friends, getting used to new physical surroundings, adapting to the climate change) and dismissed it as transitory. As time progressed, however, Zachary's state of mind became more fragile, and the conditions he reported experiencing in his new school environment proved increasingly difficult to rationalize (even though it was very much in my interest to rationalize them, since I had as much as I felt I could handle on my plate at work). Following a number of occasions when the uncontrolled weeping he exhibited after he got home (or even on the way home) from school abated after a substantial afternoon snack, I thought to inquire whether he had not liked the lunch I had packed for school. This is how I learned that these treat lunches I had intended as a midday morale booster had been appropriated and consumed by his peers. In fact, he rarely had the opportunity to pierce the cellophane of his pizza and taco kits. Giving him money to buy a drink in the cafeteria wasn't a good idea either, it turned out, because his coins were often needed to barter for a verbal agreement not to physically abuse him, a contract which, apparently, bound only the direct parties. At first I rationalized that these reported events were based on misunderstandings caused in part by Zachary's penchant for acts of impulsive generosity that he later regretted. But by and by, the welts and bruises on his back and legs begged a different interpretation: My younger son was the victim of bullying.

I don't have major lingering issues with how the particular circumstances related to the victimization of my son were resolved. A number of strategies were tried, including increased supervision in the cafeteria and at transition times in hallways, and dyadic "conversations" between individual children and administrative personnel. Some proved more effective than others, and through a process of trial and error the more pernicious aspects of my son's predicament receded over time. What remains disturbing is not the bullying of my son in a multidimensional institution characterized by flux, but rather the explanations provided by representatives of that institution to account for these circumstances.

Initially, school representatives appeared to want to ascribe the events to adaptation problems my son was experiencing because of the recent relocation. I could understand that they would want to do this: for several months I had engaged in a similar kind of problem-distancing reasoning. At the same time, I found the textual representations of this rationale unsettling. One official I spoke with offered the following: "Your son is not used to being in a school with so much diversity." I had *absolutely no idea* how to respond to this assertion. I suppose I could have refuted the proposition: having regularly accompanied me to the various sites where I conducted ethnolinguistic field work in the course of practising my trade, my son had probably had more exposure than most North American children of his age to persons who did not look or speak like him. But even then the statement did not appear significantly relevant to my little boy's circumstances.

My father had emigrated with his family from a village outside the city of Kiev, in Ukraine; and the origins of my mother's family could be traced to the same geographic area. The children who were victimizing my son were from other parts of the former Soviet Union and neighbouring countries. Eastern European history offers considerable evidence that people originating in some parts of the former Soviet bloc lack the knowledge and experience necessary for interacting with people from its other parts. But I doubt this was what the person who advanced the diversity hypothesis to me had had in mind.

After weeks of reflection, fed by detailed descriptions provided by my son concerning the ways his situation was being monitored, I realized that ungrounded assumptions were being made about the group identities of the children who were targeting my boy. I had an opportunity to test this hypothesis while dealing with the school over a subsequent incident involving the territorial needs of several students who were apparently of the mind that, if my son did not find an alternative outdoor spot in which to play, they would be entitled to "shove this ball" up his various orifices. Speaking with the same official, I asked what specific aspects of his new school culture they believed my son was not successfully engaging. I was told that Zachary wasn't used to being in an environment with "so much racial and ethnic diversity." This time I understood. I responded that the only kind of diversity relevant to my son's situation was that related to expectations about how a school's citizens are to interact respectfully. After that exchange, our situation improved.

Educators' expectations about how children are to engage in each other's social worlds represent a worthwhile subject for serious, critical reflection. Somehow, the eight to ten rules about how we are to treat our peers posted in nearly every primary school classroom don't quite cut it. ("Be kind with your words and actions. 'Check.'") I would like to highlight the underlying assumptions that provide the context for school and other institutional representatives' understandings of these sorts of phenomena.

What, for example, should one make of the following observation? At the beginning of the school year I contacted the person in charge of an afterschool program serving families from our school's catchment. After visiting the facility, I decided to enrol my children. There followed a process of filling out multiple forms—the usual disclaimers, releases, medical and school history information. One of the questions called on me to volunteer the name of my child's teacher. I couldn't remember—it was only the second day of school—and neither could my son Jacob (who remained stubbornly in summer mode for several more weeks). Unable to jog our collectively defective memory, the care provider tried another strategy: "Is he in Special Ed, or is he with the *normal* children?" So much for the religious epiphany (unless it is being seriously revised to include images of leper colonies).

My sense about Canadian schooling in large urban centres, and especially a sophisticated cosmopolis such as Toronto, is that the folks empowered to make policy are more than likely progressive, and that their enlightened views are likely to find their way into official texts which carry formal authority. Clearly something suffers in the translation from policy to implementation, not so much because of traditional theory-practice tensions, but because the rank and file haven't gotten with the program. The philosophy in which I basked, reading the correspondence from the board in my new home in the autumn of my children's first year in Canada, wasn't a result of any grassroots initiative. That letter came from soft-spoken, gentle people whose children are enrolled in schools where teaching personnel do not expend much energy making everyone feel "special," because everyone already is.

It's a quandary, all right. Progressive policies are preferable to non-progressive ones—about this I am unambivalent. One wouldn't want to go back to the reductive, monotonous world of Dick, Jane and Sally. However, I would like to see educators give greater consideration to the logical consequences of a given educational innovation and anticipate the kind of work that will need to be done for that innovation to find a receptive audience. Certainly the goals of Quest 2000, the Ontario primary-level math program, sound worthwhile. An overwhelming majority of caregivers, I am sure, would endorse our children's development of proficiency in "Number Sense and Numeration, Measurement, Geometry and Spatial Sense, Patterning and Algebra, and Data Management and Probability." However, did the authors of this program, or the officials who adopted it as part of the provincial standard curriculum, genuinely believe that parents from linguistic minorities and other disenfranchised groups, who are now expected to "facilitate" their children's homework as part of their "partnership" with schools, would be able to engage productively with the language of that text? While we are on the topic, "What is your notion of typicality?" may seem like a reasonable question for a math textbook to ask of a grade four student one is trying to initiate into the rites of logico-deductive reasoning. However, if phrased with reference to responses to a series of questions about the child's shoe-wearing practices, it is not easily answered in a situation where the child owns only one pair.

I have encountered these practices and attitudes in a community that professes diversity as an ideal and incarnates diversity as a sociological fact. Friends of mine who live in a rural area have been regaling me for years with horror stories about the local school where their daughter and son are the only Jewish students and where diversity is regarded as something that happens somewhere else. While I am sympathetic to my friends' woes, it is always tempting to tell them that this is the price they pay for not fighting city traffic. But my own experience makes it clear that living inside city limits does not provide complete protection from misapprehension of diversity.

Although plurality and diversity are now taken as givens in the ongoing conversation on the ideal role of public schooling, in fact they do not appear to be regarded as resources that lend themselves to effective teaching and learning. The enriching potential of diverse demographic groups living in close geographic proximity is not generally acknowledged, despite the enactment of multicultural policies at federal and provincial levels. Quite the contrary: I have noted an eagerness on the part of mainstream institutions and their representatives to embrace insidious hypotheses that ascribe much explanatory power to the pernicious effects of difference.

It could be argued, I suppose, that the scenarios I have illustrated represent part of a viable process for progressive change over time. First the policies need to be articulated, and then, with longer or shorter delays depending on the circumstances, they get implemented. But there are two problems with this argument. First of all, even if we can hope for a better world at the end of this process, the current schizophrenia between our official texts and the ways we act may be too high a price to pay. Second, the history of educational reforms suggests that what is involved is very likely more than just a time lag. There has been no shortage of ideas, from the New Math to destreaming, that have had a certain appeal when they appeared as articulated policies but have never successfully made the transition to classroom use.

Nor does it help to heap all the blame for these difficulties on parents. Educators, like rocket scientists, bear some responsibility for where their ideas come down. If we believe that parents' cooperation in facilitating the school's agenda is central to children's development of academic literacy, then it is incumbent on us to foster a reciprocal educational climate where the funds of knowledge observed in the socialization experiences of students from diverse backgrounds are perceived as valuable by school personnel. At present, our stance on this issue is both ambivalent and disingenuous. We require parents' participation on our terms, knowing full well that our terms are increasingly removed from the frame of reference in which family caregivers' knowledge and abilities hold currency with the children we are concerned with.

In the end, what I find most troubling is the lack of understanding of diversity and the lack of authentic commitment to it as a resource. The problem is revealed when we in unspecified ways attribute the limitations of a public community to its diverse character. We are too quick to hold our dreams responsible for our nightmares. When we do this, we call into question the original integrity of our intentions.

Family, Difference and the Socializing Process

10

One Family, Indivisible?

Boyce, Robert and Belle Richardson

Boyce:

Early in 1992 I suggested to the *Canadian Forum* magazine that I write an article on race relations.[1] I did so because I have concluded, after nearly fifty years as a scribbler, that there are two pre-eminent issues in the world today. The first is equity between nations and between peoples within nations. And the second is the maintenance of amicable relations between races. What on earth would be the use of creating an efficient and productive Canada if we descend into mutual antagonisms where we are armed and shooting at each other, as seems to be happening in parts of the United States?

I asked my son, Robert, who was at that time chairperson of the Coalition on Employment Equity in Toronto, how he thought I should approach such an article, and his response was immediate. "First, you should ask the magazine why a minority person has not been hired to write this article," he said. This led to a lively debate and a lot of soul-searching. Joined by one of his Black friends, we argued for hours in a Toronto restaurant, stopping just short of acrimony. While acknowledging that minority writers should have a chance to write about this subject, I was unable to accept that their existence implies that the subject should be out-of-bounds to me. My companions' most extreme argument was that I had been able to utter as a writer throughout my lifetime only because of my privileged position as a White Anglo-Saxon male. They said there must have been minority people who were denied this privilege, but who, like me, could have written thousands of articles if they had had the chance; therefore, my time was over, or should be.

I could not, and do not, accept any of this. Although it is true that I can never understand racism as does my son, who must be prepared to deal at any moment with being patronized, insulted or slighted because he is Black, can this possibly mean that only he, and other victims of racism, can express an opinion on the subject? I think not.

The result of our discussion was a compromise. My son and I agreed we should each have our say. My daughter, who is also Black, wanted to have her say, too.

The social climate in which Robert joined our family in England nearly thirty years ago was spelled out on the day we brought him home. The janitor of our building was a retired auto worker, a poor man who was looking after four apartments in return for a free flat in the basement. He and his wife were excited about the proposed addition to our family, and when we arrived home they hurried upstairs to have a look. He peered into the crib, and without a moment's hesitation said, in the kindliest of voices, "Ah, he's a little nigger!" Eventually, we became a family of six—four children and two adults—born on three continents, comprising three races—Caucasian, Negroid and Polynesian—and with parentage stemming from six countries. Living in such a family, I've developed a deep conviction in racial acceptance. As Rodney King asked in Los Angeles, "Guys, can we all get along?" Simplistic, maybe. But without it, what sense does life make?

We soon found that small Black kids are regarded by everyone as cute; but as they grow, those who are prejudiced find them threatening. In 1984, twenty-one years after he became one of us, Robert was constantly being hauled over and checked out by the Ottawa police, and he finally was arrested ("for suspicion," said the policeman) while walking home. We wrote a letter to the mayor accusing the police of racism (his two White brothers were never checked out). The police inquiry was over in two hours; they completely exonerated their officer (although he had done, by our reckoning, three illegal things). Welcome to the farcical world of police complaints procedure. The mayor set up an advisory committee. Seven years later, an unarmed Black man, Vincent Gardner was shot by a Nepean policeman for no apparent reason. "They haven't changed," said my son when I mentioned the incident to him.

Robert:

The image of Black people I grew up with, as a Black child in a White family, a White community and a White school, was the cartoon character Little Black Sambo. He was the guy who looked most like me. I didn't have a bone in my hair, my lips didn't reach my belly and my skin was more brown than Black, but, all the same, Sambo was my representative in the world. If it weren't for Sambo there wouldn't have been anyone at all. Even though one's family may have a positive image of Black people, being a Black child growing up in a White family in Canada has problematic effects on one's self-image.

The problem at home stemmed not from negative images but from no images of Black people. Black images at home existed only in the odd visitor to the house, or television specials depicting some exotic tribe from the dark continent, or Saturday morning cartoons with Sambo and Bugs Bunny. If you told a Black child growing up in the sixties and seventies in Canada that he was an African, you would more likely than not get a punch in the nose. It is confusing and hurtful for a child whose dominant images of Black people are those of the caricatured African to be told he is Black.

Canadian society is racist, its predominant images of Black people are negative. Perhaps in a home with strong, positive Black role models the effects of this negative propaganda can be negated. However, for a Black child in a home with no Black role models, the question of trying to ameliorate society's negative image of Black people becomes academic.

As a child, in the summers I went to a day camp. As in most of my childhood experiences, I was the only Black child at this camp. One year the camp hired a Black man, Charles, as a counsellor. Charles was young and strong and everyone seemed to like him. He taught me how to lift weights and play ball and was generally someone I could look up to. It was a great summer. The next year, looking forward to another summer and another year with Charles, I showed up at camp. But Charles didn't. I remember being told that Charles had been caught robbing a shoe store over the winter and was spending that summer in jail. I remember all the kids at camp were talking about it. None of them seemed to remember Charles as the man who had taught us to play games and lift weights. They remembered him only as someone whom they never felt they could trust anyway. They all knew he would do something like this: he was Black. I didn't say anything and tried to be as White as possible, hoping no one would notice that I too was Black.

To complicate matters, my parents adopted another child, a little Black girl. She was blacker than I was! Friends came by to congratulate my parents and tell them how pretty their little Black baby was. She grew up much the same as I had, but seemed to succeed where I had failed at being accepted into the community. She came home from school one day singing a new song, "Nigger, nigger, pull the trigger." I felt like throwing her out the window—she was Whiter than I was!

I think school was a constant source of frustration for us both. For me, because I didn't accept anything, and for her because she did. She came home from school one day happy to have a role in the school play. She was to be a railway train conductor. Her happy mood was quickly broken by a barrage of criticism from her family. I don't know if she ever did understand why we were all so upset.

Since school, I think my sister and I have both changed. While in school she had been accepted as long as she acted White and kept her eyes closed. For her these terms had been acceptable, a condition I envied. She had little contact with her heritage and possessed an ability to substitute that of others for her own. For her it didn't matter that Black people were missing from her life, her books and her history or were portrayed as criminals or caricatures. It seemed that, to her, being Black was cosmetic and no different from having big feet or little feet, blue eyes or brown. Her history and heritage was White and no one needed to tell her differently. It was when she left school, and lost her honorary White status, that it hit her. Beyond high school the rules had changed: her threats to others as a Black person and as a woman were now real, whereas as a child she had been just cute.

My sister's seeming indifference to being a Black girl in a White man's world was a trait to be envied. I was "oversensitive." I couldn't let someone call me a nigger without hitting them (unless they were bigger than me). By the time I reached high school, I had had it. I had been disciplined for fighting in every school I had ever been to and was considered an academic problem by all concerned. My ability to *fit in* was nearly nil and my ability to articulate this was less. I dropped out.

I should say that these are my perceptions, while those of my sister may well be quite different. However, the disparate methods my sister and I have used are manifestations of living in a society that is inherently racist. Growing up, we were both taught that colour is only skin deep. But while biologically we may be the same, our heritage is vastly different and the treatment outside the home is so disparate as to create a gulf in understanding not easily bridged. Growing up Black in Canada is very different from growing up White, and as a result we become very different people.

Belle:

Woman. Adopted. Canadian. Black. Ghanaian. Barbadian. New Zealander. Had I spent my life consumed by one or more of these labels, all of which could apply to me, I would have taken precious time away from the much more worthy experience of being a human being. That's not to say that gender, roots, birthright, nationality, skin colour and heritage aren't important. To be sure, they are all elements that make me who I am. I think I am sufficiently proud of each of them, but they are factors over which I have no control.

I was fortunate to become part of a family that didn't perpetuate racism. My White parents didn't ignore that prejudice existed. They simply sent me into society with no prejudices of my own. Because I wasn't raised to watch for it, I sometimes missed what might have been offensive to others, but I also didn't find it where it never existed.

Certainly racism did exist, and I didn't miss all of it. As I child I was called "spear chucker" and "jigaboo" by some of my White friends, and I considered it a compliment until I was told otherwise. When I was a teenager an elderly White man yelled at me in the health food store where I worked, "Go back to Africa, and sink lower than a ship can sink!" As an adult I had a role in a national commercial, but it was downgraded because the company decided it didn't want a "person of colour" in the lead.

Conversely, in Los Angeles, many African-Americans have criticized me because I do not know much about the American civil rights movement. While walking among the diverse crowd on Venice Beach with a White male friend, I have been harassed by Black men who have felt that—because we share the same skin colour—they have a right to judge my choice of companions.

My brother says that I had "honorary White status." That makes a good debating point for him, but I don't think it has ever been true. As far as I know, I have been Black since the day I was born, and I fully expect to be Black until the day I die. Consequently, everyone who has known me has had no choice but to treat me as a Black person. The difference between Rob and me lies not in the colour of our skins or the way we are treated, but inside our heads. Rob has even called me an "oreo." Oreo! Black on the outside, White on the inside—no great compliment!

Only one thing is certain. We may all look different from without, but if we were all cut open, within we would look pretty much the same. What matters is our humanity.

Boyce:

I started out to write the usual journalistic article, dealing with what we have done in race relations, where we have failed and what we should do next. In fact, I started the ball rolling by doing just that. I went to Toronto and talked to some visible-minority people in and out of government and tried to figure out what they thought we should be doing and where we should be heading.

I was impressed by something told to me by Enid Lee, chair of the Black Secretariat, a grassroots clearing house for information and action, of which Robert was then a board member. She complained that the media take little if any notice of the ceaseless work being done by Blacks and other minorities day after day, week after week and month after month to overcome their problems. "If you were to take a camera," she said, "and go around Toronto on a Saturday photographing every Black person who is working as a volunteer with children, you would really have a lot of photographs. No one ever gives us credit for doing that. When you read the press, you get the impression we are not doing anything to help ourselves."

A common theme among those I talked to was that most formal solutions have proven to be inadequate. Racism is, as Robert says, pervasive. Even organizations set up to combat racism have had problems of racism on their own staffs. And having more resources does not always help. For example, many resources have gone into cross-cultural training, but grassroots activists complain that the money has gone mostly to mainstream organizations that are then, once again, in a position to impose solutions.

I wrote something along these lines, and much more—my usual journalistic schtick, you might call it. But Robert found it "too impersonal." He spoke from being deeply involved, day by day, in efforts to combat racism against Blacks in Toronto. For him, the latest racist outrage, the most recent random cop shooting is not just yet another deplorable antisocial occurrence—as it tends to be for me—but a personal insult and threat. For him, all this reflection on this or that solution doesn't get to the guts of the issue. I began to realize that just by opening up this article within my own family, I was introducing an intensely personal dimension that makes my usual flow of information, facts and figures, and carefully noted contexts seem almost irrelevant.

Robert:

The Canadian way is to deny the difference between Blacks and Whites, to act as if all people are the same and should be treated as such under the law. The multiculturalism policy and *Charter of Rights and Freedoms* recognize diversity while attributing to all persons equal treatment and responsibilities. But these laws are not enforced. Even if they were, the rights and responsibilities of the descendents of the invaders who now control most of the economic and political power are very different from those of the people whom those invaders enslaved or whose lands were first invaded. Multiculturalism in Canada has come to mean the celebration of diverse cultures through special events which display different foods, clothing and dances. But for most of Canada's history, being other than European in origin has meant being other than human, and like other non-human creatures, our only recognized value has been our ability to produce product. These conditions have continued officially and legally well into this century. Oppression is an ingrained part of Canadian history, as is its denial.

Recently a vacuum cleaner salesperson came to my house. Making small talk, he asked me where I was from. I responded that I was Canadian (a lie—I was born in England).

"Yes," he said, "but where were you born?"

"In Canada," I responded.

"But where is your family from?" he persisted.

"We have been here for three hundred years," I persisted.

"I see," he said. "My family is Irish, so I guess we are all immigrants. They came over two hundred years ago. Where did yours come from?"

"Jamaica," I lied.

"I thought you were Jamaican," he said, and continued with his demonstration.

I have had similar confrontations with bank managers, teachers, store clerks, apparent friends and others. What each seems to want is to take me out of a country seen to be White and into a country seen to be Black. I vary my country of origin from time to time, but I have found that people will continue to ask me where I am from until I give them a country in Africa or the Caribbean. They will not accept that I could come from Europe or North America. There seem to be two reasons for this. The first is a simple denial that I could have roots similar to their own, since this would put me on par with them in terms of level of civilization as measured by their standards. And, secondly, if they were to admit that my roots might be as I say, then they would have to admit the history of oppression for which their families are responsible. Interesting to me is how the myth of Canadian tolerance and acceptance is so effectively sold to people on a national and international level.

Western history and culture is based on the belief that White northern European values are superior to those of other cultures, and in this society Whites have gone to incredible lengths to prove that other cultures are inferior, thus to justify the unequal privileges they themselves enjoy. Until Whites accept the fallacy of this, the pain and suffering they inflict will continue. I am talking here not only of the overt White supremacists, but also of those who claim to be outraged by them. These are the truly dangerous individuals, for while they preach equality and tolerance, they continue to accept and use their privilege without question. They speak with righteous indignation when confronted with individual instances of discrimination but do little to counter the systemic forms of discrimination that exist everywhere in their society. In Canada there is a passive acceptance of the philosophy of White supremacy while at the same time a denial of its existence to any significant degree.

There are plenty of questions White people could ask of themselves: How often do White customers in a store ask the salesperson why they are following Black customers around, while allowing White customers to go unobserved? How often do parents ask the school why their children are graduating while Black children are not? How often do they question why Blacks and Aboriginal Canadians fill Canada's prisons far out of proportion to their numbers in the general population? How often do they question why their child gets probation while a Black child committing a similar crime gets a prison sentence? Or why do high school history books lie about the development of the nation? Or why they themselves were singled out for promotion while their

Black counterparts with seniority were ignored? Or why Whites are continually asked to speak about the oppression of Blacks, and Blacks are rarely, if ever, asked to speak about the tyranny of Whites? How many ask why so few Black people work in their organization, live in their neigbourhood or are part of their government?

Race is a social construct. Racism is a reality supporting a system founded on inherent inequality. You can either attack the construction of race, or the structure which cultivates this form of oppression. If you choose to eliminate the construct, the structure will still exist. There is no reason to believe that the elimination of race as a category would substantially change the fate of those presently suffering from the effects of racism, for the structure of this society is such that it will find a new way of oppressing these same people. If you attack the structure, you attack the principal foundation of our society.

By challenging the structure, you question your own privileges and rights and the very foundation of your moral and value systems. The primary question then is: *What are you willing to do and/or give up to help create a society founded on justice and equal rights?*

Belle:

I am no less Black because I was raised by White parents and speak with a Canadian accent than is a person who has been brought up in south-central Los Angeles. Similarly, a farm worker in Alabama is no less Black than an Ashanti tribesman.

No one Black experience can be called the Black experience, or the *correct* Black experience. No one can be the judge of what is Black. Black like whom? My skin is darker than most, but that doesn't make me "more Black." The Black experience worldwide is rooted in being a minority. It would seem logical that Blacks, of all people, would be tolerant of people with experiences different from our own.

I am anxious to discover my African/Caribbean heritage, as much as I am my parents' roots in New Zealand. I empathize with those who have been oppressed, but all I can do is provide an example for what I believe our world should be—a place of inclusion, whose strength is in its diversity.

Bitch. Bastard. Nigger. There will always be excuses for people not to love me. I am obligated not to be insensitive to those who do not share my attitude. But I feel I owe it to my parents and myself not to use ignorance and segregation as an excuse for not succeeding.

Boyce:

I think I will abuse my privilege as father of this outfit to have the last word. I did not expect this article to take this form. I have always avoided writing about my family for fear that I might seem to be drawing attention to myself, and I have fallen into it on this occasion really through no wish of my own. Since Robert tried to elbow me aside as an inappropriate person to write an article on race relations, I have found the whole process revealing and at times painful. I had expected that he would use the article to outline what I might call "the Black activist political agenda," to tell us what he and others in the Black movement think should be done, what measures they hope that those of us who are not minorities will support. To describe Canada as a country devoted to a doctrine of White supremacy, as he has done, is to betray a millenarian attitude: anything short of perfection is worthless.

Though I am not by nature an optimist, I find Robert's pessimistic rhetoric depressing, perhaps because I was brought up at a time and in a place when we believed that human society, if not exactly perfectible, was at least susceptible to constant amelioration. My first memory as a sentient political being is of a Labour government whose fundamental purpose—especially when examined in the light of what is now common—was to improve the welfare of people. It became a matter of faith for me that great social movements, beginning with the labour movement, have struggled for generations against the implacable hostility of those who control wealth, towards the attainable goal that human society can be decent and can offer to everyone the prospect of a creative and fulfilling life. According to this view of the world, social and political action for change have gone hand in hand, the one inevitably leading to the other. I have always counted racism, along with class privilege, economic and social inequity, censorship and colonialism, as social diseases that human beings can cure by using all of the political and social tools available.

This faith has been severely shaken since Reagan, Thatcher and their clones such as Mulroney and Bush have worked to destroy what I have always considered to be the finest achievements of modern society—those measures of welfare that have rescued people from slum, sweatshop and workhouse.

To the extent that the ethic of collective social responsibility seems to be in full retreat in the industrial world, I share Robert's pessimism. But if the last decade has taught us anything, it is that we must hang on for dear life to the imperfect measures of social improvement that have been so laboriously put in place by people working together over the last one hundred years.

We have to accept that all our solutions will be less than perfect. The people I spoke to in Toronto who are working to combat racism every day were generally agreed that racism will always be with us. The objective has to be, not so much to eliminate it—an impossible goal—

but to moderate and control the antisocial behaviour that stems from racist attitudes. This is not going to happen overnight, but we have to hang on to the faith that people of goodwill, working together, can do it. As Robert suggests, profound attitudinal changes are needed. Our laws against racism are far from adequate. We have to push on until racist behaviour becomes as unacceptable as rape or murder.

When I began to write this, I put to paper three thousand words of information: the history of racism against Aboriginals; the changing nature of Canadian society as more people of colour come from the Third World; the many warnings we have ignored from reports and committees of inquiry; the need for more resources to combat prejudice and keep racism in check; the persistence of Canada's damaging "two founding nations" ideology, which denies the place of Aboriginals and other minorities; the passive acceptance of a growing, race-based economic underclass; the need for stronger laws and greater political commitment. But I have jettisoned all that. It might all be very interesting, but I feel that Robert's anger will give readers a better feel for what is involved than my comparatively detached journalism. And maybe Belle's calm tolerance will suggest the human possibilities.

11

Why Dad Cried When I Went to Work at "Chrysler's"

KEVIN WILSON

The plant is the last place an autoworker wants their kids to work. I know. I've spent the last five years working at the same place my dad punched a clock. It wasn't like I ignored him when he told me not to work there. I was barely in university, my degree getting more and more remote by the day. I was broke, falling behind in my studies. Making rent was touch and go. When Chrysler went retro and announced a mass hiring, I didn't hesitate to fill out an application.

Chrysler hired about 1,500 people to work in its minivan plant in 1993. The bodies were needed to create another shift to produce the hot-selling "magic wagons." Magic indeed. These vehicles have saved the company's bacon on more than one occasion. And more than one resident has had their bacon saved by the relative security and decent wages provided by the Big Three.

Whether the city of Windsor lives up to its billing as the "automotive capital of Canada" is a matter of debate. What is indisputable is the impact the car has had on this community. Situated just a stone's throw from Detroit, Windsor builds two different vehicles; GM manufactures transmissions here, and Ford builds engine blocks and finished engines.

The high level of manufacturing-related jobs has made Windsor a unique urban centre. When W.O. Mitchell came here to become the University of Windsor's writer-in-residence, he remarked that he instantly liked the city on account of the large numbers of "pregnant men." It was a playful remark about the preponderance of working-class men who sat on their porches drinking beer after a hard shift in the plants. Invariably, they were wearing undershirts. Mitchell loved the city, not in spite of the pot-bellied beer drinkers, but because of them. Windsor was, and remains, an unabashedly blue-collar city (even though some people here do bemoan the fact).

My father and I were both born here, but our formative years could not have been more different. The second youngest of thirteen kids, Dad grew up in Windsor's West End. His father had tuberculosis and was in a sanitarium when Dad was born. His mother tried to make ends meet in a houseboat moored on the Detroit River. Grandma was a devout

Catholic who went to mass every morning. Her sons had a reputation for being tough and willing to take on all comers. Grandma sent Dad to Assumption High School, which was run by the Basilian Fathers. The Basilians were renowned as quick and brutal disciplinarians. After two weeks of the ninth grade, Dad decided he'd had enough of education.

A few years later, he got involved with a Protestant girl. They got in trouble and were quickly and quietly married. My brother was born, followed by a sister a year later. I came seven years after my sister Angie. Prior to my birth, Dad had worked at a number of poorly paying jobs, including a stint in the Yukon. My Uncle Pat had told him that a fella could make a pile of money there; he'd just forgotten to tell him that it cost a pile of money to live there. Dad ended up getting hired at Chrysler. In Windsor we actually refer to Chrysler and Ford as "Chrysler's" and "Ford's," as if Walter and Henry clock into our plants just like we do.

Shortly after I was born, Dad moved our brood to Tilbury, a bedroom community fifty kilometres up the 401 from Windsor. Dad was trying to raise a family away from dope and the other vices endemic to cities. Tilbury was a great place to grow up, although the drugs were just as prevalent there as they are in Windsor. I lived in a great house, played minor hockey and never wanted for anything. Dad's wages at Chrysler provided all the amenities a kid could desire. My siblings and I may not have gotten everything we wanted, but we certainly had more than we needed.

While I was growing up, how Dad was raised was completely beyond my comprehension. My grandmother used to send her younger kids out to chase after the coal truck when it made its appointed rounds. The closest I ever came to that was chasing a puck around the town rink. Nowadays, I can't get over how much I took for granted. After all, didn't everyone live like this?

Dad started out at Chrysler's Windsor Engine Plant Two. It was a filthy nightmare from beginning to end. Men used to lose digits or limbs with alarming frequency. Twelve-hour shifts, six and seven days a week, were the norm. Dad was tight with a buck, and I've concluded that's because he never had the chance to take our lifestyle for granted. He knew how the bills were being paid. After Plant Two shut down in the early eighties, he moved over to Windsor Assembly, or Plant Three, before winding up his career at Plant Six, the big van plant on Pilette Road. He never wound up at Plant Seven, which is the common nickname for the Brentwood Recovery Home for Alcoholics. Brentwood has housed countless autoworkers over the years.

Alcohol and drug abuse used to be rampant in the "dark days," when labour and management were at war inside the plants. That wasn't specific to Chrysler. Ben Hamper, a writer and long-time employee of General Motors, chronicles his own excesses in his book *Rivethead*. Labour relations in the Big Three were so bad and the work was so unpleasant that it's really no surprise that a lot of workers turned to chemicals to cope.

In spite of our family's bucolic existence, Dad retained an extremely strong identification with the working class. Of course, Dad knew intimately how our lifestyle was being maintained. Chrysler was not exactly renowned for its enlightened labour relations during the seventies. It's not too strong a statement to say that conditions in the plant then were hellish. Even now, when new hires receive their health and safety training, they're treated to a slide show of amputated fingers and hideously maimed hands to show them the dangers of factory work.

Assembly work is dangerous on a number of levels. In addition to the risk of being mutilated, there are chronic injuries to be considered. It's also dangerously monotonous and demeaning. There aren't many jobs around where a person has to ask for permission to take a pee. In the NFB documentary, "Final Offer," there's a scene in which a worker who has been butting heads with his supervisor has to use the restroom. He hits the light that will bring his supervisor/utility man (a worker whose duties include spelling people who need to go to the washroom). No one comes. The union is called, and a grievance ends up being filed. That's what Dad lived with every day.

I think Dad tried to pass his class identification on to his kids. I never thought about it much growing up. In my second year of university, I wrote a paper on class and party identification in Canadian politics and I asked my dad whether he identified himself as middle class or working class. "Working class," he replied sharply. He seemed insulted that I would even ask such a question. I knew he would answer that way. It was Dad who got me working for the NDP when I was fifteen. I'd gotten myself grounded and he'd promised me "parole" if I did grunt work during the 1984 federal election. He occasionally talked of revolution in a manner that seemed completely out of character. He was always a supporter of labour unions. The Labour Day parade was an annual ritual for the two of us.

Paradoxically, the working class was not a place he wanted to see his own children remain. Almost from the beginning, he pleaded with us not to take the same route in life that he had. The stock speech that I (and many other children of working-class parents, I'm sure) heard was, "For God's sake, get a university education and do something for a living that you actually like to do. Whatever you do, don't end up in the plant like I did." That's a confusing message. Be proud of your class. Identify with it. But don't be so proud of it that you stay there. It's difficult to reconcile these two conflicting notions. Doubtless, there are lots of doctors, lawyers, teachers and nurses whose parents put them through university on an autoworker's salary. Are they still members of the working class? If they don't identify with the working class, are they ashamed of where they came from?

Chrysler had none of the misgivings our parents had. From the moment Chrysler made the hiring announcement, they served notice to prospective employees that the days of ninth-grade dropouts filling the plants were over. To even be considered for hire, applicants had to have at least a high school diploma. Those with college or university experience would be given more consideration than mere high-school grads. The emphasis on education is problematic. There was once a time when factory work was the last, best hope for people to make a decent living—people like my father, for example, who had an unexpected family to care for. The work might have been unpleasant, but it did pay well. Nowadays, jobs that were once a last resort are highly sought after. There are people sharing space on the line with me who have teachers' certificates, nursing degrees and all kinds of liberal arts degrees.

In the process of deciding that working in a factory isn't so bad after all, we've effectively displaced a legion of men and women who needed these jobs and might not have been able to take a crack at anything else. I find myself wondering what those people are doing, now that people like me have elbowed them out of the way. Why on earth would a giant multinational actively solicit highly educated employees to do their drudge work? For its part, my company has indicated that its employees had to be capable of adapting to a fast-changing work environment. This new workforce would have to be highly literate and numerate, and at ease with new technology.

From my perspective on the floor, this explanation is unmitigated rubbish. My input into the manufacturing process is nil, save for the work I do on the assembly line. The tools I use are no different from the tools my father used. There is more automation in the plants these days, but that's the purview of engineers and electricians.

If the corporate answer fails to satisfy us, then how should the question be answered? My own very simple reason is that Chrysler can hire whomever it wants to. Not very long ago, working at the Big Three was a vocation strongly discouraged by good parents everywhere. Factories were dirty, dangerous and populated by lots of unsavoury characters. Often, no one felt more strongly about this than the unsavoury characters themselves. Remember the plant tour? As the recessionary nineties dragged on, a trip to the Big Three seemed like a workers' paradise when compared to the minimum-wage, part-time gigs their kids were plugging away at. A full-time job in the auto industry might not have been upwardly mobile, but hanging in there was no mean feat in 1993. In effect, Chrysler got its pick of the litter.

By placing stiffer educational requirements on prospective employees, it had the luxury of narrowing down its pool of applicants. This probably saved money and time during the hiring process. My friend Dennis has a theory of his own. In his opinion, Chrysler elected to hire individuals with high levels of education because they had undergone the maximum amount of social indoctrination. This extra time in class made them less likely to question the status quo, more likely to accept consumerism as a way of life and, most importantly, "good employees."

Chrysler feels it needs a "partnership" with its workforce. At my own plant, this takes the form of "town hall meetings," in which we are briefed on our performance relative to our competitors. The workers who bother to attend these meetings (they're optional) get to see the silliest of these efforts up close and personal. Nowadays, for example, our managers no longer wear ties. In fact, they all wear exactly the same shirts. The new management shirt is a baby-blue, oxford-cloth dress shirt, with the Chrysler pentastar emblazoned over the right breast pocket. The subtext within the new management uniform is pretty laughably obvious. The foreman, once the in-house trustie of the owner, is now to be perceived as another "blue-collar" worker.

In a major assembly facility, the old Taylorist/Fordist principles are readily evident. There are high levels of vertical integration (plant manager, area managers, supervisors, assemblers). All jobs are broken into their smallest constituent elements and are highly deskilled. Absentee-relief employees can often "pick up" an unfamiliar job in less than half an hour. What is sometimes less evident are the methods that workers use to distort the Taylor/Ford model. Look first at their workstations. An observer can easily find items that the employer never intended to exist in that space. Photos of family members are often prominently displayed. Comic strips, especially ones that encapsulate the absurdities of working life are commonplace ("Dilbert" has gotten very popular in the last two or three years).

More interesting is the commonness of reading material. The nature of the material being read is not particularly important, though I'll come back to it shortly. The fact that reading material exists in a workplace at all is noteworthy in and of itself. The time spent reading represents time that an employee could be adding value to the product being assembled. To employers, it's time that's been stolen. Rightly or wrongly, the employees view it rather differently. Jobs are devised to be done in a specific time frame. A worker generally learns their job as taught to them by a co-worker. As the learning worker's movements become more economical, they are able to do their job in less time than has been allotted. The extra time is claimed by both the employer and the employee. To the boss, the extra time is a chance to enhance productivity. The employee sees the extra time as a reward for being efficient.

What results is a *sitzkrieg* of near-ridiculous proportions. In an organized plant, the contract enables the employer to eliminate jobs for a specific time period during each calendar year, generally 90–120 days. During that period, a team of industrial engineers (or IEs, in plant jargon) time every worker with a stopwatch. At my plant, the IEs generally set a target of eliminating six percent of the jobs in the plant. No one loses their jobs *per se*. People retire every year, or die, and replacements are not hired. The work that was part of the eliminated jobs is parcelled out to the workers who remain.

During the job elimination period, both sides start from extreme positions. The IE piles ludicrous amounts of work onto jobs, making them nearly impossible to complete. For their parts, workers slow down to a snail's pace before the IE even shows up on the floor. Newspapers and other visible diversions vanish. Changes in work assignments are vigorously resisted. Informal agreements between the union and management are cancelled. Once it's all over, things return to a semblance of normalcy. Over the years, my own union has bargained a reduction in the job elimination period. It used to be called the 120-day language; by the time our contract comes up for renegotiations, it'll be 90-day language. I suspect that the company agreed to this reduction because it's probably as stressful for them as it is for us. If our union hates job reductions, the rank and file hate them doubly so. On the line, a job elimination means a diminution of seniority and the loss of high seniority premium, or "gravy," jobs.

Turning back to the diversions on the line, I'll try to speak for myself only. In my own experience, I've found that thinking of only the next job coming down the pike is the shortest route to losing your mind. I once pulled a Sunday shift in my second year at Chrysler. Sometimes, if the product you manufacture is selling like hotcakes, you'll be canvassed for Sunday overtime. At Chrysler, Sunday shifts are six hours long. Since Sunday overtime is voluntary, lots of people turn the work down. Those who accept are given the option of working a six-hour shift, or pulling a double shift. The inducement here is the money, of course. Working twelve hours at double time amounts to over fifty dollars an hour when shift premiums are factored in. I really needed the extra cash, so I agreed to pull a double shift. I would start at midnight and finish at noon. The first six hours went smoothly enough, but the second half was a nightmare. I was fatigued and couldn't concentrate on anything. Before the clock had a chance to strike seven, I started looking at my watch. Clock watching doesn't have to be a bad thing on the line, but I was starting to look at my watch after almost every job. That only reminded me how much longer I had to work before I could go home. I became increasingly agitated, and to this day I still don't know how I held it together. I don't remember going home. I don't remember going to bed. I do remember my watch, and I do remember doing math in my head. In rough terms, the equation I was figuring went something like this: "When I come into work tomorrow, I will do my job about 500 times. That's 3,000 jobs in a six-day week. Multiply that by 48, and it's 144,000 jobs a year. Twenty-eight years to retirement, so I've gotta build another 7,032,000 jobs, plus the 300 or so I've got to get through today—7,031,999, 7,031,998, 7,031,997.... I remember that it felt like something was crawling just beneath my scalp.

Sooner or later, that kind of thinking will end up driving you squirrelly. It's important to complete the task at hand, but thinking about the next one or the one after that is a place where angels fear to tread. I've learned to keep my focus strictly on the job at hand and finish it quickly. On my current job, I can move up about one car length on the assembly line if I work quickly. That gives me about forty seconds out of about every five minutes to glance at a newspaper or a book. During the period that I'm chasing the line, I'm too busy to think very hard, and when I'm reading, my attention is focused on something else.

Take those few seconds away from a worker or, worse, dictate what they can and can't do in that bit of free time and fur will fly. As I write this, GM is learning that lesson the hard way. Last summer, strikes at two GM plants in Flint, Michigan, ground the entire chain to a standstill. That downtime was especially dear for GM's Oshawa facility, which was launching a new line of pickup trucks. Trucks are money in the bank for the General. When the dispute in Flint was finally settled, management in Oshawa wasted no time in promulgating a memo to employees, outlining newly forbidden "non-competitive work practices." Reading the paper and figuring out crosswords while the line is running are officially forbidden now. What's more, one employee told me that GM was handing out weeklong suspensions "like they were water."

Not surprisingly, the workers are not pleased with this. Morale, always a problem in Oshawa, has plummeted. Media reports have portrayed GM as a micromanager. According to the local union for the workers, quality has dropped since the new rules came into effect, but GM denies this. What's particularly ironic about this situation is its timing. Right after the Flint strike, GM president Jack Smith acknowledged that his company had to establish lines of communication with its unions, but the company didn't consult a single union official in Oshawa before it started giving workers the memo outlining the new rules. What's even more ironic about this is the fact that most of what workers teach themselves about economy of movement is an effort to save their own bodies. Performing repetitive motions five hundred or more times a day will wreck some part of your body eventually. Industrial workers were probably aware of this fact long before white- and pink-collar workers started suffering from carpal tunnel syndrome.

In my current line job, I've developed several techniques that the company never told me about. I'm presently employed as a fusion welder, a semi-skilled job. I have to arc-weld a dozen specific spots on every van that passes by me. Most of my welds are located on the floor of the vehicle. To do these welds accurately, I was trained to plant my feet, bend at the waist and hold the torch with both hands. After a few weeks of this, my aching back told me that there had to be a better way to do this. Eventually, I learned how to lean my body against parts of the vehicle, while positioning my torch on the floorpan. I was now able to weld without all that bending at the waist. The happy byproduct of this new technique was a few seconds of butt time. I have no firm calculations, but I'm guessing that I've bought myself a few years of freedom from workers' compensation.

Eventually everybody gets hurt, though. The sudden crippling injury happens with diminishing frequency, and occasionally, someone gets hit by a forklift or slips on an oily patch. But no one avoids the chronic injuries. Trigger finger is a near universal affliction among autoworkers. The tendons in your hands are covered in sheaths. When a person is constantly flexing their hands, as they do when they are using any kind of power tool, the tendons swell in their sheaths, making the hands stiff. When I first noticed the symptoms of trigger finger, I freaked out. I was waking up in the morning with my hands clenched up like those of a fetus. This wasn't a big deal, save for the fact that I couldn't open them up without some effort. The specialist I visited diagnosed me in about two seconds. His recommendation? "Stop working in a factory." He was deadly serious. The swelling of my hands occurred about a year later. I took this development harder, though somewhat more resignedly. My hands had been my one huge vanity. In high school, girls used to tell me that I had nice hands. Watching them turn into sausages was unpleasant, but what could I do? I'm happy to report that the swelling went down after I moved to my present job.

Thirty-two years on the line destroyed my father's back. Two of the discs in his spine have degenerated to a point where he is in constant pain. I knew definitively that he was hurting when my stepmother told me that he'd been golfing one day and had to call it a day after fourteen holes. In a previous incarnation, my dad was a guy who would drag three buddies through thirty-six holes, then play another eighteen all by himself.

A lot of people are surprised that autoworkers golf. Not all autoworkers golf, of course. Nevertheless, it's a very popular sport, both to play and to watch. Apparently, Walter Reuther, founding president of the United Auto Workers, urged local unions to form sporting leagues for their members. The objective was twofold: it exercised workers' bodies and created a sense of community and solidarity. During the winter months, bowling leagues were the norm, and golf leagues occupied the warm months. Golf was an interesting selection. While it serves the purpose of getting out in the sun and walking a few miles, golf is often perceived as the preserve of the well-to-do. I wonder if that's the reason Reuther promoted golfing to his members.

A recent acquaintance of mine, a doctor, seemed shocked when I mentioned that I golfed.

"You're kidding me, right?" she asked me.

"Nope," I replied. "I've been playing since I was a little kid. I'm not very good, but I do love to play."

She seemed really taken aback.

"You never struck me"—she was choosing her words really carefully now—"as the kind of person who golfed." She probably wouldn't have had any trouble imagining me at a bowling alley. After all, bowling is a working-class sport. That even extends into representations of the working class on television. Fred Flintstone and Barney Rubble bowled, as did their progenitors, Ralph Kramden and Ed Norton. More recently, Dan and Roseanne Connor whiled away plenty of half-hours at the Lanford Lanes. Golf is an entirely different kettle of fish.

A lot of people use routines similar to mine. Some people like to listen to the radio. In fact, summer nights in the plant mean you hear the play-by-play from the Detroit Tigers games, whether you want to or not. Some very religious people bring copies of the Bible or the Koran to work. Al, a guy I know on the door line, brings scripture passages and photos of shrines to Mary, which he sets up on his work table before the shift begins. In effect, the space that he occupies becomes a shrine to the Blessed Mother.

This kind of work lends itself to religious contemplation. It's highly repetitive, much like reciting decades of the rosary. It's possible to focus entirely on the task at hand, freeing the mind of any other external stimuli. If you take a small leap from this, you can also extrapolate about the repetitive strain injuries that are so commonplace in assembly plants. They are forms of long-term self-mortification, minus the hair shirt.

Turning back to the reading material, just about everything that can be read gets read—books, catalogues, newspapers, bibles. Porn used to be all over the place. That seems to have changed in recent years. When I was first hired on, porn seemed as commonplace as coveralls in the plant. The oldtimers say that it was even more widespread in the seventies. Back then, guys would plaster their work areas with pages and pages from their favourite skin mags. Porn is still popular reading material, but the arrival of large numbers of women in the plants has somewhat altered the rules of conduct. First, there is anti-harassment language built into the collective agreements. Second, men generally don't like to behave like idiots when there are women around. When there were just a few women in the plants, behaving badly wasn't a matter for debate. The number of women was so low that any complaints could just be ignored. But once a group enters any space in sufficient numbers, respect is demanded. It was an adjustment for a lot of men, but it went smoothly enough. For those who can't make the adjustment, the contract language is there.

That's not to say that relations between the sexes are idyllic. A lot of supervisors, particularly the ones we call the dinosaurs, can't fathom that women are capable of doing jobs in the factory. So a situation develops when a supervisor gets a female new hire in their area. Instead of being assigned a "regular" job, the woman finds herself getting stuck on some make-work project, or a "light duty" job, normally reserved for workers recovering from injuries. No one on the line likes to see the seniority system being subverted. Deliberately or not, the supervisor who engages in this behaviour is pitting workers against workers. Caught in the middle is the poor woman who just wants to do an honest day's work for an honest day's pay.

All of these little mutations in the workplace put the manufacturing and process engineers who designed the plants into something of a quandary. They probably never expected that their creations would be altered so by the people who work in them. There's not much that they can do, either. The workers occupy the space and produce the goods. They can't be fired *en masse*. Issuing a *diktat* denying workers the right to adapt their work spaces will indirectly affect the quality of the goods being produced. Perhaps some sabotage will take place, but it's far more likely that morale will drop, which ultimately affects quality.

The distortions we visit upon our workplaces have to be infuriating to our employers. In pure monetary terms, the company has to know that potential profits are going down the tubes. The important word here is "potential." The product and the process to manufacture it were designed to realize a profit for the company. As far back as I can remember, the plant I work at has been a cash cow for Chrysler. It has always met or exceeded its profit objectives. The distortions do not affect the bottom line of the company, but they lay bare potential earnings that have been foregone. However, if the company hits its targets, they can't very well expect their employees to feel that the changes to the predetermined manufacturing process are somehow harmful.

Perhaps what is at issue here is control. Theoretically, a company is controlled by its owners or shareholders. In a manufacturing environment, labour is purchased to produce the goods, which in turn realizes a profit. Thus, the machinery is owned by the boss, but it must be operated by somebody. The owner cannot possibly exert total control over the process. If the workers produce the desired result, that is, a product at the desired level of profit, then are the means that they use to achieve it important?

Management continues to try to impose their vision on the space they own. If they can't enforce it in the short term, they'll take the long view. My dad says the company will always try to break the union. Perhaps that's a little extreme, but sometimes management practices seem downright ominous, even before you start working for them. Jobs in the Big Three have become highly desirable, even coveted. Once, a rumour that General Motors would be handing out applications (just handing them out, hiring wasn't even discussed) prompted 25,000 people to line up in the dead of winter.

At Chrysler, the company contracted an outside firm to administer tests to prospective applicants. Much of the test dealt with elementary math, spatial relations, reading skills and practical dexterity. Another component was a personality profile that a psychologist friend of mine says was based on the Minnesota Multiphasic Personality Inventory. My favourite series of questions in this component centred on driving habits. All of the questions were multiple choice and we were to answer on a scale of one to five, with one meaning we agreed strongly with a statement, and five meaning we disagreed strongly. The first driving statement said, "I get really angry when someone cuts me off on the freeway," followed by about a dozen or so unrelated questions. Then, "When someone cuts me off on the freeway, I get really angry." A few other questions seemed to be thrown in to assess whether or not we would be "good" employees. Among my favourites in this category were, "I think it's important to work in a team environment," "If someone injures themselves at work, it's usually their own fault" and "When a dispute arises between me and my supervisors, I try to work it out with them." I'm not sure about the consultants, but I'm sure that our immediate supervisors know that many of the new hires from 1993 are inveterate liars. I've talked to a lot of people who took the test, and all of them lied just as much as I did.

We were "ninety-day wonders." For our first ninety days, we were punctual, obedient and, when told to jump, we asked how high. On day ninety-one, we started to assert ourselves, not satisfied with being pushed around. Day ninety-one is when our probationary period ended and we had full union protection. Since then, everyone's had their share of run-ins with management. Ruth Milkman, in her book *Farewell to the Factory: Autoworkers in the Late Twentieth Century* (1997) interviewed several current and former employees of GM's assembly plant in Linden, New Jersey. All of her subjects, she writes, have, "at least one incident of managerial insensitivity, often something that had occurred many years before, but which was so offensive to the teller that it was seared indelibly into his or her memory" (1997: 47).

My own incident took place during the job elimination phase about three years ago. At the time, I worked on the door line, installing liftgates. A team of three workers subassembled the liftgates, feeding them to us from a conveyor just off of the main line. IE made a determination that one of the subassemblers could be eliminated. The remaining two workers staged a showdown that paralyzed the entire body shop. Both workers were thirty-year veterans who had been through this a number of times. The line was crawling in fits and starts, and a cadre of managers had shown up to troubleshoot. I was enjoying myself, taking a seat and reading the paper. My immediate supervisor walked up to me and said, "I'd put those papers away if I were you." He said this in a matter-of-fact tone, as if he was commenting on the weather.

I was about to comply and asked him what was up. He completely exploded. "What's up is that you're sitting here reading the fucking paper and putting everyone in the hole." Going "in the hole" means that you're taking too long to do your job and creeping into another person's workstation. Basically my boss was saying that I was responsible for the line stoppage. Then he stalked off to join the powwow of blue shirts. I was livid and slammed my paper down on my work table. Gary, my partner, looked up from his paper and asked what was going on.

"He says I'm stopping the line by reading my paper."

"Oh," he replied. "No one else here, just you and your paper. Everyone else is reading their papers and it's just you and yours shutting the line down, right? What the fuck's his problem?"

"I'll tell you what his problem is." I was in rare form now. Raising my voice so that everyone could hear (including the circle of managers), I ventured forth with the opinion, "He's a fucking fat prick." My boss practically flew back to my area. He had turned so purple that I was afraid he was going to have a coronary right at my feet. He hissed something unintelligible, then stormed off again.

That should have been the end of it, but another supervisor approached me. "He shouldn't have gone off on you like that, but you really should put the papers away when the plant manager is around."

I was still hot and shot back: "Don't pull this good cop, bad cop shit with me. He knows goddamn well why the line's stopped, and it's got nothing to do with me. If he wants to talk to me like that, he can get my (union) rep down here."

The second supervisor was gone before I could get this speech out in its entirety. A couple of issues are well illustrated by this story. The first one is that my own experience dovetails well with Milkman's research. I will never forget this incident as long as I live. Second, incidents like this one tend to radicalize people. I rarely threaten to sic a union rep on anybody, but this situation, by virtue of its sheer arbitrariness, warranted it. By the same token, it's a pretty safe bet that I'd have been fired long before I had gotten the word "fat" out were it not for the union. I was aware of that fact long before I decided to mix it up with my boss. Third, factory work becomes even more infuriating because of the effective control of what my friend calls "discursive space" inside the plant. My boss reamed me out and then left before I could say a word. Likewise, the second supervisor walked away when I responded unfavourably to him. A worker has no such luxury.

Perhaps that's why I perceive union activism as second nature to me. My dad and his brother were ardent union men. I've often kidded Dad that the only things I truly inherited from him were his nose, a fanatical devotion to the Montreal Canadiens and the union. More fundamentally though, I became involved in the movement because I recognized that I had this job (whatever its warts) because of it.

Chrysler was reluctant to launch a third shift at the minivan plant, but Larry Bauer, the president of my local union, was adamant that the shift be added. Like my dad, he had little formal education. Bauer had risen to the presidency of CAW Local 444, probably the largest and most progressive union local in the region, and he knew that our strength in the community relied upon championing the needs of people not covered under our collective agreements. To ignore the community you exist in is to sign your own death warrant. It's not enough to just secure decent contracts for your members. If that's all you do, you engender hostility in those people who haven't secured similar benefits for themselves.

Come to Windsor and look around. There are housing co-ops financed by a CAW community development group. The university's CAW Student Centre was built with the assistance of member donations. Larry died of a heart attack in 1994. Since his death, a charity golf tournament benefitting the unemployed has borne his name. Sport Club 444 has donated thousands of dollars to worthwhile causes throughout the region. This is social unionism at its finest. Rather than just sew up favourable collective agreements for their memberships, unions have to embrace the broader community. Barricading ourselves within our homes and plants only creates the impression that we're interested in nothing but ourselves.

If I ever decide to have kids, I'll probably try to dissuade them from entering the factory, like my dad did. I'm already considered a "lifer" at the plant. There's an adage that if you spend five years in a plant, then you're there for the long haul. Nevertheless, I hope I don't have to stay here, but I've made my peace with the possibility of another twenty-five years. I do have my writing, which I've been doing a lot of in the last year. It'll probably be a moot point. University education or no university education, in the future, unless they are made out of metal, the last resort of the factory will probably not be available to anybody.

12

Chris, Chris and Zak

TARA GOLDSTEIN

Children are raised in many different kinds of families. Some children are raised by two parents; others by one. Some are brought up by grandmothers, grandfathers, aunts and uncles; others by older cousins, sisters, brothers or guardians. Sometimes children live in the same families throughout their childhood. Sometimes the families change when parents divorce and one parent no longer lives with the rest of the family. Sometimes these families change again when one or both divorced parents remarry. Often children living with two parents have a mother and a father, but not always. Sometimes children living with two parents have two mothers or two fathers.

This chapter is about two mothers raising a seven-year-old son named Zak. In December 1998, I asked Chris Higgins (Chris H.) and Chris Phibbs (Chris P.), two White women living and working in the city of Toronto, if I could interview them about their lives as lesbian mothers. They agreed. Chris Higgins is Zak's birth mother. She works for a consulting firm that organizes professional development training for people in the field of design. Chris Phibbs is Zak's adopted mother. She works at City Hall as an assistant to openly gay councillor Kyle Raye. As will be discussed later on, in order for Chris Phibbs to legally adopt Zak, Chris Higgins, his biological parent, had to give up her biological parental rights and adopt him as well. Thus, right from the beginning, Chris, Chris and Zak's experience as a family has been different from that of many other families. My tape-recorded interview with Chris and Chris was transcribed by Shawna Feinstein, a student in the Faculty of Education at York University. I then edited the transcribed interview into the piece you will read below. Except for Chris, Chris and Zak, all other names mentioned in this piece are pseudonyms.

"Tell me about your family"

Chris H.: Our family consists of two women named Chris and a little boy who's almost seven and his name is Zak, and a cat named Riley and a bunch of fish and a frog. We've been together, Chris [Phibbs] and I for over ten years, and Zak has been with us, of course, for seven. That's our family.

Chris P.: And its very much a chosen family in how we have come together and he has come to be. No part of this family has just come by chance. It is totally chosen and totally accepted both by us and by him and by, so far, most others in the world. The hardest part about our relationship [for] other people is that we're both named Chris. That's way harder for them to deal with than ...

Chris H.: Yeah, especially the little ones. They can't get how can you both be named Chris.

Chris P.: It's not that he has two moms. No. That's not the block. It's not two mothers, no. It's that we're both named Chris. That's the hardest part.

Going to Daycare and Adopting Zak

Tara: When Zak got ready to go to kindergarten, were there any issues that you were ready to [have] come up as your son went into the school system?

Chris H.: Before he went into school, [we decided] we had to bring him out in the big world and expose our family to scrutiny in some way, in some kind of formal setting. So, I think having him in daycare really helped. We went in with kind of a chip on our shoulder, going, "Okay, we are a lesbian family with a little boy. How do you feel about that?" We came out with it quite readily at daycare and they were so great.

Tara: Were you the first lesbian family in daycare or had there been others before you?

Chris P.: We were the first in our daycare and it coincided with the court battle that we were entering for me to adopt Zak.

Tara: Can you tell us a little bit about [adopting Zak]? How come that happened?

Chris P.: That happened in order for me to gain the same bundle of rights that Chris naturally has as the biological parent of Zak. In order for me to do that, I had to adopt him. In order for me to do that, Chris, for a moment, had to give up her parental rights and say,

"Yes, I will share them with you." And that took place in family courtroom and was a momentary give and take.

Chris H.: And I had to adopt him too.

Chris P.: Yes, and Chris had to adopt him too. So, in effect, we were both now adoptive parents of that boy. And we felt we had to do that in order to provide him with the same rights that all other children have automatically by being born of a man and a woman. To assign me the same rights and responsibilities to him as any other child would have, should our relationship break up, I would have to still provide the same emotional [and] financial support to him that I would were we still together, and he would still be able to demand access of me and I'd do the same with him.

Tara: What was it like to move from being a biological mother to being an adoptive mother? Was that a difficult moment?

Chris H.: The hardest thing for me was accepting that it was necessary, that any of it was necessary—the court battle, her having to adopt. For me, [at] the moment of insemination she became his other parent. I remember being at Children's Aid at one point and we had to sign over [my biological parental rights]. There was a twenty-four-hour period where anybody could come in and claim standing against what we were attempting to do. And I was signing over my parental rights to start the process. And that was scary. I was, like, walking out [of the office] going, "Oh shit, what have I done?" I mean this is kind of a weird thing to have to do. I distinctly remember having this child with her. What's the big deal.

Chris P.: But I think that's part of being a lesbian family, that we must always struggle to be treated equally.

Chris P.: And that is something that we try to teach our child. But I can't say that we ever had to not choose service from an agency because of homophobia or heterosexism. We were always very out and open, and when we started daycare it was right at the beginning of the adoption battle. We said, "You know we are lesbian parents, we are going through adoption. There may be publicity on this. There may be media on this. There may be cameras at your door." And there were and they were fine with it. You know it wasn't the child-care providers that we had to be worried about. Maybe some of the other parents, but certainly not the child-care providers.

Tara: Can I ask you about that? What kind of reactions have you experienced from other parents from different kinds of families than your own?

Chris P.: Well, certainly one of the most memorable for me was the first birthday party that Zak had when he actually had some control over the invite list and he chose the kids he knew from the daycare. So we sent out the necessary invitations and asked parents to drop off the children at the appropriate times, and these people didn't know us, but they knew of us, because word travelled quickly amongst them, through the daycare, (whispers) "lesbian parents, gay and lesbian parents." When the second child, Max, was dropped off, the father engaged me and said to me, "Do you know Diane so and so?" and I said, "No, I don't." And he said, "Oh, because she lives in the community." And I didn't understand what he was talking about, and because I work in a municipal politician's office, I thought maybe he meant the community that we represent, and he said, "No, no, no. I mean the gay community she lives in." And I said, "Oh, she's gay." And he went, "Yeah, she's my mother." Meaning she's Max's grandmother. Therefore, the child who was coming into the lesbians' house had a lesbian grandmother.

Chris H..And we thought that was big.

Chris P.: So it was no big deal for Zak's friend to be in our household. A couple more kids get dropped, and when Norman gets dropped off, his parents, both of whom come in the door, make a very concerted effort to make sure that we know that Norman's aunt is a lesbian. So to us it's a [big] deal. We're making sure that there is no heterosexism with the professionals who are teaching our children, all this kind of stuff, but the truth of it is that most of his peers think it's no big deal. Their grandmothers, their aunts, their cousins, their brothers are gay and this generation is talking about it, or is at least …

Chris H.:… exposed to it way more than I think than we were. [Growing up,] you didn't know anyone who was gay. You didn't know anyone, especially anyone's parents or grandparents. God forbid, that's probably the last thing that we considered about grandparents. It's not that big a deal for his peer group.

Growing Up within a Lesbian Culture

Tara: Have both of you made an effort to make sure that Zak had friends who also had two mums or two dads? Was there any attempt that was conscious on your part to make sure that your son had access to a community with kids who were just like him?

Chris H.: Probably more so now [than when he was younger]. We recognize that, yes, that is something that we want to be part of his life. But it happens by chance almost, because the people we socialize with are usually lesbian parents or single parents who are lesbians who have kids. We've chosen recently to come to this neighbourhood where we know more people that are in that situation, especially Zak's best friend.

Chris P.: And I can't think that we're any different than any other minority in the sense of making sure that he is exposed to his culture. And, I'm sorry, but this is his culture. You know, his culture is lesbian and he may grow up a straight man (laughs). But his culture is lesbian which may mean he wears, you know, jeans and a T-shirt. But the truth is, he's got to see that many children [share his experience] and especially I'm feeling the gender thing more and more. Many children and many boys grow up with lesbian parents, whether it's one parent or two and that is neither a good or a bad thing. You know it just is. No different from being a single parent or being of a mixed-race family or a mixed-religious family. It just is. People have different families and permutations. And certainly a lot of his friends have a hard time defining family as a man and a woman and the kids. Their definition of family is much bigger than ours ever was.

Representing Gay and Lesbian Culture in Schooling

Tara: Going back to the culture that you were talking about, do you have a need to see the school represent your culture in the classroom? Are you worried about an inclusive curriculum, or as long as your kid is safe from harassment do you feel that you can provide him with what he needs at home?

Chris H.: I do worry that he is not seeing the scope of our situation in life, our family, our type of existence, included in the normal school books or the normal teaching elements. Actually, one of the teachers, I think it was in senior kindergarten, said to us, "You know we don't have any books that show a lesbian family and since Zak is in my class, we want to include him" and asked us for books, which was wonderful, and we ran around, got books and went to the library and gave her things that she could use. But if we weren't there, we [lesbian families] wouldn't be [in the curriculum]. So, it's not a general rule of thumb to be part of [the curriculum]. It's like, you know, if there are no Jewish kids [in the classroom], there is nothing Jewish talked about. If there are no Black kids, there is nothing with people of colour. I don't know how you insist upon that. It should be the norm. It was lovely that she approached us. But she shouldn't have had to.

Tara: Has Zak ever come home complaining that he has been harassed because his family was different from other families, and, if that has ever happened, how did you deal with it?

Chris H.: Well, the best story is that Zak was being bussed to his last school and he had this older man who was driving the bus everyday. Some mornings Chris would wait for the bus and some mornings I would wait for the bus depending on our work schedules. One day, at dinner Zak said, "You know, the bus driver said to me, 'Who's that woman that was waiting with you?'" And he said, "Well, that was my mama." And the bus driver said, "Well, who is the other woman who usually waits with you?" And he said, "That's my mum." And the bus driver looked at him and said, "Well, which one's your real mum?" And Zak said, "They both are." That was probably the closest I remember of somebody going, "Hey, wait a minute, what's going on here?"—you know, that kind of attitude. But for the most part the schools have been …

Chris P.: The schools have been great. The schools have been reassuring, accepting and both the daycares and the schools have gone out of their way to try to include us, because we sit down with them at the beginning of the year and say, "When Mother's Day comes around there are two. When Father's Day comes around there is none, so don't. …" And they go, "Oh, no, no, we would never push that Father's Day thing. There's lots of kids that don't have dads at home." And we go, "Okay, just include other types of families."

When Zak Gets Older

Tara: As Zak gets a little older and gets into junior high and then gets even older and goes into high school …

Chris P.: He's going to be embarrassed about us, yeah (laughs).

Tara: Have you thought about that time? What are you worried about? What are your hopes for the schools and for him at that point?

Chris H.: I just hope he dresses well. (Everybody laughs.)

Chris P.: Oh, man. What are our hopes? I guess my hope is that he's never ashamed to bring kids home. Because I hear that when I talk to kids that are teens of lesbian mothers. They don't bring anyone home. Now, I've only talked to ones whose mums have come out really late in life.

Chris H.: After marriage.

Chris P.: After marriage, after marriage breakup, whatever, so they haven't lived their entire life with their mum being a lesbian. They've only lived their adolescent life with their mum being a lesbian and they're embarrassed to bring kids home. They don't talk about their family.

Chris H.: It's okay for other people to be gay, but my mother? Yeah, that kind of thing. They were cool about it before. Now, they're just, no, it's my mother. So I dread that. I really fear him carrying a shame about us because we did that for ourselves quite well enough. To have my child do that is a heartbreaking thought.

Chris H.: The other thing I would hope is that all [children in lesbian families] teach other kids about how to be in the world. This is my family, what does your family look like? And I think that they'll all be that way as teenagers and going on to university and that there'll be somebody who says it's just not a big deal. It's just not a big deal. This is where I come from; yeah, they're a pain in the ass too. You know, that kind of thing.

Tara: It's part of [being] a new generation, redefining family and negotiating differently ...

Chris H.: You have to hope that they will take difference as just difference as opposed to a challenge. Difference is a good thing, it's not a bad thing. Difference is good. Difference creates growth. It creates newness. It means you know different and challenging things, as opposed to a bad thing, which is what we were taught difference to be—bad. So, hopefully, to him, difference will be easy to accept.

Canadian Laws and Gay and Lesbian Families

Tara: Let's talk a little about the laws about families. What kind of changes, if any, in our family laws would make your family life that much easier right now?

Chris P.: Well, it would be good to see a change in the pension act, if the federal government would make the appropriate changes to the income tax act to allow changes to be made to the pension act. So that, should I die, Chris, as the spouse of an employee, would be able to gain that monthly stipend, whatever that would be, and Zak as my heir would also.

Tara: Because, as it stands now, that's not possible?

Chris P.: No, because we are not recognized as spouses. What other rights do we not have?

Chris H.: The whole spousal thing. I mean we just bought a house together and we had to sign a piece of paper saying we are not a spouse [to each other]. Legally, we are not spouses of each other.

Tara: Your family doesn't have legal recognition.

Chris H.: We're both adoptive parents of our son, but we're not spouses.

Chris P.: In property law, it's not automatically assumed that what is hers is mine and what is mine is hers. That assumption is not made.

Chris H.: You have to make legal agreements for that.

Chris P.: And even that can be challenged. Even though our wills and our RRSPs and our pensions at work may define each other as beneficiaries, that can be challenged in court by either of our biological families. All our wills do is say what our intent was. Our intent was to show that Chris would be my beneficiary. But that could be challenged quite easily, and certainly that is one of the reasons why we've gone to the annoyance and expense of doing wills, of doing legal powers of attorney. I know my sister and her husband do not have medical powers of attorney over each other because they don't need it. But we went out and we paid two hundred dollars to have a piece of paper which I'm sure we won't be clutching when we go to an emergency room (laughs). But we have a document should anyone try to disallow us access to each other or to Zak. So, when you ask about the laws, I mean, what would be nice is if the federal government would just accept that we are the same as common-law couples and include us in common law, and then we wouldn't have to go through either the expense or the annoyance that we do if you're trying to be responsible parents. I guess it's mostly because we have a child involved that we try to take care of those things.

Balancing the Kill, Maim, Shoot Thing

Tara: Right. Is there anything else you'd like to say about your family? What is it like to raise Zak?

Chris H.: Well, [Zak and a friend are] up there [in Zak's bedroom] shooting. You can hear that. The one thing that we're finding right now is the challenge of being women, lesbians, feminists, raising a son in this day and age, trying to balance the kill, maim, shoot thing with his more natural and better, gentler side. (Everybody laughs.)

Chris H.: It's hard, it's hard. They're [boys are] different [from us].

Tara: Have you thought about saying no to any kind of guns?

Chris H.: Yeah, and we know people that do that and …

Chris P.: We did do that.

Chris H.: We did do that for a very long time and he still is not allowed …

Chris P.: He built guns.

Chris H.: Oh, yeah.

Chris P.: How do you say no if he creates a gun? You build it out of Lego. You bite it out of your toast. (Laughter.)

Chris H.: We also decided we wanted to put him into society as opposed to having him run alongside society. There are certain things that we compromised on. We don't allow him to have guns and he knows that. But there are toys that he has that have little gun things on them.

He can watch Spiderman or Batman or something [on television]. But other shows are iffy, you know, so we have boundaries without going all the way to no television, no guns, no anything. You have to have leeway because he's got to be in the world.

Acceptance in Families of Origin

Chris P.: I still find the hardest thing about being a gay family is that the closer it is, the harder it is. I still find that our immediate biological families are way harder to deal with than the principal at school, because the principal, you can face her as a professional. I still find it harder in my family or Chris's family to [find acceptance of] us as a family unit than I do in the school system or daycare system or athletic facility system. If you're trying to join the Y or go to a rec centre, it's easy, it's almost simple to fit in. Now, I'm talking about an urban centre here. I'm talking Toronto. We're not in Penetang. We are living in a major urban centre, in downtown Toronto. I'm not in Scarborough and that is a significant difference. But I find it easier to fit into my neighbourhood than I do to fit into our biological families at times. So the school system, so far, knock wood, we're in grade two, has been nothing but exemplary. I think a lot of it has to do with where we live and it's one of the reasons why we won't move out of Toronto.

Living in a Lesbian Family: "Difference creates growth"

I would like to conclude by commenting on three moments that stood out for me in our interview. The first was when Chris Higgins talked about having to sign over her biological parental rights and adopt her own son so that her partner might legally adopt him as well. I am taken by the courage Chris showed when she gave up her own parental rights for twenty-four hours so Zak would be provided with a legal relationship with his other mother. For twenty-four hours, Chris ran the risk of losing her right to raise her son altogether. This is not a risk that we ask mothers who are not lesbians to take.

The second moment was when Chris Phibbs talked about her hope that Zak will not be ashamed to bring his friends home or talk about his family when he grows older. The shame that is associated with being lesbian and being part of a lesbian family has to do with the intensity of homophobia and heterosexism that characterizes our society. Once again, it takes courage to live as an openly gay family and constantly challenge the shame that is produced by a society that still discriminates against lesbian, gay and bisexual people and their families.

The third moment has to do with both mothers' positive experiences with the public elementary schools in Toronto. These positive experiences seem to be the result of the never-ending advocacy work that both Chrises do to ensure that Zak is well-treated in school. From talking to teachers about their family to supplying teachers with books about gay and lesbian families, Chris and Chris are constantly working with people in their son's school to dispel stereotypes about lesbians and lesbian families and challenge ideas and misinformation that create the shame associated with lesbian, gay and bisexual identities. Their advocacy work—present in every moment they speak openly about their lesbian family—creates growth, both in their own family and in the people they talk to as well. Teachers who have never read any books about gay and lesbian families grow when Chris and Chris bring them into their classrooms, as do the children who listen to the teacher read them. The bus driver who has never met a child with two mothers grows when Zak tells him both Chrises are his "real mother." Zak himself grows every time he finds himself talking about his family to different people.

As Chris Phibbs says, difference not only creates growth, it also creates newness: new ways of thinking about families and the need to find new ways of legally protecting lesbian and gay families. About one month after I interviewed Chris and Chris, a Toronto-based gay rights group named Foundation for Equal Families launched a constitutional legal challenge against some fifty-eight pieces of federal law that discriminate against lesbians and gays. Some of the laws are related to tax, some to old age security and others to spousal rights and responsibilities. Should the group be successful in their legal challenge, many of the issues Chris and Chris have raised in their discussion of the Canadian law and gay and lesbian families can be resolved. While difference creates growth and newness, fighting discrimination requires advocacy and political mobilization.

13

Negotiating Differences

Glimpses into a Canadian Interracial Relationship

BINA MEHTA AND KEVIN SPOONER

Over the past decade or so, we have spent considerable time thinking about what it means to be Canadian. Our lives are shaped by our identities within the educational system, as teachers, as researchers and as activists, but an overarching factor that ultimately shapes much of our experience and negotiations around difference is our relationship with one another as an interracial couple. Invariably, race and ethnicity have shaped how we see ourselves and how we are seen by others. This is true for each of us as individuals and also for the two of us together as a couple, living inside and outside two distinct and sometimes oppositional cultures. We find ourselves often wondering, does it always have to come down to the fact that he is white/Anglo/"Canadian" and she is brown/South Asian?

This relationship began when two individuals from diverse backgrounds and geographic locations came to study at a small Ontario university. We found ourselves in the same academic program and in the same college residence. The relationship grew out of a strong friendship that had initially developed from engaging and provocative discussions about politics and identity. At that time, in spite of our differences, it was our similarities that brought us together: a new city, new academic challenges, the first time away from home. This is a typical beginning for many university student relationships.

For the first time, we find ourselves sitting down to write about this relationship. Although in our teaching we have often drawn upon personal experiences when exploring the process of "becoming Canadian," this has usually taken place within a class we have already come to know. Telling the story of who we are is often draining and challenging, and it seems doubly difficult to put pen to paper without personally knowing the reader; it is not easy to write about something so private and personal, yet more and more common in the larger society in which we live.

We would like to introduce ourselves through excerpts from a letter written by the white guy (Kevin) to the brown woman's (Bina's) family in the summer of 1993, soon after we "came out." Because of the large size of Bina's extended overseas family, it seemed that a letter would be the best way to announce our intentions to marry. No person in either family had ever married outside their cultures, as far as we know. While Kevin's family had, early on, embraced and encouraged the relationship, it was implicit that Bina should not marry or date outside her culture. This had been something ingrained from childhood—that she must marry a Gujarati-speaking Brahmin boy in an arranged marriage. Endogamy remains a common practice in South Asian communities, even those in Canada. Because of this, we recognized that Bina's parents could encounter an intensely negative community response to our relationship. Meanwhile, Kevin's family, with its seemingly more liberal attitudes towards mixed-race couples, accepted Bina as part of their lives, commenting that her difference was unimportant. So, initially, we set aside any need to explain or justify our relationship to Kevin's family and focused instead on negotiating with Bina's family through this letter.

> July 15, 1993
> Collingwood, Ontario
>
> By now, you will have heard that Bina and I are planning to be married. I am writing to introduce myself to you. Over the six years that I have known Bina, she has spoken of her family often and I feel almost as though I have begun to know many of you....
>
> Both my Mother's and Father's families have been in Canada for generations. My Great Grandmother's Great Grandmother was born in Canada. On my Father's side, my family's roots are British, Irish, Scottish, French and perhaps Native Canadian (we're not completely sure of the latter). On my Mother's side, my family's roots are primarily British....
>
> Although we come from very different backgrounds, Bina and I have a lot in common. We enjoy vegetarian cookery. I have discovered two new favourite foods, chai and gulab jambu. Since meeting Bina I have become vegetarian.... I have been interested in Hinduism and Indian culture. I have never been a religious person—religion was not part of my upbringing. My parents felt that their children should be brought up to discover their spirituality for themselves. Now, I feel as though I am beginning to understand some of the basic ideas of Hinduism and hope that Bina and her parents will share their knowledge with me. I am already trying to learn to speak Gujarati—it will be difficult, but I'm determined. Perhaps at some time we will also have the opportunity to visit India....

I realise that all of this may be overwhelming for you, as it has been for Bina's Mother and Father. I know that they did not expect Bina to marry someone from outside of her culture, and that they did not want for this to happen. I want to assure you that it was only after a lot of soul searching that Bina and I decided to marry. We have spent many days thinking about the implications of our marriage and were aware of the difficulties that it might bring to the family. Ultimately, we know that we could not deny our love for each other and needed to be open about it. While it came as a surprise to Bina's parents, they have started to understand our situation and have given us their full support and blessings. They are concerned first and foremost for Bina's happiness. We hope that you will be able to offer your good wishes and blessings.
Sincerely, Kevin Spooner

Years have passed since that letter was written and yet, as an artifact of our relationship, it remains a powerful reminder of the negotiations that had to occur just in order for us to achieve couplehood. Coming together is something that most heterosexual, same culture and race couples can take for granted. Our differences, however, made it clear from the outset that this was a relationship that would not be normal in Canada. We still evoke shock, stares and wonder in both of our racial and cultural communities. We find ourselves struggling to belong to each other's worlds, never fully belonging in either of the communities where we began. We decided that a dialogue would be the most suitable way to share our story.

Bina: I find it hard to read that letter. It makes me feel that we are still struggling with acceptance. I can remember how awkward the *sagai* [engagement ceremony] felt; and, if I am truthful, also the *lagan* [wedding]. Even now, bringing the two cultures together makes me feel tense. It should have gotten easier with time, don't you think?

Kevin: The letter reminds me mostly of the fear in which we lived before we "came out." To me, it represents that night we finally told your parents that we would be getting married, with or without their blessing. In some ways, I see it as a symbol of our freedom from overwhelming secrecy. In a more negative way, it also provokes a profound feeling of disappointment. The letter suggests an admirable agenda of learning more about my new culture that all these years later has still not been completely fulfilled.

Bina: Sounds like we both have regrets about how we have managed in this interracial relationship—things we might have done differently, hopes that were too large and feelings of guilt. I have not become fully White and you have not become fully Indian. Maybe that wasn't the goal, but somehow I thought we'd be further ahead in feeling at home. I am at home when it is just us in our place. I belong there. I don't have to be Indian or White—I guess that means Canadian. I'm just me. But anytime we interact outside that comfortable place of belonging, there is conflict. I should be more White for your parents and for most of the society out there. I don't feel that we are Indian enough in the context of brown people. I stutter when I speak Gujarati. I feel like I translate for you too much. I don't even eat the same way as I used to when I was more Indian.

Kevin: I often wonder about the experiences of other couples, those who aren't interracial. I expect that when any two individuals get together there must always be negotiations around lifestyle and day-to-day living. But I know that in our case this process is made that much more complicated and loaded with meaning. What to wear, what to have for dinner, who to spend this weekend with are all questions that everyone faces. In our case, though, the answers to these questions will have an impact on who we are becoming as a couple. I worry about the need to strike a balance that will let us live our lives without thinking to death each and every action, and yet keep us aware of the need to preserve that which is Indian about us. The outside world is a very hostile place to cultures not in the mainstream, and I always hope that our home can be one location where we integrate our cultures rather than assimilate one into the other. It doesn't always feel this way. In fact, I think we often did a better job of striking that balance when we first got married. Have we become complacent? Have our lives become so much more complicated that striking any balance seems unattainable?

Bina: The way I see the problem is that your culture is around us practically all the time and everywhere. We have to work that much harder to include the Indian part of me in anything we do. It's not like I can turn on the television or radio and hear Indian voices. I never even see Indian people, especially here. It's not like we have to work hard at being White. If it weren't for my skin colour, we'd be "normal" in so many ways, accepted without question. And we'd probably feel more at ease and confident in our choices. But to be Indian we have to travel to where there is an Indian community. We have to deliberately and consciously make the choice to listen to Indian music or to eat Indian food or to speak Gujarati. I think our differences, though, go much deeper than all of that. There is a kind of subconscious way of living that is Indian. I can't articulate it very well. Perhaps it's an ethos of how you think about family, food, spirituality and your relationship with work and the outside. It's just different. I'm also aware that the negotiations are not merely around culture but also race and gender. In society, you are a White male and everything I know tells me that you have favoured status in Canadian society. But the moment that the outside world knows that you are married to a "Paki," your disadvantage comes through. Don't you think you are privileged in every way except by marriage?

Kevin: I am very privileged.[1] There is no doubt. My gender and race accord me advantages that I never realized or acknowledged until I began to think critically about who I am. I am reminded of this every day in our relationship. Our attempts to strike that balance that I previously mentioned demonstrate just how much privilege I have. As you say, we don't have to work hard at nurturing the White side of our relationship. If both sides were equal, as it were, this would not be the case. And yet, I think there is one other factor that has brought us together—class. There is no doubt that each of us, in our own way, came from working-class backgrounds. We grew up in environments where money (or the lack of it) was always a concern. That, I think, has been a very significant experience that has fundamentally shaped who we are as a couple. I find it difficult to envision how we would have coped with any extra pressures had we also had to deal with class differences.

Bina: Absolutely. Any more differences would have been over the top. I know that my parents wanted me to marry someone who was not only Hindu, but also of the same caste—Brahmin. Despite the fact that caste is an archaic and ancient tradition, an absurd concept in modern times, it still carries considerable importance, and its applicability is quite difficult in the modern, industrial capitalist world. But it still has much emotional and traditional pull for many Indians. Oddly enough, now that we both work as educators, we are in the typical Brahmin vocation of teaching. Essentially, you and I are very similar in terms of our working-class backgrounds and the economic status of our families. So unlike what some people might think, by marrying you, a non-immigrant, I cannot say that I have increased my opportunities for upwardly mobility on the basis of class.

Kevin: Earlier, you spoke of my being disadvantaged as a result of our relationship—being privileged in every way except by marriage.[2] I suppose that others would suggest that you are now *de facto* privileged because you married a White person. Nevertheless, we also need to acknowledge the impact of class. Any chance for upward mobility that you might have gained by marrying me is mitigated by my own working-class background. I often feel very much out of place when I attempt to live and work in a university setting; I am constantly reminded of how evident and potent differences in class can be. And yet, on the other hand, the university community is relatively more accepting of our racial differences than has been the case in the wider community of Peterborough.

Bina: Geography and place (or placelessness) certainly have played a significant role in how our relationship has developed. To not live in a large urban centre has made me even more cognizant of our differences. I expect that being an interracial couple in Toronto would be a very different experience. Our smaller community seems at times to exoticize my Indianness and at other times to ostracize us as a couple. I remember when we decided to tell my parents about our relationship and felt as though the burden of the world had been lifted from our shoulders. Walking down the street for the first time, hand-in-hand, without fear that we would be seen was like walking on cloud nine. Do you remember? What popped my balloon was that guy on the park bench who yelled out to us, "You fucking White bastard, what are you doing with that Paki woman?" It jarred me into a reality that our differences were not just cultural but also racial, and that we would not only have to deal with the problem of my family's acceptance of you as my husband, but also that of society's acceptance of us. This is the difference that has been the most difficult with which to cope. The cultural stuff like food, language and clothing can be negotiated. But racism is something not so easily negotiated. I remember thinking that my parents were racists for not accepting the White guy. For all intents and purposes, you had everything else going for you. My parents would have accepted you—well educated, loving, non-smoker, non-drinker, vegetarian, all the attributes that a good Indian husband should possess—but you were "Canadian," a euphemism for White. Not good enough. Was it reverse racism or a desire to save the Indian heritage that they saw would inevitably be drowned out by the White society in which we live? I don't know, but I understand more clearly now that marrying outside my culture would inevitably make it difficult to maintain my own Indian identity.

Kevin: How do you think your parents might have reacted had your younger brother decided to marry a non-Indian? Would their reaction have been different because of gender differences?

Bina: For sure. There is a complete double standard when it comes to sons and daughters. Sometimes sons are given implicit approval to have relationships or date, but a daughter's marriageability is something a parent would not even dare to risk by giving permission to date. As a consequence of our relationship, I think my brother is certainly well informed about what to expect should he decide to marry a non-Indian. I also think that there is a certain degree of pressure on him as the son to marry Indian, because traditionally it will be his and his wife's responsibility to care for our elderly parents. I don't think most non-Indian people would comprehend the differences in the meaning of marriage. To Indians, it is not simply a union of two individuals. Rather, it is seen as a parent's spiritual responsibility and obligation. The marriage of a daughter, in particular, is sacred and involves a link to God and heaven. As I understand it, a Hindu parent, by performing the rite of *kanyadhan* [the ceremonial giving away of the bride] ensures that their soul is given *moksha* [akin to liberation]. So while our marriage held spiritual implications, my brother's marriage is significant for my parents in terms of its practicality and the obligations of sons towards parents. In a way, none of this is very easily understood or explained unless you have grown up with Hindu ideology and values. It is perhaps no wonder that lots of young, second-generation immigrants struggle with this even when they are not in interracial relationships. There is a profound cross-cultural, intergenerational conflict which shapes the lives and identities of so many children of immigrants. This gives me some solace, that the crisis of identity and loss of culture is not solely a result of our marriage. And I do acknowledge that you have tried incredibly hard to be supportive of my need to struggle with these questions.

Kevin: I'd like to go back to your earlier point about reverse racism. There is no doubt that racism has been very difficult to deal with at times. I'm sure that many people will think that your parents' reluctance about our relationship was racist. I think that racism was a part of their response to me. Knowing them, as I do now, I also recognize that their concern was motivated at least as much, and likely more, by a fundamental need to preserve who they are and who you are culturally. For example, what you have just said about marriage has obvious relevance here. In this way, I think that culture has been perhaps even more important than race, at least in our dealings with family. As for those in the wider community, cultural pressures, while present, don't seem so immediate. Here, race is likely to be the more important factor. Those who do not know us are likely to identify us first by our race (consciously or subconsciously) and secondly, perhaps, by cultural similarities and differences. While neither of us can miss the overt racist attacks, like that of the man on the park bench, I know that you are often the first to be aware of the more subtle and perhaps insidious racism directed towards either both of us or yourself. It has taken considerable time for me to become more aware of when this is happening. I know that I recognize racism when it is happening more readily now than ever before. It strikes me that if someone as open to seeing racism as I think I am can miss it, how easy it must be for those who are not looking for it (or refusing to see it) to dismiss attempts to identify it.

Bina: I appreciate this so much because racism engenders a lot of isolation and it is so important for you as my partner to see how it happens and what kind of impact it has on me and other people of colour.

Kevin: I remember that I was always taught to ignore differences. At the time, I'm sure this seemed like a valid strategy for the elimination of racial prejudices: set aside difference and everyone is equal. In many ways, it took quite a leap of faith to set this view aside and see that in fact recognizing and accepting difference is the first step to breaking down prejudice. It now seems to me that ignoring differences or pretending that they don't exist is no better than burying one's head in the sand. Our relationship has given me the chance to see first-hand how important it is to validate who we are as individuals by respecting and fostering our cultural identities. I think this is a difficult concept for many people to see, including my family at times.

Bina: Early on in our relationship, your mum, in an effort to make me feel accepted, said that she didn't see me as different because I was Indian. She said, "We love you because you are 'Bina.'" I knew the spirit and intent of her comment was to welcome me, but I *did* want her to see my difference because that was what made me "Bina" in the first place. I know of some Indian women and men who have even changed their names with the hope of lessening perceptions of difference. Names like Inder might be changed to Linda. I'm lucky, I guess, that my name is relatively easy to pronounce. I remember wondering if I should take your last name when we married. I thought your family might see my decision to keep "Mehta" as my last name as a symbol of not wholly accepting you or them. Still today I wonder whether or not a name change will signal yet another shift in my philosophy of life. At the time we were married, I thought that keeping my Indian last name was important as a feminist and as a key to maintaining my Indianness.

Kevin: This, I think, is a really good example of how a common issue for many couples, that might be seen as primarily a gendered site of negotiation in a relationship, is actually made that much more complex by ethnicity. Cultural preservation became an important factor in the decision to keep the last name "Mehta." I'm not sure how my parents took your decision to retain your last name. If they had a problem with it, I suspect that this would have been because they perceived it as "too feminist" rather than as a cultural or familial slight. Oddly enough, my family usually does address our mail to Bina Mehta and Kevin Spooner. Mail from your side of the family often arrives addressed to Mr. and Mrs. Spooner. Naming children will undoubtedly raise this issue again.

Bina: Naming may be the least of our problems when it comes to children. I know that my parents, when they were first made aware of our relationship, worried about what kind of identity our children would have. This seems to be a common reaction when the topic of interracial relationships is raised.[3] They were probably thinking of words like "mulatto," "half-breed," "confused"—you know the list. Admittedly, those thoughts also cross my mind as we plan our family. I am so conscious of what it will mean for our child to be of mixed race. Not only am I worried about how they will feel, but also how they will be perceived and accepted as Canadian. What space does society make for mixed-race kids? Will they be wholly accepted in either Indian culture or in White society at large? Will they have an exaggerated sense of their Indianness? Will they seek the things that make them different or will they repel those differences in order to belong? In spite of our musings on this, I'm not sure that we can predict who this person (our child) will be. Maybe they will be easygoing and have the ability to cope with difficulties. Hopefully, they will have a very strong sense of who they are as a person, culturally and racially. I doubt that most Canadian couples who are planning their families think about these kinds of issues, in addition to planning for healthy, smart and happy children. Our kids will need skills and tools to help them understand and cope with the possibilities of being ostracized or excluded because of their duality. I think that they will have to be particularly secure in their sense of themselves, knowing that society looks upon difference as a deficit rather than an asset. The familiar slogan that they will "have the best of both worlds" is rather hollow.

Kevin: But I also hope that we have children who are confident enough with who they are that they are not constantly questioning and thinking on this issue. My mother often says that you and I think too much. She is partly right. I hope that our children will be thoughtful and culturally aware, but that they will not get bogged down with worries and self-doubt about their identities. This, of course, means that we will have to do a spectacular job of ensuring that they feel comfortable with both of their cultural communities—no easy task. Teaching our kids strategies for dealing with racism and confused identities will not be easy. Partly because our grandparents were so important in shaping who we are as individuals, I hope that our children's grandparents will also play a key role. This will undoubtedly help in the transmission of key cultural values. But I don't think we should underestimate the role that we will also play in the transmission of those values. We often worry about the nitty-gritty details of culture (food, dress, etc.), and it is true that often these are sacrificed in the name of convenience. I believe, though, that there are some very core values that we have developed together that have been adopted wholly from our cultures. Here I think we have done a good job of striking a balance. The people we have become in our relationship are not the same people that would have developed had we each married within our own cultures and races. We have become something new and this newness integrates values from both of our traditions, values that "fit" for us. For instance, our belief in the need for reciprocal relationships has a great deal to do with the notions of justice and obligation that have developed as a result of our Indianness. Our sense of spirituality is also grounded in Hinduism, not Christianity. And yet, our need for privacy and time for just the two of us has grown out of our Westerness. These are the kinds of significant and integral values that I hope we will pass on to our children. In this way, I hope that they will inherit the values from both cultures that we consider to be the most important. As parents, and with the help of grandparents, I hope we can do this.

Bina: It is true that we may have disappointments, regrets and guilt about what we may not have accomplished culturally since we have been married. But, and more importantly, we have a very strong world view which informs our lives. This we will be able to pass on without doubt. To return to the issue of culture, I guess we have not adequately acknowledged that culture is not a static concept and that we should desire dynamic cultures, both Indian and White. After all, cultures are fluid. I often hear that in India, women are much more progressive than their Indian counterparts here. India has moved on, while immigrants within the diaspora hold on to what was left in 1972. They expect their children to hold on to a particular culture which no longer exists in India itself. I hope that we and our children are able to move in and out with flexibility and with readiness to accept cultural change. I want from this interracial relationship a heightened sense of adaptability for living in modern society. In some ways, an interracial couple is a symbol of the modern world. Probably at no other time in history would it have been possible for a Gujarati-speaking woman born in East Africa of Indian roots to be married to an English-speaking man born in Canada of Anglo roots, with the goal of acceptance for the creation of new generations of Anglo-Indian Canadian families. Gosh, does this sound like post-colonial theory! We've used all their key words ("location," "modernity"). I know your disdain for theory, so let me ask you what you like about being in an interracial relationship.

Kevin: After all these complex thoughts, I could provide a simple and to-the-point answer: the food. Of course, there is much more. I think one of the most fulfilling aspects of our relationship has been that it has provided me with an opportunity to develop a stronger sense of spirituality. As I had said in that letter of introduction, my family was not particularly religious. We pretty much led secular lives. Christianity was a presence in the same way it is for many people in Canadian society who do not consider themselves religious. We celebrated Christmas and collected chocolate at Easter. I can vaguely remember saying the Lord's Prayer in school each morning. Spending time with you and your family gave me a wonderful opportunity to learn about Hinduism. The more I learned about it, the more I felt that it was a much better fit with my own personal values. I recognize Hinduism as a way of life, not just a religion. The beliefs, rituals of prayer and meditation provide me with an opportunity for inner peace that I may never have found had we not come together. I suppose, in this way, we have had it easier than many interracial or intercultural couples who must face choosing between religions.

Bina: For me, the greatest part of being in an interracial relationship is the deep sense of introspection that has occurred in our lives. We really do know what it means to love someone so much that we would take the risk of losing culture, family and sense of self. Ironically, we have found those things better than might have otherwise been the case. I have been told that most interracial relationships don't work, but I cannot help but think that this is untrue. If people enter an interracial relationship, then they will have to be sure that it will work between themselves, before they became public about it, because the risks are just too great. I have learned much about my own culture too. In the process of translating and explaining, I began to know things about my Indianness in a more concrete way. It has been wonderful to have the innocence of your Whiteness in relearning Hindu philosophy. It was okay to ask why with you there. As someone who grew up mostly exposed to White culture, I lost a great deal of my own teachings. Thank you for returning them to me. I must say though, if I were to choose what I like about White culture, I'd have to say that I cannot point to many foods.

> Mostly, they are bland, but with a bit of hot sauce or masala, I can always create something new. This is exciting. Curried macaroni and cheese is delicious!

Concluding Comments

Culture, race, family, religion, racism, privilege—all of these are sites of negotiation in our interracial relationship. It seems to us that this conversation addresses, in part, the differences between interracial and non-interracial relationships. There are, of course, commonalities of experience which most couples share. All relationships inherently require negotiation. As is true for other heterosexual couples, we acknowledge that our gendered life experiences have shaped our negotiations. Our socialization as male and female, each in our own cultures, is not out of the ordinary. Indeed, some essentialists would go so far as to suggest that these differences are to be expected and even desired.

Yet, for us, differences in gender are compounded and complicated by the differences in race faced by heterosexual, interracial relationships. As people continue to intermarry between cultures and races in Canada, there will be a strong need to develop further awareness of the cross-cultural implications for such couples. In our experience, both racial and cultural differences have been significant in shaping the course of our marriage. For some, however, either race or culture alone may be a predominant site of negotiation.

Interestingly, although we have been together for such a long time now, we still find ourselves sitting at the "White table" at Indian functions; while at White gatherings, we continue to recognize polite, although not entirely sincere, attempts to overlook our obvious differences, in spite of conspicuous curiosity. A friend of ours once coined the phrase "cultural purgatory." It is not without relevance for our own experience. In the end, interracial relationships offer a chance for communities and families to connect and interact in what might be the most intimate and fundamental way.

Naming Difference

14

En/Countering Stereotypes, and Gathering, in Educational Institutions

JUDY ISEKE-BARNES

"Where are you from?" "What nationality are you?" are common questions asked of me. "St. Albert." "Canadian." These were unaccepted answers which lead to further questions. "But where are your ancestors from?" Growing up in what now is a suburb of Edmonton, I have devised many answers through the years. The one I recall using most was "Heinz 57." It seemed to capture my background. My ancestors have been on this continent for millennia (Cree), for a few hundred years (Metis), for a century or so (German, Dutch, etc.) and for a few decades (English). So what "nationality" am I? Heinz 57 seemed to fit well. At some point someone told me that this answer degraded my heritage. I'm not sure whether giving my heritage the same name as a brand of meat sauce or claiming mixed-race identity was considered the most degrading. I switched to calling myself a "Real Canadian" having a "multicultural heritage." Both of these responses didn't satisfy but usually silenced the questioner. And that was usually my intent. After all, why is it necessary for me to be categorized?

Even in applying for academic positions, categorization becomes an issue. Academic applicants usually receive a request for ethnic information, particularly in the United States, where one is asked to declare if one is a "visible minority," "Native," woman, "disabled," etc. I never really knew how to fill out those applications. In considering the absurdity of these forms, a friend and I mused about what it would take to fill in all the boxes. As a woman with an Aboriginal heritage, I was both "visible" (an "other" rather than a "minority," but that didn't seem at the time too much of a stretch) and Native (in some sense of the word). Now all I needed to do was to figure out how to fit into the "disabled" category and I could check all the boxes. Of course, what this musing pointed to are many questions about categorizing. What are the dividing lines? Who is inside and outside of these lines?

In my academic career, I have had many experiences of being an insider and an outsider. I began my academic career in St. John's, Newfoundland, a province which is 98 percent of Anglo/Celtic descent. I was told by neighbours and colleagues that issues of "diversity" are not even in the consciousness of the people. The indigenous people of this region, the Beothuk, "disappeared from existence" or "became extinct," I was told. Somehow these descriptions are reminiscent of discussions about endangered species. Being in Newfoundland, I never felt so "brown" in all my life. And while living in Edmonton, many times I was reminded that I had a "browner" skin tone than most, but I generally didn't think of myself as "white" or "brown," but just as me. But here I felt very "different."

Newfoundlanders called me and my family CFAs—"come-from-aways"—outsiders because we did not speak with the Newfoundland accent. My students said my language had that "western drawl." It lacked the sounds of the English and Celtic influences which Newfoundlanders have come to expect. But I didn't feel too offended, because students, colleagues and people I met in grocery stores and restaurants told me that they could usually tell what region of Newfoundland a person was from by the sound of their accent. So it wasn't just my western drawl that they picked up, but they were very aware of "accents" of many kinds, sometimes with very subtle differences. Somehow it was recognized that all people spoke a language in the way of their region, so we all spoke with an accent.

In Newfoundland, I found myself listening more closely to words spoken by my students—partly because many spoke quickly and partly because, when they talked informally, especially with people from the same region, the words became incomprehensible to me. I sometimes wondered whether my words were incomprehensible to them. In formal discussions, they spoke a more formal English. As one student described it, he "toned down" his "accent" so I could understand him. In a lighthearted and friendly manner, students laughed at me when I asked them to repeat phrases and expressions I could not comprehend. To all of them their words were as "plain as the nose on your face," and yet I could not understand them.

Three years ago, my academic career moved me and my family to Toronto, the city at the "centre of Canada," as advertisements on television declare, and a city described by the United Nations as the most culturally diverse city in the world. It is interesting to teach and work here, because when I walk down the street or I visit classrooms in schools in the region I find students who speak many languages, whose skin tones are of many different shades and who clearly give me the sense that I am in a very diverse setting. But when I walk the halls of the academic institutions in which I work and when I engage in pre-service teacher education, there is very little apparent diversity. The invisibility of "minorities" is significant. I am told that only 10–15 percent of students identify themselves as "minority" in some way.

In my experiences, some students are extremely intolerant of students who appear to be of a minority group. For example, in one of my classes, students engaged in slanderous comments about students who entered the program through an access initiative (a very minimal program in this institution which is meant to encourage students from diverse backgrounds to enter the field of education). The comment made was "The unqualified ethnics are going to get the jobs, not me, because I'm White." This comment was taken personally by a student who had identified herself as Canadian of Chinese descent but whose classmates called her "Asian." She said she had been admitted in the same way they had been (she had not entered the program under an access initiative) and was tired of the assumption that she was unqualified to be here (despite her entry as a student of first calibre from her undergraduate program). She began to cry. In my efforts to deal with this situation, I talked about my own ethnicity and the need to change the ethnic mix of teacher education. Another student suggested that, in her opinion, access initiatives for faculty and students just let in the "riff-raff," a classification she assigned to me. From this point forward, students would not work with each other and some did everything in their power to disrupt our classes. I have sometimes described my role in this situation as being just "too Indian" for some students.

I have also experienced incidents in Toronto that made me feel that I am "not Indian enough." In a meeting of people interested in indigenous education, a graduate student singled me out and said that I was not hired as an "Indian." She questioned my involvement with indigenous issues and any claim I might make to an Aboriginal background. In later discussions in this group, I was told that in Toronto, much to my surprise, there are a number of stereotypical gradations of Indianness, with "from the reserve" meaning a "real Indian," particularly if you speak the language. If you are "urban," then the stereotype is that you are "less Indian." If you are Metis, then you are stereotyped as just like other mixed-race Aboriginal people and told that you should just ignore any knowledge of your heritage. This is particularly true if you can "pass" as White. This reminds me that in Canada "there are seventeen different classifications of Indians. The Indian Act still makes distinctions between 'Indian' and 'person'" (Mercredi and Turpel 1993: 24). Given recent changes to legislation and ongoing land claims, are new classifications of "Indians" being created by government structures? For example, the historic decision of the Nisga'a (pronounced "Nishka") and the newly created territory of Nunavut may well create new classifications of "Indians." I was told recently by a woman at Indian Affairs (who asked me about my heritage but did not ask this question of the rest of my party) that there is a court case going on right now that will determine if Metis peoples are Aboriginal. One member of our party stated, "As if it is up to them." In another example, in the past, "Indian" women who married "White" men were stripped of their status. Did they stop being "Indian"? Some of these women are now being reinstated. Are these women resuming "Indianness"?

There appears to be little recognition of the Metis nation as a nation amongst the Ontarians I've met. But, then again, there appear to be multiple political agendas being played out in multiple First Nations in the region. A First Nations woman told me of her story of failing a course in "Aboriginal World View" offered at a particular post- secondary institution because she would not espouse the views of the instructor who was of a different First Nation. Since it was a required course, she took it again but the second time begrudgingly gave the instructor what he wanted and passed the course.

As one of my students, Bonita Lawrence, has shown me, Metis is a regional designation which exists only in Ontario and westward because of the timing of treaties and government declarations. Anyone from east of Ontario has no status as a Metis person but is just known as a mixed-race Aboriginal person. In Ontario, the designation of "Metis" may well be marginal in both Aboriginal and non-Aboriginal settings, given the limited recognition and funding available. This lack of recognition seems to contrast with the necessity in Ontario (and apparently elsewhere as well, e.g., Alberta) to provide proof of family affiliations and genealogical records in order to become a member of the Metis Nation.

What is most interesting to me these days is that since I am now recognized in some official way as an "indigenous" person at the academic institution where I work, I have begun to be called "a woman of colour." I keep wondering how this designation came to be? I certainly have never made this claim. And exactly what colour is that anyway? I recall the remarks of a graduate student who questioned the designation "red." She said, "My skin isn't red but brown. What is all this talk about redskins?" I find the distinctions of "White" and "Indian" really troubling because both of these terms suggest that colour and racial identity are fixed and narrow categorizations.

And academic institutions are increasingly interested in brokering identities based on narrow categorizations. A senior academic suggested, in reviewing my grant proposal, that I should indicate that I have a Metis background because the proposal was about Aboriginal peoples. And in a recent publication submission, a colleague of mine wrote that I was Metis, leaving his own background unspecified. I was asked why I was offended by the inclusion of my background. Again, my question of why I should be classified arises.

I recognize that identity is complex, being formed through many relations and situations. To be simply described as a Metis person is inadequate. My background is complex, and so to identify me in this way feels like essentializing. Gerald Vizenor, a mixed-blood Ojibway, questions the orientation of many with a mixed-race Aboriginal background to "go Indian," taking up the identity of the idealized Indian portrayed in museums, photographs, paintings and in cultural practices which have worked to create what he characterizes as the "invented Indian" (1984). He suggests that it is important to counter this stereotype (for a discussion of Vizenor, see Blaeser 1996).

> The dominant society has created a homogenized history of tribal people for a television culture. Being an Indian is a heavy burden to the *oshki anishinabe* because white people know more about the *Indian* they invented than anyone. The experts and cultural hobbyists never miss a chance to authenticate the scraps of romantic history dropped by white travelers through *Indian country* centuries ago. White people are forever projecting their dreams of a perfect life through the invention of the Indian—and then they expect an *oshki anishinabe* to not only fulfill an invention but to authenticate third-hand information about the tribal past. (Vizenor 1972: 15–16)

Valaskakis (1993) describes "a discourse which constructs what outsiders, and Indians, know about Native peoples in representations of Indianness: tribal and traditional, other and unequal. In the words of Deborah Doxtator, "People growing up in the 1950's and 60's were conditioned to believe that 'Real Indianness' had something to do with not talking very much, never smiling, wearing fringed clothing, being mystical, being poor, riding horses" (Valaskakis 1993: 159). I had a graduate student ask me how is it that I am an "Indian," comparing my responses to those of her family, as she is a non-Aboriginal person with status through marriage. She suggested that my outgoing personality and talkative nature are more "of my French side than my Cree ancestors." But my family and many Metis, Cree and Ojibway people I know are very outgoing and talkative. They laugh a lot and enjoy life. So I wonder how this stereotype was created. But then again, how is any stereotype created? What I think are important to counter are these stereotypes of the invented Indian.

Countering Stereotypes

Inside educational institutions it is increasingly important to counter stereotypes. In a recent meeting of the Center for Integrative Anti-Racism at my institution, a colleague, Sherene Razack, suggested that we change the institution by writing on it with our bodies. All faculty members in this group are "counted" as "persons of colour" by the institution. Our very presence at the institution, as a lobby group and reminder of the need for change, causes the institution to rethink itself and its goals.

Another group that is working for change in the institution includes faculty members focused on equity studies. The fact that they have decided to read about equity rather than act as a political lobby group is limiting, but at least they are talking about the many ways people are marginalized in the institution (by race, class, gender, sexuality, ableness etc.). Several networks of students and staff do serve as a political lobby, including the anti-racist network and the Indigenous Education Network (IEN).

At a recent gathering I helped to organize for the IEN, we had a traditional Aboriginal teacher come and open our gathering with a prayer and blessing. She spoke in Ojibway to those assembled and explained her blessing in English to those of us who could not understand. We then heard an Aboriginal women's drumming group who sang songs given to them by singers from many traditions. Their joy in the songs lifted all our spirits, and their strength in singing these songs filled us all with courage. Representatives of the dean's office and department chairs then welcomed a new Aboriginal faculty member, Laara Fitznor, who spoke of her mission to bring awareness of Aboriginal issues to the institution at every level. The Ojibway teacher closed the meeting and then we enjoyed bannock and other treats provided by a local indigenous caterer. To the surprise of the IEN organizers, sixty people gathered at this event. They were members of the academic community, representatives of Aboriginal organizations and Aboriginal educators from local schools. One of my colleagues called this a "gala opening."

Gathering like this in the educational institution is politically important because it provides a sense that Aboriginal education does have a place there. It is also important spiritually because it creates a place for Aboriginal spirituality to be present in the institution (which is exceedingly uncommon given the nature of institutions). A gathering is also an opportunity to create community and awareness because it provides contact amongst peoples from multiple locations and allows them to focus in public on the presence of Aboriginal approaches to education. A gathering brings the community together to experience the teachings and medicines (tobacco, drums, blessings). A gathering is not just a meeting of people, but a coming together of people for a purpose. It recognizes the power of people acting together and signifies that "things are happening." As Fitznor (1998: 29) says, "me-you, we give and we take what we can with what we know and we work with it in an interconnected way."

After cleaning up at the gathering, we all dispersed in various directions to resume our daily activities. But I noticed that new and old associations were rekindled by this event and that people who might not have associated with each other left together engaged in conversation. As I left I spoke to a graduate student. He and I walked through the lobby where a bookseller had his wares set up; the Graduate Students Association organizes this event as a fundraiser several times each year. As we walked through the lobby past the tables of books, we discussed the importance of raising awareness of indigenous issues. I said, "See what I mean?" as I picked up a children's book with the picture of a wrinkled, red-skinned man with a feathered headdress. As we flipped through it, we saw more stereotypical images. I put it down and the student said, "I feel like I should speak to someone about this." I thought for a moment and then picked up the book. As I took the book towards the temporary sales counter, the bookseller said: "I'll take you over here," moving towards the cash register. I introduced myself as a member of the Indigenous Education Network and said: "This book presents a stereotype of Aboriginal peoples which is no longer relevant. Indeed, it never was relevant." Then I pointed to a painting hanging right next to us which the IEN wanted to have moved last year because the garbage cans end up under it during the book sales. I had spoken to the physical plant people on behalf of the IEN. When I was describing this Morriseau painting to the physical plant coordinator, he called it the "Indian painting" and said it had been at the institution since its inception about thirty years ago. I told him that Morriseau, an Ojibway, is the most influential painter from the Eastern Woodlands region of Canada, whose works have inspired a generation of painters. His paintings incorporate the spiritual beliefs and world view of the Anishnabe people and are of great cultural, historical and artistic significance, as well as of monetary value. The physical plant people now ensure that garbage is no longer located underneath this painting, even during special events.

I said to the bookseller, "This painting is a Morriseau, an incredible piece of art by an incredible indigenous artist." Then I pointed once more to the book and said, "This is not. I just wanted to bring this problem to your attention, as I'm sure you weren't aware." Then I turned to my colleague and said "Good evening" as we parted.

Now, one does not always have a Morriseau painting to provide such a stark contrast with simplified and stereotypical images of Aboriginal peoples. But it's sure nice to have this painting present in our building. This painting is extremely valuable for many reasons, not the least of which is that it signifies the presence of Aboriginal peoples at the Ontario Institute for Studies in Education at the University of Toronto (OISE/UT) and serves as a reminder of Aboriginal knowledge in our midst. I believe it is incredibly important that such complex and diverse cultural presentations are made accessible in order to provide contrast to the simplistic and problematic images so prevalent in our society. The IEN is now considering rededicating this painting to Aboriginal peoples at OISE/UT.

I have begun a project of collaborating with Aboriginal educators from across this country to engage in a conversation about what Aboriginal education might mean. The most profound thing for me is the diversity in this conversation. No simplistic or stereotyped images are possible because multiple images and perspectives are continually presented. Meanings are continually renegotiated and transformed in these representations of living culture. I believe that awareness of the multiple and diverse narratives of Aboriginal peoples will assist all of us to counter our own stereotypical understandings of Aboriginal peoples and to resist simplifications.

15

The Home Visit

DENNY HUNTE

Rusty nails and broken staples protrude from the wooden door of the Queen Street East address. I knock four times with my pen.

"Who is it?" a female voice asks.

The westbound Queen streetcar moves toward Parliament Street. Traffic lights flash red. Streetcar wheels screech.

"I am Mr. Maynard, from Social Services."

"Who is it?" the voice repeats.

A few seconds later, the loud pounding of feet echoes behind the door. The lock on the door clicks, the knob turns and the door opens to the full extension of the safety chain. A puff of smoke explodes in my face. I cough. Through the thinning smoke, a White woman in her early twenties with light brown, shoulder-length hair and a small, round face peeks from the other side of the door.

"What do you want?" she says.

I look at her, I look at the number on the apartment door and I look at the top left corner of the home visit request sheet in my hand:

Applicant: Ms. Nancy Davies
Age: 19
Status: Single parent

"Are you Ms. Davies?"

She stares. I pull a calling card from my jacket pocket and hand it to her.

"I am here to complete Ms. Davies' application for social assistance. Does she live here?"

The young woman stares at the calling card, glances at me and then rereads the card.

"Ms. Davies phoned the office yesterday and requested a home visit. She gave this as her address."

Without speaking or making eye contact, she studies my face. Her gaze descends to my chest, my stomach, my legs, my shoes and returns to my face. My cotton toque is pulled down over my forehead and ears. Our eyes lock as I step back from the door.

"You're the welfare worker?" she asks loudly.

I nod. "Yes, I am."

"You got something with your picture on it?"

I take off my toque, revealing my locks, squeeze the toque under my armpit, reach into my pants pocket, pull out my wallet and show her my employee ID card. She stares at my photo, taken ten years ago when I had closely cropped hair, smiles and releases the chain latch.

"Come on in."

I stare at her. "Are you Ms. Davies?"

"Oh! Yes. I am Nancy Davies." She smiles. "Please call me Nancy. Everybody calls me Nancy."

I nod.

"I didn't expect a worker to be here this early."

I glance at my watch: 8:35 am. At the last staff meeting, the area manager reminded us to start home visits within regular working hours; 8:30 am to 4:30 pm. If a job-related incident occurred outside normal hours, the department would not be liable.

Ms. Davies walks up the flight of wooden stairs, and I walk behind her. The stairs squeak. She is wearing a long blue housecoat and one pink slipper. Midway up the stairs, she glances over her shoulder.

"To be honest, I didn't expect you to be.... I expected ... you know ... I expected someone else." She smiles. "You don't look like a welfare worker."

"Thank you. I think I'll take that as a compliment. But what does a welfare worker look like?"

Ms. Davies stops and turns. Holding onto the wooden railing, she stares at the ceiling, takes a drag of her cigarette, holds her breath for a second and then exhales.

"Well. You know. Somebody who is like ..."

"Like what?" I ask. "Taller? Female? Older?"

She smiles. "You remind me of someone," she says.

"Is that so?"

At the top of the stairs, Ms. Davies slips her left foot into the other pink slipper.

"This is the apartment."

Ms. Davies ushers me inside. She throws the cigarette butt in the kitchen sink and points to a small table and four chairs. She nods toward a partially closed door across the room.

"Do you have to see Shaun? He is asleep in the bedroom. He has a bad cold."

"No, not really."

Nancy Davies and Shaun, her two-year-old son, live with Nancy's mom. Dance music from WBLK pulses from the bedroom.

"He kept me up all night. My mother leaves for work early in the morning. She says if I am going to stay with her, I'll have to pay half the rent, buy my own food and live by her rules."

Nancy walks into the kitchen, dampens a used jay-cloth, returns to the living room and wipes the plastic table cover and mats.

"Excuse the dirty dishes. Mom is a neat freak. She gets upset if I leave dirty dishes in the sink overnight. I have to wash them before she gets home from work."

Crumbs fall from the table into her cupped hand and onto the unswept wood floor. Ms. Davies tosses the jay-cloth towards the sink where it settles in an unwashed, yellow plastic dish filled with soapy water. Water beads on the plastic table mat. I place the application forms on my thighs and start the interview.

"Can I see a verifiable ID, please?"

Ms. Davies reaches into a glass fruit tray filled with colourful plastic fruit and pulls out a small leather wallet. She puts the wallet in the centre of the table opens it and hands me her Canadian birth certificate.

"And do you have your son's birth certificate, Ms. Davies?"

She places her hand over her mouth and glances at me.

"Is something wrong?"

"Not really. But it sounds so strange when you call me Ms. Davies. Like I said, everyone calls me Nancy."

I nod.

Nancy lifts the fruit tray and removes a plastic birth certificate.

"And how have you managed financially until now?"

"I was living with friends for the past six months. I just moved back home less than a week ago."

"Do you have any assets?"

Nancy shakes her head. Silver earrings cut in the shape of Africa hang from both ears.

"Do you have any income?"

She knits her brow. I smile.

"Do you expect any income in the future? How have you survived financially until now?"

Nancy sighs as she exhales. She glances into the kitchen, looks out the living room window and taps on the table top with her long, polished nails.

"Are you on your mother's lease? How much rent do you pay your mother? And what is your mom's name?"

"Why do you need to know about her? She is not applying for welfare. She doesn't even know that I phoned the office."

"I need to record your living situation."

"Her name is Erma Davies."

I hear a key in the apartment door lock.

"Nancy!" a woman calls from the hallway.

Nancy raises her hands to her mouth.

"That is my mom," she says. "She is gonna be mad at me."

A woman stands inside the apartment door and glares at us. Nancy looks at me and I look at the woman.

"I told you not to bring anyone in my house," the woman says.

Erma Davies' eyes dart back and forth from Nancy to me. Her face is round like her daughter's. Tramlines streak her forehead.

"This is how you got in trouble in the first place. I didn't accept this kind of behaviour then and I won't accept it now. Like I told you, if you can't live by my rules, you are going to have to move." Nancy's jaw tightens. "One mistake is not enough? You can scarcely care for one child."

Nancy blushes. Her mother slams the front door and walks toward me. I stand.

"Where is Shaun?" Erma Davies demands.

"He is in the bedroom sleeping," Nancy says. "And this is ..."

"And this is how you're looking after a sick child?" her mom interrupts. "And you haven't even cleaned up the mess you left in the kitchen last night."

Erma Davies glimpses at her watch, holds her head high, turns to avoid me and continues down the hallway.

"I want him out of my house right now," she says.

I pick up the partially completed application form from the table.

"But Mom, this is not what you think. This is the welfare worker."

"The what?" Erma Davies stops walking, turns, stares at her daughter and then at me.

"Mr. Maynard is a worker from the welfare office," Nancy says.

Erma Davies squints as she stares at me and starts walking toward us.

"You are a welfare worker?"

I nod.

"Have a seat, Mr. Maynard," Nancy whispers.

I glance at Nancy, at the chair, then at her mom.

"I'm sorry," Erma Davies says. "For a moment, I thought you were someone else."

I extend my hand. Erma Davies shakes it weakly. I sit. I unfold the application forms and rest them on the now dry table mat.

"Who did you think I was?"

Erma Davies' voice becomes almost inaudible. "You look somewhat like Shaun's no-good father."

Nancy smiles and then raises her hands to cover her mouth and nose.

"But now that I look closer, he may be a bit thinner and is not as, ah, dark," her mother says.

"That's what I wanted to tell you, earlier," Nancy whispers.

As I uncap my pen, Erma Davies walks toward the table, stands behind my shoulder and looks at the application form. Nancy sits on the other side of the table.

"Does Shaun's dad pay child support?"

Nancy shakes her head.

"Do you have a court order for support for Shaun?"

"I wish," Erma Davies says.

Nancy glares at her mom.

"If she had listened to me, she wouldn't be in this situation. She would still be in school getting an education instead of applying for welfare. I didn't think about getting welfare when I had her. I raised her alone and without asking for or getting a dollar from anyone, not from her father or from the government."

Nancy sighs. She stares at the ceiling. She stares at the unswept floor.

"Shaun's father, what is his name?"

"Jerry Padmore," Erma Davies says.

"Where does he live?"

"Only the good Lord knows," Erma Davies says.

"Mom! He is talking to me, not to you." Nancy says firmly.

I glance from Erma to Nancy. Their eyes lock.

"Excuse me, Ms. Davies," I say. "Nancy has to answer these questions since this is her application."

Erma Davies rests her hands on her hips. Then she points her finger at me.

"Mr. Maynard, you welfare people are part of the problem," she says. "These children learn from an early age that you will give them welfare. This is why they get themselves into all kinds of trouble. If you ask me, you guys make it too easy for them to get money."

A cry comes from the bedroom, "Mom! Mom!!" A little boy with a light brown complexion, curly black hair, big dark eyes and sturdy legs, and wearing a Toronto Maple Leafs T-shirt stands in the doorway. He cries. His nose runs and mucus drains into his mouth. The boy looks at his mother, at his grandmother, then at me. Nancy pulls a tissue from the box on the cabinet and walks towards him with outstretched arms.

"Come to Mom, Shaun. Come."

Shaun stops crying. Nancy bends to pick him up, but Shaun circles away from her outstretched arms and runs towards me. He wipes his runny nose with the back of his hand in mid-stride. Drool from his mouth falls onto his chin, onto his already wet T-shirt and onto the floor.

His arms flail at his sides.

"Dad-dy! Dad-dy! Dad-dy!" he shouts.

Shaun grabs my knees and climbs onto my lap. His wet hands grab the table, smudging and wrinkling the application forms. They fall to the floor. Lifting him onto my lap, I glance at his mom. Nancy blushes and then rushes towards me. Shaun tightens his already firm grip on my shoulders and cries. The tears rolls down his cheeks and into my shirt. His grandmother stares at me, at him and at the forms that lay scattered on the floor. Erma Davies leans forward and gathers the welfare papers.

"I am so sorry.... I am so embarrassed," she says.

Erma Davies places the forms and my pen on the table and then stares at the ceiling. Nancy stares at the table.

"It's all right," I say as I place my arms around Shaun's back and hug him. He stops crying. His wet face feels warm against mine.

16

A Perspective on How Deaf People Perceive Being Different

David G. Mason

This chapter examines how we Deaf people see ourselves as fitting into the grand scheme of everyday life. Generally speaking, members of minority ethnic communities view themselves as being different from those of other minority communities based on language and/or socio-cultural values (Christensen 1993). However, diversity, tempered by understanding and tolerance, is ultimately balanced by sufficient similarities to ensure "macro-mosaic community" cohesion. But there are fundamental differences between the way hearing people perceive the Deaf and how we perceive ourselves (Lane 1992). This is the heart of the matter under discussion here. There is little doubt that this difference in perception has had a profound effect on Deaf people and the way we interact with others.

The way I see it, people associated with an ethnic or orientation-linked community likely have a sense of what being different from others means, yet they remain secure in the knowledge that they meet the requirements of membership in the larger mosaic community. In a nation where human rights legislation is valued, such citizens are apt to tolerate and appreciate the uniqueness of a distinct community, partly because they themselves identify with their own unique communities. This appears to be the underlying foundation of egalitarian thought. It is not difficult to embrace an egalitarian way of life such as that enjoyed in Canada where socio-political harmony and stability under common law prevails. This soothing, even placating, egalitarianism remains intact as long as fundamental differences do not appear to be too different, especially when it comes to language and culture. This is where we Deaf people are said to deviate. Before elucidating, I must hasten to add that it is purely the above-implied mentality from which we deviate.

Where opportunity presents itself, people invariably speak their familiar ethnic language of choice while doing their best to acquire the majority language for use in the broader societal context. While the world is full of linguistic variation, there is a common thread which ties all spoken languages together, and that is the modality by which they are transmitted. They are all oral-aural languages. Not as much so with signed languages. Using one's hands, face and body to communicate is especially different in the eyes of the hearing majority. However, ethnic and Deaf community members are similar in that they enjoy many benefits from being part of their minority communities within the larger mosaic macro community.

The "Deaf community" is made up of "culturally Deaf," hard-of-hearing, deafened, and "oral Deaf" people who feel comfortable with and value the use of signed language and appreciate being part of this community. (The use of a capital letter in the word "Deaf" indicates an affiliation with the Deaf community.) "Culturally Deaf" persons see themselves as part of the Deaf community. They feel comfortable using sign languages such as American Sign Language (ASL) with others who sign, and recognize that they, consciously or unconsciously, have many attributes that help to define Deaf culture as a naturally emerging and evolving socio-cultural phenomenon. Culturally Deaf persons also use English and interact with hearing people. Culturally Deaf persons are more likely to have a bilingual and bicultural lifestyle than a monolingual and monocultural lifestyle. Many "oral Deaf" persons have learned to see themselves as persons with the ability to do so well with oral communication that they feel they do not need to acquire and use a sign language. They often identify with the world of hearing people and avoid interacting with those who sign.

Almost every member of an ethnic community within the larger mosaic community is hearing, which means that she or he speaks, hears and values an oral language as the main means of communication and, understandably, expects this to be the language of education for his or her children. This language is central to community life and is the underlying basis of community cohesion. Deaf people do not take issue with this. Spoken language so permeates hearing people's personal and social lives that it is often difficult for them to understand how a community could exist without it. In fact, Deaf people use a sign language such as ASL much the same way their hearing counterparts use their spoken languages to experience being part of a community. The Deaf may also rely on their ASL-English bilingual skills or take advantage of competent interpreters or translators to benefit from being part of a larger community.

At this point, I feel compelled to shake the foundations of egalitarian thought by posing a few simple questions:

1. Since most hearing people rarely have contact with or exposure to people who use ASL rather than oral English as their important language, is it realistic to expect them to understand and appreciate that ASL is a language?

2. Can hearing people be expected to understand the significance of the Deaf community as a viable and productive component of the same macro-mosaic community they're part of?
3. Do hearing people realize that most Deaf people are part of both the Deaf and hearing communities and use two different languages, English and ASL?
4. How have hearing people influenced the way Deaf people perceive themselves within the larger community?

For a moment, let us take a closer look at the makeup of the overall population. Most hearing people can be said to be naive or ignorant about what it means to be Deaf, which is not surprising since the majority of people have no experience of deafness. Most of them probably feel awkward when meeting Deaf people who sign, attempt to vocalize English with what may sound like a foreign accent (Hoffmeister 1992), or attempt to write back and forth what they want to say or ask. As a general rule, Deaf people become used to and sympathize with hearing people in such situations; and the sympathy is often reciprocal.

"Intermediary" individuals make up a much smaller percentage of the population. These are hearing people who are comfortable, at least, with the notion that ASL is a second language and enjoy interacting with Deaf people and being part of the Deaf community. Siblings, parents, relatives, children of Deaf parents, interpreters, spouses, playmates, teammates and teachers are among those who are usually better informed about the significance of the Deaf community within the larger community and have a deeper understanding of the uniqueness of Deaf persons' experiences and values.

A third, relatively small but powerful group within the general population is comprised of people with a "missionary mentality." Members of this group typically employ tactics which trivialize and even attempt to dispel the notion that the Deaf community is a bona fide minor community. It is not uncommon for these people to occupy positions of authority which allow them to strategically set directions for young Deaf children and their families, discouraging contact with the Deaf community, tolerating or encouraging their use of one or another type of signed communication as long as it is not ASL, and often restricting their communication to the spoken language of the culturally detached macro-community. For all intents and purposes, their mission appears to be to discourage Deaf people from being Deaf altogether and to urge them to adopt and identify with the more generic socio-cultural values of the larger community. "Missionaries" have often been known to manipulate public sentiment by enlisting the help of the media in their campaign to eradicate all vestiges of the Deaf community. Occasionally, media reporters interview Deaf persons to get their stories or views; however, it is not unusual for the same reporters to double-check with such missionaries and include their counter-opinions, often with a portrayal of a mother with her child as part of the same article. The "missionaries" seem to have no difficulty procuring powerful financial and political backing, nor are they ever at a loss at how to win over an audience with quotes from literature created by others with a similar mentality.

Within this elite circle typically are ASL-incompetent or inadequate hearing educators of the Deaf who feel threatened by the prospects of Deaf professionals becoming their equals in the field of Deaf education. Consequently, they are adverse to supporting bilingualism—that is, ASL and English proficiency—which allows Deaf people to interact well with both Deaf and hearing colleagues and acquaintances (Mason, in press). It is truly a baffling phenomenon. Often, even hearing people from ethnic minority backgrounds have difficulty recognizing and celebrating the Deaf community and Deaf bilingualism.

In recent years, writers have come up with the term "audism" to denote the means by which the "missionaries" wield power over their Deaf associates. As defined by Lane (1992: 43), "audism is the corporate institution for dealing with Deaf people, dealing with them by making statements about them, authoring views about them, describing them, teaching about them, governing where they go to school and, in some cases, where they live; in short, audism is the hearing way of dominating, restructuring, and exercising authority over the Deaf community." Proponents of audism ("audists") are somewhat similar to technocrats (Saul 1993) who control, manipulate or regulate aspects of a bureaucratic body but are absolved from having anything to do with how this body functions as a whole and as part of the larger community. Audists with technocratic power seem to quickly deflate and become ordinary persons when they come closer to empowered or independent Deaf adults in Deaf community activities and become more authoritative with their own missions the farther they distance themselves from them. This implies that they rarely have an opportunity to learn about and share the intricacies of Deaf persons' experiences and values.

Deaf people throughout the ages have demonstrated remarkable resiliency and adaptability. Nevertheless, the struggle goes on in many forms. For someone who does not deal in "sound," it is no easy task to open up lines of communication with teachers, politicians, business people, church people or even one's own family. By working hard to acquire some speech and aural listening skills, they can establish some contact, but they often need something more to forge meaningful communication links. Lucas and Valli (1988) discuss the notion of contact language between English- and ASL-using people, explaining how both adapt their language skills to enable themselves to understand and be understood without having to compromise the integrity of their own languages. The authors stress that such a communicative structure is so unique, because it does not compromise the integrity of either language, that it does not and cannot have the characteristics of either a creolized or pidgin language. Livingston (1997) emphasizes that dealing with meaning constitutes the essence of interactive communication. Mutual respect for others' languages while trying to solve one's own communication problems is th essence of a collaborative effort to even the playing field and meet the common need to understand and be understood.

I feel that I have been part of a smaller Deaf community within a larger hearing community ever since my childhood. During my early adolescence, I was somehow led to perceive that I was different from and more special than "those of the Deaf world," but not without experiencing my hearing peers' unwillingness to allow me to enjoy camaraderie even with some of them who had adequate signing skills. For example, one time during my early adulthood I returned for a visit to my alma mater, looking forward to meet and have a brief chat with my favourite hearing teacher whom I had not seen after my graduation. When she saw me approaching her with anticipation and excitement, she quickly gave me the disdainful look only "those Deaf adults" could possibly relate to, turned around and walked away. That experience made me wonder if it had been just part of her institutional obligation to encourage her Deaf students to reject the Deaf world's socio-cultural values as inferior to those of the hearing world and to identify with the latter. Her actions made me aware that hearing people do perceive Deaf people as being different from them, and that Deaf community is a minority group within the hearing-dominated community. That experience also made it not difficult to infer that the tendency of people to identify with others with common experiences and values is an intrinsic force that conflicts with external forces that act against the tendency. As a Deaf member of the hearing-dominated educational profession, I have met many young Deaf and hard-of-hearing persons who struggle with these conflicting forces.

One way or another, much of my adulthood has been spent in academia, first as a teacher in junior and senior high school programs, and now as a university professor. I feel that I have considerable insight into what being different means from both Deaf and hearing perspectives. Certain things have become crystal clear to me. I am about as familiar with the objectives (mainly hearing) educators have for young Deaf children and youths as I am with the outcomes of such objectives among Deaf adults, who have shared many of their stories about the positive and negative aspects of past schooling experience. The inconsistencies between professional objectives and real-life outcomes cannot be overlooked. For example, many Deaf persons acquire ASL and value being part of the Deaf community years after being trained to identify with the spoken language and socio-cultural values of the hearing world. They have told stories about their sincere efforts to reach the objectives set for them and to be as much as possible like hearing people. They have told stories about their struggle to speak clearly and be understood and their eventual realization that their speech was not as good as their teachers or therapists had encouraged them to think it would be. Mather and Mitchell (1994) suggest that this would be an example of a Deaf child being a victim of "communication abuse."

In the final analysis, many Deaf people find that they will never become full members of the hearing world. Many eventually acquire sign language and come to appreciate being part of the Deaf community.

Long having been a member of both worlds, I have acquired a knowledge of what being different means and a firm belief that most hearing people are not prepared to accept that the Deaf community is unique in a way similar to an ethnic or orientation-linked community. I feel compelled to add my belief that the Deaf community needs to be and *is* more creative, productive and active at the local, regional, national and international levels than almost all other minority communities. This is because Deaf people work to compensate for their limited or loss of access to many privileges hearing people have. By organizing Deaf community activities, for example, Deaf people shoulder responsibility for things they would otherwise miss out on. The Canadian Deaf Sports Association connects local associations with the International Committee on Sports for the Deaf (CISS) to give Deaf athletes an opportunity to compete with their peers from other countries in the World Games for the Deaf. These associations also give them many opportunities to develop leadership skills and fellowship. Deaf leaders interested in the socio-political issues faced by Deaf people can become involved in local or provincial associations affiliated with the Canadian Association of the Deaf, which is in turn affiliated with the World Federation of the Deaf. Local cultural associations have a connection with the Canadian Cultural Society of the Deaf, which gives Deaf people with exceptional talents an opportunity to show what they can do. Unfortunately, most hearing people are unaware that the Deaf community is alive and vibrant at all levels. I feel that audists with the missionary mentality would rather trivialize Deaf community accomplishments that might stand in the way of their patronizing agenda for Deaf children and youths.

No doubt, some hearing people have thrived on speaking and acting on behalf of Deaf persons since the beginning of time. But their poor track record in trying to make Deaf children over in the "hearing image" should concern them. Carver (1989) and Johnson, Liddell and Erting (1989) point out that Deaf people who attempt to follow the audists' agenda lag behind their hearing counterparts in literacy and educational accomplishments. Where is the justice for the Deaf children of this world who find it necessary to undo all that indignity?

17

The "Situated Knowledge" of Helpers

ELIZABETH MCGIBBON

Incorporating awareness of issues of oppression into the practice of health professionals appears to be a slow and painful process, and this difficulty seems to be reflected in other professions as well. My paid work experience has been entirely in the health field, and in recent years I have begun to lift myself out of the fog of attempting to "treat everyone equally," as if society really treats everyone equally, and notice that most health professionals carefully avoid explicit discussion of issues related to race and social class. Discussions of different identities and experiences are usually placed under headings such as "client/patient environment," "client/patient culture," "client socio-economic status," "culturally sensitive care" or "cross-cultural practice." The notion that helpers and clients may have different experiences of social class, gender and racial dominance has scarcely been addressed by helpers in the health field, and the implications of the social class, gender and race of *the helper* have barely been mentioned. Unlike in the human service fields of education and social work, the dynamics of unequal power distribution have yet to enter the discourse of many health professionals, and we have not yet begun to "situate" ourselves and dominant societal structures in our everyday work.

This chapter is a discussion of the "situated knowledge" of helpers, and corresponding ideas about "situated practice." I focus on mainstream health care in Canada, my experience as a nurse, and how my identity as a White woman of working-class heritage has come to situate me in my work. How are my knowledge and experiences intimately situated in my practice? How do the dynamics of dominant ideologies and the dominant culture shape the practice of workers in the health field? What might "situated practice" look like? I will share my experiences of how gender and class are a part of me and my practice; my reflections on race concern White privilege and my own stance as a White person. Although many forms of oppression are central in the work of persons who define themselves as helpers, I focus on those oppressions that have touched me the most. Through my stories and reflections, I hope to give voice to a much neglected area of investigation in the practice of health professionals. What might be the relationships between the social class, gender and racial identities of helpers and those of the people they presume to help? How do these identities take shape in practice?

Situated Knowledge, Situated Practice

The concept of "situated knowledge" has been discussed in many fields, including sociology, anthropology, geography and education. Qualitative research in these fields and others, including nursing, has begun to make the self-positioning of the researcher, educator and practitioner more explicit. Proponents of situated knowledge claim that the construction and dissemination of knowledge occurs within many different contexts, including personal and individual, institutional, societal and historical contexts. This view contrasts with traditional scientific thinking that generally views knowledge as objective truth, regardless of the origin of the knowledge or how it was produced. If we think of knowledge as "situated" we are free to examine an entirely new layer of meaning in research, education and practice.

In the personal and individual context, when I have the intention of situating myself in my nursing practice, a different kind of knowledge results. I may ask myself questions such as: How does the fact that I am a White woman position me when I am working with a Black woman? How does being a woman and a nurse situate me in the hospital hierarchy? How does my particular situatedness affect my ability to advocate for myself and for patients? If being a nurse and a woman has placed me in a unique position of oppression, how does this experience help me to understand the plight of women who have been oppressed in their lives? How is my experience of sexism, as a White woman with a steady job, different from the sexism experienced by young women who have lived on the street? More importantly, how might my own personal understanding of sexism enrich my work with young women, without trivializing the sexism they have experienced?

These kinds of questions create a conscious practice milieu where situated knowledge is made explicit on a personal and individual level. When I practise within a framework of situated knowledge, I attempt to understand my own identities as a White woman of working-class heritage, and how these identities position me in my practice. Similarly, the identities of the people we presume to help are also situated in our practice. Social class, gender and race are part of all interactions, *especially* when the client's identities do not mirror the identities of a practitioner. An individual's cultural identity includes multiple characteristics such as age, ability, race, gender, spirituality, ethnicity, social class and sexual orientation (James 1996).

If I explicitly situate my identities in my practice, I am working within a conceptual framework of "situated practice." In contrast, for example, I might choose to operate on the premise that "I'm not racist" and enter into work with African Canadian persons with the conviction that skin colour should not matter and that I should strive for objectivity in my work. Similarly, I might talk with a gay young man without concern that my own sexuality and heterosexism will affect my practice. The knowledge and identities that the client and I bring to the encounter, as well as the potential shift in knowledge and identities produced by the encounter, are not then considered to be particularly dependent on their *context*.

It is important to note that an individual's identities are not necessarily consistent with each other. One of the contradictions in my life is that I enjoy the game of hockey. I have exquisitely fond memories of my family, including my uncle, gathered around the television set on Saturday night to watch hockey games together. I know about sexism and racism in sports, including hockey, and I see these played out in each game. Yet I enjoy the playoff games in much the same way as I did when I was a child.

There are many interesting examples from the health field of how knowledge is historically situated. When I first started practising nursing, homosexuality was still defined as a psychiatric disorder that might be ameliorated through treatment. This diagnostic category was presented as *truth,* in the same way that current psychiatric classifications are viewed as objectively true. A more recent example of the historicity of health knowledge is the realization that in order to understand women's health, we need to do research *on women*. For example, not so long ago, cardiac research conducted exclusively on men was considered to be a valid clinical guide when working with women. Now we recognize that what was once considered objective truth about women's cardiac care is open to critical analysis and modification.

The societal context within which knowledge is constructed is similarly fluid. The dominant culture influences and shapes the work, lives and identities of all members of society on a daily basis. It is this larger context that warrants further discussion.

The Societal Context

In the helping fields, many of us tend to focus on the situation at hand: working with a family in crisis, supporting a woman through her childbirth experience, being consciously present and supportive during the last hours of a child's life, advocating for a young homeless man to help him find shelter late at night, and countless other circumstances that mark the powerful immediacy of human experience. The ability to be fully present and effective is the helper's optimal goal. These qualities are essential if we are to assume the capacity of helper.

However, we often have difficulty placing these situations in a larger, societal context. This larger context, including the socio-political, economic and ecological realms is not yet a substantive or even explicit part of the theory and practice of many helpers. For example, we may determine a family's income and how it may influence health, but we do not generally make ourselves aware of how shifts in political ideology are often *the* key element to understanding the economic hardship experienced by a growing number of Canadian families. Consequently, helpers generally do not practise in a proactive way that challenges the political ideology of the dominant culture.

Yet, every individual struggle is inherently situated in the larger, societal context. The socio-political circumstance of a country is reflected in all levels of society: the individual, the institutional and the systemic. In countries around the world where women have increased access to formal education, the pregnancy rate is correspondingly lower; there is clearly more at stake than the individual woman's desire to have or not have children. Larger societal forces influence each individual experience and each individual life; these forces include the state of the country's economy and the country's political will to advance the human rights of women. This view starkly contrasts with much of the current thinking and practice in the health fields.

Nursing and other health fields have begun to recognize that some socio-political forces are as important, if not more important, than biophysical factors in determining health. However, I think this recognition has not yet influenced theory and practice in any substantial way; for the most part we are still practising within an apolitical conceptual framework that emphasizes the problems of individuals, families or communities and corresponding solutions that fail to go beyond this level. Why are we health professionals having difficulty broadening our analysis? The answer lies partially in the fact that our identities and practices are shaped by the same forces that shape the society in which we practise; dominant ideologies and the dominant culture are an integral part of what positions us in our practice.

Shaping Situated Practice: Examining Dominant Ideologies and the Dominant Culture

In order to understand our everchanging identities in the larger, societal context, it is helpful to examine some of the dominant ideologies that affect the health field, and the dominant culture within which ideology is translated into action. Although there are many dominant ideologies in Canada, such as capitalism and Judeo-Christianity, for the purposes of this discussion I have chosen to examine the dominance of medical ideology. I believe that medical ideology is a powerful deterrent to creating a framework that encourages helpers to situate themselves and clients within their unique identities and life experiences and the larger societal context.

Medical Ideology

I have often been perplexed by the ideology that currently guides most of the "helping" health fields. We spend countless hours in the pursuit of understanding the dilemmas of "others" whom we most often refer to as "clients" or "patients." Our analysis is most often based on some sort of "wrongness" that needs to be fixed. For the most part, we function within this dominant medical ideology, in the mental health field, as well as in the physical health realm for which the medical model was originally devised. Although many practitioners strive to shift their views from a mechanistic model to a holistic or "whole person" model, the fact remains that mainstream health delivery is still heavily steeped in medical ideology. As a society we have become accustomed to accepting that this is the way things should be, as if the current medical ideology existed *a priori*, and it is very difficult to remove ourselves far enough from this way of thinking to sufficiently question its validity.

Historically, medical ideology has been based on two assumptions that continue to have a profound effect on practice in the helping fields: (1) the belief that the totality of human beings may be expressed in terms of the sum of their individual parts, and (2) the belief that practitioner objectivity is both desirable and possible. The conceptual framework of medical ideology began to dominate health service delivery in the mid-nineteenth century, as physicians lobbied politically to have themselves declared the dominant arbiters of health knowledge. Midwives, native healers, herbalists and communities' natural helpers were gradually removed from their centuries-old helping roles. Following the medical model, human beings were then viewed as the sum of various separate body parts, with each part having a particular set of potential maladies and corresponding treatments. To this day, acute care health service delivery is organized according to body parts: the heart, lungs, uterus, brain and so on. This is not to say that if grandmama has a heart attack, we do not want a skilled cardiologist to be one of the people who guide her to wellness. The point is that this "body part model" tends to be used to address every alteration in the human condition. Only in the past few decades have consumers, especially mental health consumers, and practitioners begun to challenge the use of the medical model as the officially sanctioned mode of conceptualizing human health and experience.

My experiences as a hospital-based psychiatric nurse are permeated with examples of the potential inadequacy and destructiveness of psychiatric medical ideology when it is used to assist persons who are experiencing mental health difficulties. I recall the hospital admission of a thirty-four-year-old woman whom I received from the intensive-care unit. She was transferred to the psychiatric service and diagnosed with "Brief Psychotic Episode." "Anna," as I shall call her, was described as having persistent delusions that someone was trying to kill her; she was afraid to go outside and frequently examined her hospital room for signs of tampering. The psychiatric staff were unable to connect her mental state with her recent experience of having been stabbed in the chest with a lead pipe. The perpetrator was Anna's boyfriend, who was known to be an influential member of a national motorcycle gang, and it was known on the street that he was actively looking for her. This woman left the hospital with a psychiatric diagnosis instead of with help to leave her abusive relationship if she chose to, or help to exercise her right to legal counsel. My inability to successfully leverage my relatively low status as a nurse, along with the staff's difficulty with seeing beyond diagnostic categories, meant that I was ineffective in my attempts to advocate for Anna. A framework of situated practice would help me to acknowledge the violence and misogyny in Anna's life; *engaging* in situated practice would help me to relate the misogyny I have experienced in my own life to my own cognitive and emotional reactions while working with Anna; I would also be able to identify the power dynamics when Anna struggled so persistently to tell us that she had a *real* reason to be paranoid, while staff gave her knowing looks that said "Yes, dear."

The second tenet of medical ideology is that the practitioner must strive to be objective at all times. Objectivity, or refraining from allowing such things as one's own opinions and biases to affect practice, is believed to be not only desirable but actually possible. Practitioner responses to patients, however powerful, pleasurable or disagreeable, are to be "put aside" so the practitioner may deliver the best possible care based on scientific objectivity. Helpers tend to operate within a conceptual framework that values objectivity and detachment; we are the observers and the patients/clients are the observed. The patient is consciously maintained in their status as "other." This applies to all the various definitions of patient or client: the individual, the family, the community, the ecosystem and so on. The "otherness" of patients/clients serves to reinforce service providers' view of themselves as somehow not part of the encounter. We are not actually situated in the encounter; we are beside it or above it, functioning as objective experts. Yet many practical experiences make helpers acutely aware of the impossibility of objectivity.

Several years ago I worked with "Maria," who was in the last stages of having her gender changed from a man to a woman. Maria entered the mental health system in search of support during this profound transition in her life. Her file was a rather confused mixture of snippets from her "old" life as "Greg" and her current life as Maria. Staff, including myself, were completely perplexed about how we should talk to Maria, or how we should address questions from other clients about everyday things such as the use of washrooms. Although we had the intention to work with Maria in a compassionate and caring way, our education and socialization as health professionals made it difficult for us to let go of our attempts at objectivity. Imagine how different Maria's care would have been if we had been able to *start* our work with her in a context of subjectivity and acknowledgement of some of the complex identities, ours and hers, that formed the basis of our relationship.

Fortunately, Maria was often able to see the humour in our clumsiness. She was amazed by our relentless attempts to pretend that we were somehow removed from the situation, and that we could "carry on as usual" when working with her. Maria was also on social assistance and had been for most of her life. Staff were angered that she had "wasted good money" on changing her sex when there were so many other people truly deserving of society's help. Gender and social class were inseparably situated in all of the work that we did with Maria; the two identities were interlocked to produce a myriad of reactions in helpers, most of them unkind. Maria's story also illustrates that gender discrimination is not necessarily only towards women. In a similar way, racism is not about skin colour alone, as demonstrated by the racism experienced by people with Jewish ancestry.

In the everyday work of nurses and other helpers, the dominant medical ideology exerts and reinforces itself on many levels. On an individual level, countless examples—from where workers are situated on pay scales to who gets the preferred hospital parking spaces—all remind workers, in a very personal way, of the dominance of medicine. On an institutional level, the decision to use disease-based medical diagnostic categories, even in mental health, continues to be a powerful symbol of the dominance of medical ideology. On a societal level, provincial and federal governments reinforce this dominant ideology through their decisions regarding health-care resource allocation. Non-profit community agencies continue to struggle on shoestring budgets to provide community development–based approaches to health as an alternative to traditional and vastly more expensive medical clinics. Although these new approaches are proving to be effective in providing meaningful and equitable front-line services across the country, funding sources consistently choose to support medical clinics as the most common entry point into the health care system in Canada.

Medical ideology creates specific constraints that greatly affect nursing practices. Amid the debate about medical ethics, and its concentration on high-profile issues such as abortion, the right to die and euthanasia, lie the almost invisible ethical dilemmas of nurses. In part, these dilemmas are about not being able to successfully advocate for patients when both patient and nurse disagree with medical opinion; one dilemma occurs because the physician has been mandated with the "final say." Mental health nurses, including myself, often have stories about disagreeing with a physician about "committing" a patient (i.e., taking many of the patient's human rights away and locking them up). Although the physician writes the "order" for committal, it is the nurse who has to enforce the committal in her everyday work, whether or not she agrees with the decision. This places her in an ethical double bind when she tries to work compassionately with committed patients. The nurse's position as a woman and a nurse situates her in a very particular way in her practice; the outcomes of her practice are a reflection of the power imbalance between physicians, whom the dominant medical ideology situates as the ultimate "knowers," and nurses. Patients, in turn, occupy a subordinate position below both nurses and physicians. These unequal power relationships are part of every health-care encounter. It is awareness of this kind of power set-up that helps to create situated practice.

The Dominant Culture

The dominant culture is that which most influences our individual lives, as well as all institutional and systemic structures, including government, educational, judicial and health care systems in Canada and elsewhere. The dominant culture values the "upper" classes above the "lower" classes, maleness above femaleness and lighter coloured skin above darker coloured skin, and dynamic systems actively maintain these preferences. In health care, the social-class, gender and racial preferences of the dominant culture are continually reinforced and recreated. For example, we already have a health care system that requires consumers to have a cash base in order to access health care. Working with homeless persons has taught me that if you have no cash, you remain on the edge of the health care system in Canada. Everyday things such as bus fare to get to appointments, money for prescribed medications or treatments, or money for sunscreen or special baby needs are out of reach to most, if not all, homeless persons and families. Political decisions throughout Canada in the past decade have explicitly created our two-tier health system which separates the quality of health care into two separate categories: one for those who have money and one for those who don't.

Communication across social-class boundaries in the health fields has received little attention in the literature. This lack of analysis affects the therapeutic relationship in several ways. First, it sets up a therapeutic milieu that ignores the fundamental influences of class on helpers and clients. In doing so, it reinforces the position of client or patient as lower on the hierarchical ladder that is so fundamental to traditional therapeutic approaches, thus reproducing the power imbalance of social class in the dominant culture. Second, the lack of class analysis obscures the fact that working-class people have not generally taken part in the framing of the therapeutic discourse of health professionals (McGibbon 1999). According to Baker (1996), when we therapists and health professionals address the experiences of the working class, we are using *our* words to describe *their* experiences.

I often feel like a cultural insider when I work as a nurse with working-class clients. I have come to notice that class is a powerful part of communication in the health professions. I have seen and have myself treated patients differently when they had the markers of being in the middle or upper social classes. I notice that health professionals tend to take the concerns of working-class clients less seriously and are more likely to attribute problems to lack of intelligence or credibility. I have no research evidence to substantiate this statement; what I know about class and health care is based on my own experiences of growing up in a working-class family. I have often wondered why health professionals do not view class as an important part of the experiences of clients.

Although I am now middle-class, my own working-class background largely affects how I view the world. I have always considered class as a major factor in the shaping of life experiences, probably because I see class in a way that people of middle- or upper-class heritages do not. I have learned as an adult about the niceties of social class: where all those extra spoons and knives go at the dinner table, how to select pastries from the little cart when it is wheeled up to my table in a fancy restaurant, how to unlearn my working-class propensity to end words in "in" instead of "ing," how to socially navigate a room where everyone is dressed to the nines and, of course, how to nurture the ability to learn about markers of class so I won't feel like a cultural outsider.

My practice is full of markers of social class and the difficulties of communicating across boundaries of class. Some young people who have lived on the streets have been quick to stop me when I express empathy about their situation. "How would *you* ever know about what it's like? *You* have a steady job and *you* have an education." These young people have taught me how to express compassion without being patronizing. I have found my nursing practice especially complex when one of these young people has been of Native Canadian or African Canadian heritage. Then I have to think about how to acknowledge the oppressions of class *and* race without being patronizing. Regarding class, I can relate beautifully to some of what the young people have said about their teenage years, but I can never really *know* about experiences related to race. In this way, I have learned that communicating across boundaries of difference does not happen in a linear way. The oppressions experienced by clients are interlocking, as are the oppressions experienced by helpers. When client and helper communicate, they may or may not have portions of their identities in common. In my case, I have a class heritage in common with many clients; however, my current middle-class status changes the dynamic of this identity in our communication. In both situations, the dominance of the middle and upper social classes, and of Whiteness, are central in the therapeutic encounter.

Nursing, performed by a predominately female workforce, is powerfully influenced by the gender bias of the dominant culture. Nurses, although by far the most numerous of health care workers, and those who spend the most time with patients, have been devalued to the point where in several Canadian provinces, including Nova Scotia, casual nurses make up over 50 percent of the nursing workforce and have no benefits and no job security. Governments and institutions have mandated this situation through legislation, layoffs and a profound restructuring of how bedside nursing is delivered across the country. Nursing is still viewed as women's work, and as such is undervalued and underpaid. The societal view of nurses' work parallels the societal view of women's work, much of which is invisible and not considered worthy of entering into the country's economic analysis of what counts as real work. Several authors, most notably Rachlis and Kuschner (1994), have expressed sheer amazement at how the country has stood by and watched the deterioration of the working conditions for nurses. The literature increasingly identifies the individual and systemic treatment of nurses as a gender issue, both historically and currently (Campbell 1992; Carter 1994).

As I wrote in a local newspaper, *Street Feat: The Voice of the Poor* (McGibbon 1998), discussion of where race and racism are situated in health and health care has received relatively little attention among health care administrators and providers. The dominant culture generally supports the maintenance of race as a rather invisible or insubstantial issue. Since the health care system is shaped by the dominant culture, race is most often discussed in terms of "celebrating diversity" or "honouring the multicultural nature of the Canadian people." A few years ago, I presented at a large three-day workshop for students of the health professions. The topics were pretty standard fare, with various invited speakers from the community. One of the presenters was a man who described his experiences of growing up as a Black Nova Scotian, including his experiences with the health system. I was struck that this was the first time I had heard anyone speak about racism in health care from their own experience, for more than a few minutes.

After the presentation, the entire group of four hundred students and facilitators met in smaller groups, one of which I facilitated. The students soon began to discuss "John's" presentation and one said, "What the heck did that have to do with anything?" I found myself trying to legitimate John's stories, as if he somehow needed my help, instead of helping the students to confront their difficulties in understanding him. I now understand that some of my unease came from how I was positioned as a nurse attempting to "teach" medical students. At that time, the emotional and intellectual baggage of years of being required to legitimate my mental health knowledge to primarily male physicians was still very close to my heart.

I later learned from the other facilitators that many of the students had not liked John's presentation and said they preferred "more relevant" speakers. There are many possible reasons for why this happened. It is unlikely that there was any anti-racism content in the course work of any of these students; they were hearing about racism for the first time from John. It is likely that health issues related to racism, if discussed at all, were placed under the heading of "multiculturalism and health." Notions of privilege and power were probably never addressed. It has been my experience as a White person that, because we live in a profoundly racist society, I could not begin to address racism or even accept that racism exists until people began to help me *see* it. This continues to be a challenge for me, because my Whiteness allows me to look the other way. I can choose not to notice that the faces in the hospital's patient information booklet are almost all White, or that the "skin tape" used all over the hospital is my skin colour or that the materials used in occupational therapy for making arm and leg splints would go relatively unnoticed if I had to wear them against *my* skin.

Outside the hospital, when I buy pantyhose with "skin color" written on the label, it is my skin colour; when I buy shampoo, it is specially formulated for my hair. When I buy these items at the drugstore, I can be pretty sure that the faces of the pharmacists and the faces looking up at me from the packaging of almost all of the products will have my skin colour. I have the privilege of not having to think about these things. This is unlike my friend Althea, who has very dark brown skin and was recently told at a local drugstore that the hair-care products for "her type of hair" were locked up and that they would have to get the key from the manager if she wished to buy these products. These examples illustrate how racism in the health care system is a reflection of racism in the dominant culture. The education system that trains helpers is similarly influenced. For example, the books used to educate health professionals depict mostly White bodies. Health professionals themselves are mostly White; even Nova Scotia, with one of the largest indigenous Black populations in Canada, has disturbingly few Black practitioners. All of these influences have shaped my socialization as a health professional. Unless I work in a "situated practice," it will be difficult for me to locate my Whiteness as an identity that confers unearned power.

Thus, situated practice operates on many levels:

- the *individual* level, where my Whiteness, femaleness and working-class background form who I am;
- the *relationship* level, where my identities and the identities of clients are inextricably linked in any given encounter; my White privilege and my current middle-class status often differentially situate me when I am working with clients because I have these societally preferred identities;
- the *institutional and systemic* level, where such things as philosophical underpinnings and political affiliations shape the structures we practise within; for example, some institutions are committed to affirmative action according to Canadian Human Rights Commission guidelines and some are not; and
- the *societal* level, where the powers for dominance and the desirability of the subordination of certain groups are maintained according to preferred identities.

It is essential to recognize that these various levels of situated practice are not discrete entities which merely add to each other in layers. Rather, each level helps to shape all other levels in a dynamic way.

Moving toward Situated Practice: Implications for Practice, Research and Education

The concept of "situated knowledge" has profound implications for research, education and practice. Situated knowledge has been examined extensively in the field of qualitative research, as has situated learning in the field of education. This chapter has focused on how situated knowledge relates to situated practice, a concept that is relatively new to the health field. I believe that nurses and other helpers in the health field are uniquely constrained in their ability to situate themselves, their clients and the larger societal context in their practice. This constraint is, in part, based on the interwoven nature of medical ideology and the dominant culture.

In broadening this analysis, we have begun to examine other possible worlds. For example, many of us have come to know the power of gender as a force that intimately shapes all of our therapeutic work. Conversely, the influence of racism in the lives of clients has barely begun to surface in the discourse of helpers. Similarly, we do not yet seem inclined to address social class, except for the endless studies since the 1970s that have determined that economic status, one of the clearest markers of social class, is by far the best predictor of health. Racism and social class as issues in the experiences of clients are not usually viewed as part of the fabric of helping, no matter how much we say they are in our mission statements and professional codes of ethics.

If we have difficulty thinking about the social-class, gender and racial identities of clients, how can we even begin to situate *ourselves* in terms of these oppressions? However, this task is a necessary one. We will be better positioned to understand the interlocking oppressions experienced by clients if we first examine where *we* are situated in relationship to these oppressions. How effectively can I address racism as it applies to my practice if I have not begun to address the power of White privilege in my own life? If I have not begun to address how misogyny has shaped my own life, how can I understand how my background might affect my work with women who have experienced sexual violence? These kinds of questions help us enter into a dynamic inquiry that can lead to a "situated practice."

Reflections on Moving toward Situated Practice

These reflections represent a work in progress. If I am working toward engaging in situated practice, I may:

- Continually seek to discover and clarify my own identities;
- Attempt to be aware of how my identities enter into every encounter in my practice;
- Recognize that my ability to understand and respect the identities of clients in my practice is enhanced, or limited, by my ability to discover and acknowledge my own identities;
- Try to see the identities of clients from *their* perspective;
- Recognize and address societal forces that influence me, my practice and the people seeking my help. I do this by situating these forces in the everyday happenings of the lives of clients and of my own life. For example, if a Black woman expresses difficulty with not being able to find adequate skin care products for her children, I can question whether this relates to systemic racism, as opposed to a supply problem at the local cosmetics counter;
- Be conscious of the possibility that if I do not engage in a situated practice that recognizes oppression, I may be reinforcing these oppressions on an individual and societal level. Conversely, engaging in situated practice can help to undermine these oppressions;
- Engage in a critical examination of how being a helper positions me in my practice. I am in a "power over" situation in my practice, where the patient/client occupies a position of less power than me. Even the word "patient" connotes a power imbalance, which includes who has the preferred health knowledge and under what conditions they are willing to share this knowledge.

These reflections bring discussion of the helping practices to a different place, compared to current theories of helping in the health field. Health practitioners are still held firmly by the dominant ideologies and dominant culture, which makes it difficult to move from a stance as objective observer to a stance that challenges oppression in everyday practice. Situated practice goes beyond *learning about* social class, gender and race, or about *other* cultures and cultural sensitivity. As Sherene Razack points out:

> pluralistic models of inclusion assume that we have long ago banished the stereotypes from our heads. These models suggest that with a little practice and the right information, we can all be innocent subjects, standing outside hierarchical social relations,

> who are not accountable for the past or implicated in the present. It is not our ableism, racism, sexism, or heterosexism that gets in the way of communicating across differences, but *their* disability, *their* culture, *their* biology or *their* lifestyle (1998: 10).

Translating situated knowledge into situated practice means that helpers explicitly critique how oppression is situated in practice.

The concept of situated practice has far-reaching implications for research and education. Research with practitioners who form alliances in situated practice will be essential in addressing therapeutic boundary issues; if I am to situate myself in my practice, what implications does this have for therapeutic disclosure? The notion of therapy as a political act is also relevant to situated practice. What are the links among identities of difference and working for social change to undermine oppressions related to these differences?

The education and professional socialization of workers in the health fields is perhaps the most crucial area for further examination. It is here that the power dynamics of the dominant culture are often translated into clinical practices that reinforce existing oppressions. Fields such as social work have already engaged in teaching anti-oppressive practice; health professionals may also draw upon additional rich bodies of experiential and academic knowledge in their move toward situated practice. Most importantly, situated practice can help us to provide equitable and ethical care that undermines oppression in the health fields and in the dominant culture.

Moving into and through Difference

18

Moving into Difference (with Echo)

CELIA HAIG-BROWN

This story—two stories really—is about moving into difference: moves made by choice, out of privilege and curiosity, and for love. It is a somewhat untidy, occasionally excessive story of how such moves disrupt, challenge and force a person to arrive at new beginnings, a place where history starts over again. It is a story of how ideas and bodies travel through time and space, and how complex those journeys can be. In their new contexts, ideas and bodies invent and are reinvented through interactions, magic, energy and desire. This is work done alone, and with others, work bringing despair one minute, a sense of coming home for the first time in another, with hints of promise scattered throughout—history in the making.

Thinking of Moving

When I was thinking of moving to Toronto, to so-called Central Canada, from my home in what they call the West and I call B.C., I had the privilege of having dinner with Dorothy Smith, an internationally known sociologist, who had in the course of her academic career also made that move. While acknowledging that it was something she has never regretted, she looked at me across the table and said in her grey-haired wisdom, "The hardest part is that you lose your history." Those words have echoed in my head on many occasions since then as I try to find my way in this new world, creating history as I go, often feeling flung back to a form of infancy, a time of constantly needing to prove that I am trustworthy, useful, thoughtful, more than the "one issue person" a colleague accused me of being during my first year.

This is a story about another kind of shift: about ignoring boundaries, refusing categories and imagining new spaces—a move that can occur without even leaving home although once you make the move, home is never the same place again. Perhaps it is not really a story at all: instead it is all transition, all movement, a gradual scene change: fade out and then in, be with that moving vibrancy. Perhaps it is a story after all—of adventure, with tragedy, comedy, love and a moment of resolution still unfolding—with a beginning, a middle and no end in sight.

An irony lies within the idea of losing history, an irony based in one of the ideas that is central to my scholarship and the way I make sense of the world. The history I claim in this country is brief and has always felt tenuous. Through my work with Aboriginal peoples, I have posited—partly for the sake of argument, but more fundamentally because it embraces geographical and historical truth—that there are two kinds of people in Canada: those of Aboriginal ancestry, and immigrants and their offspring. While those of immigrant ancestry have vastly differing histories in Canada, having come over time from across the earth, none can claim much beyond five centuries of living on the land and, most, far less time than that. This recognition is the place to begin to construct a personal history and geography in this colonized country—always in relation to the land and the Aboriginal people. Whatever circumstances brought us foreigners here, this land is the space we came to, and Aboriginal people are the original people who have lived continuously with the land on which we all now dwell.

"Land" is more than a word. People walk on it, they literally put their feet on it, sometimes insulated by layers of concrete, pavement, flooring and shoes, sometimes barefoot on bare ground. Everyday we walk on the land. How our feet come to be here and who walked here before us connect us to who we are, have been and can be. These are the varied histories fundamental to the nation and the people in it, inescapable histories for anyone who takes the need for common recognition of national history seriously. Some came as slaves, some came as refugees from slavery, some as workers with hope for prosperity in what they were told was a new and "empty" land, some with desires to rule and exploit (Warren Crichlow, personal conversation). As Canadians, many of us are only now coming to admit that, unlike the world portrayed in the lies which lured so many people to move here, this never was an empty land. Aboriginal peoples have named, lived in and travelled through this space for at least thousands of years—since time immemorial, some say.

In an urban context such as Toronto, where a claim to sophistication apparently desires and demands new myths, our memories may be disrupted by changing landscapes and a feeling of distance from the land. Yet one need only observe the changes in wardrobe that accompany the seasons, breathe deeply on a downtown sidewalk, walk beside the decaying Humber River or hear of one more friend with asthma or cancer to know that we all remain deeply related to the land, air and water around us—the environment—and the treatment we give it. We cannot escape it, no matter how hard we city dwellers pretend that we are disembodied cyberbeings who rarely touch the earth.

Touch the earth: touch is part of moving. As you are beginning to see, this "other" story is messy; it leaks untidily into the surface story. It slithers along just below the surface and then insinuates itself onto the page. Good stories are tidy. They make a point, evoke a moment, pin history down. This story refuses to be good: it is about losing history and gaining history, about losing even the words and returning to them.

As a rural child of English and American immigrants, I was taught by my family and have continued to see a responsibility to know a land-based Canadian history that begins first with the original peoples and includes the racism which has been integral to this nation's establishment. It has been a long and disturbing process; some see it as perverse. As a child, I was conscious that the riverbank where we played had a canoe landing which the Kwaguelth people had used long before us. I knew something of Japanese internment. I was taught to see inequity and injustice around me and to want to use privilege against them. In 1950, when I was three years old, my father, Roderick Haig-Brown, wrote in his book, *Measure of the Year*:

> Yet Canadians are the most intolerant people I know. Almost any Canadian has a pet intolerance, probably several, that he [*sic*] will expound upon at a moment's notice. I have heard Canadians hating Catholics, Jews, Americans, Irish, English, Scottish, Ukrainians, Poles, Japanese, Chinese, French-Canadians, English-Canadians, Germans, Mennonites, Doukhobors—the list, for all I know, may cover every nation, race, religion, and activity on the face of the earth.... Vicious exchanges between Ontario's Protestants and Quebec's Catholics lessen the nation. Prairie hatred of Ukrainians is often vicious and dangerous. Pacific coast hatred of the Japanese, founded on economic jealousy, used the war to strip them of their homes and property and liberty.... I am not happy about Canada's treatment of Canadian Indians. It was benevolently conceived, paternalistic, in some degree protective; but it is hopelessly outdated, it is narrow, based on ignorance and misconception, and at this stage of the twentieth century it is oppressive.

Years later, as an academic, I pursued research on the paternalistic—I prefer the word "genocidal"—residential schools created for children the federal government calls "Indian." As I read more widely in anti-racist scholarship, I learned of incidents that were never part of history classes: the *Komagatsu Maru* incident, efforts to segregate children of Chinese ancestry in Victoria in the 1920s, the Chinese Exclusion League, the Ukrainian persecution on the prairies—the list was endless. (I hadn't read my father's book, and when the essay called "Canada" was used in my grade twelve English class, ministry officials edited out the passage quoted above). These disturbing incidents and situations are B.C. stories: they happened in the Aboriginal lands I lived in and came to know and love. As problematic as they seem, these are the understandings on which I base my work and my sense of self. How and where does one begin to develop such understandings in a new context?

I am grasping for the words with which to tell you a story in motion. I want words that refuse specificity and location, words that don't name—because too often to name is to fix, and this story is about refusing to be pinned down. I want to keep the tension of not knowing exactly alive in the reader as long as possible. Here's a flat fact or two to keep you going. I moved from the lush B.C. coast to the arid interior to teach high school Biology and English in 1970. I married the next year and stayed that way for fifteen years, giving birth and life to three children along the way. In 1986, I went back to the Pacific coast, taking three children, leaving one husband in a log house in the rolling hills of Shuswap territory. I began doctoral work as a single (swinger) mother (pariah).

In his examination of the works of Nikolai Leskov, Walter Benjamin wrote of two kinds of storytellers:

> "When someone goes on a trip, he has something to tell about," goes the German saying, and people imagine the storyteller as someone who has come from afar. But they enjoy no less listening to the man [*sic*] who has stayed at home, making an honest living, and who knows the local tales and traditions. If one wants to picture these two groups though their archaic representatives, one is embodied in the resident tiller of the soil, and the other in the trading seaman. Indeed, each sphere of life has, as it were, produced its own tribe of storytellers (1969: 84–85).

Never mind that there is nary a woman in sight in this excerpt. I aspired to be the resident tiller of the soil: the one who stays home and delves deeply into that place in ways that, when articulated, allow the people who live there to see what has slipped by unmarked because their familiarity, discourse and limits of imagination have kept from them the wonders of the everyday world. The language of the storyteller, with its precision based in patient observation, opens eyes to what has been taken for granted. I prided myself on being a provincial person. I grew up in B.C., went to school in B.C., and found a job at the other university when I completed my work at the one I had always attended. I did move around the province, but that just gave me more familiarity, a chance to know relationships more deeply, and, anyway, the rivers, the sea and the salmon connect all the people, Aboriginal and immigrant, and places there. To be provincial was to be focused, to be building a connection with and a history on a land, seeking a depth of experience that no world traveller could ever achieve.

How paradoxical that somewhere in the fragility of these roots developing, there was also a desire to be the travelling storyteller—a restlessness, a curiosity, an ache to know and live differently.

A yearning to be something different, a creeping sense that the dream dying hard was impossible and that only new dreams could allow the intensity to continue. As soon as it began, this story about moving has refused to be confined to any singular identity or issue. It appears on the page pointing to something beyond itself, insisting on excess, insisting on a truth that can never be the whole truth. It directs the reader to the silences, the gaps, the absences—seeking to fill the spaces by evoking moments of similar sensations in their own stories. It calls the listener to a new place in another old history: "Let's just touch fingers and faces."

A desire to be in Ontario at the beginning of Mike Harris's term hardly seemed politically different than the tumultuous years of Social Credit control with which I had grown up. But there were more fundamental differences. While still Canada, Ontario is a different land: the Niagara escarpment, the ancient mountains of the Canadian Shield, the lakes, the factories, the acid rain. It has a vastly different history as a colony. The Aboriginal people in the south experienced the encroachment on their land much earlier than those in B.C. What was the deeper significance of the treaties and real estate deals (of questionable nature) of which I knew little or nothing? What would it mean to start again to build a history with this land and the Aboriginal people of what is now called Ontario?

About this time, I had another conversation with Becki Ross, who had just made the opposite shift from Ontario to British Columbia. When I asked her why she had done so, she responded that she wanted to see if ideas travel. Shifting theory—what happens when we take ideas from one context and consider them in another? Would my sense of the importance of starting all my work in Canadian educational research from a focus on land and Aboriginal people transfer to a new context and make any sense to people with histories different from my own?

I should acknowledge that much of the research for this chapter qualifies as "research as chat"(see Haig-Brown 1995: 31; Bishop 1996).

During my doctoral research, I was taken with the notion of research as conversation as part of my love affair with ethnography. Ethnography is probably what lured me back to academe, which I had left in a fit of resistance to reductionist statistics which had so little to do with making sense of life. It had been a course in biometrics which had finally done it for me. I enjoyed math but had left the discipline in order to get closer to life in biology. When, not only in my biometrics course but also in my ecology course, I found that I was to divide the world into measured squares, count and then crunch through statistical tests all that I found exciting, I knew this was not for me. Research as ethnography spoke openly of being in the place with the people, learning the language of the people and coming to understand with them the meanings they made there. My tendency to flee research and seek life soon led me away from the structured interview to free-flowing conversation and from there to recognizing that some of the most intense moments of research came within these casual everyday conversations as I moved through the worlds of the people with whom I was working. In this chapter, there is a continuation of this love of research as chat. Many of the references are to everyday conversations with colleagues, friends and families. It appeals to the way that we make sense of our lives and the various shifts we make.

If one were to identify the moment when the shifting began, it could be said to start with Adrienne Rich's article "Compulsory Heterosexuality." The continuum: at least that's what brought first focus and then flashbacks to allow a revisionist personal and social history. Lesbian, Lesbos the island, women loving women so much that they touch each other.

Moving

Learning Differences

I am learning to say subway instead of sky train
board walk instead of sea wall
(although I see some of the "boards" are made of concrete not wood).

I am learning to say lake instead of ocean.

but on the last day of November walking on the boardwalk
this could be either beach:
the greyness is the same and the solitude.

How soon these Eastern people confine themselves to
buildings, houses and apartments
perhaps sitting near a propane fire place
on a peacefilled Sunday afternoon
or in front of a television set
or hanging out at the mall
where late twentieth century North America has brought us
a home away from home,
familiar repetition from town to town to city,
the only form of community we know for sure
(and that "we" is all of us—across classes and races and all those other things):
bright colours, endless consumption, a world of artificial needs.

but back to the beach which is a lakeside one, not an ocean beach
the inevitable discolouration of late fall:
leafless darkened trees, only a trace of red in their bark,
grey-brown sand,
grey-blue water lapping at the somber shore,
and endless grey sky seemingly displaced
from the Pacific Coast.

Why were we taught such subtlety is not beauty:

a dark duck farther out in the water
sleek grey gulls overhead on fall search
looking down the lake to all those places—Mississauga, Etobicoke, Toronto
good words, words of the land and the original peoples—
now caught in grey: high rises, boardwalk, sea, land, and sky.

I am learning to say lake instead of ocean.

I arrived in Toronto. I came by choice to the place I had stereotyped as a grey place—Anglo, conservative, with long winters, without ocean, with no mountains to speak of, in other words, drab and boring. (Yes, I have done some work on cultural self-hatred. I recognize the tendencies: an Anglo who finds Anglos as a group bland and embarrassingly staid and reserved. I know I must not generalize, not even about my own people.) Visits to Toronto had already challenged my prejudices and I knew it was no longer the place I had imagined, if it ever had been. I knew that there were people from all over the world: the subways hummed with many languages. I knew also how little I really knew of the people who lived in Toronto, including the Aboriginal people of the area.

I began my life and my work in Toronto with a persistent question: "Whose traditional land are we on?" Not content to be the traveller anymore, this move required serious relocation. I had to begin a long process of locating myself in relation to history, in relation to shifting geography through the simple starting point of connectedness to the land. My colleagues, without exception, could not answer my question. I began my research. Which sources? Where to look? Who to trust? In B.C., where there are twenty-six Aboriginal languages; I usually knew whose land I was on and who had written respectfully of those lands and peoples. Here it was slow slogging. I read, I talked to newfound friends and Aboriginal students. I went to the Lands office of the Department of Indian and Northern Affairs and slowly I constructed my answer: York University is on Mississauga land; at least they are the people who signed the treaty. Other sources (including Mona Jones, personal conversation) told me that the land had earlier been used by many nations as a sort of "harvest bowl." I needed to know more. When colleagues asked me to speak to their classes on my work in Aboriginal education, I continued to talk to students about my B.C. experiences but also told them of the progress of my work in coming to know a history through getting located in my new setting.

Not only do you lose your history, you find yourself displaced in others' history, not common history. "No, I don't remember when...." There are conversations which you can contribute to only by interrupting with weak, unshared connections to a time, place and people thousands of miles away. I look closely at the faces around the dinner table and see incomprehension and occasional resentment at this intrusion into the shared story of camaraderie they have built over years. And neither of the stories I am trying to tell you here fit easily into the established histories.

At some point in my second year in Toronto, perhaps in response to the (dis)located work I had been doing, I had a dream. I was with a large class of teacher candidates in the final year of their program, probably in Foundations of Education, and I had been working with them on the notions of land and Aboriginal people as central to our considerations of Canadian education. On this day in class, we were watching a video that depicted Kwaguelth ceremonial dancing; I imagine it was "Potlatch, A Strict Law Bids Us Dance" produced by the Umista Cultural Society of Alert Bay. I was enthralled thinking of the dances I had seen as a child and the renaissance that was occurring in Kwaguelth territory since the lifting of the potlatch ban in 1951. Lost in thought, I became increasingly aware that the students were chatting to one another, not watching the film and exhibiting total disrespect for the gravity of the cultural moment they were witnessing. At first I didn't know what to do and then I stood up and began talking over the film, angry, wanting them to pay attention and realizing even as I was doing it that my teaching had failed, that it had done the worst, which was to bring into a classroom dimensions of Aboriginal culture and subject them to the disrespect which has greeted them in so many circumstances since explorers, entrepreneurs and settlers arrived in Canada. As I talked, I began to hear a low chant coming from the room but not identifiable as coming from any place, a groundswell of "Sieg Heil, Sieg Heil." Despair and horror overcame me as I awoke, wondering how I could continue to imagine bringing what I had respectfully learned from Aboriginal people in one context into the classrooms in a land I was only beginning to know.

I continue to ponder the dream of the disrespectful students. Do ideas travel? There is always the concern that a little learning is a dangerous thing. So often, well-intentioned teachers have found that their efforts at multicultural education—the field trip to the Sikh Temple, the food and festival days—reinforce negative or romantic stereotypes rather than challenge them. Is it possible for a non-Native person committed to anti-racism to introduce an awareness of the central role of Aboriginal peoples in Canada currently and historically in a way that promotes respectful understandings? African-American singer/songwriter/ theorist Bernice Johnson Reagon, in a landmark article, writes of "coalition work," work which people can do together from very different locations and identities to address injustice, especially the racisms on which the new North American nations have been built. She says of such work, "You don't go into coalition because you just *like* it. The only reason you would consider teaming up with someone who could possibly kill you is because that's the only way you can figure you can stay alive" (1983: 357). She talks of spending a limited time in "a little barred room ... where you sift out what people are saying about you and decide who you really are. And you take the time to construct within yourself who you would be if you were running society" (1983: 358). But when the nationalism that such spaces can nurture becomes reactionary, she says, it's time to open the doors and begin the real coalescing:

> Coalition work is not work done in your home. Coalition work has to be done in the streets. And it is some of the most dangerous work you can do. And you shouldn't look for comfort.... You don't get fed a lot in a coalition. In a coalition, you have to give, and it is different from your home.... If you feel the strain, you are doing some good work (1983: 359, 362).

In Reagon's terms, is "coalition work" for a common goal—in this case, some form of social justice—with people who are "not just like you" really possible? I have no answers to this question except the one I give myself which refuses essential "race-based" separations and insists on the importance of starting somewhere. We White people cannot succumb to the luxury of doing nothing simply because what we do and have done is so fraught with current and historical problems. We need to risk being wrong and standing corrected and to move along on the project together with those who know better about their own experiences.

In my classes I meet gay and lesbian students. One night, standing with my lover in a downtown bar, the pair who had happily sat in my class the week before pass by, totally engrossed with each other, on their way to the dance floor. Is it appropriate to say in the next class, "Saw you at Tango's on Saturday"? What's the relevance to learning? I devour my partner's papers on sexuality and teaching and find no need or reason to come out in class. With more self-confidence or commitment than I, the student from the bar, in one of her course papers, crosses out her self-description as "woman" and writes in "lesbian." I respond with an article I have been reading on lesbian teachers, discreetly folded so the title is not visible to the students sitting near her.

In this new context, I found several ways to begin. I continued to do my B.C.-based research and on sabbatical focused my interest on Aboriginal-European relations in a trip three B.C. chiefs made to London in 1906. This work also provided an opportunity to nurture my fledgling knowledge of Aboriginal Ontario. In Penny Petrone's book, *First People, First Voices*, I came across an account by Nahnebahweequa, also known as Catherine Sutton, who in 1860 made her second visit to Queen Victoria, this time to plead the case for her land. In London, I came to know pieces of her history. Full texts of her speeches are recorded in newspapers and magazines. I found records of the people with whom she had stayed and, eventually, in the memoirs of her hosts that, in addition to meeting the Queen and giving many powerful speeches to groups of thoughtful supporters, she had given birth to her fourth child while she was there. Owen Sound, the location of her home, took on a very different meaning for me.

Several months later, I connected coincidentally—*Do we really still believe in coincidence?*—with Darlene Johnston, Land Claims Research Coordinator for the Chippewas of Nawash and Saugeen, who is working in the area of Nahnebahweequa's homestead. We exchanged information and planned future meetings to share information and continue discussions around education. Other contacts with Aboriginal educators—Shirley Williams at Trent University, Kaaren Dannenman of Red Lake and Laara Fitznor at the University of Toronto—are giving me the feeling of starting to arrive in this land. Of course, there is work to be done here in Aboriginal education, rights and land claims. There are injustices to be addressed and, just maybe, I can find some opportunities for participating in coalition work, always starting from the land and Aboriginal peoples. Just maybe, ideas—at least this one—can travel.

Uncategorically moved

Refusing to be pinned down,
I am learning to be circumspect.
I am learning not to even try to offer the whole truth
to try to read the moment
to decide when and how much to say
"Why would anyone move from B.C. to Toronto?
Especially at times like these?"
to see if ideas travel
to see what it means first to lose and then to make a new history
for the promise of stimulating colleagues
for a lover …
Hmmm,
How much do you really want to know?

19

On Becoming an "Other"

Carolyn Ewoldt

> "I wish I had a magic wand," he said as I walked out of his office. My heart twisted with pity for this kind, reserved doctor who had tried so hard to save my eyes. I wanted to hug him, but we had maintained a polite distance for almost eight years and he would be embarrassed. It had been hard enough for him to face me and say that he didn't know what else to do. So I thanked him and carried my thick file to the receptionist. (journal entry, February 5, 1997)

I have composed many journal entries over the past ten years. The poetry and journals I write are like road maps through new emotional territory (Hebb 1954), beginning with the diagnosis of a rare form of glaucoma ten years ago. The story begins with the day I experienced great relief on learning that the brain tumor my doctors had been so certain about did not exist—I was only going blind. Of course, I didn't really believe that I would lose my vision. My doctor informed me that the simple application of eye drops would likely keep the condition under control. There were many drugs to be tried, laser treatments, and surgery as a last resort. But the condition proved to be impervious to treatment. Each new test revealed a greater loss of sight, the destruction of nerve endings progressing from the periphery to the centre of my vision. Each increment of loss added to my sense of urgency. I rushed from one doctor to another across Canada and the United States in what I later learned was a typical search for the magic cure. I experienced "the vacillation between hope and despair [that] is perhaps the most difficult or painful pattern to cope with" (Schulz 1980: 52).

In a hospital in Vancouver I met a woman with a similar eye condition, and we talked incessantly about our common experiences for two days while undergoing tests. I recall that experience even now as an uplifting one, even though it did not result in any great revelations about my vision problem. Elkins (1996) speaks of drawing as a dialogue with blindness. Like the artist, the writer's marks move into blindness and leave a path of sight. Through writing of my experiences, I have looked backwards and have undertaken the difficult "memory work" necessary for self-understanding (Haug 1987, cited in Norquay 1993).

One memory I have reclaimed, an uncomfortable one, was buried for many years: a woman on a plane with a monocular on her head (a device for enlarging print) was attempting to read something with obvious difficulty. On seeing her, I felt a welling-up of unreasoned loathing, one of the strongest emotions I can recall.

Monbeck (1973) describes some of the theories that have been offered to explain the negativity directed toward people with disabilities, particularly toward those who have low vision or blindness:

- The social, cultural, religious and historical roots of our prejudices are passed through generations as part of the socialization process.
- The prejudices are embedded in our current literature, television and movies and in Western culture's emphasis on "the body whole, the body beautiful."
- Freud's theory of castration anxiety is often cited as an underlying factor. The eye is equated with sexual organs.

As Neumann (1954) suggests:

- Night fears and dreams are dispelled by light, experienced as emanating from above and giving guidance and orientation.
- Light has come to symbolize consciousness, and dark, the unconscious (to see is to understand; to be blind is to be blinded to the truth).

A further explanation is that sighted people do not want to be reminded that they themselves might become blind (Schulz 1980), and I suspect that is at least a partial explanation for my reaction to the woman on the plane, because I had severe myopia, though no hint of glaucoma, at the time.

The woman I later encountered in the hospital was no threat; I was already like her. Then, when I met Jean Little, the well-known author of books for children, I confess to being impressed by her celebrity and strong personality, which helped a great deal to dispel any negative reaction toward her blindness. She was a "privileged" woman like myself. Thus, when my ophthalmologist offered to refer me to the Canadian National Institute for the Blind (CNIB) so I could stay ahead of my continuing vision loss, I was more receptive to the idea of association with "others" than I would have been before I met Jean. However, I still felt threatened. To suppress this feeling, I attempted to intellectualize the experience. I proposed a leave of absence from teaching so I could research my own process of learning Braille at the CNIB. I would also contact professors who were blind to discover how they conducted their classes. I would do a study of the literacy preferences and experiences of people who were blind. Many services were now available to me as a CNIB client—talking books on tape, directory assistance, mobility instruction, Braille lessons.

As an American transplanted in Canada, I also felt, for the first time in many years, a strong Canadian cultural identity. I was making friends and contacts among other people who were blind or had low vision. I felt a sense of community and a commonality of experience. More importantly, I had great affection for my new friends. I was also grateful for my sighted friends who regarded me as a "person first," a phrase which indicates that a person with a disability has many unique characteristics, of which the disability is only one (Wright 1960). This is not to deny that I was at the same time experiencing frustration and anger. Some former friends now seemed to find me too much trouble; others did not know how to react. As Jean Little wrote to me during that time, "If you are not angry, check your pulse; you might be dead" (personal correspondence, January 12, 1996).

I also suffered a severe loss of self-esteem. Academic achievement had been a primary means of maintaining or increasing my self-esteem. I had achieved a degree of recognition for my research into the literacy process of people who are deaf or hard of hearing. Now I had to recognize the irony of going blind when my reputation had been built on my work with people who were deaf. Once I dreamed that I was standing beside a moving sidewalk, watching a younger woman in a business suit and carrying a briefcase who slid silently and rapidly past without noticing I was there. The field was moving ahead, and I was being left behind, wishing I could have become deaf instead, and wondering how to fill the remaining academic years.

I was shocked when an acquaintance who is blind suggested that I "go on welfare" since I was so apprehensive about returning to the university. Again, a prejudice of which I was unaware burst out into the open. I was not one of "them"! And I was forced to confront the ways in which I had constructed less privileged people as "others." Gunn (1981) says that the significance of the autobiography lies not in the obviousness of its answers but in the strangeness of its questions. Having believed that I had overcome the prejudices of my Southern upbringing, I felt that I was asking myself a strange question, but the answer was obvious: I had been an ableist, and an elitist as well.

As I attempted to reinvent myself within the world of academia, I turned to the education of children who are blind as an area of possible research interest. At the W. Ross Macdonald School for the Blind in Brantford, Ontario, I was delighted to see young people using Braille and adaptive devices for reading and writing. I was touched by a video produced by the National Association of the Blind (n.d.), in which adults who were blind talked with great regret about their having been denied the use of Braille as children. When I attended the International Conference of Educators of the Visually Impaired in Sao Paulo, Brazil, I was angered to hear speakers refer to "the blind" and their lack of qualifications for guiding educators regarding the needs of children who are blind. Comments were frequently made to the effect that Braille was unnecessary and that those who promoted its use did so because they wanted to keep the field mysterious, thereby saving their jobs. These speakers were unmoved by passionate pleas from conference participants who were blind to keep Braille alive, and unimpressed by the speakers who read their presentations in Braille with ease and fluency.

The similarities between the prejudices of sighted educators of people who are blind and those of hearing educators of people who are deaf were striking. Both American Sign Language (ASL) and Braille have been denied to many children, based on the beliefs that people with disabilities should be "normalized," and "failures" are the fault of the children and their parents. This realization led to collaboration on an article with David Mason, a colleague who is Deaf (the capital indicating a cultural affiliation with the Deaf community). In the article we explored some of the common assumptions underlying and supporting the continued involvement of TABs (temporarily able-bodied people) in the fields of education of people who are deaf or blind (Mason and Ewoldt 1999).

One such assumption is the "use it or lose it" fallacy. Many educators of children who are deaf believe that the use of ASL will prevent children from developing and using oral language. Studies from 1971 (Vernon and Koh) to the present day have shown that children who use ASL are no different from children who are trained orally in their speech and speech-reading abilities, but these studies have had little effect on the negative attitudes toward ASL held by many hearing educators. Similarly, I was told during a vision assessment that I could not get a screen reader (an audio output component) for my computer because, "We believe that if you don't continue to use your vision, you will lose it." It is inconceivable that a person with vision would not use it. Aristotle recognized our love for sight. Even when we do not need vision for a particular activity, we prefer sight over any of our other senses. Almost half of our cerebral cortex is devoted to sight, more space even than that devoted to language (Magee 1995). Furthermore, I had been using my vision for many years but I was still losing it!

I began to take on an advocacy role, serving as a volunteer at the CNIB. I constructed myself as a friend of people who were blind, but I still had quite a lot of vision. (Many people are surprised to learn that few clients of the CNIB are totally blind.) I could still stand outside whenever I wished. I had yet to realize that, in my self-appointed role as advocate, first for the Deaf community and later for people who were blind, I was interpreting people from my own standpoint and that this is a feature of cultural imperialism (Graveline 1998).

However, an incident on October 10, 1997, thrust me more firmly inside. I was making a left turn out of a shopping mall when a man suddenly appeared in front of my car. Until that moment I had not seen him. I had been driving slowly; there was no dramatic screeching of brakes to inform the pedestrian that he was in danger, but it was a momentous event in my life. I never drove again. Giving up a car and all it represents in Western culture—independence, spontaneity, privacy and status—was devastating. Nothing I had ever experienced before made me feel so deprived. Every relationship was now altered by my dependence on others for transportation. I would always be in the inferior position of passenger, never in control of the radio or heater, always feeling compelled to engage the driver in conversation as the price of a ride. Even taxi drivers can drag one into unwanted conversations. The quiet reflection afforded one who drives alone was denied me.

Once again, I came up against a self-realization that was uncomfortable. I had been contributing to our unhealthy environment by driving alone and now felt miserable at not being allowed to continue! I also had to overcome a lingering negativity surrounding the use of public transportation. In my own defence, there was a reason for my reluctance to use buses. The first time I had ventured out on a bus alone, the driver had deliberately (so I believe) misinformed me about the bus's destination and left me stranded at a busy intersection far from home. Of course, as one accustomed to power, I reported the incident with the expectation that I could raise the bus company's awareness of the needs of passengers who have low vision. As I made the call, I realized that I had just begun to inhabit the other side of oppression where so many people, even in Canada, live daily. For them, such ill treatment is the norm, and they would not have reported the incident with the same expectation of effecting change.

I have since experienced other instances of marginalization, ignorance and indifference. Now I know the isolation of entering a room and not being able to determine who is present or make eye contact or exchange a wave, to have to wait and hope that I will be approached by someone I know and be engaged in conversation. Sighted people do not realize that it is difficult for me to make the first move. I know how it feels to be dragged to places you have no wish to go, to be talked about as though you couldn't speak for yourself ("Is she for the handicap bus?"), to be informed that someone else "will tell you what you need." I was surprised to discover, on attending a support group meeting at the CNIB, that years after becoming blind, people were still talking about the thoughtless remarks of sighted people and how to interpret and respond to them. Sighted people often make the mistake of trying to avoid words related to vision when conversing with people who are blind. Phrases such as, "It's nice to see you," are quickly swallowed, even though they are not offensive to the person who is blind.

As a person with low vision, I have had the opposite experience. I am frequently asked, "What *can* you see?" "Do you see that?" Or conversely, "I thought you said you couldn't see," when I pick up something from the floor or remark on something I have seen. These are common problems of people who are partially sighted: to be reminded of the limitations of one's vision and to be given the impression that others suspect one is "faking it." I have taken to carrying in my purse a picture from a textbook which depicts the visual experience of a person with glaucoma. However, it is difficult to explain the vagaries of my vision. Little puzzle pieces are fairly clear, and some days or at some times during the day might be very clear, but I cannot depend on them to be available. And, my vision continues to deteriorate. Thus, I live an Alice-in-Wonderland existence in which there is no visual stability.

I have learned, however, that most of the difficulties I face are not the direct result of losing my vision but of the handicapping environments that are imposed on people with disabilities. It is society which renders a disabling condition a handicapping one. "Using disability as a social construct means understanding the economic, political and social forces which restrict the lives of the disabled" (Duval 1984: 635–36). With this understanding, I moved from advocate to activist. I joined a task force to look into barriers faced by people with disabilities who are attempting to start their own businesses. I became involved in drafting a response to the government regarding the proposed *Ontarians with Disabilities Act*. I joined the board of directors of my local CNIB. I developed a graduate course dealing with society's response to people with disabilities. I also recognized once again my own privileged position and the fact that, had my disability surfaced much earlier in life, I would not now enjoy the position I hold.

Parallels have been drawn between ableism and racism. "Like racial prejudice, a belief in the social incapacity of the handicapped disguises ignorance or bigotry behind what we 'see' to be an obvious biological fact" (Gliedman and Roth 1980: 23). However, the view that people with disabilities are in need of treatment rather than rights impedes their achievement of minority-group status (Biklen 1988), with its greater solidarity and political awareness.

Adherence to "traditional definitions of culture that are dependent on intergenerational transmission" (Linton 1998: 103) has also contributed to the lack of cohesiveness. The culture and history of disability are seldom shared and, when made available, are more likely to be transmitted from adult to adult than from adult to child. As well, many parents of children with disabilities will not allow them to associate with other people with disabilities. Or a person with a disability may not wish to be identified with a marginalized group. Others may choose not to be politically active or may not feel empowered to be (Scotch 1988).

Social and geographic dispersion often work against collective political action. Geographic diversity can be especially problematic for people who are blind or use wheelchairs, as transportation continues to be an almost insurmountable barrier. There are many architectural barriers as well. For example, people who use wheelchairs have reported that they were unable to enter polling stations because of the lack of accessibility.

The oppression of people with disabilities is multidimensional, for some people must face racial and/or sexual oppression as well (Oliver 1990). A person who is a member of a racial minority and also has a disability is doubly "visible" and heir to all the prejudices and oppression associated with both groups. In addition, men are expected to display stereotypical masculinity but are feminized by society because of their disability. Women with disabilities often suffer from a double dose of patriarchal hegemony.

Taking their cue from the black power and gay liberation movements, members of the Disability Movement celebrate difference and have adopted similar strategies, including de-euphemizing (flaunting the most degrading terms, such as "cripple"), repudiating societal values which serve only to perpetuate marginalization and promoting revolution against the oppressive aspects of rehabilitation. The Disability Movement is growing stronger and more cohesive (Linton 1998), crossing boundaries between marginalized groups to foster community activism. Alliances are being formed, not along racial and gender lines, but through the "felt collectivity" of people for whom a particular aspect of our identity, our disability, may be openly declared and important in one setting and carefully protected or irrelevant in another (Fiske 1990).

I am becoming stronger in my resolve to contribute to the cause. I am, however, beset by contradictions. As a professor in the Faculty of Education, I feel a responsibility to my students and to their students to raise awareness of disability issues, but I still struggle with a sense that my attention to disability issues will be regarded as self-serving.

When I requested that my undergraduates submit their papers in large print, the word came back to me that some students were complaining about the cost of additional computer paper and ink. Compared to the price of markers, glitter, poster board and other paraphernalia that I tried to discourage in favour of more thoughtful, questioning student presentations, the cost of using large print seemed to me to be minor. I responded by devoting a class session to discussion of disability, reminding the students that there would likely be children with disabilities in their classes and that such attention to their needs would be required. Some students' reaction to the "disability talk" was to target me as the problem, as Graveline (1998) has also observed while teaching about Native Canadian issues. I have yet to internalize the fact that a reaction of this kind may be typical of those whose privilege is most threatened, and that it is those topics which students speak about with emotion that are most in need of discussion.

Another area of contradiction is the political agenda of the Disability Movement. Stressing the independence of people with disabilities, the Disability Movement attempts to remove the perception of TABs that people with disabilities are a drain on society. It is important for able-bodied people to recognize that the cost of removal of barriers to employment and full participation will be repaid many times over by the contributions, financial and otherwise, that people with disabilities will make (Oliver 1990). And yet, I feel at times that this emphasis on independence imposes a great personal burden to achieve, and that dependence, though necessary to human existence, has become politically incorrect for people with disabilities. As well, the Disability Movement promotes a recognition by able-bodied people that having a disability is not a tragedy. My sympathy with this message troubles my own need to speak occasionally of my disability with dismay. In fact, Fine and Asch (1988: 334) called for "more reflective, less inspirational accounts" of people who have acquired a disability later in life. This duality of need, this contradiction, is difficult to address. Others like me who are acquiring a disability need the messages of strength and hope offered by the Disability Movement, but we also need to know that we are not alone in our experiences of fear, frustration, anger and grief. I am also concerned about how to mesh feminist and disability issues in ways that will not diminish the positions of either movement. If feminist theory argues against dependency, how does one reconcile this value with the lives of women who are severely disabled? (Hillyer 1993). Perhaps what is needed is a new perspective on the independence/dependence continuum that recognizes the individual's right to position herself or himself at any point at any time.

There is a great deal more "up to go" (Ciardi 1988). Reinventing myself requires understanding how to overcome my own constructions of loss and how to listen to new voices. This is the next part of the climb. "For a vision of the future functions less as the predictable outcome of all our forward-straining energy than it does as the lure for it" (Crites 1986: 165). In this process I remind myself that I must not allow activism and the concomitant view of myself as a disabled person to overshadow the progress I have made toward becoming a person first, a person who is more closely connected to those formerly constructed as "other."

20

Beamers, Cells, Malls and Cantopop
Thinking through the Geographies of Chineseness

GORDON PON

Siting Chineseness

> Go to Vancouver or go into the Chinese quarters in New York and see the Yellow Peril in all its aggravated forms; let him go no further away than his own city, Toronto the Good. A visit to the gambling haunts, the heavily curtained, evil smelling opium joints into which white girls are lured (*Jack Canuck*, February 10, 1912: 9).[1]

The other day, while riding the TTC,[2] I drifted through what felt like a millennium. In one afternoon of Christmas shopping in the Greater Toronto Area (GTA), I moved through a geography that reflected one hundred years of the ever-changing landscape of Chineseness. Beginning in "Chinatown" in downtown Toronto, I wove my way through cramped, cluttered and always aromatic Spadina Avenue. Here the *lo-wei-kuo* (the old overseas Chinese)—the Toisanese and Hoipingnese,[3] who first established this district one hundred years ago—have increasingly given way to more recent, Chinese-speaking Vietnamese entrepreneurs. But like old masters of survival, the Toisanese patriarchs perch outside on the ledge of the Dragon City Mall in the heart of "Chinatown," surveying what once was the battleground of their daily struggles against White racism. As if in one last stand against erasure, one last attempt to be free from anonymity, there they sit.

Aboard a TTC bus, I now head for the Pacific Mall in Markham, leaving behind the Toisan seniors. Moving away from "Chinatown," I feel relieved of the insatiable desires for non-erasure that are embedded deep in their Toisanese and Hoipingnese dialects. When I arrive at the Pacific Mall, I am awed by its abundantly spacious, pristine and postmodern ambience, an ambience characterized by a fusion of Hong Kong, Mainland Chinese, Japanese and North American cultures. As I settle into the stream of shoppers I am struck by the fact that most of them, like the hundred or so stores and store signs, are Chinese, and the many voices around me speak in Cantonese. I am thrilled to see so many Chinese youth and I am mesmerized by the pride they show in their language and culture—their "Chineseness." The fact that this mall has come to fruition is especially gratifying when I recall the furor it created among local White residents. In the ongoing debates about the increasing Chinese presence, former Deputy Mayor Carole Bell remarked, in her now infamous but honest exhortation, that the citizens of Markham (read "Whites") were feeling besieged by too many Chinese. Remembering this, it gives me great pleasure to see that the Chinese entrepreneurs were not deterred.

The mall's unabashed insistence on meeting the needs of Chinese consumption utterly rebuffs Carole Bell's concerns and, in fact, thumbs its nose at the Deputy Mayor, xenophobia and other particularities of White fright. For those who do not understand Cantonese, the mall seems to shout out: "Well, that's your tough luck! We're here, we speak Cantonese; we read and write Chinese; so get used to it." Herein lies the powerful resistance of these Chinese entrepreneurs and consumers. By refusing to assimilate into English-speaking retail protocol, these Chinese people inscribe themselves firmly into the landscape of Markham, refusing erasure; refusing to defer to the anxieties and desires of those unsettled by the sites and sounds of Cantonese.

This powerful and inspiring resistance counters the prevalent Chinese "model minority" stereotype in many ways. This stereotype is part of a larger discourse that emerged in the 1960s in the United States, championing the success of Chinese-Americans, in contradistinction to African-Americans, who at the time were mobilizing to effect vigorous demands for civil rights. The implication was that the "troublemaking" minorities should model themselves after the Chinese-American's hard work ethic, self-reliance and willingness to assimilate (McKay and Wong 1996; Lee 1996). Critics of that stereotype note that it promotes the idea that Asian North Americans have overcome historical barriers such as poverty and racism and now form a uniformly affluent and successfully assimilated group. The flipside of this stereotype is the belief that Chinese people are quiet, overly passive, nerdy, conformist, willing to assimilate and exceptional students, particularly in the maths and sciences (Wong 1993).

At first glance this stereotype does not seem all that bad. Indeed, it even seems positive when compared to the prevalent stereotypes of Blacks and Natives (James 1997b; Monture-Angus 1996). However, it is often quite harmful. How can it be harmful? After all, one might ask, what is wrong with having people, especially teachers, believe that one is smart and gifted in math? For instance, while attending elementary school in the 1970s, I recall the day my grade-six teacher paired up Chinese students with non-Chinese partners. When a curious and rather puzzled White boy ventured to ask why, the teacher replied that Asians were superior at math and would therefore assist the other students. Later, outside in the playground, we Chinese students all gathered together, including those who could barely add, and raved excitedly about how smart the teacher was! We took a real liking to this teacher thereafter, feeling that he was really "with it" and knew the "truth" about the intellectual prowess of us Asians. I remember one Chinese boy, who was particularly bad at math, remarking to the effect that "of course we're the smartest. Look at how little body hair we have; that's because we're the most evolved." As our reactions as youngsters show, there is indeed something very seductive about the stereotype.

It was only as I got older and progressed into the higher grades that the harmful aspects of the stereotype would increasingly trouble me and its seductiveness would begin to wane, and even to haunt. By the early 1980s I was attending high school, and math had become my weakest subject, while English, particularly writing, had emerged as my passion. Yet from grade eight and onwards to grade twelve, my English teachers would often query me in class as to whether or not I had written the essay assignments myself or solicited someone else to write them for me. When I reassured my teachers that it was my own work, they looked at me oddly, perhaps with suspicion, perhaps bewilderment, but certainly with unease. Rather begrudgingly, the teachers would return my essays to me with grades ranging from a B to an A-, but never anything higher. It took me years beyond high school to figure out that my essay-writing skills, which were quite strong for my grade level, ruptured the dominant stereotypes of Chinese students, particularly the belief that we are all math whizzes. Stereotyping particular groups such as the Chinese places limits on what is expected of them and inhibits an understanding of the complex differences among the members of that group. Thus the stereotypes my English teachers held of Chinese people resulted in an expectation that I was supposed to be good in math, but not English!

At the Pacific Mall, things seem to be so different than my own experiences of growing up in Ottawa. The most obvious reason for this is that there are about 335,000 Chinese people in Toronto and only about 9,600 in Ottawa (Statistics Canada 1996). But more than anything, what is striking to me is the class difference. The Chinese students at my high school were, like myself, predominantly working-class, Canadian-born Chinese (CBC) who spoke the Toisanese dialect of Cantonese. The Chinese students in Markham are increasingly Cantonese speakers from Hong Kong and, according to local perceptions, are middle- to upper-middle class.

The class privilege of some of these more recent Chinese immigrants in Markham is remarkable. For instance, visiting the Pacific Mall,

I am struck by its surrounding well-to-do neighbourhood, which is increasingly populated by Chinese. The stellar single homes are recent constructions and their three-car garages stand like testaments to grander wonders within. Indeed, there is a striking array of vehicles—BMWs, Volvos, Mercedes Benzes—parked outside many of these beautiful homes. At the mall itself, many of these elite cars snake their way through the crowded parking lot. And just as striking as these vehicles are the young shoppers, especially the Chinese youth, dressed in high-priced designer fashions like Calvin Klein, Gap and Club Monaco.

The seemingly well-to-do status of these youth of Markham contrasts markedly with the Chinese youth of Ottawa. For instance, my high school was also located in an elite upper-middle-class neighbourhood. However, it had racial and ethnic minority students who came primarily from the adjacent working-class neighbourhood which was neatly divided off by the major highway that cut across Ottawa. We, the working-class youth, went to this high school because we desired to enrol in advanced-level courses not offered in the two high schools in our immediate neighbourhood. These two local schools were vocational; one catered to the female-dominated trades such as secretarial work and bookkeeping, while the other focused on male-dominated, technical vocations such as auto mechanics and carpentry. Thus, every morning the predominantly White, middle-class neighbourhood would experience an influx of working-class Toisanese, Lebanese, Italian and Vietnamese youth as we walked underneath the highway overpass making our way to school. By late afternoon the neighbourhood would return to its monocultural state as we "minorities" made our way back home.

Cantopop, White Flight and "Model Minorities"

A shopping centre like the Pacific Mall certainly might tend to confirm aspects of the Chinese "model minority" stereotype, particularly the belief that the Chinese are rich. Even among Toisanese there are stereotypical beliefs that the Hong Kong–born Chinese are very affluent. Yet, this stereotype can be deleterious because it overlooks the large numbers of working-class Chinese, including many who are Hong Kong–born, living in a city like Toronto (Das Gupta 1996).[4]

Observing the people at the Pacific Mall, I could see how easy it might be for a non-Chinese person to slip into ways of thinking about the Chinese that are stereotypical, overgeneralizing and homogenizing;[5] for example, that we are wealthy people who are only concerned about "Beamers" (BMWs), "cells" (cellular phones), high-end fashion and monster suburban homes. Therefore, I feel a certain ambivalence when I'm in a place like the Pacific Mall. On the one hand, the Chinese youth who frequent the mall seem comfortable with their Chineseness in a way I find awe-inspiring, especially given the fact that they live within a larger society that pushes them to assimilate. Yet, on the other hand, I am unsettled by their apparent obliviousness to the racism and societal structures that mitigate against them.

My ambivalence was heightened when I wandered into a record store. The unmistakable upbeat dance rhythm of Hong Kong pop music, or what is often referred to as "Cantopop," boomed through the loudspeakers. The store was buzzing with young Chinese men and women who were sorting through a vast selection of CDs and DVDs. I recalled David Parker's (1995) writings on Chinese youth cultures in Britain. He argues that British Chinese youth listen to a hyper-commercialized Hong Kong pop music that tends toward formulaic love songs and few elements of explicit political comment or resistance. As I listened, unable to discern much of the lyrics with my limited Cantonese, I could not help but wonder if the song was *à la* Cantopop—depoliticized, formulaic and lacking in resistance. I thought to myself: "If Cantopop does not challenge the status quo, then does it reinforce the 'model minority' stereotype?" Likewise, I contemplated: "Can it be that the Chineseness of the Pacific Mall is a necessary phase that will one day foster increasingly critical cultural productions?"

As I looked at the designer fashions worn by many of the Chinese youth, I understood how easily non-Chinese people could resent or envy the fact that these youth can afford to purchase such expensive clothing. I contemplated whether this ability to own designer fashions was part of the sinophobic sentiments that trouble the suburb of Markham. I wondered whether many of these Chinese youth were cognizant of the increasing xenophobia and anti-immigrant sentiments that frame their lives.

I could not help but lament the fact that despite the ongoing tensions around issues of race and language in this neighbourhood, Cantopop seems to speak little to these issues. I wondered if they think about issues like "White flight"? If so how did they feel about the "White flight" from their schools and neighbourhoods? What are their reactions to Carole Bell? Are these Chinese students even aware of these issues? Likewise, I wondered if English-speaking Anglo-Canadians ever admonished them for speaking Chinese in public spaces? How do these Chinese youth feel and react when people admonish them to speak English? How does their music resist contemporary forms of sinophobia and xenophobia?

Unable to contain my curiosity, I queried many of the youthful shoppers about these issues. In response to my questions about whether they experienced racism or resentment in their lives, most, if not all of them, stated that they did not. These youth remind me of a recent study at York University which found that many Chinese students see themselves outside of race and what it connotes. That is to say, these students do not want to be marked by racial categories. Also, these students have very positive outlooks on life and do not regard racism as a barrier to their abilities to secure employment in Canada.[6] Is it possible that the class privilege that many of these Chinese people enjoy shields them from racism?

While I am grappling with this question and scanning the record store in search of another youth to approach, the Cantopop playing over the store speakers gives way to a rap song sung in English. I ask the youth next to me who this band is. I wonder to myself, "Is this a Cantopop singer who can sound so Black?" The young man tells me with a smile, almost as if he can read my mind, "Its Leon!" He points to a CD with a picture of a young, handsome Chinese man on the front. The youth informs me that Leon is a very popular singer from Hong Kong. I pick up the CD and check the back for song titles and see both Chinese and English songs. I locate the rap song—"Police Station Rap: Black versus Yellow," about the pleas of a Black male who has been arrested by a police officer. The man laments that not only has he been physically assaulted by the Chinese, but they have also moved into his hometown. Some of the lyrics are as follows:

> Yo! Yo! Officer you see these Chinese people
> Coming through like they new ...
> This one hit me in my lungs
> With their kung-fu
> Woo-chee-woo-chee ha! ...
> I can't figure out what they were sayin' ...
> I'm doubly oppressed ...
> They come to my hometown all smilin'
> Me and my man CK
> Just sitting down frownin'[7]

I ask the youth if this is Leon rapping, and he laughs, assuring me that it is not. Intrigued, I ask the sales staff and other youth in the store if they know who is performing the rap song. No one knows and the persistent staff peruse the liner insert of the CD, but to no avail. Unable to tell who it is or where this rap song comes from, I make several assumptions about it: the male rapper sounds like an African-American; the song is probably borne out of a large urban American context that is undergoing substantial Chinese immigration; this has given rise, most likely, to economic and social tensions that mirror those currently between African- and Korean-Americans, like those articulated in rapper Ice Cube's "Death Certificate" CD in which he warns Korean-American merchants of violence if they are disrespectful to African-Americans.

The inclusion of this rap song on this CD shattered much of what I thought about the "depoliticized" nature of Cantopop. I could not help but wonder: What does it mean and represent to include this rap song on a Chinese CD? What politic does this inclusion engender? How are these Chinese youth relating to the "Police Station Rap" song? Is it not primarily the White people of Markham, not Blacks, who contest the Chinese presence? How do they deal with the fact that in the GTA, it is middle-class Whites, not Blacks, who most resent their Chineseness?

These questions help me to realize that what I find particularly interesting about the Leon rap song is what it fails to acknowledge. For instance, it does not acknowledge that the nature of racism in sites like Markham, is not black versus yellow but rather white versus yellow. Moreover, it is a particular suburban middle-class whiteness that is at play here—as mentioned earlier, it is the White middle class that feels "besieged" by the Chinese. Bearing this in mind, I recognize that the Leon rap song "misreads," in a provocative manner, the situation in the GTA. In its global circulation, the rap gets mired in casting Blacks against Asians, not so much out of context, as in a return to the "model minority" stereotype. In an epiphany, I suddenly understand how the Leon CD declares, "We're not Black."

Perhaps part of Cantopop's appeal is its ability to differentiate its listeners in the diaspora from the musical cultures of "other" racial-minority youths. As such it plays a central role in forging distinctive Chinese identities. Many of those who identify with and enjoy Cantopop may not necessarily be looking for critical race consciousness, nor are they desirous of the social and political commentary one might find in other forms of music.

However, I can't help but think, "Wait until they get into the real world. Once they bump into racism in the labour market, Cantopop will do little for them."[8] Perhaps Cantopop, unlike much of the music of working-class Black and South Asian youth in North America, is not as informed by critical and powerful ways of knowing and understanding society. Nonetheless, Cantopop in the GTA, like the Leon CD, stakes a claim on the public domain; like the Chinese entrepreneurs who stake a claim in the Markham Mall, the youthful listeners of Cantopop are thumbing their noses at the Carole Bells, White flight and the CBCs. For those who do not understand Cantonese, the youth seem to remark: "Too bad! We're here and we won't be erased! We love who we are, our community, our Chineseness, our language, and our Cantonese pop singers! So get over it!" Herein lies the remarkable resistance of these Chinese Canadian youth and their vibrant, diasporic Cantopop culture.

"Speak English! This is Canada!"

Recently I returned to Ottawa, a city characterized by an economic implosion of sorts, a city of predominantly White civil servants under siege by their own elected representatives. In a conversation with Philip (a pseudonym), a Toisanese friend I have known since childhood, I spoke about the differing sense of Chineseness in Toronto. I talked to him in particular about how in teacher's college, teacher candidates frequently debate schoolwide English-only policies. I also shared with him the feelings of both Chinese and non-Chinese students who tell me that occasionally in the GTA, a non-Chinese person will tell Chinese youth to "Speak English! This is Canada!"

With this, Philip's eyes open wide in obvious disbelief. "They say what?" he asks horrified. I repeat myself and Philip inquires angrily, almost desperately,

"What do the Chinese kids say?" And before I can reply, he adds with a smirk, "Do they fight?"

I am surprised by his last question and find it odd, for I realize that it's the first time I have ever heard it.

"No, they don't fight, " I reply after a moment's thought. But given that my comment might be regarded as overgeneralizing, I quickly add, "I haven't heard about any fights." Philip looks perplexed.

Philip's perplexity makes me realize that he grew up with different investments in the learning process than the more recent, Hong Kong–born Chinese students of Markham. The more recent arrivals came to Canada in part for the schooling opportunities. Thus, they regard education as an important means of securing upward social mobility. Accordingly, racism, like limited English language proficiency, is regarded as an obstacle they must endure and overcome. Philip, on the other hand, like so many Toisanese working-class CBCs, is haunted by the ironies of nation-state building and struggles for family reunification. Indeed, the famous Chinese railway workers who constructed the western segments of the Canadian Pacific Railway (CPR) were recruited from the Toisan and Hoiping counties of Guangdong province. First the gold seekers and, later, Toisanese and Hoipingnese railway labourers arrived in Canada in the late 1800s. Pitted against the odds of a "Chinaman's chance," countless Toisan Chinese died during the construction of the CPR. The "Chinatowns" that arose upon completion of the railway belied any notions of the sojourning nature of this labour force. But the name "Chinatown" continues to express the deeply embedded White desire for us to one day return from whence we came.

Growing up in a working-class Toisanese family, youth like Philip and I were but a few decades removed from the racism of the *Chinese Exclusion Act* and the atrocities of the Head Taxes (Li 1988). We were privy to the continuing struggles of Toisanese immigrants to secure a living in Canada. We were all too cognizant of how our resistant Toisan parents and elders worked, suffered and sacrificed. Thus Toisanese youth committed ourselves to the belief that we have a right to be in this country, despite the dominant society's insistence upon constructing us as "other," as foreigners. Our stakes in the learning process were characterized by tremendous ambivalence: we desired an education and its promises of upward mobility but were frustrated by its otherization of Chinese people. Given this history, it becomes clear why Philip responds the way he does to tales of admonishments to speak English. Moreover, he sees no difference between himself, a Toisanese CBC, and the Hong Kong Chinese youth of the GTA. This leads him to regard hatred expressed towards Hong Kong–born Chinese as hatred directed toward himself.

Like Philip, I sometimes overlook the differences among the "Chinese." A few months ago, I was in a GTA high school watching a student talent night. The population of this school is predominantly Asian and most are Hong Kong–born Chinese Canadians. The majority of the performers were Chinese and many, if not most, of the songs were sung in Cantonese. Midway through the talent show my heart sank as the MC announced that the window of a BMW parked outside had just been smashed. Oh my God, I thought, it must be some White students who are pissed off at all the Cantonese music being played! I was suddenly ashamed of my ambivalence towards the Chinese youth and their music—I realized their vulnerability and innocence as never before. I struggled to control a feeling of rage, as suddenly for the first time this evening I felt very "Chinese." The assault upon the vehicle felt like an assault upon me, upon my racial group, the Chinese people. It then struck me that it was equally plausible that a CBC had smashed the window.

My momentary erasure of the differences among Chinese youth was interrupted by a realization that many CBCs do not identify with their Hong Kong–born peers. Philip, in contrast, overlooks this intragroup tension and strongly identifies with the Hong Kong Chinese youth of Markham. Philip's identification with these youth makes me suddenly angry at the many Hong Kong-born youth who would readily refer to a Toisanese like him as a *"juk-sing." Juk-sing* is a pejorative term used frequently by Hong Kong–born Chinese youth to describe Toisanese Canadian-born Chinese. It literally means the empty spaces inside bamboo. The term alludes to the way CBCs are considered to be stuck in a void—neither fully Chinese nor fully Canadian. This term is analogous to the label "banana, which is often used by Chinese people to refer to someone who is considered "yellow on the outside but white on the inside." How, then, do you explain Philip's rage, hurt and bewilderment?, I want to ask this question of a youth who would call Philip a *juk-sing*. But more importantly, I wonder, how do I begin to tell Philip that his rage feels somehow out of place; like an anachronism of sorts. Philip has different stakes than the Chinese youth of Markham. I want to tell him that the youth at the Pacific Mall are not much like he was at all. For instance, while I'm sure the youth who are admonished by non-Asians to speak English do not find this totally innocuous, I don't think they find it half as enraging as Philip does. In a way I suspect that many of these recent immigrants strongly want to acquire greater English language skills. In fact, such admonishments may not depart much from Chinese parental exhortations.

For an instant, I want to tell Philip that he's a dinosaur. The youth who are admonished to speak English in the GTA have an innocence that is forged at the intersection of adolescence and class privilege. This innocence plays itself out at the mall as that simple, quintessentially adolescent wish to be somebody, to be seen, to be heard, to have fun and, of course, to be desired. These youth of Markham are the new, young Chinese immigrants of our postmodern world. They, like their Cantopop, are part of the increasingly global, stateless and rapid movements of capital, culture, goods, knowledge and labour. In comparison, Philip and I are like old Toisanese remnants of the contradictions of the nation-state.

I most feel the disparity between myself and the Chinese youth at the Pacific Mall in the fears and anxieties I bring to bear on their race politics—my inability to "chill," really. I am old in my fears, old in my worries, old in my understandings of racism and its brutal, transforming and chameleonlike powers; powers that could depict us Chinese-Canadians as a "Yellow Peril" (Pon 1996) one day and "model minorities" the next. Why on earth should I expect a fifteen-year-old Chinese youth armed with a Calvin Klein top, a cellphone and the latest Leon CD to care about racism? Why would they care if its black or white versus yellow? If anything, the Markham Chinese youth highlight how our Toisan ways of refusing erasure and resisting racism are often rudimentary at best, and embarrassing at worst. My greatest fear is that this is what Hong Kong–born Chinese youth mean when they refer to us as *juk-sing*. Perhaps they clearly see how the deeply ingrained desire among

Toisanese for equality and acceptance among Whites continues to infuriate us when this goal eludes us.

Mutiny on the "Slow Boat" and Our Schooling Experiences

Talking with Philip, I recall our experiences of schooling and suspect that they are very different from those faced by Chinese students in GTA suburbs. Many of the recent Chinese immigrant youth face the tremendous struggle of attending school in a language that is not their first. This is a struggle that we did not have to contend with as adolescents.

Our teachers challenged us in ways that were disturbingly blunt in their racism. In grade nine, my math teacher, Mr. Heinz (a pseudonym) would always joke about sending the Chinese students who gave incorrect answers back to China on the slow boat. Sometimes when students got the answers wrong, he would inquire if they were Italian. The class would break into uproarious laughter, while we Toisanese Chinese exchanged looks mixed with pleasure and pain—we would be laughing and also coaxing our Chinese peers to talk back. In our braver moments, one of us would blurt out, "Oh, mi Gott, not the slow boat!" in a rather pitiful attempt to mock our teacher's German ancestry.

The incident that all the Chinese students from my high school will probably remember forever is the day Jason Wong (pseudonym) challenged Mr. Heinz to a fight! Whether tired of Mr. Heinz and his racial and ethnic slurs, or maybe just sick of math, Jason became a chronic skipper of the class. Once while skipping the class, Jason showed up outside the classroom and from there, hiding himself just enough to elude Mr. Heinz, but in full view of most students, motioned for some of us to join him. Before any of us could respond, an Italian student upstaged his ploy with a loud, "Oh, hi Jason!" Immediately Mr. Heinz snapped to attention, and with his eyes almost bulging out of their sockets, he screamed: "Jason Wong? Jason Wong?" Jason turned to run, but Mr. Heinz, who moved with a speed that surprised us all, caught him by the back of his neck. The two grappled and jostled as Mr. Heinz literally dragged Jason into the classroom. The class looked on in shocked silence, instinctively backing off toward the perimeter of the classroom as the grappling was ferocious and desks and chairs were being toppled and pushed about. Finally, Mr. Heinz let go of Jason. With his face flushed red, perspiring and breathing heavily, Jason exclaimed with more terror than conviction:

"You can't do that! You can't touch me!"

"I can so," replied Mr. Heinz, who strangely seemed no worse for wear.

"No, you can't! You can't touch me!" Jason repeated again and again.

Finally Jason raised his clenched fists. At the sight of those fists, his raised chest and the mad rage in Jason's eyes, the class suddenly went berserk with shouts of approval. We cheered and screamed in a cathartic, high-pitched frenzy bordering on lunacy. Spurred on by the students, both Jason and Mr. Heinz stood resolutely toe-to-toe, each challenging the other to throw the first punch.

In the end, despite the bizarre display of bravado on the part of both teacher and student, and much to our chagrin, not a blow was exchanged. Mr. Heinz refused to teach a grade-nine class ever again, and the Toisanese and Italians would vie for years over who deserved more credit for the turn of events. And Jason Wong never completed his high school education.

Geographies of Chineseness

In concluding, I return to discuss the two geographies of Chineseness represented by the downtown Toronto Dragon City Mall and the Pacific Mall in Markham. I find it fascinating how in traversing from Spadina Avenue to the Pacific Mall, one can see how a hundred years of Chinese Canadian history has unfolded and continues to unfold. In "Chinatown" the Toisanese seniors of the Dragon City Mall harken back to a time when Chinese people were in demand for the cheap, transitory labour we represented. Indeed, the title of the mall and its invocation of the "dragon" conjures up a particular "Chineseness" often associated with exotic mysticism, kung fu films and a forlorn nostalgia for Chinese martial supremacy. Today "Chinatown" remains a predominantly working-class neighbourhood with newer Vietnamese and working-class Hong Kong, Mainland Chinese and Taiwanese families settling here.

At the Pacific Mall, the story of Chinese-Canadians plays itself out differently than in "Chinatown." Here it is clear that the newer Hong Kong–born Chinese have come to Canada without the historical hangups the Toisanese have. As such, they have a resiliency in the face of "White fright," racism and xenophobia that is unshakeable and very evident in the fervour and energy that infuses their mall. Thus, admonishments to speak English, for example, are but minor irritations in what is otherwise the daunting but exciting task of forging a new life in postmodern Canada.

Walking through the Pacific Mall, I realize that its name, invoking the "Pacific," aptly reflects the rising economic momentum of the Pacific Rim. Unlike the nostalgic nationalism and nativism invoked by the

"Dragon City" Mall, this suburban space is enraptured in the notion of the Pacific Rim as a nascent star of global capitalism. Its name calls attention to new circuits of immigration and consumption in the shifting world economy. As I peruse the multitude of shops here, I recognize that the store operators understand these new circuits of immigration and the related postmodern penchants of today's consumers. Many of the stores sell products linked to new technologies: DVDs, cellular phones, "private" karaoke studios and the latest in personal computing hardware and software. Other stores market clothing fashions and cultural productions, such as movies, music and comic books, that capitalize on the increasingly global cultural village afforded by such things as the Internet, e-business and satellite television. These shop owners are "with it" and know what Hong Kong Chinese youth consume and desire; and these young Chinese shoppers spend their dollars in a way that enables them to feel right at home, here in Canada.

The postmodern savvy of the Pacific Mall differs greatly from the other Markham shopping centres I pass while riding the TTC. Passing through this geography of suburban Whiteness characterized by familiar Canadian landmarks such as The Bay and (formerly) Eaton's, I find it mundane in comparison to the lively fervour of the Pacific Mall. At that mall such familiar Canadian retailers or department stores are nowhere to be seen. Despite the weight of NAFTA, The Bay and (formerly) Eaton's strain and cling desperately to more glorious times gone by. Their retail knowledge of postmodern consumption is staked not so much on globalized culture as on nostalgia for a now more subdued Anglo-Canadian aesthetic, epitomized by The Bay's introduction of a Wayne Gretzky line of clothing. Indeed the bankruptcy experienced by Canadian retail establishments such as Eaton's reflects a more general decline of the White Canadian middle class.

Members of the White middle class in places like Markham are perhaps reminded daily by the Chinese presence that they themselves are increasingly under threat of erasure. In comparison to the newer homes constructed by some Chinese residents, their own homes now appear ordinary, even parochial; their summer cottages are now as precarious as their tenuous middle-class jobs; and their steadily increasing tax bills are as unfathomable as their diminishing real disposable incomes.[9] No longer the "kings of the hill," certainly not in Markham, they are now running with their children in tow toward newer, more distant and "less diverse" hills.

Reflecting on this "White flight" I think about whether or not a White resident would even visit a place like the Pacific Mall. After all, nothing here would be familiar to them. What might it feel like to an English-speaking Anglo-Canadian to shop at the Pacific Mall? Would they feel marginalized and left out? Would they feel besieged?

21

Provincially Speaking
"You don't sound like a Newfoundlander!"

Susan A. Tilley

I have always felt connected to the ocean. I think that comes with being an "islander." I walk around the seawall in Stanley Park appreciating the time to think and breathe. As I walk along, my thoughts turn to the Atlantic Ocean; I want to smell the air off the ocean in Newfoundland. I reminisce about Middle Cove, going there as a child with my father and siblings during the caplan run. We would all race down onto the beach as the tide went out and snatch up caplan flopping on the rocks. Sometimes we had rubber boots, sometimes small nets, but most times we were in our sneakers holding plastic bags that we would fill with the few caplan we managed to grab up in our hands as the water charged back up the beach. As each of us took our turn having our shoes filled with water, or tripping and falling on our knees, we would laugh so hard it hurt. My memories of childhood are inseparable from my memories of home and all that I miss.

While growing up, I didn't think much about the fact that I lived on an island, or that this island was not attached to the rest of Canada, to the "mainland." I wasn't aware of the boundaries within which we lived our lives. My world occupied a very limited space. My family's travel was confined to Sunday trips, by car, to visit my maternal grandparents who lived in a small community on the Avalon Peninsula, two hours away by dirt road now only fifty minutes on not-so-smooth pavement.

As a young teacher in Labrador, the mainland portion of the province, I became more aware of my island status and the fractures within the province's population. During that time, I was often asked if I was from the island. My uncles living there with their families no longer identified themselves as islanders but classified themselves as Labradorians, often ignoring the fact that they were "come-from-aways" who had intruded on the Aboriginal populations living there.

Newfoundlanders have a history of moving away from the island. My uncle John, as a young man, travelled to Boston to take up work building high-rise structures of steel, while three other uncles moved to Labrador to work on an American base. Newfoundlanders continue to leave the island to find employment opportunities elsewhere, setting up house away from home.

When people I knew started to move away, I began to think more about travelling. My first plane trip was when I was sixteen years old and went to visit my sister who had moved to Ottawa. Over the years, I developed a strong desire to travel which I nourished whenever time and finances were available to me.

I began to be aware of my deeply embedded provincial identity as a result of my extensive travels and the opportunities I had to meet people from other countries. I spoke to them of being a Newfoundlander first and a Canadian second. Meeting fellow Canadians supported and strengthened my developing provincial identity while educating me about the stereotypical notions of Newfoundlanders embedded in the national psyche. Before that time, I wasn't aware of how deeply held these images were or how they affected the ways I was perceived by others. In this chapter, I will try to make sense of the impact my identity as a Newfoundlander has had on my everyday experiences, while recognizing that pieced together with my provincial identity is that of a White, middle-class, heterosexual woman, sister, aunt, friend and educator.

Provincial Identity

> Many differences among us are linked to our historical beings, living in particular places at particular times, subject to particular interpretations of our physical characteristics and activities. (Spelman 1988: 12)

My dictionary lists two definitions of "provincial": ... 1. "relating to, or coming from a province.... 2. limited in outlook: NARROW b: lacking the polish of urban society: UNSOPHISTICATED." The first definition relates to the straightforward declaration I make when others ask (and often even when they don't), "Where are you from?" and I inevitably reply "Newfoundland," adding Canada as an afterthought when I am outside the country. I declare my provincial ties loudly. The second definition matches my memories of hearing people described as having an "island mentality," having limited knowledge of the world, being set apart from the rest. Both definitions inform my identity. The latter definition relates closely to stereotypical images of Newfoundlanders held by others in the country and sometimes by Newfoundlanders ourselves. Media representations of Newfoundland and Labrador have helped create and support these stereotypes. They continually focus on Newfoundland's poverty, unemployment and dependence on the rest of Canada. Charles Lynch, a *Globe and Mail* columnist, once suggested the island be dragged further out into the Atlantic Ocean and set adrift, that no great loss would be suffered by the rest of the country. I have internalized as well as resisted other's perceptions of who I am. Over time, I have become more aware of my identity as a Newfoundlander and the ways in which that self-identification affects how I understand myself and am read by others.

"You Don't Sound Like A Newfoundlander!"

When I met Tom, an American from Dallas, Texas, in Singapore, I told him I was from Newfoundland. He was really interested in finding out about my home, asking many questions about economy and lifestyle. His interest was genuine. I explained to him how refreshing our talk was compared to conversations I seemed to have regularly with other Canadians I met while travelling. I described to him the typical scenario. I meet people who say they are from Canada. I ask from where and they name a city or province. I say I'm from Newfoundland and they inevitably reply, "You don't sound like a Newfoundlander." He suggested I might be exaggerating the number of times this occurred. Two people joined our table during lunch in the crowded food market. As they settled in, the man turned to us and introduced himself, adding that he and his partner were from Canada, and in Singapore on holiday. I joined the conversation, telling them that I was from Canada as well. Immediately, based on hearing me say two sentences, they both declared in unison, "You don't sound like a Newfoundlander." I kept a straight face but couldn't resist kicking Tom under the table.

I first heard the words "You don't sound like a Newfoundlander" from other Canadians I met as a young woman travelling in foreign countries. I continue to hear similar comments from people I meet in Canada. For a long time I didn't question people who made such a statement, although I always felt uncomfortable hearing it. As I grew older and wiser, I began to ask the speakers what a Newfoundlander sounded like. Often an uncomfortable silence would ensue, maybe a little colour to the cheek and a sputtering beginning of an explanation. "Well, you know!" As I pushed to get a response to my question, inevitably a reference would be made to the comedy group Codco, "This Hour Has 22 Minutes" or the voice of a fisherman on the radio. No one mentioned Clyde Wells, E.J. Pratt or Rex Murphy, our resident Rhodes Scholar who hosts a weekly show on CBC radio. The worst-case scenario was when they'd try to imitate what they thought Newfoundlanders sounded like, obviously believing we all sound the same.

During an earlier period of my life, when I was willing to give people the benefit of the doubt, I would initiate a discussion around accent and dialect, how they differed, suggesting the improbability of all people from one province sounding the same whether that province was Newfoundland or British Columbia. In later years, I would go into a tirade about how you could hear more of the historical Queen's English in areas of Newfoundland than in the heart of London, and might the speakers not need a trip to the east coast for a lesson or two? I attempted to force the speakers to name their stereotypical beliefs, to acknowledge their narrowness and provincialism.

Through my interactions with other Canadians, I began to understand the complexities of this unrehearsed but tip-of-the-tongue statement. When they told me I didn't sound like a Newfoundlander, they were complimenting me. I didn't have to admit to coming from the island. I wasn't provincial-sounding; I spoke standard English. I could "pass" as someone "from away" while others could not.

I think a lot about a friend who described to me some of her experiences while studying at graduate school. She had made the grade, been accepted into a graduate program, had the necessary papers. She had an extensive and successful working career as an educator in Newfoundland. However, she was marked by her use of dialect in everyday speech. She repeated comments made to her indicating that judgements were being made about her based on how she spoke and not necessarily on what she said. She grew up in a small community; I was a city girl. While I was being told I didn't sound like a Newfoundlander, she was often judged negatively because she did.

When considering how Newfoundlanders continue to be judged because of their use of dialect, I think of my father. When I was younger, my father told me about some of his experiences attending first-year university in Newfoundland. I no longer remember all the details, and he is no longer here to ask. However, what I do remember is his description of being taken aside, with others who came from rural Newfoundland, to be taught how to speak properly. When he told me this, I began to understand his practice of correcting my speech, a practice that served to silence me, as well as to develop my understanding of the use of standard English. Many years after, when I began teaching and working in school districts, children were also being told that their spoken language was wrong, in need of correction, substandard. Stereotypes of Newfoundland, for the most part built through media discourse, hide the complexities of the rich cultural, historical and dialectical history of the province and its people, of which I am very proud.

Provincially Speaking

A co-worker meets me in the hallway to let me know that a Newfoundlander has taken a position with the same company as her husband. She explains to me that she doesn't understand a word he says. She says, "He sounds like a real Newfie." I guess that means I don't, that I'm not an authentic representation. I just listen, tired of having the same mundane conversations. I meet her a week later and she explains how the Newfie is losing his accent. She talked to him on the phone the other day and she is starting to understand what he is saying. I respond by suggesting that it seems unlikely this person is losing his accent within a week, that possibly she is starting to pay more attention to what he is saying and not to how he is saying it. She might be the one changing, not him. I stop there, not willing to expend any more energy for the cause.

I wear my provincial identity on my sleeve, understanding that I can resist the stereotyping—push the cause—because of my privilege as a formally educated woman who has learned to speak "properly."

Moving Away

> My main intention is not to argue with the stereotypes but to think about them. (Francis 1997: 5–6)

When I drove across the country to begin graduate studies in Vancouver, I had already been sensitized through my previous travels to the stereotyping specific to Newfoundland, but I had no idea of its depth or implications. Settling down on the west coast was the catalyst that forced me to begin to reflect and theorize, and develop deeper understandings of identity and difference. I was aware of the gender inequities I experienced in my everyday life, but knew I was not marginalized in ways I had witnessed many of my friends to be, specifically those classified as different from the "norm" based on race, class and sexual orientation. I arrived assuming that I would slip into place, easily recognizable as belonging to the dominant Canadian culture. I was prepared for neither the dislocation I experienced from my shift in geography, nor for the realization of how, in Canada, Newfoundlanders have often been ignored and considered "provincial."

The headline of the Vancouver Sun *for August 15, 1995, reads "Newfoundland spends more money on cultural funding than British Columbia." I read this and ask myself, "Why is Newfoundland the headline grabber when this article is about British Columbian support of the Arts?" British Columbia lags behind almost every other province in Canada per capita for cultural funding. So why is Newfoundland given the headline space? The irony that "Even*

Newfoundland invests a dime more per capita than we [British Columbians] do," is not lost on the western population. And neither is the reporter's ignorance of Newfoundlanders' appreciation of the arts and their rich cultural heritage lost on me.

Thought of as different, Newfoundland, the last province to join Confederation, has on occasion been exoticized, the peoples and the culture seen as endangered. When the Canadian Society for Studies in Education was to hold a conference there in June 1997, a number of people explained to me that they were going to go because they had never visited the province and this would be an opportunity to experience the east coast. The conversations included talk of quaint communities, fishing villages, friendly people they would be sure to meet, crafts, pubs, lobster dinners and the different accents people would have. Much of the talk smacked of voyeurism—the "other" province would be brought into view. Newfoundlanders are both laughed at and exoticized depending on context.

My move away from the familiar created the space I needed to recognize the depth to which I was personally marked by culture, history and language. I was able to get to know myself a little better than before and began to uncover the roots of experiences I now claim to be part and parcel of my identity as a Newfoundlander.

Newfie Jokes

My sister has told me that I have no sense of humour because I refuse to encourage the telling of Newfie jokes. Since settling in Vancouver, I have heard more of these jokes than I care to tally. Most times, the telling happens so fast that I have no time to interject and politely state that I would rather eat nails than listen to another Newfie joke. I find it hard to fathom why the telling of Newfie jokes is high on the agenda of people first meeting someone from Newfoundland. Is it supposed to make us feel more at home? I find myself in the awkward position of biting my tongue and marking it down to the speaker's insensitivity. When I had opportunities to state how I felt, I was told to lighten up, that jokes are told about people in all parts of the country. I argue that you can be told a Newfie joke in the remotest areas of Canada but are unlikely to hear a joke whose central character is a stereotypical British Columbian.

When I returned from a visit with my brother in Edmonton last spring, I brought back a Newfie joke he had told at the supper table. I wanted to repeat it (with a little twist) to my hairdresser because he was always trying to get me to laugh at the jokes he told while working on my hair. I vividly remember sitting in his chair and beginning my joke. I had decided to change the laughable Newfoundland bumpkin into a Vancouverite. As I got deeper into the telling, the more irritated I felt. I finally realized that the joke wouldn't work because there was no stereotypical image of bumpkin Vancouverites. The joke worked because it was about a Newfoundlander, whose image anyone across the country could relate to.

While my sister suggests I don't have a sense of humour, I push her to think of the implications of the stereotypes that are reinforced with the telling of these jokes. I ask her to consider what we internalize about ourselves and what the rest of Canada comes to understand about Newfoundlanders in light of these humorous anecdotes. These jokes are tools to mark our provincialism. Although couched in the cloak of "It's only for fun," they are used against us.

Degrees of Connection

I resisted giving up my licence plates when I switched insurance companies. I argued vehemently with the car insurance representative who insisted I had to give up my Newfoundland plates before they would give me new ones for B.C. He didn't understand that he was taking a little bit of home away from me. Of course, later I became aware of the underground market in licence plates and the large collectors' shows where a Newfoundland plate could garner a high price because of its rarity!

My first year living in Vancouver, I decided to drive to Alaska. A friend travelled from Newfoundland to join me. One of my vivid memories of that trip was the number of times my friend corrected me when I told people we met that I was from Newfoundland. She kept butting in and reminding me that I was from Vancouver. I tried to explain to her that I might live in Vancouver at the moment, but that I was from *Newfoundland, and that when people asked where I was from, they were interested in my origins, not just where I was living at the moment. I don't think she was ever really able to understand how strongly I felt about the issue. I chalked it up to the fact that she was a "come-from-away."*

I am not making essentialist claims; my experiences are not necessarily those of other Newfoundlanders regardless of the similarity of our provincial and other backgrounds. There are various degrees of provincial identification. Some people move away from home never to return, while others visit with varying degrees of regularity. Some Newfoundlanders may consciously choose to distance themselves from their provincial roots to escape the impact of well-established stereotypes.

Longing for the Familiar

I get fall fever in Vancouver. I miss the colours the season brings at home in Newfoundland. The trees in Vancouver don't change colour to the same degree. When my west-coast friends talk to me of the impossibility of living in a place like Newfoundland because of the climate, I think of fall and the exciting winters, of what they are missing. I miss the extremes of weather that brought variety to my life, challenges in the everyday. Now, I realize the influence climate has had on shaping my provincial identity—the differences that become apparent as I settle into the west-coast weather.

When I was teaching in Newfoundland and bad weather was reported in the forecast for the next day, I would go to bed with my fingers crossed, wishing for an unscheduled holiday. Snow and sleet would beat against the windows; by early morning, everything would be hidden in a deep white snow. I would turn on the radio at about 6 am and wait for the announcement, anxious as time passed, knowing the chances for a holiday were thinning out. I would huddle in the warmth of my quilt, loving the feeling. Sometimes I would get lucky and be able to stay in my bed. More often than not, I was forced out into the weather anyway.

I was reminded of home during the Christmas storm of 1996. The familiar faces I saw as I walked around the seawall suddenly lost their glaze and became friendly. The storm was so extraordinary that a video recording the event was produced and sold. Everything in Vancouver was buried in snow. Cars were marooned where they had been parked before the storm began—not a new experience for me, but one I had missed.

I pulled on my skis and started my trek around the seawall. Numerous people were out, with family and friends, exclaiming wonder at the winter weather. Some people were on skis, others on snowshoes and some on foot. Everyone was friendly, with many hellos. I was amazed at the difference. While jogging or walking around the seawall, I had seen these same people, but it had often been difficult to catch their eyes, to receive some acknowledgement. I have chalked it up to people being more reserved than I am used to. This storm has pushed me to think about connections between people and climate. How does a harsh or mild climate shape the person? Am I missing challenges the weather produced for me in the east? Does climate shape identity? I'm beginning to think yes.

I long for things familiar—family and friends send me care packages filled with my favourites that are hard to find in the West. I receive peanut butter kisses and peppermint knobs made by Purity Factories, and partridgeberry jam. I read books such as Bernice Morgan's *Random Passage*, which I recommend to friends over Annie Proux's *The Shipping News*, stressing that a Newfoundlander has written the former.

For my graduation party, I had a cake baked in the shape of a puffin resting on a map of the island of Newfoundland. To have a piece, each person had to provide a location in Newfoundland. Most people were able to remember the humorous and unusual names of places—Come-by-Chance, Hearts Desire, Hearts Content. When I travelled to Hadai Gwaii, Queen Charlotte Islands, to teach, I was delighted to find a gigantic wooden, yellow-tufted puffin perched in front of a gift shop.

During the Vancouver Film Festival, I went to see "An Extraordinary Visitor," a full-length movie filmed in Newfoundland, whose actors and scenery were familiar to me. During the film, the infamous Mary Walsh (of "Codco" and "This Hour Has 22 Minutes") announced that she was "as crooked as sin." Her declaration took me back to the times when I had first arrived in Vancouver, when I would speak those words without realizing they were not commonplace here. Over the last few years, I have used this phrase and similar everyday Newfoundland phrases less often. The movie is full of familiar streets, houses and beautiful scenes of the harbour at night. I scan seats checking to see if there are any faces I recognize. I know the room is full of Newfoundlanders when many laugh at a reference to Fort Pepperal—a reference only those very familiar with St. John's could possibly know.

Nothing Much Changes

I keep hoping that the powerful image of the stereotypical Newfoundlander will diminish. Newfoundlanders living in B.C. and elsewhere in Canada clearly contradict the images often held by others and ourselves. However, my experiences tell me change is hard to come by.

May 1998: The bookseller at a conference in Ottawa is selling Joey Smallwood's Encyclopaedia of Newfoundland. *I tell him I'm from Newfoundland and he replies, "You don't have to apologize for it" and continues on talking about book prices. I'm silenced and leave, too angry to respond.*

May 1998: I begin teaching a university course. Individuals in the class take turns introducing themselves. I give them a little of my history. After the class, two of the students tell me, "You don't sound like a Newfoundlander." When I ask them what a Newfoundlander sounds like, I again get the usual focus on media representations. My comments make them defensive. They suggest that nothing is meant by that comment, rather than engaging in an examination of what they have said.

September 1998: While attending a university meeting where I identified myself as coming from Newfoundland, an individual approached me and commented, "When you were speaking I couldn't hear any accent like the Newfoundlanders I've heard on the television."

Hopeful Signs

September 1998: I listen to the last section of the CBC *"Out Front" radio program. Questions like "What is a Newfoundlander?" and "What is a Mainlander?" are being discussed. Is the difference between the two a question of geography? The speaker focuses on different circumstances—the person born in Newfoundland who moves away as a child and then returns, the person who settled in Newfoundland over twenty years ago. How long do we have to live somewhere before it is home? It is surprising yet comforting to hear this discussion on national radio.*

September 1998: During an interview on CBC *radio, David Suzuki speaks of the tremendous life force of the Atlantic salmon. I think a similar life force, of energy and strength, can be observed in many Newfoundlanders, most of whom will never be on television or radio, and who contradict the stereotypes that persist. Suzuki suggests that the Atlantic salmon are moving into the oceans of the West; they need to be taken seriously because "their power to survive makes them incredible predators." Is a similar warning in order for those individuals who continue to construct stereotypical images of Newfoundlanders?*

September 1998: While sitting at my computer writing this chapter, I receive a phone call from my sister in Newfoundland. She says she has a surprise for me. All I need to do is sit back and listen to a recording she has made. I hear a man's voice introducing the play my twenty-year-old niece wrote during her first year at York University. Sarah received high praise and awards for the one-woman show she wrote, produced and acted in. When in Newfoundland this past summer, she presented her play to a home audience. My sister had recorded the opening monologue in which my niece describes her initial experiences at York University. The opening line in her monologue refers to her irritation with being constantly told, "You don't have a Newfie accent."

My niece has no idea I am writing about similar experiences. We've never talked about these things. I am anxious to speak to her, to find out her thoughts, to ask how she deals with her irritation and disenchantment. Does she feel the same dislocation? What of her provincial identity? Does she miss the same things I do? To talk across the years would be exciting. I think of this as a sign. If my niece is also concerned about making Newfoundland stereotypes visible, then maybe so are others her age. Maybe things will change through their efforts.

22

Beyond Breaking the Silence

CATHY VAN INGEN

> It is true that putting people into categories like "gay" oppresses or at least limits them, but it is also true that it gives them power and political cohesion, that it strengthens their collective resolve to fight back against homophobic campaigns to strip them of their basic civil rights (Harris 1998).

In 1998, I was attending my first gay pride rally in Edmonton when I heard about a national survey (Samis and Goundry 1998) being conducted on the experiences of Canadian lesbians, gays and bisexuals. This seemed auspicious, since two months earlier the Supreme Court had ordered Alberta to protect gays and lesbians from discrimination. My partner and I each picked up a survey to fill out later. Answering it, I realized that the questions framed many of my own experiences within homophobia and raised important issues I would have to negotiate in the future. In this chapter, I want to explore some of these questions, as they reflect injustices that sexual minorities face while living in a homophobic society. I want to discuss the ways in which lesbian identity and sexuality are denied and continue to be silenced even after an individual's "coming out."

When I write about sexuality and homophobia, I write as a graduate student who has access to certain bodies of literature, theoretical framings and notions of sexual identity, and as a lesbian who has access to my own situated knowledge and lived experience as a member of a sexual minority group. All of these ways of knowing inform and shape my understanding of sexuality. Filling out the survey was a deeply personal experience, as it required that I reflect on the ways in which my sexuality has been silenced, regulated and all too often ignored.

I want to begin by discussing the value of such a survey being undertaken in the first place. This survey is called the "First National Survey of Lesbians, Gay Men and Bisexuals in Canada." It was funded by several departments of the Canadian government, the national organization EGALE (Equality for Gays and Lesbians Everywhere) and the Canadian Human Rights Commission. This survey is significant, as it is the first time gay, lesbian or bisexual Canadians have had the opportunity to share their diverse experiences. The Canadian Census does not address sexual orientation issues or same-sex relationships, so little has been known about our experiences. The information from the survey will be used to inform advocacy groups, the government and the courts to act on issues that affect the lives of queer people in Canada.

The existence of a national survey like this raises several questions. Is it necessary to survey gays, lesbians and bisexuals exclusively? Why is sexuality such a focus? Isn't this survey defining gay and lesbian individuals almost entirely by their sexuality? Why isn't homosexuality accepted in the same way that heterosexuality is, instead of being recognized as a moral issue on which everyone is usually expected to voice a vehement opinion? There is more to lesbians, gays and bisexuals then sexual orientation, but we live in an overwhelmingly homophobic culture where gays, lesbians and bisexuals form a minority group—a sexual minority.

Collecting information of this kind is an important first step in tracing some of the inequities that profoundly affect sexual minorities. But what is more important is that the survey provides an opportunity to discuss ways heterosexuality is assumed to be a "neutral or unmarked form of sexuality" and the ways same-sex desire is regularly problematized and marked as deviant (Jagose 1996: 17).

Questions of Identity

Filling out this survey gave me an opportunity to reflect on my personal experiences and it highlighted several things for me. I am extremely fortunate that I have not been exposed to some of the acts of intolerance and discrimination addressed in the survey. My experiences are a reflection of the fact that I am a member of a largely invisible minority group, and they are mediated by the fact that I hold membership in several groups that hold significant power in society: I am White, from a middle-class background and able-bodied. My "identity" as a lesbian in Alberta and Canada, and my experiences with equity, inclusion, privilege and oppression, are all mediated by membership in these identifiable groups. Although homophobia impacts on many of my social interactions, I do not face the same kind of discrimination faced by people from other racial or social backgrounds.

Several axes of difference other than sexuality are involved in framing my identity, including gender, race and class. Yet, simple acknowledgement of these cultural markers is not enough. Stating which identity categories I inhabit only provides a shopping list of my "multiple identities." None of these categories is insignificant, and each needs to be understood as possibly participating in the legitimization of oppressive social practices. For example, my Whiteness allows me to discuss my experiences with homophobia without discussing the ways in which my sexuality is also raced. My Whiteness is unmarked and, being a culturally created category, is falsely naturalized. Queer theory offers a theoretical framework that unpacks the complicated process of identity formation. Within this framework, "differences" are reconceptualized in a way that reveals how they are divided, hierarchized and enforced.

Queer theorist David Halperin explains how "others" are conceptually produced through binarisms like heterosexual/homosexual: "Each consists of two terms, the first of which is unmarked and unproblematized—it designates "the category to which everyone is assumed to belong" (unless someone is specifically marked as different)—whereas the second term is marked and problematized: it designates a category of persons whom *something differentiates* from normal, unmarked people" (1995: 44). Postmodern understandings of identity demand that normative, unmarked identity categories be challenged. Exposing the privileged invisibility of heterosexuality is necessary in order to resist and denaturalize normative understandings of sexuality.

All identity categories are inherently risky, yet identity categories such as "gay" or "lesbian" have very real material effects. Being "lesbian" is not a stable, fixed identity, although that is what is often understood. The work I am engaged in as a graduate student involves framing identity as a performance rather than as coherent and unified.

Thus, my identity is always incomplete since "it is a process rather than a property" (Jagose 1996: 79). Within a post-structuralist climate, all assertions of identity are problematic. Using this theoretical lens enables me to explore sexuality not as "an essentially personal attribute but an available cultural category" (Jagose 1996: 79). This rather simplistic and hurried explanation is given here to explain that same-sex desire has

been traditionally framed in specific cultural formations and that significant limitations arise when "lesbian" is used as an allegedly universal term. It is not my intention to further the reification of any single lesbian identity. Rather, my intention is to show the work required to enforce the cultural category "lesbian," based on my own experiences.

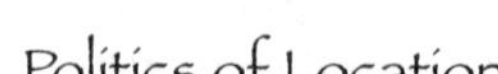

Politics of Location

Homophobia informs the lives of all sexual minorities. However, it is important to acknowledge that significant regional differences in Canada create vastly different climates for sexual diversity. This "politics of location" plays an important role in determining what types of support and legal protection are available. For instance, Alberta is known as a province highly intolerant towards lesbians and gays. Other provinces, such as Ontario, have more inclusive provincial legislation. In larger urban centres, such as Toronto, gays and lesbians have claimed public spaces; "gay ghettoes" provide spaces for the formation of gay organizations, for increased security and for contact, pleasure and the celebration of queer lives. Queer spaces such as Toronto's gay village are important because they offer representations of queer experience and imagery; there, memorials, public spaces and billboards depict aspects of queer lives that which are virtually invisible outside of these communities. However, despite these progressive locations, lesbians and gays continue to face discrimination and intolerance. Regional differences form only one thread in the complex fabric of discrimination and oppression.

Questions on the national survey ask about the ways that geography impacts upon and informs my sexual identity. Several answers to survey questions reflect where I live in Canada. The forms of discrimination that I record are often rather subtle. They are the daily and insidious reminders that I am an "other" and that I repeatedly have to negotiate my presence because of my sexual orientation. My answers reflect the expectation that I separate the public and private in my life in ways heterosexuals don't have to. As I read the survey, I thought about how the issues I face and will face in the future are mediated by geography and social climate. On this basis, I wonder: Will my partner and I be entitled to the same employee benefits that heterosexual couples access? Will I be able to designate my partner as the beneficiary of a pension plan? Will I be denied visitation privileges to my partner in a hospital, or access to information from a hospital? Will the neighbourhood I live in be safe and accepting? Will my relationship ever be legally recognized in the way that heterosexual marriages are?

In Alberta, only since April 2, 1998, have gays and lesbians been protected under provincial human rights legislation. The Canadian Supreme Court ordered Alberta to protect gays and lesbians from discrimination and ended a seven-year court battle to insert the words "sexual orientation" into Alberta's *Individual Rights Protection Act.* The case involved Delwin Vriend, who was fired from his job at a post-secondary institution because he was gay. After winning the case, Delwin said, "I think it is extremely shameful that the government of Alberta kicked and screamed and whined for the last seven years all the way to the Supreme Court in an effort to ensure that discrimination against gays and lesbians continued" (Laghi and Makin 1998). The discrimination that Delwin was referring to in Alberta included job loss, being denied housing or being evicted without notice from rental accommodations, failure to recognize relationships, violence and gay bashing, and many other acts of discrimination.

Of course, the formulation of legislation that condemns discrimination based on sexual orientation does not ensure equality. Several individuals and organizations continue to create a climate of intolerance. After the court ruling, a spokesperson for the Canada Family Action Coalition stated that, "By every objective measure—economic income, cultural influence and political clout—Canada's homosexuals are a privileged, even pampered community, carrying none of the natural burdens of families" (Laghi and Makin 1998). Statements like these send a dangerous message that it is permissible and even acceptable to discriminate against gays and lesbians. The belief that homosexuals receive "special rights" continues to fuel homophobia, hatred and intolerance.

Since the *Vriend* decision, government departments have been asked to review how it impacts upon provincially administered laws. As the courts continue to make decisions to protect lesbians, gays and bisexuals, the provincial government continues to resist. It is now promoting the concept of "legislative fences." This involves changing Alberta laws to exclude lesbians, gays and bisexuals so the province will not have to follow court decisions. If these "legislative fences" are created, then each law would have to go through the courts individually to be challenged. The intolerance towards lesbians and gays in Alberta is, in no small way, attributable to the practices of the provincial government.[1]

Respected Prejudice

Homophobia has accurately been called the most respected of prejudices (Wilton 1995). Indeed, intolerance toward sexual minorities is tolerated and encouraged in Canada in several ways. Lesbians, gays and bisexuals are often excluded from receiving basic civil rights. For example, in Prince Edward Island and the Northwest Territories, discrimination against gays and lesbians is still not prohibited in human rights legislation. One basic privilege of heterosexuality is the right to marry, yet this right is denied in every gay and lesbian relationship in Canada. The first time the issue of same-sex marriage was the subject of a vote in the House of Commons was in June 1999, when the vote was overwhelmingly (216–55) in favour of a motion opposing same-sex marriage (EGALE 1999). In many parts of Canada, employee benefits are not granted to same-sex partners, medical decisions cannot be made on behalf of a same-sex partner and adoption by same-sex couples is not allowed. Does our culture single out any other minority group in such an overt and systematic way?

Although the federal government has been slow in introducing comprehensive laws to recognize queers and our relationships, many important steps have been taken to secure legal recognition. Quebec became the first province in Canada to change the definition of "spouse," in thirty-nine provincial laws and regulations, to ensure common-law status. British Columbia recently added new same-sex laws and already provides for equality in same-sex adoption, spousal support and pension benefits (EGALE 1999). Although many inequities remain entrenched in Canadian law, persistent efforts are being made to establish protection from discrimination based on sexual identity.

Homophobia is pervasive and operates not only through civil law, cultural representations and institutions but also informally in personal relationships.

My Own Homophobia

My responses to the survey would have been vastly different three years ago. I doubt that I would have even felt comfortable picking up such a survey, let alone responding to the questions. Like many other gays, lesbians and bisexuals, I had internalized dominant homophobic values. I had learned to loathe homosexuality long before it became necessary to acknowledge my own. I never had an opportunity to develop a positive understanding of same-sex relationships, because I had grown up in a culture where prejudice and homophobia are a matter of course. My values and understanding of homosexuality flowed from my experience within a heterosexist culture. Exclusion, devaluation and stereotyping informed my understanding of "queers." My parents, my church and the mass media told me, both directly and indirectly, that homosexuality was deviant and immoral. Thus, my own homophobia was cultivated early in life.

It is only through my own struggle with homophobia that I have come to understand the complexity of oppression. Within the last few years, I have become increasingly aware of the way homosexuals and bisexuals are often obliged to live in silence. This need for secrecy comes in part from not being entitled to the same social recognition and resources as heterosexuals. It is "normal" to grow up without any knowledge about gay and lesbian history or the gay rights movement. Sexual minorities, like other oppressed groups, have been almost entirely ignored by historians, educators and textbooks.

When to Tell: "Coming Out"

One section of the survey, entitled "Outness & Self Censorship Issues," asks questions that deal with being "out" about being gay, lesbian or bisexual. The response choices for this section range from being "Totally out" to "Not out at all." The number of questions and range of possible answers highlight how complicated sexuality is in our culture. Can you imagine a straight individual having to "tell" others that they are heterosexual? Yet, just about every gay, lesbian or bisexual individual has to negotiate coming out to their mother, father, brother(s), sister(s), other relatives, children, friends, neighbours, doctors, co-workers and many others.

Coming out is a difficult process. There are even those who question why it is necessary to tell anyone at all (this question is most typically asked by a straight person). Isn't sexuality something private and personal? One of the most common statements I have heard in discussions about sexuality is that gays and lesbians make such an issue about the fact that they are homosexual; most also say they have no problem with homosexuals as long as they keep their relationships private. Yet, all one has to do is turn on the radio or TV, watch a movie or open practically any magazine and one will be flooded with representations of heterosexual relationships. After winning a sporting event, such as the Grey Cup, it is common to see the athletes hug their opposite-sex partners in celebration. Yet, after winning Wimbledon, Martina Navratilova was criticized for hugging her female partner. There are very clear boundaries, both overt and covert, in place for gays and lesbians. What is socially or legally tolerated between heterosexual couples is often violently suppressed when it comes to same-sex couples. The obligation for secrecy is often brutally unequal for sexual minorities.

Coming out as lesbian is a continuous process. Every time I develop a new friendship or join a new sports team, I have to negotiate telling all over again. And, even after you do break the silence and "come out," there is still incredible pressure to blend into straight culture. There are still many silences after "coming out." Yet, many people seem to believe that the visibility of being "out" and routinely declaring a lesbian identity will successfully neutralize homophobia. This approach is flawed—other visible differences such as race or gender have not eliminated racism or misogyny. While it is important that lesbians and other sexual minorities insist on the right to be themselves in public, it is also important to realize that visibility itself will not be enough to denaturalize the cultural forces that seek to control and regulate our "difference" based on desire.

David Halperin (1995) draws on the work of Michel Foucault and

Judith Butler to argue that homophobia cannot be refuted but only resisted. Liberationist strategies such as voicing previously denied and silenced lesbian and gay identities and sexualities are not an effective means of challenging homophobia. Halperin elaborates on the contradictory notion of "coming out":

> To come out is precisely to expose oneself to a different set of dangers and constraints, to make oneself into a convenient screen onto which straight people can project all the fantasies they routinely entertain about gay people, and to suffer one's every gesture, statement, expression, and opinion and to be totally and irrevocably marked by the overwhelming social significance of one's openly acknowledged homosexual identity (1995: 30).

Indeed, "coming out of the closet" can be an important personal act, but it does not address all of the discursive structures that determine the production of sexual meaning. The act of coming out needs to be carefully negotiated.

When Not to Tell: Concealing and "Passing"

Despite the fact that I am "out" to my family and friends, there are still times when I continue to conceal that I am a lesbian. For example, when house or apartment hunting, my partner and I are careful not to reveal our relationship when we feel that a homophobic response from a landlord might prevent us from being offered a place to rent. At job interviews, I am careful to word my responses in a way that will not reveal my relationship and possibly prevent me from a job opportunity. However, the most common time I conceal my sexuality is when I am in a public place with my partner. I find the most routine forms of discrimination the most intolerable, because they become a daily reminder that I am an "other" and am expected to be closeted in public. Displays of affection between two women or two men, such as holding hands or kissing goodbye in public places, is often seen as an act of public defiance rather than as a simple expression of affection between two people.

The survey asks a series of questions that focus on experiences with discrimination when someone knows or suspects I am lesbian. Questions are asked about situations related to housing, accessing public services, and situations at school or work. The forms of discrimination included range from name-calling, being refused service in public facilities and being discouraged from discussing issues related to sexual orientation at work to being physically assaulted. Considering all the forms of discrimination that sexual minorities can and do experience, it is easy to understand why some gays and lesbians "pass" themselves as heterosexuals. "Passing" is done for a variety of reasons—because of our own internalized homophobia, other people's homophobia, to keep jobs or to avoid the very real dangers posed by intolerance and hatred such as verbal, physical or sexual assault. But the security attained by "passing" is fragile and often illusory because being lesbian, gay or bisexual remains taboo.

Violence is an important reason why sexual identities are concealed. The survey asks questions about violence committed by strangers and by people who are known to the person, and about violence within same-sex relationships. The responses reveal the continuum of violence that exists—from homophobic slurs and threats to physical and sexual assault and property damage. Such incidents can occur virtually anywhere: at school, work, on public transit, in a recreation facility or bar, in gay-friendly or non-gay-friendly environments.

The fact that I am not easily identifiable to the general public enables me to conceal my sexual orientation in public places. And my partner and I do not hold hands and walk down the street together in Edmonton out of fear of reprisal, but I, like many of my friends, would love to feel safe enough to do so. In a heterosexist culture, simple actions can place you at risk. I would have vastly different experiences with discrimination if I were completely out. But even not doing anything explicitly queer does not prevent discrimination and verbal or physical harassment. I have several friends who have been subjected to homophobic slurs while simply walking down a street in Edmonton. They were presumed to be lesbian and therefore became targets. Discrimination and the threat of violence persists and the safety attained by "passing" is indeed very fragile.

Negotiating Other People's Responses

The survey also asks how other people respond to my partner and our relationship, another area of questioning that demonstrates heterosexual privilege. The first two questions focus on my parents. I find it difficult to find the response that best fits my parents' attitude and feelings about my relationship. Before I came out to my parents, my mother collected information about homosexuals from newspapers and magazine articles. She was active in organizing a petition to the Supreme Court to keep lesbians and gays out of the *Charter of Rights and Freedoms*. I knew my parents would never accept my relationship. My parents now know that I am a lesbian and they know my partner, but they believe our relationship is inherently wrong. When I came out to my parents, they told me that they still loved me, but that one day I would stand before God to face judgement and be held accountable for my *choice*. Why is it that no one chooses to be heterosexual but they just are, and that anyone who is gay or lesbian has supposedly chosen homosexuality?

I have two sisters who have had very different responses to my relationship. One sister has been very accepting, fully supportive and happy that I have found someone I want to share my life with. My other sister's reactions have closely mirrored my parents'. There is always tension when my partner and I are at family gatherings. My second sister has let me know that she has already told her three children that homosexuality is a sin. My nieces were eight, six and four years old when they began to learn that same-sex relationships are wrong. They have not been told that their aunt is a lesbian yet; my family would like that to remain a secret for as long as possible. My partner and I have been asked not to display any affection for each other in front of my nieces. We are also not allowed to be with my nieces without another (straight) adult around. Before my sister knew that I was a lesbian, I was asked to be a godparent; now I am treated like I am someone potentially harmful.

One of the questions asks how other relatives outside of my immediate family respond to my relationship. All of my relatives know, and most of them have also met my partner. They have been quite accepting of our relationship. My partner feels welcomed and is included in the same way that other "in-laws" are. In fact, most other people in my life, both gay and straight, have been very accepting of my partner and our relationship. Having to consider and respond to other people's acceptance or disapproval of their sexuality and relationships is something that gay, lesbian and bisexual people have to deal with on a regular basis. But heterosexual privilege protects straight people from having to negotiate how other people respond to the same areas of their lives.

Beyond Breaking the Silence

In the introduction, I discussed some of the issues raised by the survey of lesbians, gays and bisexuals. In closing I would like to return to this discussion.

Is it necessary to survey the queer community as a group? Yes, because the voices of lesbians, gays and bisexuals have largely been overlooked, denied and rejected, and the importance of these voices cannot be overlooked. Audre Lorde (1984) describes transformation of silence into language and action as an important step in self-affirmation. Breaking the silence surrounding the lives of lesbians and gays alone is not enough to effectively challenge homophobia and heterosexism, but this survey allows lesbians, gays and bisexuals to address important issues that impact on their lives in different ways. As a minority group, our experiences have long been submerged and unacknowledged, and omission has been a powerful tool of oppression.

Why is sexuality such a focus? Doesn't the survey define gay and lesbian individuals almost entirely by their sexuality? These are interesting questions because they suggest an attempt to silence the representation of gays and lesbians. Lesbian, gay and bisexual people have been discriminated against and oppressed entirely because of their sexual orientation. The survey puts the lives of lesbians, gays and bisexuals front and centre, instead of relegating sexual orientation to the periphery. In doing so, the survey illuminates the pervasiveness and complexity of homophobia and heterosexism in our culture. The oppression of gays and lesbians is complex and the survey allows the airing of multiple voices and experiences.

This survey is one important step in addressing and challenging the oppression and marginalization of members of the queer community. The questions in the survey reflect distinct forms of oppression that lesbians, gays and bisexuals face. It is imperative that these questions be asked. It is important that lesbian, gay and bisexual Canadians continue to break the silence and expose injustices and discrimination that are often tolerated and accepted as normal, and in doing so expose the "work" required to sustain this discrimination. Breaking the silence is just the beginning.

The "First National Survey of Lesbians, Gays and Bisexuals in Canada" provides one way to track some of the inequities that impact on the daily lives of queers in this country. Other steps need to be taken to ensure the denaturalization of dominant understandings of sexual identity. Perhaps the real value of this survey lies in its potential to frame the multiple ways that lesbian, gay and bisexual identities are produced as "different," thus exposing conditions that maintain heterosexual privilege.

Equity, Diversity and the Politics of Difference

23

Talking Equity
Taking Up Differences in the Classroom[1]

Didi Khayatt

On Saturday, October 24, 1998, the *Toronto Star* ran a front-page story entitled "How 28 bar exam failures became lawyers." The story outlines the decision of the Law Society of Upper Canada to license twenty-eight young lawyers who failed the bar exam. Although the decision to pass them was based on a 42–2 vote, the *Star* presented it as extremely controversial. It turns out that the law society, to mark its two-hundredth anniversary, had "committed itself to making the ranks of Ontario's lawyers as diverse as its people—to include more minorities, aboriginals and the under-represented." While the treasurer of the society called the decision "leadership," others called it "politics." The whole of this rather long article was devoted to the controversy that ensued. Who exactly failed the exam but were licensed is not specified but the *Star* reflects on a longstanding concern of the law society's that "'a disproportionate number' of students who fail the bar admission exams are 'aboriginal, visible minorities and students from the French language division.'" Whether this gesture was justice or politics, what is important to note is that, although we know only that a concern was articulated regarding the above-mentioned people, the *Star* assumed that all twenty-eight of those who failed belong to one of the groups named. An entire year's worth of graduates who are Aboriginal, French or people of colour are thus tarnished by this article, even though the *Star* stresses that we do not actually know who failed. And it is only in the last paragraph that York University law professor Camille Lee is quoted as saying: "There are many white Bay Street lawyers who failed the bar admission course and were subsequently admitted to the bar. These white beneficiaries were not made to feel inferior" (1998: A25).

My problem with this newspaper article is not the controversy presented as by the *Star* but the nuances and the assumptions it leaves hanging in the air: that people of colour, Francophones and Aboriginal peoples are somehow unable to measure up, but for political reasons it is necessary to pass them without merit. It is no wonder that those deemed "special interest groups" by those in power are often perceived by Joe and Jane public as always getting something for nothing! At no point in the article is there any mention that sections of the examination may have been irrelevant to these people; nowhere does it mention that there may have been difficulties with the language of the examination; at no point are we advised whether there are any law-school resources or supports for students whose first language is not English. It is important to remember that tests, like knowledge, have a history, perspective, objective and political agenda, all of which are hardly ever made known to those being tested.

The issues generated when testing is used without reference to the context of those being tested remind me of when I was admitted to the American University in Cairo at age sixteen several decades ago. I had just passed my General Certificate of English examinations and was accepted by that university. It is an entirely American institution right in the middle of Cairo: American professors teaching out of American textbooks about American subjects. Although my education had already been almost entirely in English, it was British culture with which I was most familiar. My first contact with the American University was an intelligence test administered *after* students are admitted. I arrived in plenty of time for this test about which I knew nothing, found a place in a classroom of fifty mostly young Egyptian students and sat down. We were informed that there was no passing or failing this test. The stern-looking professor administering it asked us to divest ourselves of our belongings since they would provide us with everything we would need. We all complied and papers were distributed. We were told not to touch them. Pencils were given to us and we were asked not to touch them. The professor then explained to us that this was a timed test, that we would be told exactly when to begin, when to pick up our pencils, when to turn the page and so on. Well, if you know anything about Egyptian culture, you know that we are a people who are often nonconformist. We do things our own way, even if not always efficiently. The test began. The first set of questions were general knowledge questions that asked you to identify who discovered or invented what. Easy. I had a vast general knowledge thanks to my mother's insistence that it was important for heavens knows what. "Put your pencils down," shouted the professor forbiddingly. Already? I had only done seventeen out of the twenty questions. I sneaked one more in and put my pencil down. "Turn the page," ordered the professor. We did as we were told. The next test was a series of one hundred sums. I did two or three to show my proficiency at arithmetic and then turned back to the more interesting first page with the general knowledge questions. After several hours of such "odd" games, many of which made no sense or had any relevance to me at the time, the test was over.

In my second semester, I wanted to take Philosophy and was told I could not. My friend Soraya and I had gone to see our advisors and were both told we absolutely could not take our course of choice. We did not think much of it and went on to complete the four years for our B.A., including several courses in Philosophy, and finally we graduated. It is only when we both graduated and received copies of our transcripts that the intelligence test finally surfaced again. Beside my overall average of 81 percent was a small notation that my IQ was 64! I was lucky! Soraya graduated with an overall average of 96 percent, even though her IQ was listed as being in the forties. We both have our Ph.D.s now, she from Berkeley and I from Toronto, but those B.A. transcripts live on to remind us of our "intelligence" level, or perhaps, more accurately, of the absurdity of tests whose contexts are unfamiliar to those taking them.

The above anecdote illustrates my understanding of and approach to issues of equity. I could even claim that my interest in this topic was generated by such incidents in my early life in colonized Egypt. My awareness of social injustices has stemmed from the classed, racialized and gendered positions I have occupied, first in my native Egypt and then as an immigrant to Canada.

Allow me to explain what I mean by "equity" within the classroom. I use this term with my students, regardless of their level of study. Unlike the term "equality," which refers, to a certain extent, to sameness or equivalence, equity allows for individual differences while working toward a goal of social justice for all. Achieving equity can be accomplished mostly through systemic changes, in addition to alterations in individual values and beliefs. Classrooms are part of an educational system and often reflect power structures of the larger institution and of society itself. Within a classroom there are often shifting, sometimes contradictory and always complex relations of power between students and teachers and among students, based on race, gender, sexuality, size, age, ability/disability, access to material possessions and so on. Therefore, to ensure that we are working toward equity in the classroom, we must take all these factors into consideration when selecting our reading, deciding on our assignments or constructing our curriculum. Teaching is always a political enterprise. Knowledge has a perspective, and when we teach particular information, we are bringing together, consciously or otherwise, an historical context, a certain frame of reference, a discourse, an expectation of previous comprehension. We are also leaving out other knowledge. It is this tension between what we choose to teach and what we actually leave out that I call political.

One day I was driving to my university thinking about my impending lecture to student teachers. I was listening to the radio in my car and the discussion was about Thanksgiving—where we got that tradition, why we celebrate it and what it means to us as Canadians. One of the radio commentators reminded listeners that Thanksgiving originated in the United States when the first settlers were facing their first winter. Aboriginal people, seeing the "innocence" of these pioneers, their lack of knowledge of the land and of the severity of the winter ahead, provided them with necessities that would see them through the cold months. On some level, I knew this, although I did not (and do not) know from where or how Canadian Thanksgiving was established. I went to class with the idea of finding out what my students knew about that celebration and how they would deal with it in their classrooms when they became teachers. To my amazement, not a single student mentioned the "Indians" who had helped the White Man through that first winter. All answers centred on "giving thanks to God," recognizing our bountiful nation, turkey, mashed potatoes and stuffing, family, the harvest, the end of fall and so on. After that class I wondered to myself: Had I not been introduced to Celia Haig-Brown's work on Aboriginal education that year, would I have even "heard" that story? Would I have brought it to class? How often had I, up to that point, ever thought of introducing my students to the history of residential schools as part of their foundational knowledge of education? Why is it that I had known more about English and French settlers than I had about the place of Aboriginal peoples in this society? How can I, a recent immigrant to this country, understand the special place the First Nations of Canada occupy when I cannot even place myself in the diversity of populations that have come to live here in recent years?

Several years ago, I wrote an article, later published in Carl James and Adrienne Shadd's book *Talking about Difference* (1994), in which I discussed the intersections of race, class, gender and sexual orientation in an attempt to increase our understanding of these complex representations and identity locations. I told the story of how, as a graduate student in the early eighties, I was learning a sociological method that begins from the experience of women. The discussion in class one day revolved around the term "immigrant women." We were being shown how to begin from the perspective of these women rather than from a sociological category. The debate had been raging for nearly an hour when finally the professor was asked to give her opinion regarding what constituted an "immigrant woman." She smiled and told us that we had an immigrant woman among us, and nodded in the general direction of where I was seated. The gaze of the whole class turned toward me, and I also looked behind me. I had not recognized myself as an "immigrant woman," because, although, as Celia Haig-Brown would remind us, everyone who is not of Aboriginal descent is an immigrant to this country, there is a common-sense understanding of the term that precludes someone like myself—of the upper class, educated and relatively white-skinned—from recognizing herself in that term. As Roxana Ng says:

> In common sense usage, however, not all foreign-born persons are actually *seen* as immigrants; nor do they see *themselves* as "immigrant." The common sense usage of "immigrant women" generally refers to women of colour, women from Third World countries, women who do not speak English well, and women who occupy lower positions in the occupational hierarchy" (as quoted in Khayatt 1996: 78).

I had not seen myself in that term on that day. But, I ask myself, how many people who are White and middle class, and speak either English or French as a first language, ever think of themselves as immigrants, especially if their family has been in Canada for several generations?

When integrating equity into my teaching, I insist that my students trouble or disrupt the taken-for-granted terms, the unarticulated assumptions, the presumed. I ask them to be conscious of their own location in society, for how else would they understand the oppressions or privileges of others? Social location is, by definition, relational, or, as Baudrillard aptly put it, "In the desert, one loses one's identity" (quoted in Rutherford 1990: 10). It depends on the "other" against whom we measure ourselves. I discuss with my students how those in positions of relative social power, who occupy hegemonic locations because of their race or gender or sexuality, remain unnamed. "Eddy is white," says Toni Morrison (1992: 77), "and we know he is because nobody says so." Those who provide us with the standard measure, what I call the "default position" in society— be they White, male, able-bodied, heterosexual or economically privileged—while they do not and do not *need* to name themselves, have the power to define others. Others' identities— as a person of colour, female, lesbian or gay, poor or disabled—provide them with a binary opposite location against which theirs can be established. In other words, the identities of those in power rely on their relationships to those against whom they define themselves. For instance, "masculinity" cannot be valid as a concept without "femininity," since there would be no need to distinguish it; to establish masculinity, you would have to invent femininity. Likewise, "Whiteness" and "heterosexuality" exist because of their presumed yet sometimes unarticulated binary opposites: those "other than White" and those who are "homosexual." It is those "others" who are measured against the hegemonic position who always come up short, because it is generally not they who are doing the describing and ascribing of characteristics. Consequently, traditionally they were seen as needing to be defined, studied, categorized and reflected upon as "problems": the problem of women, the problem of people of colour, the problem of the disabled and so on. Today, we talk about "issues" rather than problems: the issue of gender (meaning women only—but as I told my class, men have genders too!), the issue of race and ethnicity, the issue of sexuality (again that term seems to apply only to those whose practices are outside of the norm of heterosexuality).

I tell my students that, yes, it is good to have those issues in mind when you teach children, but people are not issues. People do not come in neat little categories, nor do they have but one identity. People are multidimensional, complex beings with identities that shift, grow and change with the context. My students learn to deal with the whole person, who may incorporate a number of the above-named issues, girls who may be both Black and lesbian, for instance. Dealing with issues does not necessarily provide real understanding of what this young person confronts in her daily life, the insults and discriminations, the teasing and taunts. Nor does dealing with issues permit my students to understand that same young girl's joys and triumphs, laughter and accomplishments. Dealing with a young Black lesbian as a set of issues cannot possibly allow us to comprehend that she does not go around in life being one issue at a time: she embodies her gender, race and sexuality always at the same time; it is we who judge or merely observe her who put one or more dimension in the forefront. Those of my students who are truly concerned with making their classrooms inclusive, who look carefully at their curriculum to insert relevant pieces on race, ethnicity and gender, still often manage to obliterate the reality of many of the children they teach. They do not do it on purpose but by presuming knowledge about the children or youths which flattens their differences. In their teaching, they often presume a young student to be male (as in "Why Johnny Can't Read"), they presume Whiteness despite the apparent and observable evidence to the contrary in their respective classrooms, or they presume heterosexuality because acknowledging that their students might be otherwise may be too threatening.

I teach a graduate course called "Feminist Pedagogy." Students often assure me they are not feminist, even though they are taking that course. They say feminists are only interested in girls' and women's issues, and that they want to care for all of their students. They prefer to call themselves "humanists." I have taught that course for six years in a row and every year there is at least one Education student who makes this comment. I have to explain that the term "feminist" in this context refers to a theoretical perspective that acknowledges that our society systemically favours and recognizes one gender over another. Feminism recognizes and, one hopes, works to redress this power differential. It is also a political perspective that considers, through the lens of gender, other diversities than gender, since women come in all races, sexualities, abilities, sizes, ages and social classes. My undergraduate students do not outrightly reject the label "feminist," especially after our discussions in class, but they often inform me that in the "outside world" the term "feminist" is not perceived as positive. They also assure me that when they teach little kids, they love them all equally and they see them all as the same. I question that affirmation: How can they not notice a child is brown, or that she does not speak English very well, or that she is not a boy? These are all markers that define us, that allow us to conform to some social category, whether we like it or not, and thus we are identified by others or identify ourselves.

I went to the dry cleaner's the other day and she recognized me because, although I had just moved into that neighbourhood, I had lately come into the store a number of times. We exchanged names, I learned hers and that she was originally from the Philippines, and I told her my name and that I came from Egypt. "Oh," she exclaimed, "I would not have guessed it. You must have come to this country many, many years ago." This exchange is one I have had numerous times. Consequently, I now understand that it is not my skin colour alone that determines how I am perceived by most people; I think it has more to do with impressions of who I am, based on how I dress, speak, hold myself and so on. These impressions happen as much in the classroom as they do on the street. We are embodied. We are perceived through our gender, our race, our evident access to material goods and our presumed sexuality. Whether we like it or not, our bodies are texts that are read by others and recognized, interpreted, slotted or ignored. Likewise, we look at others and read their bodies as well. We think we can tell a person's ethnicity (cues include names, skin colour, way of dress), gender (we think that might be easy, but we ignore transgendered and transsexual people), language(s), academic ability and possible successes or failures— all from the very first glance. We then refine our presumptions and shift our expectations accordingly. Racism, sexism and homophobia are based not only on our slotting of each individual into a particular race, gender or sexuality, but also on the ensuing assumptions we attach to these categories.

Teaching equity is based on understanding and acknowledging the power relations and politics of the classroom. Many of my students are very well meaning and want to learn how to create a socially just classroom climate. They make sure they call on as many girls as boys to answer questions or complete a chore, they choose with care what books will be introduced to the students, they reflect on the needs of students who are diagnosed as "special," and on the whole they do the right thing. The problems that may arise for them often materialize when their classroom politics are challenged by the realities of their lives: Who will get a job at the end of the year? Will some boards exercise employment equity policies (despite Mike Harris)? and Who will be chosen for what position? If, for example, two students are shortlisted for a particular job and the one who is accepted happens to be brown, the white one who did not get the job seethes with feelings of injustice. Situations of employment equity—what used to be called "affirmative action"—are covered in my classroom because my students are interested in and directly affected by these issues, from hiring to equivalent-pay schedules for work of equal value. It is very difficult to convince most, however, that there is a certain justice in attempting to rectify the very low number of teachers of colour, if only to reflect the racial composition of the student population in Toronto. Most of my students assure me that they believe we have reached a certain modicum of justice in this society and do not need special policies to ensure diversity in the hiring of teachers. They maintain that many women now work outside the home, that women reach all kinds of positions of power and that people of colour are represented in all the professions. And they may even know of gays and lesbians in the teaching profession, though they also know that these teachers tend to remain in the closet. I always remind them to look at the boardrooms and the senior administrative posts in Canada and count how many Aboriginal people they find, or how many women CEOs or senior officials in the top government positions, or how many people of colour are hired to teach in proportion to their numbers in society.

Discussing employment equity in class invariably results in at least one student arguing that they know of a White young man—usually the brother or cousin of a friend—who took a test to become a firefighter or join the police force; that White man achieves an 85 percent average and yet the job goes to a person of colour or a woman who tests lower. I have heard this same story so often that I now come prepared to explain by analogy the justice of that situation, even though I do not quite believe that it actually happens in that way. I ask them to imagine a racetrack where a race will go on for many laps. The inside lane is the shortest distance around the track, and therefore the rules of racing dictate that the starting point of the runners in each lane has to be staggered to make up for the distance gained by being in the inside lanes. Once they have run once around the track, the athletes are allowed to elbow their way into that inside lane. Let us imagine a track where the rules are such that only one relatively privileged group, let us say, for instance, White, middle- or upper-class heterosexual men, are permitted to run on the inside track. They run around unencumbered by any other group, and do so for many rounds, so ultimately, of course, they find themselves ahead of all other groups. Although still competing amongst themselves, they are inevitably winning the race. Imagine all the other people having to run and jostle in the outside lanes, competing with each other, fighting for a chance to run in the lane closest to the inside one but never being able to get into the inside lane. Then let us imagine that, by some decree, the walls crumble between the inside lane and other lanes and everyone now has access to the inside track. The White men have been there for a long time, so they continue to be in a winning position because they know the track, and they help and encourage those who look like they do. When new White male runners join the race after the walls have crumbled, they look at those like them and expect similar privileges, but now they have to compete with all who have been let into the inside lane: women, black, brown and Asian peoples, Aboriginal peoples, disabled people, gays and lesbians and so on. They feel entitled to similar privileges and so question all other competition as unfairly disadvantaging them (for instance, declaring that women or new immigrants are taking their places).

Problems arise because the inside lane is now filled with all kinds of people, and several things happen. First, so many more people are trying to run in the inside lane that not as many of the original group are able to come up ahead except those select few whose connections to the original group are unmistakable. Second, since they have been running in that lane for a long time, the original set of White men are winning in any case, and consequently the new ones assume they are entitled to win too. But they are not doing as well as they would expect because of the relative increase in competitors. Let us also imagine that, since the privileged White men are winning hands down, the new rules would state that, for the sake of fairness, whenever two people finish the race at the same time, if one is from the disadvantaged group, he or she will be deemed to have won the race. Finally, we realize that in this race, even with the barriers to the inside track demolished, the disadvantaged runners can never gain on those who have been running on the inside track for so long, and so we decide to give them some support or encouragement to strengthen their performance, despite the outcry from the advantaged group that this is unfair. It is these two last rules that constitute the "affirmative action" or equity policies that existed for a while in Ontario.

I will not belabour the point of this analogy any further. My students work with it, question it, analyze it, deconstruct it and absorb it to varying degrees, but it does bring home to them how systemic injustice works in our society. It also allows them to comprehend that their ideas of implementing an inclusive curriculum and of being "fair" to all their students is a political stand that has to extend beyond the classroom into the rest of their lives.

After many years of teaching about equity and teaching from a feminist perspective, I find that one of the most difficult topics to broach in the classroom is the subject of sexual orientation. I have written at length about it and am perpetually attempting to find a way to discuss it, even beyond my students' objections that this is not a topic for the classroom. I believe it is. Our sexuality is present in the classroom in the wedding or commitment rings some of us wear, in our talk about husbands, wives and partners, in pregnancies, holiday talk and in other tacit ways. Most often, when I bring up the issue of sexuality, my student teachers are interested but claim they will not be allowed to teach about sex. Sex is taught in the schools, I assure them, only very badly. It is talked about under the rubric of health and hygiene, or in some schools under religious education; we mention sexually transmitted diseases, we teach about protection, and of course, we instruct students about marriage and family values and all these entail. So, we do teach about sex in schools. What we do not mention is sexual desire. My students would argue that this is an inappropriate topic, that they would need to wait to be asked by the children or adolescents, that it makes them uncomfortable, that parents will object, that religious organizations would terminate their contracts, that it would lead to universal teenage pregnancy and so on. They strongly believe that sex as desire is to be left at the entrance to schools, that it should never cross the threshold of their classrooms. This all makes it very difficult to speak about sexual orientation.

What are categorized as perverse sexualities are maintained on the periphery of what is considered normative through factors such as the mainstream media's relative silence, curricular disregard and, more often than not, the failure of those concerned with equity work to recognize that sexuality deserves as much attention as race, gender, ability and class. Consequently, I have made a point of integrating this topic into my courses.

Any mention of sexual orientation brings "homosexuality" to people's minds, as if heterosexual individuals do not have a sexual orientation. Usually, the perception is that heterosexuality is the norm and the problem is homosexuality, and therefore mention of sexual orientation must automatically refer to the problem. My students, however, are not alone in their heterosexism. As with "Whiteness," heterosexuality is the taken-for-granted sexuality, the orientation less discussed because most of the discourse deals with "other" sexualities. Like "Whiteness," heterosexuality is now under scrutiny. Students in my classes are asked to engage and grapple with its history, social construction and normativity.

They are invited to analyze how compulsory heterosexuality functions in our society, what discursive and ideological supports exist, what legal and institutional structures are in place to maintain its hegemony, and how perverse sexualities also have a history and a discourse that categorizes and defines them, and often keeps them extraneous to normative sexuality.

In materials presented to students in classrooms, lectures and lesson plans, the general presumption is that everyone is or will be heterosexual. This is especially so in younger grades where teachers presuppose that students have no sexual desires and may not even know the terms "lesbian," "gay" or "queer" and assume that their teacher is married or soon to be. Needless to say, for a place deemed devoid of sexuality, school culture is rife with often unarticulated desires.

At first in my classes, I used to ask students what they knew about "homosexuality" in schools. It is a subject about which many undergraduates seem to have an opinion but few have much knowledge. Having noticed that any talk of non-normative sexualities produced acute discomfort in my students, I began listening carefully to their objections. Very often their disapproval centred on religious beliefs. I do not quarrel with these, but I do attempt to disrupt their thinking if only for a moment. I ask them, What exactly do you think God hates about homosexuality? Answers range from "It is not natural" to "It is an abomination." Over the years, I have referred to various religious texts so as to be prepared to respond to their concerns, and have noted that, in particular, male homosexuality is discussed in at least three religious traditions. Consequently, instead of bringing up the topic of sexuality in the classroom and causing my undergraduate students to begin the discussion with their objections, I have recently taken to giving them a chance to reflect upon the topic among themselves first. This exercise is a modification of one I learned from my colleague, Deborah Britzman. I divide them into groups of four and assign them four short stories. Each then has to pick a story on which they will lead a discussion and prepare questions. On four consecutive weeks, I lecture and teach for two hours and then ask them to go to their seminar groups to discuss their short stories. They all read the same story, but only one is assigned to present it, lead discussion, and record what transpired. This student then has to write a short paper, describing what went on in the discussion, to hand in the next week. I have found that by the time they have read, discussed and educated each other, they are ready for a class discussion that happens very late in the semester.

The four short stories all concern social issues. One deals primarily with anti-Semitism, the second with fundamentalist Christian narrowness, the third with memory and age, and the fourth with a child who is facing a choice between living with their father or mother after a divorce. Each story has a character who is gay or lesbian. Although sexuality is not the central theme of the stories, it is present and has some bearing on the outcome. My students, invariably, read each text *only* within the framework of sexual orientation. By the third week, they have had enough of that discussion and begin to complain that they covered the subject of homosexuality at length. It is then that I point out to them that they are focusing on one issue, the one they can deal with least, at the expense of all others. Suddenly they begin to read about people, characters who are multidimensional, who are more than the sum total of the issues they embody. Their gaze shifts and often, but not always, their thinking follows.

Understanding and working with equity in the classroom means attempting to incorporate the entire spectrum of differences, looking at people as whole, multidimensional human beings, and not presuming to know how people identify themselves, or assuming comprehension of their particular experiences without asking them about it. It is work toward social justice. It is respect for others, but not at the expense of justice.

The last story I want to share is about teaching an introductory women's studies course several years ago and talking about violence in the home. One young man challenged me with the comment, "In my country, it is within the precepts of my religion that men must beat their wives to keep them in line." There was total silence in the room, and all eyes were on me, awaiting my answer. I felt it was more important not to antagonize the student, by attacking him or what he was saying, than to prove him wrong. I felt my reply had to show respect for the religion to which he was referring, yet point to the injustice perpetuated by those beliefs toward women. I didn't want to threaten the student or put him on the defensive, because it was essential that he remain in the course if he were to change his attitude. I was curt in my answer because I knew to what religion and culture he was referring, and while what he was saying was true, more progressive interpretations of its ancient texts have recognized women's rights. What I said was that our adopted country, Canada, has specific laws that deal with the human rights of individuals and we should abide by those laws. Suddenly the tables were turned because, had he pursued his line of reasoning, his religion and culture would have come across as regressive. He did not want that to happen nor did I want to force him to do that. This student not only continued the course but chose to enrol in other women's studies classes.

Roger Simon suggests that one can practise what he calls "the pedagogy of possibility." I like the idea of equity in the classroom being taught as a pedagogy of possibility. Simon cautions that there are no "abstract or decontextualized answers to the question of which practices constitute a pedagogy of possibility," but he does have some suggestions: "One might begin with a critique of the explicit, implicit, excluded, and unarticulated notions of curriculum, assessing each for its implication in the unjust diminishing of human possibility" (1992: 58). And that is exactly where we must begin.

24

Being Me in the Academy

Maxine Bramble

> Monkey mus know weh him gwine put him tail before him order trousiz" (Bennett 1993: 90).[1]

In September 1990, I entered university, one year after immigrating to Canada in search of educational opportunities not available to me in the Caribbean. I had taken my night school teacher's advice to apply to university as a mature student, rather than wait until I had completed upgrading courses he felt I did not need. I was thrilled when I was accepted to university. Though I did not know what I wanted to study or what career I wanted to pursue, I knew I wanted a university education. The thought of being stuck in my mind-numbing, clerical day job did not appeal to me. I wanted to engage with new and different ideas, to gain more knowledge and to get a degree in something. Since I enjoy debating, I relished the thought of discussing all kinds of issues with students and professors and exchanging ideas with them. University was going to be a place where I would come into contact with different people, develop new ideas and learn new things.

The image of university I had was supported by the information package I received with my acceptance letter. The package promoted the university as a place where students explore issues of personal interest with the guidance of professors, where differing ideas can be expressed and where people's voices are listened to. It seemed to indicate that the university is a place where diversity thrives and where differences in ideas and bodies are accommodated. The package outlined a range of programs and courses available to students and pointed to the possibility for students to create individualized programs based on their own interests. In the orientation sessions I attended in the weeks leading up to the beginning of classes, university personnel spoke of the university as a place that promotes equity and accommodates difference and diversity. They spoke about the increasing diversity of the student population and about programs that have been initiated to respond to this diversity and attract students of different backgrounds. Since I did not have any friends in university and had never spoken to anyone who had attended one, my perception was based largely on this information and the popularly held belief that this institution promotes intellectual engagement with a range of ideas.

I entered university excited at the thought of what lay ahead and ready to take on the challenges I knew I would face there. As a non-White, or, to be more specific, Black, working-class Caribbean woman in a predominantly White, middle-class institution, I knew that there would be obstacles. However, I was unprepared for the dissonance I experienced between the university's apparent commitment to diversity and equity and the way this commitment played out in reality. Although I represent the new kind of body the university has been trying to attract and accommodate, I later discovered that there is little or no space for me to be me in academe because of the contradictions this institution embodies.

The idea of being me in the academy is about inserting the personal—the self—into the academy as a fundamental, recognizable part of the knowledge that is produced and disseminated there. It is about doing work that is personal, work that is related to my ethno-racial community, work that subverts the historical configuration of knowledge in the academy. Such work sees the body as central to the process of knowledge production and positions identity as a central part of one's inter/actions, whether identity is named or not. Moreover, it sees identities as the products of meanings that are ascribed and attached to bodies in social inter/action, as well as the lived experiences of these bodies. Implicit in this is a conception of identity as relational and shifting, fluid, always in a process of change.

What follows is an examination of my experience of academe. I look at the ways in which the university is dealing with the challenges posed by the entry of bodies like mine. Since these bodies bring with them knowledge that comes out of their experiences, they make demands on the university to respond to the differences they embody. In an era of talk about accommodating difference, reflecting diversity and promoting equity, I question the extent to which the university is in fact ready for a range of different bodies and what they represent. My analysis is framed around the following questions: How are questions of equity, difference and diversity taken up in the university? How does the university's understandings of difference, diversity and equity take into account the fact that knowledge is embodied? To what extent does the university really accommodate difference, reflect diversity and promote equity?

"That really wasn't me"

> *In September 1997, I sat in a classroom with eight other graduate students and a professor, in the first session of a year-long seminar. As a standard operating procedure, we each introduced ourselves, including in our introduction information about our background, intended area of interest and the focus of academic work we have done in the past. As I sat listening to the other students' introductions, I carefully planned my own so that I/it would sound articulate. I opted to go last and stumbled through my well-rehearsed introduction in a less than articulate manner. I spoke about my academic background, my previous work on Caribbean sayings and proverbs and about my plan to continue working in this area. Later that day, as I reflected on the seminar proceedings, I remember thinking that the person I introduced and personified in that class* really *wasn't me.* (Bramble 1999:273)

What do I mean when I say that that person really wasn't me? Who was the person I introduced if not me? More importantly, who is this me I think I am?

My feeling that the person I introduced wasn't me is linked to the absence of the personal from my introduction and inter/actions in the first seminar. I introduced myself as if I were defined by my academic interests and background. The identity categories I generally use to define myself were absent. These categories—Black, working-class, Caribbean and, of course, woman—do not constitute all of who I am but are central to my sense of self and the way I experience life. Paul Gilroy's articulation of how Black identity is lived captures the way I live these identities. Gilroy notes that "Black identity is lived as a coherent (if not stable) experiential sense of self" (1993: 102). Hence, I felt that to introduce myself without mention of my sense of self was akin to disembodiment, a kind of disassociation from self that is revealed in the statement, "that … *really* wasn't me." Moreover, I had come to doctoral studies intent on asserting my identity as a Black, working-class Caribbean woman and on marking the academy with my presence, but I did not do this in my introduction. I also planned to enjoy the academic as well as the social aspects of doctoral studies, since I had not enjoyed the two years of my master's degree. Instead, I followed the standard operating procedure and said nothing else about myself apart from speaking about my academic interests and background. Similarly, my colleagues did not reveal any personal information about themselves that I could use to form a social relation outside of the classroom setting. It is no wonder that I socialize largely outside of the university. But I digress.

Clearly the person I introduced was me, but it was me in relation to a particular context—a graduate seminar. Within this context, the identity available for me to assume was that of the "graduate student." To be a graduate student, I had to act as if markers of identity such as race, class, gender, ethnicity and culture were absent, invisible or of no significance to my inter/actions in the seminar. The unstated rule seemed to be: Leave all talk about identity and, by implication, talk about difference out of your discussions because it interferes with intellectual work. How can the university claim to accommodate difference when it asks me to leave my identity at the door before I come in to engage in intellectual activity? It seems to me that the university employs a very narrow definition of accommodation that stops short of acceptance of non-White bodies like mine. So, while I have been granted entry into the university, there is no space for the differences my body represents.

I have found that there is a general unwillingness to raise questions of identity in classes where I am the only non-White student. Throughout the course of the seminar, questions of race and gender were rarely discussed and when they were, we never spoke about the implications of the fact that I am a Black woman and that the others, with the exception of one White male, were all White females. The silence about race and gender and questions of identity is not surprising, given that our introductions in the first class set the tone for the type of inter/actions that would occur throughout the year; we would interact with each other as "graduate students." Even the jokes that we shared and the conversations we had prior to discussing assigned readings focused on things related to academic work. For example, we spoke about upcoming academic conferences and guest speakers, talks we had attended and recently published books or journal articles. No one spoke about family or pets or events we had attended in our own communities. This unwillingness to speak about the self and the larger social issues we engage with daily is probably a matter of personal choice. But I sometimes wonder whether it is related to the fact that Black women (and other historically marginalized people) bring with us discourses that challenge the historical configuration of the university.

One such discourse is that of class, and in particular a discourse critical of the middle-class culture of the university (Gardner 1993). In the seminar this discourse was foreclosed and the fact that bodies are inscribed with class-based meanings was overlooked. I was struck by this, given that in Canadian society, my body marks me as working class on a number of bases. As a Black person, I am seen as working class because of racist stereotypes that portray Blacks as uneducated welfare recipients or blue-collar workers, criminals and the like. As a Black person, I am also perceived as an immigrant (read: "newcomer," "non-

Canadian") because all Blacks are seen as newcomers whether they have been here for seven generations or seven days. Since newcomers tend to be at the bottom end of the socio-economic scale (Porter 1965), and Blacks are perceived as newcomers, I am cast as working-class, even though I may have some of the trappings of the middle class. The same is not true for European (read: White) immigrants, who are cast as "Canadian" even though they may see themselves otherwise. When I speak, my non-Canadian accent identifies me as an immigrant/newcomer, and therefore working-class. While it is still possible to have a non-Canadian accent and be middle- or upper-class, (as is the case with some Hong Kong Chinese immigrants, for example) the reality is that the majority of Black people in Canada occupy working-class status; therefore I am seen as working-class as well. "A recognition of my Blackness and my non-Canadian accent by my colleagues would mean acknowledging not only class differences but the fact that race is classed and class is raced, that race is 'immigrant-ed' and that immigrants are classed" (Carl James, personal conversation, August 1999). This recognition is outside of the parameters set out by the university to understand difference, therefore it could not be imagined.

The assumption within educational settings that class difference is obliterated with education, provides another way of looking at the silence about class. Working-class people are told that they will become equal (read: middle-class) if they get a university education. The fact that my colleagues and I had attained or were well on the way to attaining graduate degrees therefore meant that we were all equal. Thus, for my colleagues, to acknowledge class differences would be to admit that the university's promise of equality does not hold true for working-class people, particularly when our bodies are "raced." Moreover, it would be to admit that we were not equal because of class and other differences we embody. The stark reality is that no matter how much education I receive, as a Black person I will always be seen as working-class because of the social configuration of Canadian society and the meanings attached to my Black body. Yet, the assumption that everyone is middle-class permeates the university, particularly at the graduate level and beyond. This assumption prevents engagement with issues of class difference.

If the university is to promote equity, the recognition and naming of differences is a necessary prerequisite. Yet, in the seminar there was a fear of naming our differences, apart from our differences in opinion on issues raised in classroom discussions. This fear was not unlike the general fear of naming differences (particularly racial differences) that is common in the larger social context. It is not uncommon to hear some White people say that they do not see race or colour, they only see people. It is almost as if they fear they will be labelled that dreaded "r" word—racist—if they acknowledge that they see race or colour. As Ng (1994) argues, there is a common belief that only racists see colour. The failure to name race and other forms of difference suggests that difference is bad and needs to be erased at best, or contained at worse. Thus the university's engagement with difference continues to exclude historically marginalized peoples. But this exclusion is different from the historical exclusion of bodies; it is an exclusion that stems from a failure to critically engage with the differences embodied in bodies.

"Who me? Essentialist?"

Last summer, I took a research methods course that focused on the politics of interpreting data and by extension of interpretation in general. Inadvertently, the issue of identity surfaced in this class. It came up during a discussion on research methods that followed a discussion on the insider/outsider debate about who should study, or is best suited to study, whom. The course director stated that she did not know if there was a difference between feminist research methods and Latina or Black women's research methods, since the research methods that these women use resemble feminist methods. I interjected, arguing that while this may be so, what was important was the knowledge that is produced from Latina or Black women's research. Arguing that knowledge production is situated in the body, I maintained that the knowledge produced by Black or Latina women about their own communities differs ontologically from that produced by researchers who are not from these communities. I went on to argue that as a Caribbean woman, my feeling of Caribbeanness and my knowledge of Caribbean culture influence the way that I employ research methods and interpret data from research with Caribbean people. In response, one of my colleagues, an all-Canadian woman (read: White, middle-class) asked me to define "Caribbeanness." I replied by stating that I did not see a need to define it, but that Caribbean people know and feel what Caribbeanness is. My colleague, who had just returned from the Caribbean where she had been conducting research, then suggested that I was being essentialist. Like so many other times, I wondered why my assertion of difference always seems to unsettle someone. I felt tired of having to engage yet again in the essentialism versus anti-essentialism debate.

My colleague represents the voice of many people I have encountered in the academy who take particular theoretical orientations that allow them to charge others with essentialism. I have been repeatedly accused of being essentialist, particularly when I speak about identity and use categories like "Black women" and "Caribbean women." "What do you mean by "Black women? You are overlooking the differences between Black women," is what I am told. Or "You can't speak about 'Caribbean women,' because there is so much diversity and their experiences are so different that to put them all together masks these differences." Of course, I know that there is diversity among Caribbean women and that our experiences are different. After all, class, race, sexual orientation and a number of other variables work to structure our experiences in different ways. But to argue that I cannot use categories like "Black women" or "Caribbean women" is equally as essentialist, for, as Martin (1994) argues, while such categories do not reveal everything about the people they define, they do not conceal everything about them either. My use of these categories does not assume that identities are fixed, as the charge of essentialism and the often concomitant request for a definition implies. Rather, it assumes difference and diversity, and acknowledges that all categories simultaneously mask and reveal difference and diversity.

Why are charges of essentialism so common in the university? Martin's (1994) argument that the label "essentialist" is often a way of silencing others offers a possible response to this question. She notes that a critique of one's work as essentialist puts a seal of disapproval on it and implies that it is not good. In the current post-positivist era, where "grand narratives" that claim universalism have been dismantled, maintaining what appears to be an essentialist position is the most deadly intellectual sin an academic can commit. Such an offence can have a negative impact on the work White scholars choose to do; and Martin (1994) points out that it can also affect women and other marginalized scholars who take particular theoretical positions. Since many non-White scholars choose to do work related to their ethnocultural communities, these judgements can be debilitating and can discourage us from doing much-needed work on our communities.

Given my argument for the insider research perspective, scholars with research interests in communities other than their own tend to think that I am challenging their academy-given right to conduct research on topics in which they are interested. By doing so, they miss the point of my argument as well as that of the insider/outsider research debate; namely that the body is central to knowledge production. Although the insider/outsider research debate is generally framed in terms of value judgements on the quality of research and the knowledge produced, at heart the debate is about recognizing the body as central to the production of knowledge. The debate is based on the assumptions that there are insiders and outsiders to any group or setting, and that these subject positions (and by implication the experiences they make possible) enable different kinds of research and produce different knowledge. The insider position holds that those who live the experience and are part of a culture—the insiders—know it better than the outsider, who comes in to study that culture and may not be familiar with its nuances. In contrast, the outsider position holds that those who are on the outside are better able to see things that an insider may not be able to see because of the insider's closeness to the setting and the biases that this position engender. My real concern in arguing for the insider position is about the tendency to divorce knowledge and its production from bodies.

My argument for the insider research perspective was part of my assertion of the need for non-White scholars to do research on our own communities. Historically, knowledge about non-White peoples has been produced by outsiders who have access to resources (power) and are given legitimacy, cloaked in the garb of "objectivity." Conversely, when we non-Whites study our own communities, our work is often dismissed as biased by those who do not see themselves as embodying their own knowledge. By arguing for the insider research perspective, I am arguing for an equitable research practice that will see more non-White people having access to resources to study our communities. I am also arguing for knowledge produced by, rather than about, non-White peoples. This does not foreclose the possibility of White researchers conducting research on non-White people, nor does it attach a value judgement on their research. My position calls on White researchers to take the historical reality of knowledge production into consideration. It also calls for an acknowledgement of the strategic use of essentialist categories as a means of mobilizing for change.

I find it interesting that the charge of essentialism and the accompanying anti-essentialist position is popular at a time when universities are grappling with the concept of equity and talking about accommodating difference and diversity. On the one hand, the university recognizes that particular bodies have historically been excluded and is attempting to address this exclusion, yet on the other hand, it fails to recognize that these bodies are imbued with knowledge. Is this a coincidence, part of the natural evolution of theories? I am not sure, but I do know that the fact that universities are grappling with these issues has not come about by chance. It is a testament to the decades of struggle by non-Whites and other minorities for space within the academy. The gains made through these struggles appear to be threatened by those who uncritically champion anti-essentialist positions and denounce essentialist ones.

"Where are the professors to deal with my subject area?"

Towards the end of the first year of my master's degree, I began to look for professors for my thesis committee. Since I had switched topics and had decided to do my research on Caribbean sayings and proverbs, I had to look for different professors than the ones I had previously identified as possible members of my committee. Though my department was one of the largest, there were no Black professors and I could not find a professor with any substantive knowledge of the Caribbean to sit on my committee. I decided to find a supportive supervisor who would be willing to work with me and then look outside of my department for someone who had the knowledge that I needed. I asked a professor—a White male of Caribbean heritage—who I had taken a course with during my undergraduate degree and he agreed to be on my committee. When I approached the graduate program director about it, he informed me that I would have to petition for permission to have this professor on my committee since he felt that I did not require someone with substantive knowledge of the Caribbean to be on my committee. I was dumbfounded by his response as was my supervisor, a White woman, but at least he did not ask me to change my topic to make it compatible with the work of people in the department.

Like many of my female friends who are pursuing graduate studies, I have chosen to do work related to my ethno-racial community. My decision to do this work was as much a political statement aimed at challenging what counts as knowledge and how it is produced, as it was a logical choice. Since my interest is sustained by work linked to something to which I can relate, focusing my research on my own community was an obvious choice. However, as I came to realize during my master's program, it may not have been the wisest choice because of the difficulty that I had finding thesis committee members. This experience is not unique to me but is shared by many of my Black friends; though the females always have more difficulties than our male counterparts. Our research interests are often circumscribed by the possibility of finding a supervisor to work with and departmental policies that limit our choices. We frequently have to work with people unfamiliar with our research topics but supportive of our work. In my experience, not only was this so, but the person who actually supervised my work could not be named officially as the supervisor. While half a loaf is better than none, in an institution that espouses equity, Black women should have the option to choose whether they want half a loaf or a whole one.

For Black women like myself, the university is a site of struggle, a place where we have to fight to get our voices heard, to have our work recognized and to be seen as competent (Carty 1991; Collins 1991; hooks 1993 and 1990). Our struggle is exacerbated by the lack of bodies like ours in the professorate. The absence of Black women professors is especially glaring in Canadian universities. In universities that espouse equity and boast of being racially diverse, very few full-time, tenured, Black woman professors are to be found. If universities truly believe in equity, how is this possible? Why isn't the diversity of the student population reflected in the professorate? Why do I not have the option of working with a Black female professor? Don't get me wrong, I am not saying that a Black female professor is the best person to supervise the work of Black female students, or that I needed a Black female professor to supervise my work. What I am saying is that it is likely that a Black woman professor would have the background or experience necessary to deal with my subject area. After all, knowledge is not divorced from bodies but is embodied in people; therefore a diverse group of people would reflect the diversity of knowledge of the academy.

Thinking of this incident, I am reminded of a statement made by Professor Himani Bannerji at a 1995 forum on minority women in the academy. Speaking about the issue of hiring more minority faculty, she stated that "bodies in space are political." Like Professor Bannerji, I am gesturing to the fact that the presence of Black female professors is a political statement. To Black female graduate students, a Black female body in the professorate is a statement about what is possible; namely, that they too can become professors. At the same time, the absence of such bodies is a reminder of the alienation and exclusion that Black women face in the academy.

The exclusion of Black female bodies from the professorate is compounded by the denial of the relationship between knowledge and lived experiences. In this regard, the notion of what constitutes knowledge and, in particular, theory does not represent the experiences found within a diverse student body. This became clear to me in the first four weeks of graduate school when I sat and listened to professors and graduate students speak about "grand" theories and refer to well-known theorists, most of whom were White males. These theories were wrapped up in complex language and were available in printed form in books, journals and the like. Many of them sounded like the theories that my grandmother used in her everyday interactions, but hers took the form of sayings and proverbs. However, the professor's presentation of theories as those which are housed in books excludes those of my grandmother and the knowledge she passed on to me through her use of sayings and proverbs. In effect, my professor's conceptualization excludes me, because my grandmother's theories are part of the knowledge I bring to the academy.

Let me return to the program director's assertion that I did not need anyone with substantive knowledge of the Caribbean to sit on my committee. Can this be an example of a White male's failure to acknowledge the situatedness of knowledge in bodies? In other words, is it possible that he was saying that the theories embedded in sayings and proverbs are comparable to other mainstream theories, therefore any professor with knowledge of how theories work could conceivably be on my committee? Would this make his response acceptable? While this might make his response more palatable, it certainly does not make it more acceptable, particularly since it fails to recognize and accommodate the difference that my work represents. Moreover, it supports the exclusion of Black professors from university faculties. For, by suggesting that I did not need anyone with substantive knowledge of the Caribbean for my committee, the program director is implying that a Black woman (or Black man, for that matter) who might have this knowledge is not needed in the department. This reflects the inability of the university to understand diversity. Diversity is not only about having Black bodies like mine in the student population, it is about having the resources to respond to these bodies.

Difference Makes a Difference

After completing my undergraduate degree, I enrolled in a one-year teacher education program that would certify me to teach at the elementary school level. I was happy to be part of this program since it espoused equity as its cornerstone and made explicit the notion of diversity. This was the only teacher education program like it around. In the year that I spent in the program, we were immersed in diversity and difference, from the diverse bodies of the teacher candidates and the students in the schools in which we did our practicum, to the slogan "until difference makes no difference" that we adopted. Yet, I left the program disappointed.

My disappointment with the program had to do with the way in which we took up questions of difference and diversity. Throughout the year, our discussions focused on recognizing and naming difference but failed to take into account the socially ascribed meanings of difference and their relations to power. Difference was conceived largely in terms of cultural differences. For example, we spoke about religion, language, food, dress and holidays. Culture was seen as located only in certain bodies—largely non-White bodies—and individuals were seen as representatives of whole cultures. Moreover, differences within cultural groups were collapsed, rendering these groups homogenous, thereby erasing differences. So, we engaged in a process of recognizing differences, only to turn around and erase them. In other words, we dropped the "until" from our motto and seemed to be saying that "difference makes no difference." This way of taking up difference is reflective of the dominant multicultural discourse that permeates the larger Canadian society (James 1999). Clearly, the university is not immune from the effects of this multicultural discourse.

Our engagement with diversity was equally problematic. Diversity was conceptualized in terms of race, gender and, to a lesser extent, sexual orientation. On the odd occasion when we addressed issues of class, they were always overshadowed by race. This is so even though the schools in which we did our practicum were located in an "inner city" (read: working-class, immigrant, poor) neighbourhood and class differences were obvious. I have found that the overshadowing of class by race when talking about diversity within the university is a common occurrence. I have also found that people from working-class backgrounds never raise the issue of class themselves. Even I am complicit in this, as I became caught up in focusing on race to the exclusion of class during my year of teachers' college.

The university's understanding of difference and diversity obviously impacts on its ability to truly promote equity. When difference and diversity are framed in ways that simultaneously recognize and name yet exclude and collapse differences, the extent to which the university can promote equity is circumscribed. It was therefore not surprising that, despite teacher candidates' embrace of the values of difference, diversity and equity espoused at teachers' college, when the time came for hiring new teachers, all our talk about equity seemed to be for naught. White teacher candidates were angry by the perception that non-White teacher candidates were receiving more job interviews. Professors were at a loss as to how to deal with the tension that engulfed the class. So much for equity!

Some Closing Thoughts

The experiences that I have related are not unique to me, nor are they peculiar to the institution I am part of. Over the last few months, I have been conducting research with second-generation Caribbean-Canadian women living in Toronto, and I have found that their experiences of other institutions are similar to mine. The inability to adequately accommodate difference and diversity and to promote equity transcends the university. This inability has to do with the failure to acknowledge that bodies are imbued with knowledge and that different bodies embody different knowledges. Consequently, institutions like the academy that wish to promote equity and the accommodation of difference and diversity must deal with the increasingly different bodies that enter their midst.

25

Lived Experiences of an Aboriginal Feminist Transforming the Curriculum[1]

FYRE JEAN GRAVELINE

I grew up in the northern bush country of the Prairies—harsh, untamed, isolated country. As the rebellions and the resistance movements of the 1800s were squashed by the hanging of Louis Riel in 1885, my people were scattered south to the States, and north to the Shield. The Metis are a Nation in diaspora, as are the Acadians of the eastern seaboard and the Blacks of Africa.

Located throughout the Prairies there were/are pockets of Metis culture, resisting, remembering, retelling the stories of Louis Riel, of Gabriel Dumont, of John-Baptiste Lagimodiere, my relations, my Elders. Metis peoples model resistance as a survival strategy, resistance as a culture. Our culture has been continuously under creation, given environmental pressures and survival demands.

Culture is not only the ancestral stories told, told and retold through the ages, it is also the day-to-day living out of our lives, our identities, as we are embodied. Today, as cultural workers, we embody a commodity, a commodity sought by the post-secondary industry, "required" under the legislation of "equity." We want to believe that our voices and our gifts are desired but find that the "open door" policies quickly become "revolving door" realities. Revolving door realities.

We, the too few in number, are charged with the mission to create change in Eurocentric patriarchal universities. We are held continuously responsible for curriculum development on diversity and difference. We represent our stories and our selves in an effort to address issues of gender, race, class, sexual orientation. A pain-full reality, a highly contradictory relationship of visibility and appropriation. How do I take the risk to speak when I know not how or by whom my words will be taken?

The stories I share today are excerpts from a collection of healing and teaching stories I am writing about my lifework as a Metis woman, teacher, activist, healer, located within; as an "Outsider within" (Collins 1991) post-secondary institutions in Canada. My work is highly contradictory, very personal and ultimately political. It takes courage to examine the uninvited, uncomfortable, threatening, confusing moments as they erupt in my life, in our workspaces. As Marie Battiste reminds us, "Contradiction and incoherence are inevitable and indispensable to successful transformation" (Battiste and Barman 1995: xiv).

I'll tell you a story now—one most notable teaching story, one I'm still learning to tell because of how hard, how strong a feeling I have for it, a trickster tale, a dream tale. A dream of a Native-run, Native-controlled school done "our way," based on Native traditions administratively and pedagogically, set in a beautiful sacred valley nestled in the precious mounds of Our Mother.

I dreamed this job, although I couldn't see my face, and the vision gave me a chill. Chill wind blew through me. I thought, decided, wanted it to be just the fierce wind blowing off the Atlantic. I accepted the surface picture, the lovely valley, the dream. I took a risk. The Native-controlled college was not. It was bureacratically White. This was the biggest heartache, the biggest disappointment of the dream. As I unmasked the oppressive relations to myself and with others, my classroom became a site of this struggle, of this learning and teaching paradox.

I was teaching the theory of oppression around the Medicine Wheel. It took all morning. We had a double class that day. I began the afternoon saying, "Now, does anybody have an example we can work with?" A few were mentioned. One woman spoke at length. She knew about oppression and she had a story to tell, a story she had to tell. She had to tell it.

Here she was, a single parent, a full-time student, who worked part-time at the school. That day at noon, when she went in for her cheque, she was told "You are laid off."

"I'm laid off," she gasped. "But why? Why?" she asked.

"Now that you are student council president, it is a conflict of interest," they said.

"Conflict of whose interests?" she asked.

"You cannot possibly have time to fulfil the duties of both studies and politics, and juggle paid work. Especially being a mother and all," she was told. She was told.

She protested to us in class later: "I need the job. Why should they decide what is best for me, anyways? Why should they decide? Why should they? Should they?"

It was a classic example, a teachable moment. I listened respectfully to the story as the gift that it was. When she was done, I went to the board. We began to work. "If we take this model, the Wheel of Oppression we developed this morning," I said, "and apply this problem, what do we get?" We worked all afternoon. Everybody was energized about it.

It was all drawn out—right there on the board—the socio-political, gender, race, class and historical context of her "personal" problem. We strategized then: "Given the analysis," I asked, "how can this picture be changed? How can she get what she needs? Who would she have to talk to and how?" By the close of the afternoon, she had the know-how to act on her own behalf, and the support of her peers to do so. She did lobby the administration, and she did get her job back. She got her job back.

It was a beautiful lesson. I was proud: proud of my work, proud of her courage. It was a well-worked-through, clear and compelling example, right in their daily lived experience—with analysis, action and a happy ending. A happy ending—well almost.

Until later, I heard … I heard …

There was someone lurking outside the open window as the lesson progressed, a "spy" from the White administration, who reported what little she had seen and heard, what little she had seen and heard, out of context, out of context. What I taught then and in what form in my classroom became contested terrain.

It seemed to me that they had hired a Native teacher, but they really didn't want one—really did not want one, didn't want one with a Red Heart. They wanted a token. They were building their lives and careers as "Great White Leaders of the Native Education Movement," a pattern which I had learned to recognize and resist, recognize and resist through my other political efforts—resist with my head, resist in my heart. I learned then and know now, over and over, over and over again, I learn—resistance produces backlash. Action is taken by challenged authorities. Activism big or small has risks.

All of a sudden, the administration began to mention to me, "Maybe you are unhappy here."

"I was unhappy?" I parroted back with a question mark attached.

"Maybe you are not comfortable here, not 'Fitting In.'"

I partially agreed. "I am not happy, not happy. I am dis-enchanted. My workload is too heavy, too heavy. And things, things are not as they had appeared. No. But I am surviving, thank you, and even having good days, at least good moments in my teaching. I am making nice connections, good friends in the community and learning and teaching lots and lots inside the classroom and out. Both inside and out," I clarified.

In a short time, the message went from I was unhappy to I was leaving. I was leaving? I had resigned? Maybe fired? What? I was leaving because of conflict, because of complaints from/with students. What? I was confused. "What students? When?" I asked anyone I could. I was dizzy. I was sick. It was all happening too fast, much too fast for me. Who? Who? Who said what? To whom? When? Why? Where?

What? Who? Who? This is too much for me, much too much for me. What to do? What to do? Grandmothers help me. What to do?

I was acting "as if" I was in a Native environment, where our ways—Circles, stories, ceremony, experience—could be used as pedagogy and our history experiences and traditions as content to understand the White institutions of social work and education. I had felt safe. I was open with my politics, open with my beliefs, my practices. Open. Teaching from my heart. My Red Heart open.

Some people express very firmly, "You are to teach in the expected mode, exactly what the calendar says." Why is White mono-cultural reality now the expected norm on our ancestral lands, I want to know. Why do I find myself frequently counselled by those in positions of institutional power, "It will be less trouble if you just learn to get along." Just learn to get along. What about equity in Uni-versity? Where is Diversity? I find Domination by an overriding culture a pain-full experience. What about freedom? Academic freedom? Cultural freedom? "Power is the ability to do what one chooses. The more power one has, the more options one has," Adair and Howell (1989: 220) say.

I will resist. Means says, "It is natural to resist Extermination, to Survive" (1980: 31). I will teach skills, tools, attitudes required to heal Aboriginal peoples struggling to recover from abuses of colonialism. Accreditation demands: "The curriculum shall ensure that students have an understanding of oppressions and healing of Aboriginal peoples" (Carniol 1998).

I am always unprepared for the backlash of White authority. How the words and actions of myself and my students were twisted and used against me. Twisted and used against the students. Twisted and used against our traditions. I could not rest. I could not rest. Students were turning against students as gossip fuelled the division between administration, students and me. Mostly I withdrew. I withdrew and listened, listened and waited, waited and burned Sweetgrass every day. Every day. I was hurt. Hurt and sad, sad and mad.

I did go out to see Elijah Harper when he came to town to speak—a moment of light, inspiration in a dark time. After, I saw an Elder downtown, a beautiful woman who "worked" at the school. "How are you? How are you?" She asked touching my arm, a soft, care-full caress.

"What to do? What to do?" I asked. "What to do?"

"If you call a Circle, I'll come," she told me. She told me, call a Circle.

So I did. I put word out to the Community—students, colleagues, administration, family/Community relations, Elders. I especially invited some Medicine Keepers to help with the Circle, as I felt too shaken, too empty. Too empty. I knew I would not be able to properly attend to the process, to give full energy to the Circle. I would need to be attended to. I would need support myself.

Finally, the day came. Everybody was all in a Circle, about fifty in all. A big Circle, most of my students, many Community supporters and some "admin" members. A Medicine Keeper, the husband of my student, a friend, came and burned a special Sage Smudge in their traditional way to open the Circle. A Pipe Carrier, my student and friend, brought his Medicine Pipe. He offered blessings to the Four Directions and passed the Pipe, giving us each the opportunity to create our own Circle of Personal Responsibility within the greater Circle today.

A Talking Feather was passed to the Elder woman who spoke first, as is the Rite of the Elder. She spoke from her Heart, giving us her example, of her concern for me, for her grandchildren, my students, for her community, for the school, for the beautiful land that is their home, showing the Interconnectedness of all of us in the Circle today. She said we should speak openly of our Hearts and voice our part in the Story, so we could all see the Web of Interconnectedness holding us together during this time of struggle.

Moving to the East, in clockwise manner, the Traditionalist who burned the Smudge spoke next about the rules of Circle. "Everyone speaks in turn," he said, "the Circle going round, and starting round again till everyone has spoken what needs to be said. When I come to Circle, I talk about my Heart. This is what we talk about here. Heart talk. We talk about our own selves, and what we know, each of us." And he did. He did and we all did. We all did.

As the Circle progressed, it seemed to be bogging down, bogging down. Two people had spoken and left the Circle, spoken and left the Circle without listening, without listening to others speak. This was considered very rude behaviour by some who knew better. Some knew better.

And the Medicine Woman came with her Eagle Feather Fan, and she swept the air clear. She swirled and twirled. Swirled and twirled and she flew, flew around the Circle and moved the air. Moved the air and changed it and charged it, re-charged it and us. The pain lessened, ssshhh. The air lightened, aaahhh. I/We could breathe easier, aaahhh. We all felt better. All felt better. She worked as we worked. She worked as we worked. We worked as she worked to create new positive energy out of this horrible, horrible time, out of this struggle. Let us each learn the lessons that we need to know, learn our lessons so we can walk on our Path. Walk our Path with clear knowingness of our past experiences. "Grandmothers, what do I need to know?" I pray silently.

We all talked for as long as we were able, as long as we were able. The energy was ebbing. Yawn. Time went on. I/We were getting tired.

One student/friend/wife of the Pipe Carrier and mother of other students had the Talking Feather. She spoke the collective consciousness, the Voice of the Circle: "I'm tired, I need a hug. I want to close the Circle. Does anyone here still need to speak?" She held out the Feather. No one needed to speak. All had been said. All had been said for now.

The closing began. She turned to her daughter and hugged, moved on to her husband and all around the Circle. As she did the Circle followed her. Her daughter, then her husband, then all of us in turn. All circling. All circling and hugging, hugging and talking, talking and crying, crying and laughing. And the Medicine Woman was flying.

As you face each person to connect, hug, handshake, speak, any or all, you say or do whatever you need to say or do and move on. Then, as the Circle circles back, each person faces each other person once to talk and once to listen. Beautiful energy. We felt Community in that Circle, Community I carry in my Heart today. Ceremony intends to integrate: "The person sheds the isolated, individual personality and is restored to conscious harmony with the universe," says Gunn Allen (1986: 62) Harmony was restored in my Universe, in that moment, on that day.

Many of these sacred tools I carry myself and use in my healing and teaching experiences: the Smudge, the Talking Feather, an Eagle Feather Fan, a Sacred Pipe. I love Circle work. I love Circle work. I had been applying it as pedagogy, had used it in political collective building, had experienced it in healing ceremonies and conflict resolution for others. But this Circle was for me. For me and with me. With me and intimately about me. Me and my self-in-relation to others. My sense of my self as a Person, as a Traditionalist, as a Teacher, had been called into question.

I stood strong on tradition and called on support from that base. In my greatest need I felt the Power of that Circle, that Collective Knowing. The Power of generating a Circle with that much help: the Smudge, the Pipe, the Elders, the Medicine Keepers, the Feathers. The strength of all the family members who knew the Power of the Circle, who knew through experience how to intensify it, through words, the Power of Voice, to speak from the Heart. Through Silence, to listen respectfully, to pay mindful attention, to really hear what each person has to say. What each person has to say.

The Circle remains a central foundation of my healing and teaching practice. Circle talk is a beautiful way to allow Voice, to create a space for people to claim their "First Voice" (Graveline 1998). To speak with Power, with authority of their daily lived experience, as an act of resistance. Circle is a place where all voices can speak if they wish to. Uninterrupted. Unanalyzed. Unargued. Unchallenged. We all speak our own truth.

The Elders teach: We all have a story to tell. We all have a story to tell. I've learned, especially since using Circle in mainstream classroom settings, that not all voices, not all stories have the same healing and teaching value. Not all are rooted in the same consciousness, history or experience. Some voices need expression. Some voices need silencing. It is a personal / political / privilege thing.

Yikes!! Did I say that?

"What you say? What? Isn't that against the 'emancipatory' voice? Against the rules of collectivism? The notion of immanence?" My internal critical and cultural voice dialogues. Let me tell you a story about Voice and silence.

Sometimes, giving Voice, giving voice to my identity, my politics, my Aborigina1 consciousness, paradoxically can be a lesson in silencing, of me or others. In Circle, having Smudged and called the Directions, I am in "Aboriginal Consciousness," but when I am also in a Western university classroom—oooppps—it can be dangerous ground.

One time my "Circle voice" declared a colleague to be racist in his use of "voice." He had constructed his "teaching stories" in class using overtly racist language. Students argue: It's okay, because he is the professor and must be right. Because he says the word, that makes it "acceptable" vocabulary for further use in the classroom and elsewhere. I respond: It's not that we all haven't heard the word or don't know what the word means. We just wish we didn't. Wish we didn't. Can we all agree: Racism does not require bad intentions. Impact not intent says the law.

That night I had a nightmare. Nightmare. Tossing and turning. Talking. I wake up. I wake up in a cold sweat, a terror. I am dreaming. Dreaming. Dreaming other dreams, other realities of calling "racist," of giving voice to this word—racist—the "r" word. Using "it" to describe authority, particularly White male authority, and being hurt. Being hurt and being fired. Being fired and being trashed. Oh, no. Oh, no, I don't want to. I don't want to. I don't want to be in the middle of this battle right at this time, right at this time on the shifting new grounds of employability. "What to do? What to do, Grandmothers?" I pray.

I know how news about "What the Prof said" travels fast. I know who will ask who to clarify my "Aboriginal meanings" in the student lounge. I contact my Native students / friends and tell them. I tell them about the Circle. The Circle and what I said in "Circle voice." How I called the word "racist," and how I dreamed. How I dreamed and how I was afraid. How I was afraid, and how I prayed, "What to do? What to do, Grandmothers?" We thought. We talked. We strategized. We knew what had to happen.

Because I had to fear, had to fear because of my past experience, history. I / We decided to encourage silence: encourge silence, emphasize to students that what was said in Circle is meant to be kept in Circle. What is said in Circle is meant to be kept in Circle. Kept in Circle. Invoking the ethic of confidentiality. Confidentiality becomes a code word. Code word for silencing. I encouraged silence. Don't talk about what I talked about. Don't talk about what I talked about. Silence to cover the fear behind my giving Voice. Cover my fear of Voice, when what was needed, what was needed to intensify and provoke change was lots of talk. Lots of talk to silence his voice. But I was glad. I was glad it turned out as well as it did. The student chit-chat settled down, the problem remained, but I escaped being caught in the middle—being the martyr—for a change. A change, at least for that moment, I was relieved of the burden.

Anyway, the struggle about whose voice is a common one in society and in my classroom: I did one day inadvertently silence many of my students, silenced many of my students.

I had been feeling upset, angry, hurt about how class was proceeding and had decided that rather than swallow it, swallow it and try to continue to affect change in subtle ways, I would speak out about my feelings in Circle. Speak out in Circle as is the Aboriginal way. Students were being, in my estimation, highly disrespectful, highly disrespectful and generally not paying attention, not paying attention to the process. While I recognized this to be in part related to their Eurocentric consciousness, I felt little effort, little effort, was being made to even understand, to even understand the expectations of Circle. I saw and named, saw and named this ignore-ance as an act of privilege.

I had spoken twice about it in Circles but had not been heard. Had not been heard. I began to discuss it with others. "They are just like that," I heard. "It's not just your class." I knew respect was a much-needed lesson in this classroom community. I prepared a "speech," and during "Circle time," I spoke from my Heart. My Red Heart. I spoke from my Heart about my feelings, about how I had been experiencing class, about how my/our history was contributing to my feelings and experiences. I shared how I had been dreaming about the class, and the ways I felt they were showing disrespect to my/our ancestral traditions. I let them know that I was beginning to feel like we were appropriating tradition rather than honouring it, and if attitudes and behaviours did not change in specific ways, I would continue to cover content, but we would not be using Circle, not be using Circle or other sacred ways in class.

My "speak-out" was a very profound experience for everyone, including me, especially me. Students talked about it for weeks. It was the talk of the school, except in class. Except in class. The following week, I passed the Feather, passed the Feather to give opportunity for

Voice. Only a few spoke, the Black and Aboriginal students and one White male, none of the others. None of the others spoke. They were silenced. Silenced. I was surprised but did not respond except to say, "I did not mean to silence you."

As I reflected on it, at first I thought maybe what I had said was profound, so profound it provoked Silence. Maybe it was. But what was really profound for me was realizing that what silenced them was not necessarily my Aboriginal "Voice" teaching them respect for tradition, but the power invested in the professorial voice. That's what was important to the students—that I the professor had said it. That's what made it school talk. School talk. They talked and they talked. They talked to students, to Aboriginal students. "What did she mean? What did she mean? Maybe she's just angry and taking it out, taking it out on us," some said. "She's right. I did it myself," others confessed. Some students learned that silence was necessary to learn to practise proper conduct in Circle. Some continued to be their same old rude selves.

Being silenced often as a student very much affected my teaching style and my reaction to the students' reactions. I was shocked. Shocked at myself to be thinking about silence/silencing as a positive thing, a good lesson. I have since contextualized the idea and know it to be rooted in Aboriginal pedagogy. Not the act of silencing, but the Power of Silence. The Power of quietly observing. Quietly observing. Not questioning. Not asking why, why, why? Just sitting quietly, usually out in Nature: Being in Silence. In Silence. Learning by observing. They didn't get it. Did not get it. They had to be told. They had to be told.

I am getting better at recognizing "cultural differences" between students and myself, and being more clear about expectations before the conflict arises, before conflict arises. This is an ongoing struggle. I am learning—learning from my teaching—lessons about life, about who-I-am-in-relation: to my students, to my professorial authority, to my Aboriginality. I recognize that I am political. My Person is political. I am a challenge. I will challenge all to acculturate to Aboriginal norms. I will not sit in rows. I will not leave my Spirit Guides at the door. I will not quietly nod nor smile as they speak ignorantly of "those people": Natives, Blacks, women, gays and lesbians, poor people, "clients." I will make visible the societal structures which serve to oppress. Oppress some like us—my people—and privilege others like them.

"If she initiates a process challenging the worldview and view of self of her students, she will surely—if she is doing her job—become the object of some students' unexamined anger," theorizes Culley (1985: 213). Anger missiles are projected at me, a never-ending arsenal stockpiled throughout years of blind obedience, blind obedience to the status quo. Bad enough to be a Native female in an authority position, but to openly contest Eurocentrism, to unveil White privilege and revitalize ancestral practice—is this simply too much to take? Too much to take in a Western educational context?

We all bring our cultural background, personality and past experience to any learning experience. Our Selves are ever-present, ever present "like a garment that cannot be removed" (Peshkin 1988: 17). Should an educator be "neutral"? Can an educator be "neutral"? What is neutrality but the norm? Freire teaches that all education is political: "Educators who do their work uncritically just to preserve their jobs have not yet grasped the political nature of education" (1985: 180).

Critically reflect on the construct of "comfort." Singleton (1994) found *faculty comfort* a critical deciding factor in whether racially relevant material was actually covered in the curriculum. Finding comfort speaking in the university classroom about racism and oppression is a journey. Comfort in the face of well-developed denial and defensiveness is difficult. Denial and defensiveness are highly complex, highly complex physiological, psychological, sociological manifestations. They appear, disappear and reappear in each and every encounter in challenged systems.

Mohanty theorizes, for universities to continue to conduct "business as usual" "problems" of race and difference are formulated into "narrow, interpersonal terms"; historical and contextual conflicts are rewritten as "manageable psychological ones" (1994: 157). How quickly structural issues become personality problems. Anticipation of and recovery from occasions of outright racial harassment is ongoing. According to Weir, "When the classroom becomes a site of anti-racist political struggle, the racism present massively among white people will be spoken" (1991: 24).

How far are we prepared to go to ensure our own comfort? Or the comfort of those around us? To whose comfort level are we consciously / unconsciously trying to adapt? Confronting racism, sexism, classism, homophobia and ableism creates uncomfortable feelings for some. What about the uncomfortable feelings for others? Others who are targeted daily, targeted daily for being. Being who we are.

Discomfort is a critical political issue today. Be aware of massive implications for academic freedom. Institutions are increasingly driven by market demands. Commodified learning means "satisfy the customer." When students / faculty / administration are uncomfortable, dis-satisfied, challenged to critically see what they have been conditioned to ignore, I cannot ignore it. My livelihood is challenged. My academic freedom is conditional. Should satisfaction of every student, every student in every class, unconditional acceptance of every colleague, be required for tenure? Only for some it seems.

We often experience backlash as personal assassination. It is decisively political, a critical bargaining issue. Creating change can pose threats to some. It can bring a counteraction to "Others," to our Selves. In my book *Circle Works* (1998), I storytell about my own experiences of backlash. Backlash can cause us to spiral into hopelessness and helplessness. Fatalism, Leonard proposes, has been "culturally constructed to serve the dominant order of things" (1990: 3). Resist Fatalism to Survive.

I have learned to sustain my Spirit of Resistance through engaging in Aboriginal ceremony. Visioning enables us to transform that which is, to actively create more potent lives for ourselves and our children. We can tap into the strength of our Ancestors, the energy of Earth Mother. Visioning helps us not to get so caught up, "caught up, bogged down, oppressed, beat up, by everything that's going on in our day to day" (Fyre, in Graveline 1998: 280). Visioning gives us direction, hope, desire to enact change, power to survive, to survive backlash.

Let's stand strong. Stand Strong Together for Community Healing and World Change.

To all my Relations, Megwetch.

26

Reflecting on Difference
A Concluding Conversation

Carl E. James and Celia Haig-Brown

In this final chapter, Carl, the editor, and Celia, one of the contributors, colleagues at York University, reflect on the book and the chapters within it, its intents and revelations. They name a number of considerations around difference which emerge from the writings: denying difference, collapsing difference, naming and acknowledging difference, ranking difference, refusing categorization, disrupting "privilege as usual," infiltrating cultural space, and working with and through difference as a vital responsibility. In the final analysis, the two agree that difference is socially constructed, relational, contextual and contentious.[1]

Carl: Let's start with your question to me, Celia, about the danger of putting all these differences into one book. We have differences based on gender, sexuality, age, class, race, religion, ability, ethnicity, family composition and geographical areas from where people have come. Are we minimizing these differences? Or are we saying that all these differences are similar and therefore it's possible to analyze them in one volume, have everybody react to their experiences and see ...[2]

Celia: ... that everybody is struggling against something ...

Carl: Everybody is struggling against something, and if there's a common person or structure against which everybody is struggling, we can all get together and struggle together? Well, it's not like that; it cannot work that way. I'm still thinking through this whole idea of why put all these differences in one volume.

Celia: You have to answer that, you're the one that put all these differences in one volume. How *do* you feel about that now?

Carl: I wanted to look at the whole question of difference, and especially your question, "When does difference make a difference?" I know that sometimes difference is seen as a disadvantage and sometimes difference constitutes privilege. Rather than just simply saying that everybody is struggling against something, I want to start thinking about how we can think through all these differences in a more complex way, so that we do not simply say we all experience the same thing. Because we don't experience the same thing. The point is, what can we say theoretically in our struggle against oppression, when all these differences matter so much in so many different ways to different people?

Denying Difference

Celia: Reading the essays, one of the things that spoke to me is the notion of denying difference. For instance, Gordon Pon's chapter talks about the Chinese students who do not want to be marked by racial categories or claim that racism is an issue for them. And it came up again in Didi Khayatt's chapter, around the notion of "immigrant woman" when the professor said to her, "We have an immigrant woman among us" and nodded in the general direction of where Didi was seated. As all the other students looked in her direction, she too looked back to see who was there. Because of the degree of privilege from which she was coming, the term "immigrant woman" with its implications of class and colour could not possibly apply to her. Carolyn Ewoldt's chapter also brought into focus the idea of resisting degrees of difference, or, in seeing difference, not wanting to be associated with it. She writes about seeing the person using a monocular, a lens for enlarging print, and feeling repulsed by it, holding to the notion that "this has nothing to do with me," despite the fact that, at that time, she was severely myopic. From positions of relative privilege, one can refuse to acknowledge the relationship between an identified difference and one's own experience.

Carl: Another example of denial of difference, or attempts to minimize it, comes up in Leanne Taylor's story about her father. This is an excellent example of how difference is very much contextual, very related to individual experiences....

Celia: ... gender ...

Carl: ... gender, and colour and complexion. What's also interesting about her story is how her brother sees difference, and his experiences with racism compared to hers. There are times when he experiences racism and she doesn't.

Celia: Although they're both the same colour.

Carl: Yeah, her brother did not get away with some of the things she did. Yet her brother's experiences have not made him negative towards Whites. In fact, he finds White women more attractive, while Leanne tends to be more attracted to Black men. This example shows how difference is related to personal experiences in growing up.

Celia: I think that example is further complicated because their family makeup seems to have some implications in whom they find attractive. Since the father's Black and the mother's White, the kids may be identifying with their parents' relationship and reconstructing it in their own. He sees the woman you marry should be White, and she sees that the man should be Black.

Carl: I am thinking about another example of denying difference. I got an e-mail two days ago from a friend and colleague who just graduated with his Ph.D. in Sociology and whom I have been trying to get to write an essay exploring what his "Portugueseness" means for him. In conversations with him, I get the impression that it is important to him. I was encouraging him to conduct research on Portuguese students, because here in Toronto, while there's much talk of Black and Aboriginal students not doing well in school, board of education studies continue to show that Portuguese students are not doing well either. In this case, ethnicity and class, more than colour, are likely the issue. My friend agrees that there is a problem, but he writes to me saying that one of the reasons he has very little interest in researching the Portuguese is because he does not want to be seen as an "ethnic sociologist," somebody who only researches ethnic issues. Then he goes on to say that he likes the work of Paul Gilroy, Stuart Hall and bell hooks, who are Black and write about issues concerning Black people. While he sees them as great scholars and he likes using their work, he doesn't want to concentrate on Portuguese issues for fear of being labelled as an "ethnic scholar." So he distances himself. The irony is that he was hired to teach race and ethnic relations, but he is more interested in teaching the sociology of work. I guess the university he's at saw him as able to work in the area of race and ethnic relations despite his resistance to recognizing his own ethnicity as relevant to his work.

Celia: Why might he be seen as Portuguese? Does he have a Portuguese name, one that sounds Anglo?

Carl: Yes, his name might be a giveaway. He even said that, at one time, he toyed with changing his name. Evidently, mediating all this is his "Portugueseness," something he is not confronting.

Celia: So, here is an example of refusing to be named but being unable to escape an identity being ascribed to you. All around you, your ethnicity is being named.

Collapsing Difference

Carl: One way of denying or minimizing difference is to collapse differences into one another. This comes out in assumptions such as thinking that being in a marginalized position enables us to understand other marginalized positions. In other words, because you're a woman, or because you're gay or lesbian, you're able to understand the impacts of racism. Similarly, we tend to question why one group of marginalized people doesn't understand the experiences of other marginalized people. Why aren't people able to see things in others that they feel for themselves?

Celia: As you were talking, two things came to mind. One day I was driving along with a long-time friend, a woman of Aboriginal ancestry, and we were talking about our upbringings. Quite often, people ask me why, as a White woman, I am working in and conducting research in Aboriginal education. In response, I find myself thinking about the way my parents raised me with a fundamental respect for Aboriginal people, their place in and relationship to this land. Because my father was a conservationist long before it was fashionable, my family lived with respect for the land, and an understanding of the limits of private land ownership and the significance of the interrelationships of rivers, land and the air we breathe. Aboriginal peoples were respected because their traditional lives are based on similar principles. My friend looked over at me and said, "How I wish

I had been raised like that." In other words, her experience of societal structures, including systemic racism, had mitigated against anything that her family or a disrupted Aboriginal community could do to convince her that she and her heritage were worthy of respect. The message from Canadian "mainstream" society was just too strong: Aboriginal people were inferior.

Another incident that comes to mind related to collapsing oppression was an experience I had with a Kurdish graduate student. He was in Canada as a political refugee and was still working to address the plight of his people, looking for ways to build coalitions, solidarity and support for the cause. One day, he asked me what I thought the chances were of finding support within what he saw as the politically active gay community. He was clearly impressed with the degree of organization of the gay and lesbian movements at the time. My immediate response was that it was unlikely that he would be able to garner much support because the majority of gay White men that I had encountered are very much focused on their own issues and the politics related to them. While there are clear exceptions, for the most part, they don't have the time or interest to take their activism for gay rights in all its complexity and work in any other area. At the same time, their struggles do provide important insights for social action in this country.

Carl: And isn't it very common among human beings to think, "My struggle so consumes me that I have no time to take up other people's struggles?"

Naming and Acknowledging Difference

Carl: We could also say that this idea of collapsing differences was captured in a different way in Denny Hunte's chapter, "My Home Visit." What I liked about his piece is that it is a story. It's an example of the different ways in which people talk about difference.

Celia: His story focused on class, but on the other hand …

Carl: … race was very much part of it.

Celia: I don't know why, but what stuck in my mind is that the author/social worker looked so much like the father of the child and that the child himself runs to him saying, "Daddy, Daddy," and climbs on his lap. The mother had a hard time getting past that and, as a reader, I too wondered about how to make sense of the moment. I suppose that was because of the racist notion that all Black people look the same, and yet in the confusion, for the child whose absent father is Black, it is something quite different.

Carl: Denny's story clearly presents those often-heard words, "You all look alike," which obliterate individual differences and unique experiences. It also represents refusal of non-group members to learn about and recognize the diversity within groups. Because of these things, group members, like Denny, are likely to experience negative or embarrassing situations related to the actions of other group members for whom they should not have to take responsibility. Experiences with police officers come to mind here. The fact is, if we are to work seriously with difference, we have to recognize and acknowledge differences and not lump people together on superficial bases. I also want to mention the idea of recognizing difference in ways that some might consider positive. In that case, you might wonder if lumping members of one race together works to their benefit. I am thinking of Gordon Pon's chapter and what he says about the geographies of Chineseness. Shouldn't we be happy about some of the differences that get constructed for us—you know, the "educated," the "model minority"? There might seem to be no problem with that construction of Chinese identity.

Celia: He talks about how the mathematics students went out into the school yard at recess and "raved about how smart the teacher was ... to know the 'truth' about the intellectual prowess of us Asians." It's a lovely moment. Especially the boy who was bad at math who said, "We are more highly evolved because we have so little body hair." [Both laugh.] I think there are some big problems with positive stereotypes as well. [More laughter.]

Carl: Aren't some constructed differences good?

Celia: I think romantic stereotypes are as problematic as negative stereotypes. With Aboriginal people, stereotypes are built on the understanding that these are people who come from the land, therefore they should know how to live harmoniously with nature forever. A lot of time has passed since most of these indigenous societies were intact, and exactly what it means to be Aboriginal in the current context is being worked out by those who are committed to recovery. None of this is to suggest that Aboriginal people never had a different relationship to the land than Europeans, but to simply assume that is far too simplistic. I'm not going for model minorities at all.

Carl: Also, with regard to the issue of being a minority, Maxine Bramble's discussion brings us close to home in terms of her experiences of being in university.

Celia: Her essay is not just talking about making invisible the experiences that matter to her in her own introduction of herself to the class. It also speaks to us as faculty in our role of making space for difference in the classroom. I never want to take the position that I cannot see a person's body in front of me because it threatens my theoretical or scholarly position, where my need to have my theory work better, or be uninterrupted or more seamless makes me blind to the students with whom I am working. I am already aware that my socialization will keep me from being as open as I would like to be: it's a continuous struggle to work against our induction into and collusion with society's norms and the mores of racism, heterosexism, class bias and sexism.

Carl: What I like about Maxine's essay is how she has dealt with class and race and being an immigrant, showing how difference is complicated.

Celia: I also really liked what seemed to be a fundamental point she was making, that when she introduced herself in that context, she wasn't even in her own introduction. Difference was erased; it wasn't allowed to be present. Difference vanished, as she said, but it was more like it was banished. It wasn't erased, it was still very much there, but it wasn't allowed to enter the discourse.

Carl: Doesn't it get back to the point of how being constructed as different sometimes means that difference should not be named?

Celia: You might not take it on, but the fact that people kept naming you in other contexts as being different may push you to say, this is what I am. Their gaze makes difference explicit.

Carl: It's important how difference gets constructed in relational terms. For example, students see you as feminist because of what you teach; you get labelled as such and then you take it on.

Celia: This also relates to a point that you and I have talked about before—as well as to your example of the academic who did not want to address his Portuguese ancestry in his work—which has to do with being seen as an advocate or a one issue person. And the whole question around "Should you come out in class?" (Khayatt 1997). I know in classes where I have been leading a discussion on sexuality, where I was not out, the nature and quality of that discussion would have been incredibly different if I had been. Students stated in the class, "I have never met a lesbian and so therefore …" Well, [laugh] it's a strange situation to be in, but in order to facilitate the discussion, I continued to allow them to think that they had never met a lesbian. And despite the fact that I knew there were lesbian students in the class. You have talked about being conscious about which texts you use, because you are cognizant of being seen as a person using your position to advocate for anti-racism for Blacks.

Ranking Difference

Carl: I want to get back to the point about putting all these differences together in one book, and to talk about the tendency to rank differences. Of course, we must not, should not and cannot rank differences. But at the same time, we cannot deny that in certain situations, differences are resisted. I was having a conversation with a friend recently and we were talking about possible reactions to a Black man being hired to teach a group of grade seven students, for example, and how White, middle-class parents would react to a Black man teaching an all-White class of twelve-year-olds. Parents might object, but at the same time I think they might be cautious about voicing their objections, because even though racism permeates our society, we know we're not supposed to be racist. But it is possible that in the same community, if the principal hired a gay person, the parents might more openly challenge that hiring. So, we are back to your question: When does difference make a difference?

Celia: It depends on context, clearly.

Carl: It depends on context. So, then for me, the purpose of putting all these differences in one volume is to open up the idea that context informs or influences many of these experiences. When we listen to people talk about their experiences, we have to relate them to context and think that, placed in other contexts, they might not have the same kind of experiences. If we use Susan Tilley's experience, for example, in Newfoundland, who cares about her accent? But in another context, when she is "away," she gets the comment, "You don't sound like a Newfoundlander." I think this volume demonstrates that context is an extremely significant factor when we think more deeply about difference. Context will determine whether race is going to result in privilege or marginalization, whether sexuality is going to bring privilege or marginalization and so on. And another dimension is, Who is doing the looking, and who is doing the seeing? Your own experience will inform how you read some of these experiences.

Celia: Geographical location is clearly an issue in what Susan Tilley is discussing, but another way of looking at her situation is as one of shifting contexts. Many chapters in this volume are developed around a temporal shift, such as looking back at things. So Kathryn Alexander remembering what it meant to be a twin then, and what it means to be a twin now—it's an entirely different experience than when she was age five or ten, whatever.

Carl: So what you're introducing is that difference is not static …

Celia: Exactly.

Carl: It's constantly shifting. So it might be that I move from a situation of being a professor in the university to another context where I'm more privileged.

Celia: Though, we were already privileged as professors in the university system.

Carl: But at the same time, even in the university, here's the point, you're presumably among scholars like yourself, so other things kick in to construct your difference—differentiations such as the ranking of professor, associate professor, assistant professor, and things like race, gender and publishing record.

Celia: Oh yeah, the full professor. I forgot about those distinctions, which are very often connected to the other differences to which we have been alluding. And again it goes back to the question, When does difference make a difference? There is always a question of time implied, a temporal shift in the significance of difference.

Carl: If that's the case, can we hold onto difference? Someone might say, because I'm a Black male, I experience society's racism. But someone else might say, well, you're a professor and you enjoy many privileges, therefore, what are you complaining about?

Celia: And the fact that I live with another woman is not significant partly because I have a family for whom it is not an issue. On the other hand, there are times that it does make a difference. We were talking about shifting contexts: if I decided that I wanted to go back to teaching in public schools, I would be subject to quite a different set of rules about where I should go, how I should behave in public, how open I should be about who I am. You may be walking some place and thinking you want to put your arm around the one you love and you can't do it—well, you can do it, but it's complicated. I absolutely agree with you, gays and lesbians in schools are in a very delicate situation. If you are quiet about it, that's fine. It's another example of certain rules applying in one context and not in others.

Carl: You have to deal with the consequences.

Celia: Yes, and that example takes me back to talking about minimizing oppression, which can be seen as a dimension of ranking. I think ranking is both a survival technique and an issue of slight blindness. It's not useful to rank oppressions or to get into competing oppressions. You might choose to have one as your emphasis, but try not to lose sight of the others.

Carl: But other people argue that we have to start somewhere. What if the starting point is social class?

Celia: You can start with class, but then you would want not to lose sight of other dimensions of oppression. That's where education comes in, because there is a tendency for people to be single-minded and self-serving even as—perhaps especially as—they're working with certain groups.

Refusing Categorization

Carl: The question of refusing categorization is an important one. When I call someone and say, why don't you write an essay placing yourself as a woman at the centre, or as a Black person in the centre, or as a lesbian or gay individual or working-class person at the centre. Given our postmodernist view of shifting identities, we might hear the person say that this is not something he or she can do, or wants to do. While it's true that we're not locked into a category, that we do move around—after all we have been saying about context and relational aspects of difference—I don't think we can go anywhere without naming difference.

Celia: Yes, the postmodern notion of "shiftiness" is present in our talk. But the ability to take up and put down difference depends on what the difference is, of course, because it's really hard when you're Black to say that you're not Black today. But if I want to say I'm uncategorically sexual today, I can use those words to refuse simplistic categories and being named as different. There's a huge gap between the two situations. Forget it, not naming difference is a dangerous practice.

Carl: We have been saying that difference is socially constructed, so race and gender are socially constructed. Why then is it so important to name difference?

Celia: One of my favourite Halperin passages in your book, *Seeing Ourselves* (1999), says that all these differences may be socially constructed, but "people live by them after all—and nowadays increasingly, they die from them." So we have to take, as you said, political action if we are going to have social justice.

Carl: So you're arguing that we have to name difference and we have to take political action if social justice is our objective.

Celia: Yes, never losing sight of the fact that those names are social constructions and they can shift, but time and history and place—in other words, circumstances—influence those shifts.

Carl: How then do we get people with disabilities, Black people, gay and lesbian people, and working-class people organizing against various forms of political "oppression" to understand that structural inequality is a barrier for all …

Celia: … in places outside their own difference?

Carl: Yes.

Disrupting "Privilege As Usual"

Carl: In thinking about difference, we have to think about privilege, oppression and marginalization at the same time. We have to ask ourselves, How does this difference that I have translate or work with the privilege I have? Is this difference marginalizing us or adding to the privilege that we have?

Celia: Or at least not affecting the privilege we may have. I was thinking about the senior administrator in the video made at University of Western Ontario called "The Chilly Climate." He's the guy selected to head the equity committee who says, "I started the first meeting by saying I'm not sure why we're having this meeting about a chilly climate. In all my years at Western I don't know of any experiences of racism or sexism." And then he goes on to say, "Five years later, I realized that was a very stupid thing to say." Well, for that guy—White, male, senior administrator, privileged—what he said was doubtlessly true: the "'isms" had not been part of his experience, so he could not see them. If he has engaged in any racist or sexist actions, they don't affect him in noticeable ways, they only affect the person who is on the receiving end. Or maybe he really is a good guy and he knows not to behave injustly, but he's not in a place to experience those sorts of discrimination in his position of power.

Carl: There is also the issue of privilege that is evident in Cathy van Ingen's essay.

Celia: In reading her chapter, I was thinking about her life "coming out" and fighting the big political battles. In contrast, my move into lesbianism was in most cases not a big deal for the people around me. I am an older White woman in a secure, tenured position in a university, where there is usually more tolerance for difference than other places. So I don't have to spend a lot of time thinking about my circumstances because I'm in a position of privilege. So it seems to me that one of the times difference can be denied is when people have a degree of privilege, whether it's class privilege or privilege of position or material privilege. There are people like those students who frustrate Gordon Pon. You sense that frustration in his chapter when he says, "Hey, really listen to that song you're playing: it's saying something that you should be thinking about," but they don't care. They've got their Calvin Klein clothes and their three-car garages, and considerations of race and racism are not useful to them.

Carl: So the idea of difference must be weighed against privilege. It's not just difference in isolation.

Celia: Yeah. There's the chapter where Bina Mehta says, "I appreciate this opportunity to talk so much, because I experience racism and gender in isolation and it's important for you as my partner to see how it happens, what kind of impact it has on me and other people of colour." Kevin Spooner says, "I remember I was always taught to ignore differences." There again is that privileged place where a person can ignore difference. Who is it who gets to do that? Only some people—those with privilege.

Carl: And when you buy into that, you begin to think that you're no different. And because people want you to feel included or to be a part of their group, they claim that they do not see you as different. They refuse to think that you are Black or disabled or whatever the case may be, because it's a way of fitting you in. Do you think privileged people—because they want to protect privilege, because they want to protect the status quo, and because they do not want to see themselves as racist, sexist or homophobic—are the ones who constantly say, "Oh, I don't see you as different?"

Celia: Yes, I do. Another story. I was talking about the racism I had seen in Red Lake, Ontario, to a miner who was working there. And he responded, "Well, I grew up in northern Manitoba and one of my best friends was Metis. I was never conscious of this guy being Metis until I came to university. I used to go to his house, eat bannock; he came to my house and ate perogies When we were at university, somebody said to me, "Where is your Indian friend?" and I said, "What are you talking about?" In all the time he had known his friend he had never realized that he was Metis. He told me this story as a way to show that he was not racist. I see that moment of ignoring difference as fundamentally …

Carl: … racist …

Celia: … denial. Absolutely racist. To know somebody or a people without knowing anything about who they are, about their histories, about their cultures, is a way of protecting privilege. But I think it comes out of a profound ignorance. I don't think people are consciously saying, I'm going to protect my privilege by not knowing. And in schools, that's what we should be doing something about.

Carl: It's reflective of a society that trains us all to think that we're all nice people.

Infiltrating Cultural Space

Carl: Another thing that comes up when we talk about difference is the idea of people borrowing terms. For example, Kevin Spooner and Bina Mehta talk about "outing." Susan Tilley read that and asked me what I thought about it. What do you think about them using the word "outing"? We associate the word "outing" with lesbians and gays. People sometimes think that's cultural appropriation. What do you think about that?

Celia: I love people playing with language. I have been thinking a lot about the distinction between appropriation and learning, probably because I'm in the field of education and I conduct research with Aboriginal people. Very often people learn from one another by taking language and ideas to new contexts and societies. I think it can be respectfully done, if people acknowledge their sources and the connection to those other places and peoples. That is important. Maybe that's the distinction with people who are appropriating: they simply take and use something in another context without acknowledging it. So, I like the idea of learning, and I think it ultimately suggests respect. What do you think?

Carl: I think words are there to be used. And I think sometimes use of language in another space provides a powerful way of communicating, because words are so nicely developed in one group. If it's easy for people like Bina and Kevin to use the word "outing" in their conversation about being in a mixed marriage, then it's okay. It's easy to understand the word.

Celia: In some ways we might think of this phenomenon as a form of "reverse colonization," when a word like that gets taken up by many different groups and makes its way into the mainstream. Another word like that is "passing," a totally fascinating word, and one that I've often used in contexts beyond those addressing sexuality. Because I work with Aboriginal people and maybe because I have brown eyes, sometimes people think that I'm Aboriginal. There are moments when its tempting to "pass." Usually "passing" is taken to mean the other way around: where you pass as a member of the mainstream, but especially when I am in Aboriginal gatherings with people who don't know me well, it is often a tense moment when I dispel their hopes and admit that I am White.

Carl: And we can connect that to difference, because what you want is to deny your difference.

Celia: Yes, exactly.

Carl: And here's a difference that gives you the privilege. So you can use the difference when you want it and you can also deny the difference when you don't want it. So some people have the privilege of difference. In one context you're different but sometimes you can quickly translate that difference into "I'm part of," therefore giving you privilege.

Celia: Something related came up in my chapter: Why would a White person want to pass as Aboriginal? What's going on there? I was doing a piece of research in an institution for Aboriginal adults going back to school. During a workshop run by a social worker on the topic of "cultural self-hatred," I was the only White person there. The students were engaged in thinking through specific instances of negative reinforcements they were getting through systemic racism. As this work was going on, I became more and more uncomfortable, wishing I were not one of the group which had perpetrated, and continues to perpetrate, the racism the students were attempting to address. Because of the work I'd been doing for so long, I knew the history of White Europeans on this continent and around the world. I realized that I had a good dose of cultural self-hatred myself. I could romanticize all kinds of ideas about being Aboriginal, being non-White, whatever, and I actually had to do some quite serious work in that workshop to get to the point of being able to say, "It's okay to be White." I realize this may sound self-indulgent—"poor little White woman of privilege"—but that work enabled me to articulate my position and to think more clearly about ways to use the privilege I have to work for social justice. So the notion of "passing" as an Aboriginal person when you're White does bring in considerations of cultural self-hatred and its unhealthiness.

Carl: At the same time, though, there's a privilege that can mask it.

Working with and through Difference: A Vital Responsibility

Celia: I'm reminded of experiences of sexism I have had in my life. I spent a lot of time denying the impact of sexism, again out of privilege. If I wanted to do something, I just did it. Being female was not going to stop me. I had family support, I had financial support, and if I needed help or was desperate, I knew I could always call on mommy and daddy. So one goes along to a certain degree not aware of experiencing sexism. To acknowledge sexism for many young women is to risk being identified as feminist and to endanger their relations with young men. Similarly, successful career women say, "Gender has never been an issue for me." It was in university that I began to feel that sexism was blatantly keeping me from certain things I wanted to do. When I decided to offer a course called "Gender Equity Issues in Teacher Education," it came to a head. By this time, I had spent quite some time working with feminist theory and was ready to do some scholarly work, which actually became political work within the context of where I was working. When I tried to get course approval, sexism was suddenly thrown into relief. I could see it permeating the place. The questions about my course began with the associate dean who said to me, "I'm not sure how you can mount this course. Is there a literature you can draw on?" And it went on from there. Well, that incident struck me hard. Yes, indeed, sexism is alive and well and living in academe. I could then look back at a whole series of sexist incidents that had been too dangerous to acknowledge before. After that they had become too dangerous not to be acknowledged. So what about that? What if we refuse to pay attention to oppression?

Carl: I think one reason we don't pay attention to oppression is because we are not trained to see it. It is only when somebody upsets us or challenges us that our blinders fall away. It's possible for people to challenge us many times, but we'll never feel the challenge until we are ready to feel it. Because we have agency, we can sometimes …

Celia: … resist and sometimes act in ways that aren't appropriate to the circumstances. People who are serious about social justice need to recognize and address injustices that have served them, that they have been party to. This need is particularly important for people who presumably cannot afford not to consider their complicity in a system built on injustice.

Carl: This means that they have to take political action seriously. Kathryn Alexander, in her excellent discussion of gender differences, doesn't talk about sexism directly, but some of her comments relate to how sexism is learnt and experienced, which should indicate a need for political action. I think many of the things she talks about are noteworthy examples of sexism.

Celia: The place where I really noticed her point about sexism was when she looked at the certified family genealogy, and her brother was named as the first-born male and she and her female cousins weren't even there. She writes, "It was the first time in our lives that I faced cultural truths about how girls really do not count or, more accurately speaking, were not counted." She's definitely using the experience of twin-ness to get at sexism.

Carl: Her essay can be used to teach about how school socialization contributes to the gendering of students.

Celia: Not just school.

Carl: Yeah, society in general, because as twins, they grow up thinking of themselves as loving each other, holding hands and going to school, but they quickly learn that's not okay. And there were times when she brought home the difficulties she had in school with males; like when she and her brother were not to touch each other.

Celia: And there was her concern when she asked her mother if she had to marry her brother when she grew up. [Both laugh.] She writes, "I knew I didn't have to marry my brother when I grew up, but the alarm in my mother's voice indicated that I had to marry someone else's brother." [Laugh.] I love the stuff she pulls out of the book *God of Small Things* about twins' use of pronouns, "Esthappen and Rahel thought of themselves together as Me, and separately, individually, as We or Us." (Roy 1997: 4). It also resonated with Jean Graveline's piece and her discussion of a world view that comes tied up in language. There is a non-twin world view of Me and Us in the standard use of English.

Carl: The essay by Karen Meyer about girls in science is an excellent example of gendered schooling.

Celia: I noted the place where she writes, "Silence is the recourse for many girls [in science classrooms]. In the end, the passwords are the glossary at the back of the textbook or the parroting of definitions as if they were lines from a travel phrase book. The issue is, science as a second language acts as a liability to participation and communication, making access and inclusion problematic."

There are many places in the essays where an unusual notion of second language comes into play.

Carl: On another aspect of difference, David Mason talks about how schools and teachers deal with deaf students. More generally, David's chapter relates very well to the point about our responsibility to work with and through differences. In reading early drafts of his essay, I wondered about what living deaf in a hearing world must be like when everything, particularly the subtitles of human interactions, depends so much on hearing and seeing. From David's essay, I've recognized how much I know from being a hearing person, including things that I cannot read about and that I get informally. Then I started thinking of how we in the academy expect deaf individuals to produce pieces of work in the same way that hearing people produce work. In that context, I considered my own expectations of conformity. So, I wonder, do we have space for that kind of difference, where we give consideration to the fact that it is impossible for a deaf individual to relate in the same way as hearing people?

Celia: That relates to the point we were considering about people being able to recognize and work together across their differences. The ability you've just talked about, to be able to put yourself in another person's shoes is essential. If we can't make an effort to do that (and I don't think we can ever fully achieve the position of the other person), working together is doomed. But if you don't even try, then the likelihood of working together through our differences is vastly reduced.

Carl: In his essay, David draws comparisons between ethnic-minority and deaf communities, inferring that since we respond to ethnic communities in particular ways, we should do the same for the deaf community. I think suggesting that similar approaches are applicable to both communities doesn't necessarily further the kinds of understanding and political action that are needed for both communities, because ethnic and language minority communities are not necessarily going to agree that they have common issues. I'm trying to communicate that differences are not necessarily similar. We cannot make simple connections just because we want other people to do so, just because we hope that, in making connections, they will be able to make sense of each other.

Celia: I think there's a huge difference between what you're describing now and what you were describing initially in your reading of David's essay. What you were doing at first was not to imagine a connection to an ethnic-minority community, but rather to get yourself to a place inside his community to make a connection. That's a big distinction, because to go the other way is presumptuous. It's presumptuous to assume that the differences are the same.

Carl: And that's why we just can't say, if you're a working-class White person then you can understand the demands that racialized people make on the system. That would not necessarily work. You have to first admit that you're working-class, whatever that means, and then try to understand your relationships to privilege and your relationships to marginalization and how the other person's relationship may be constructed differently or similarly.

Celia: What you just said flashes me back to Paulo Freire and his efforts to take his literacy campaign from Brazil to Chile, and then Guinea-Bissau. The latter, according to some people, was not a terribly successful event. However, in the introduction to his book, *Letters to Guinea-Bissau* (1983), he says what we learned in Chile was that we couldn't do in Chile what we had done in Brazil, despite the fact that they were both literacy campaigns. And that piece just hangs in my head non-stop in terms of critical pedagogy, in terms of education in changing contexts, and in terms of developing relationships within new contexts. Over and over again, when I go to a new context, usually in an Aboriginal community—that's where I do my research—I have to start from the position of knowing that I know nothing, absolutely nothing. I can't go there assuming that what I saw in Secwepemc territory or what I saw in Tsimshian territory is going to play out again in an Anishinaape territory in Manitoba or Red Lake. Most important in entering a new place—rather than leaping to conclusions and seeing similarities—is an acceptance of not knowing, and an openness to wanting to know.

Carl: I think the major point you're making is that we should not be so quick to construct similarities. A starting point then, are the questions, What is this context? What's this context all about? And what do I know about this context? And we have to wait for answers before saying there are similarities.

Celia: It is not that there aren't similarities, for those similarities may come and you'll see them. But these are very specific and limited, and there will always be huge differences. And if all you are trying to do is see similarities, that's what you'll see, and you'll miss all of the richness of the distinctions.

Carl: In thinking further about the issue of working through differences related to disabilities, Carolyn Ewoldt's essay comes to mind. I remember reading her chapter and thinking of some experiences we're blind to because we're not there. For example, she talks about driving and the things we take for granted.

I keep thinking of that. I do lots of important thinking while being in my own company when driving, and I can take the car and drive whenever I want to and wherever I want, but I've never given much thought to how privileged I am in that way.

Celia: Not only do you do your own thinking there, but you have very important conversations with your son when you're driving.

Carl: Yes, Carolyn awakens me to those taken-for-granted things that we have in our everyday lives. I think that exposing ourselves to the complexities of each person's "differences" is very important. It helps us to make sense of our own differences and what we take for granted.

Celia: Can there ever be a time and space where we can see other people's differences through a recognition of our own? I think Fyre Jean Graveline speaks to that point very clearly. She takes us through some of the incredible difficulties she's facing within an institution that's reacting against her use of Aboriginal knowledge. In order to survive there, she goes to a ceremony—to an identifiable Aboriginal space—so she can come back to the institution with the strength and humility to continue to say, "We have to find ways to work together." There is no romance in what she writes. She's given us a harsh look at reality, and she does not let us fall into the trap of thinking this work might be easy. One thing I worry about with a book like this is that somehow people will put a romantic twist to it, saying with conviction, "See, we all have differences; we just need to all work together." It's important to know how hard that work can be. Graveline's piece makes that point with lucidity. It's heart-rending as we work through the pain we cause each other, and it's Herculean to sustain the desire to do that work.

Carl: I'm thinking that this book also shows that, despite what we might think about other people's differences as being the same as ours, we can never be in another person's body or have the other person's experience, as Jean Graveline illustrates, moving between her different worlds. I know that I can never have another person's experience, so how could I say my difference is the same as that other person's? I have to appreciate the difference and the experience that comes with the difference and see where we connect.

Celia: Yes, to keep recognizing the importance of going out there into the grey, but also finding times when you can be with people more like you, when you can sit and talk through those issues, or just be in a place where you don't have to be explaining to someone how different your difference is from theirs or be silent because the differences threaten to overwhelm you.

Carl: I want to reintroduce the notion of privilege in this discussion about working through difference. Elizabeth McGibbon's essay is a good reference here.

Celia: This is the woman who writes, "Notions of privilege and power were probably never addressed in the class.... I could not begin to address racism or even accept that racism exists until people began to help me *see* racism. This continues to be a challenge for me because my Whiteness allows me to look the other way."

Carl: That's a very good statement. I keep thinking of why is it that the marginalized person has to do ...

Celia: ... do the educating. [Both laugh together.] As Judith Moschkovich, a Latin American Jewish feminist, writes in *This Bridge Called My Back* (1987), "It is not the duty of the oppressed to educate the oppressor. If you White people are really interested in learning about me and my culture, go to the bookstore, there's some really good books there. Go to the music store and buy some music and learn. Go and inform yourself and when you've learned from all the texts you can find, then come and have an informed conversation with me about difference." The idea that you have to find a lesbian to educate you about homophobia, or you have to find a Black person to educate you about racism, is far too simplistic and irresponsible.

Carl: But don't you think that one of the reasons we do not often engage with each other's difference, and why so often we remain ignorant, is because somehow, even in university, we give no space for the discussion of experiences? We just simply talk about the information, the objective truth ...

Celia: ... and we theorize whenever we can. We don't want to let experiences get in there and mess with the purity and clarity of the theory. Too often, we try to force people's experiences to fit our theory, so it can become more and more refined, more and more unassailable. And this is not to say that rigorous theorizing can't come out of experience. It …

Carl: … has to come out of experience. And we have to base our theories on experiences, on the diversity, complexity and fluidity of our experiences. We have to see ourselves as constructing people as different, understand how we're doing so and why we're doing so.

Political Action

Carl: Do you think that a book like this that opens up questions of difference, and the ways in which different people are experiencing difference, can move us to think about political action, to understand the ways in which different people engage in political action, and identify how we might build coalitions?

Celia: Yes, although not everybody in the book is engaged in organized political action. Some might be said to be engaging in "individual" political action—an oxymoron if I ever heard one. I do think that serious engagement in political action is always a matter of education, not necessarily formal, of course. But it is a matter of conscious effort: people need time to talk together about not getting stuck in their single agenda; although some people should stay within their single agenda because there's so much work to do in all of those areas. For some people to have one issue as their sole focus is probably fine as long as they never lose sight of the fact that they are choosing one focus from many possible. I think about class structure, union struggles, Marxist organizations, and of the inability of those organizations to address sexism. They may be doing a little better, but then moving from there to do anything around racial or ethnic difference seems to be incredibly difficult for them. And I am referring here to those unions dominated by White folks.

Carl: I don't think we can really engage in political action unless we name the oppressions. If we are to engage in political action against sexism, how can you not name "women" and the issues women experience? To engage in political action against racism, how can you not talk very deliberately about race and examples of racism, such as saying, because of my race, this and this happened? Unless this is done, racism is not going to be dealt with.

Celia: We're assuming that people want to engage in political action, of course. [Both laugh together.] There are real reasons for you to assume that there are people who don't want to make waves, who just want to go along without disturbing things. If they can pass, they'll pass.

Carl: Well, if that's the case, then probably we'll get nowhere. The situation for marginalized people—and for some more than others—will remain the same.

Celia: Well, that depends on so many factors. Political action can also start with only a few knowledgeable and committed people. Practically speaking, you have to name things to make change. I think that's also what Cathy van Ingen gets at in her essay. There were moments in her chapter when I wasn't sure in which direction she was going with her politics because she was objecting to a questionnaire designed specifically for homosexuals and she spent quite a lot of time saying, "Why are we the subjects of this questionnaire. Why doesn't everybody do this questionnaire?" But, in the end, she comes back and says there are some policy implications here and they matter. Now, in a group I'm working with at York University, one of the issues that keeps coming up is the whole business of not keeping track of "ethnocultural diversity," as we call it at York. And that whole business of people not having to identify themselves is really important, and if you were an applicant to a program, would you want to indicate that you're Black? Is that going to have an effect on your application? Would you want to leave that off given a chioice? All those questions related to privacy and implicitly concerned with normalist gatekeepers seemed to have been taking precedence over the importance of keeping track of, for example: How many Aboriginal students do we have in this university? What's happening with the Aboriginal students we have? Are they successful? What are the good things that are happening? Where are they falling through the cracks? That business of not naming is having an impact on how things unfold and can also be seen as a political move.

Carl: Oh yes, and I would think it's also a political move to maintain the status quo.

Differences Are Socially Constructed, Relational, Contextual and Contentious

Celia: Okay, now I want to ask you: You've gathered all these differences together, you're obviously fascinated with the notion of difference in all of its aspects; if you were asked to hit the high spots of what theorizing one can do based on these texts—theoretical moments that stand out for you in this particular collection—what would you say?

Carl: I think of the notion of context. I hope readers see the significance of context and how it operates. And closely related to that are the relational aspects of difference. You move from one context to another, and depending on who you are relating to, difference takes on particular meanings. So difference is never without a context, or independent of people and our interactions. For me, the idea of putting all these differences in one volume is not to state how similar these differences are, but how differences must be thought of in relational terms and as related to context. How we name a difference is very much based on the fact that it is socially constructed in relation to everything around it.

Endnotes

7: "You're doing it for the students"

1. I see the socialization process as one way in which youth are not invited to think about understanding their own possibilities but told what they *should do*, what they *should become* and whom they *should be like*. In this process, role models represent, as Crichlow (1999: 2) puts it, "fixed images of achievement and ideologues of 'politically correct' socialization."
2. The paradox of Black History Month activities is effectively discussed in Althea Prince's essay, "Black History Month: A Multicultural Myth, or 'Have-Black-History-Month-Kit-Will-Travel.'" Prince points out that "we" participate in the month's activities "in the name of the community and history, for our children, for ourselves, for our society" (1996: 167). It is an opportunity that is seized because it is the only time such space is open to share, explore and discuss the history and experiences of Black people. Yet it is understood that a month's activities are not the way to build an inclusive curriculum. But, as Prince goes on to say, "it feels sometimes that we are in a bind. For if we continue to enable the ghettoised version of our history as a people, allowing it to be relegated to one month, then we are complicit in the perpetuation of a hegemony that denies our existence" (1996: 169).
3. The profile of the communities from which the students came is quite significant, for it plays a role in the perceptions that educators and others might have of the students, seeing them as people needing role models.
4. This term is borrowed from Regina Austin, who points out that "role models are typically viewed as an antidote by those who deem a given community diseased." She was referring to a court ruling that favoured the position of the Omaha Girls Club. The Club held that Crystal Chambers, a single African-American woman, was dismissed from her job as a craft instructor when she became pregnant, because she "could no longer serve as a positive role model to African-American girls who participated in the club" (cited in Britzman 1993: 38).
5. The experience of a teacher candidate, Lynette (a pseudonym), with whom I worked, is illustrative. Lynette recalled being "brought up to believe that one of the problems for Black students was that we did not have enough role models," and that as a "successful" high school student in one of Toronto's famous so-called "inner-city communities," she was encouraged by her teachers to pursue a career in teaching. But a recent incident involving some members of her grade eleven (advanced) class of "predominantly" Black students, nearly 90 percent of African-Caribbean background like herself, reinforced the point that "students do not appreciate you simply because you have 'made it' having come from a community like them." Lynette reported that she met a number of her students at a roller skating rink across from the school one Saturday night. This was considered inappropriate enough that some students requested that Lynette not return to teach them, claiming that she could not be a role model and be "partying

with them." Her host teacher and principal did not agree. But as Lynet said, working with the students thereafter was a struggle for they saw h as someone "from the ghetto," who had not earned their respect. At the en of her teaching practice, after they had grown to appreciate her and he knowledge, interest in them and dedication to teaching, in a parting comment to her, one student said: "Miss, don't go to any more parties." What happened? Lynette had breached the moral conventions and expectations of a role model that the student had come to accept.

6. Fisher points out that the existing role model discourse works because it obscures structures of inequality that maintain the status quo and resist change (cited in Crichlow 1999).
7. The experience of Deidré R. Farmbry is an example. She tells of her struggles to connect with her Black high school students on the basis of her Black identity. Contributing to the struggles was the students' reading of her physical appearance and "language style" as "different," "foreign," "correct," "proper" and "white" (1993: 273).
8. There were less than four Black teachers at the school of about eighty teachers.

8: Classroom Doors at Christmas

1. Although Christianity began as a Jewish sect and for a long time sought converts primarily from among Jews, when Christianity separated from Judaism, much of Christian theology sought to discredit traditional Judaism and establish Christianity as the one true religion. Jews who would not convert were seen as rebels against God's purpose. Since some explanation had to be offered for why many Jews would not accept Christ as the son of God sent to earth in human form, Jews were labelled as heretics and agents of Satan. Images of Jews having horns and tails were among the popular beliefs that identified Jews as "other," inhuman, and as a people to be feared and hated. Perhaps the longest and most damaging myth can be traced to the Fourth Gospel, of John, in which Jews as a group are held responsible for the death of Jesus, thus establishing the concept of "deicide" in New Testament teaching. Until very recently, many Christians were taught that the Jews killed Christ. What actually did happen remains speculative and many of the reports in the Gospels were written several decades later by people trying to discredit Judaism and appease Rome. It is clearly stated by most sources, however, that Jesus was tried, convicted and sentenced by Roman law and Roman judges, and crucified by Roman soldiers. It may be that some of the leaders of the Jewish community saw Jesus as a threat to their own power, but they were not representative of the larger portion of Jews at the time who were living under the harsh domination of Roman law. And even if a few Jews did encourage and support the conviction of Jesus, it is inappropriate to make all Jews forever responsible. Despite how problematic this thinking is, the myth of deicide was used as an excuse for the persecution of Jews over the course of history in Christian Europe (Weinstein and Mellen 1997).

For a discussion on Hanukkah and Christmas celebrations by Jews, see the story entitled "My Hanukkah" in Letty Cottin Pogrebin's *Deborah, Golda and Me: Being Female and Jewish in America* (1991).

3. I want to thank my colleague Judy Iseke-Barnes for this insight about the common bond that celebrating Christmas has for Christians
4. Once again, my thanks to Judy Iseke-Barnes for this insight about "loss of innocence." As briefly explained in footnote 1 above, throughout history Jewish people have been persecuted for not converting to Christianity. In addition to the myth of deicide, other myths and libels, such as charging Jews with kidnapping Christian babies and using their blood for religious purposes, were repeatedly used in later years as rationales for attacks on Jewish communities and the mass murder of Jewish people. For example, the Crusaders killed tens of thousands of Jews on their way to the Holy Land, the Spanish Inquisition killed thirty thousand people and one hundred thousand Jews were massacred in Poland between 1648–1655. This strategy set the stage for Hitler's "Final Solution" during the Second World War (Weinstein and Mellen 1997).

10: One Family, Indivisible?

1. This essay appeared in *Canadian Forum* in October 1992, and also in James and Shadd (1994).

13: Negotiating Differences

1. My notion of what it means to be privileged has been informed in part by Peggy McIntosh (1989: 10–12).
2. An interesting exploration of the implications of interracial couples and notions of privilege, class and disadvantage can be found in Pui Yee Beryl Tsang (1994: 221–29).
3. A useful assessment of the impact of race on children of mixed parentage can be found in a book by Barbara Tizard and Ann Phoenix (1993).
4. For an examination of complementary racial identities see Katya Gibel Azoulay (1997).

20: Beamers, Cells, Malls and Cantopop

1. For a discussion of how Canadian media such as *Jack Canuck* fueled discourses of the "Yellow Peril," particularly in relation to Chinese masculinity, see Pon (1996).
2. TTC stands for the Toronto Transit Commission, the public transit system.
3. Toisanese and Hoipingnese are people from the Toisan and Hoiping counties of Guangdong province of mainland China. Prior to the late 1960s the majority of the Chinese people in Canada spoke village dialects of Canton-

ese, such as Toisanese and Hoipingnese (see Yee 1993 and Woon 1998).

4. In fact, 25 percent of all immigrants from Hong Kong live below the po erty line, compared with 15 percent of those who were born in Canada ar 19 percent of all immigrants (see Carey 1996). Also, Chinese-Canadian male earn on average 30 percent less than Canadian males overall and Chinese Canadian females earn 40 percent less than Canadian females (see Das Gupta 1996).
5. For instance, the prevalent stereotype that the Chinese are all rich is evident in Don Gillmor's (1997) article on the Pacific Mall which appeared in *Toronto Life*. Perpetuating the more recent "model minority" stereotype and reinvoking older stereotypes of the "Yellow Peril," he describes the mall as being populated by rich "satellite kids," extortionists and unassimilated businesses. This article was nominated for the 1998 Chinese Canadian National Council Media Awards under the Stinker Category.
6. See Grayson, Chi and Rhyne (1994). It is important to note, however, that York University has a cohort of Hong Kong–born Chinese youth who are extremely politically active. These students write and publish campus newspapers and are regular contributors to critical Chinese youth journals such as *Young Renmin*. This particular journal can be accessed on-line at youngrenmin.at.hkid.com.
7. From the song titled "Police Station Rap: Black vs Yellow," which appears on the Leon CD (1998) called "I'm Waiting to See You Again," Sony Music.
8. It is important to note that many Chinese-Canadians have very optimistic outlooks about the labour market and do not regard racism as a barrier to their career aspirations. For example, surveys conducted at York University found that a large number of Chinese students who spoke Chinese in the home do not consider themselves members of a visible minority group. In subsequent focus group meetings it was found that many regarded the term "visible minority" to be derogatory. Some students equated the term with affirmative action programs and these students opposed such initiatives due to fears of backlash and aversion to reverse discrimination; belief in meritocracy as a basis for hiring; and feared organizational consequences (see Grayson, Chi and Rhyne 1994).
9. Attendant to free-market globalization has been an increased disparity between the rich and the poor, and a shrinking of the middle class. Rapid movements of transnational capital have made many middle- and working-class jobs tenuous. This results in part from the rise in new technologies, "capital flight," corporate and government downsizing, increased American corporate competition and a general dismantling of the welfare state. Teeple (1995) argues that this decline of Canada's working and middle classes is linked to the New Right corporate agenda. He contends that globalization allows corporations to reduce taxation by playing nation against nation. This has resulted in global restructuring, so that the working class, particularly the lower and middle strata, bear a larger and rising share of taxes. Corporate taxes have not only declined sharply, but state loans, grants and tax deferrals to these companies have risen tremendously since the 1980s.

22: Beyond Breaking the Silence

Several legislative changes continue to occur across Canada. On February 11, 2000 the Federal Government introduced Bill C-23 (Modernizing Benefits and Obligations Bill) in order to extend to both opposite-sex and same-sex couples the status of "common law partners". Bill C-23 affirms that same-sex relationships are entitled to equal treatment under the law and provides equal access to income tax, pension benefits, and employment insurance (EGALE, 2000). This Bill is intended to ensure that the human rights of lesbians, gays and bisexuals in Canada will not depend on where in the country we happen to live. Yet in March 2000, one month following the first reading of Bill C-23, Alberta voted into law Bill 202, or the Marriage Amendment Act, which bans marriages between same-sex couples. This is one example of the Alberta government using the notwithstanding clause to pass legislation that discriminates against lesbian, gays and bisexuals and prevents further challenge under the Canadian Charter of Rights and Freedoms (Cudmore, 2000).

23: Talking Equity

1. A different version of this chapter was first presented as the 1998 Florence Bird Lecture, sponsored by the Pauline Jewett Institute of Women's Studies, Carleton University. I am grateful to Katherine Arnup for inviting me to speak and for Celia Haig-Brown for inspiring me.

24: Being Me in the Academy

1. Translated literally: "Monkey must know where he is going to put his tail before he orders trousers." This Caribbean proverb advises individuals to think things through carefully before acting. These words of caution have kept me out of trouble on many occasions. But I don't always heed the advice of proverbs; I sometimes throw caution to the wind and hope that, when I need to, I can find a safe place to put my tail. Although I know that it is potentially dangerous to be critical of an institution while I am still a part of it, I have decided to throw caution to the wind and write about my experience of academe.

25: Lived Experiences of an Aboriginal Feminist

1. This narrative is based on a collection of experiences throughout my life as a faculty member in different institutions across time and space. An earlier version of it appears in Graveline (1994).

26: Reflecting on Difference

1. The taped conversation was transcribed by Mirella Guido, who was carefu to capture not only the words but also the tone and tempo of our interaction and communication, such as the way we built on each other's sentences and the laughs we shared. We really appreciate what Mirella has done.
2. The use of elipses at these points in our conversation indicates places where we interrupt one another or build on each other's ideas. They are significant to us as points where our thoughts at times coincide and at times diverge. The reader may find it informative to examine these places as points where knowledge is actively collaborative even as it may disrupt.

References

Adair, Margo, and Sharon Howell. 1989. "The Subjective Side of Power." In J. Plant (ed.), *Healing the Wounds: The Promise of Ecofeminism*. Toronto: Between the Lines.

Anderson, Laurie. 1994. *Stories from the Nerve Bible: A Retrospective, 1972–1992*. New York: Harper Collins.

Askew, Sue, and Carol Ross. 1988. *Boys Don't Cry*. Milton Keynes: Open University Press.

Azoulay, Katya Gibel. 1997. *Black, Jewish, and Interracial: It's Not the Color of Your Skin, but the Race of Your Kin, and Other Myths of Identity*. Durham, N.C.: Duke University Press.

Baker, N.L. 1996. "Class as a Construct in a Classless Society." *Women and Therapy* 18(3–4): 13–23.

Bannerji, Himani. 1991. "But Who Speaks for Us? Experience and Agency in Conventional Feminist Paradigm." In H. Bannerji, L. Carty, K. Dehli, S. Heald and K. McKenna (eds.), *Unsettling Relations: The University as a Site of Feminist Struggles*. Toronto: Women's Press.

Bartky, Sandra Lee. 1996. "The Pedagogy of Shame." In C. Luke (ed.), *Pedagogies of Everyday Life*. Albany, N.Y.: State University of New York Press.

Battiste, Marie, and Jean Barman. 1995. *First Nations Education in Canada: The Circle Unfolds*. Vancouver: University of British Columbia Press.

Benjamin, Jessica. 1998. *Shadow of the Other: Intersubjectivity and Gender in Psychoanalysis*. New York: Routledge.

Benjamin, Walter. 1969. "The Storyteller: Reflections on the Works of Nikolai Leskov." In W. Benjamin, *Illuminations*. New York: Schocken Books.

Bennett, Louise. 1993. *Aunty Roachy Seh*. Kingston, Jamaica: Sangster's Book Stores.

Biklen, D. 1988. "The Myth of Clinical Judgment." *Journal of Social Issues* 44(1): 127–40.

Bishop, Russell. 1996. *Whakawhanaungatanga: Collaborative Research Stories*. Palmerston, N.Z.: Dunsmore Press.

Blaeser, K. 1996. *Gerald Vizenor: Writing in the Oral Tradition*. Norman, Okla.: University of Oklahoma Press.

Bornstein, Kate. 1998. *My Gender Workbook*. New York: Routledge.

Bramble, Maxine. 1999. "'That really wasn't me': A black, immigrant, Caribbean woman's attempt to belong in the academy." *Canadian Woman Studies* 19(3): 134–40.

Britzman, Deborah P. 1993. "Beyond Rolling Models: Gender and Multicultural Education." In S.K. Biklen and D. Pollard (eds.), *Gender and Education: Ninety-Second Yearbook of the National Society for the Study of Education*. Chicago: University of Chicago Press.

Bryson, Mary, and Suzanne deCastell. 1995. "So We've Got a Chip on Our Shoulders: Sexing the Texts of 'Educational Technology.'" In J. Gaskell and J. Willinsky (eds.), *Gender In/Forms Curriculum: From Enrichment to Transformation*. New York: Teachers College Press.

Bull, Ray, and Nichola Rumsey. 1988. *The Social Psychology of Facial Appearance*. New York: Springer-Verlag.

Butler, Judith. 1997. *Excitable Speech: A Politics of the Performative*. New York: Routledge.

———. 1990. *Gender Trouble: Feminism and the Subversion of Identity*. New York: Routledge.

Campbell, M. 1992. "Nurses' Professionalism in Canada: A Labor Process Analysis." *International Journal of Health Services* 22(4): 751–65.

Carey, Elaine. 1996. "Skilled, Young, Wealthy and Loyal to Canada." *Toronto Star*, November 10, B1 and B4.

Carniol, Ben. 1998. "Racial Ethnic and Cultural Diversity and CASSW (Canadian Association for Schools of Social Work) Accreditation Standards." Report to the CASSW Advisory Committee on Racial, Ethnic and Cultural Issues, January 6.

Carter, H. 1994. "Confronting Patriarchal Attitudes in the Fight for Professional Recognition." *Journal of Advanced Nursing* 19: 367–72.

Carty, Linda. 1991. "Black Women in Academia: A Statement from the Periphery. In H. Bannerji et al. (eds.), *Unsettling Relations: The University as a Site of Struggle*. Toronto: Women's Press.

Carver, R. 1989. *Deaf Illiteracy: A Genuine Educational Puzzle or an Instrument of Oppression?* Ottawa: Canadian Association of the Deaf.

Christensen, Kathee. 1993. "A Multicultural Approach to Education of Children Who are Deaf." In K. Christensen and G. Delgado (eds.), *Multicultural Issues in Deafness*. Toronto: Copp Clark Pitman.

Ciardi, J. 1988. "How to Tell the Top of a Hill." In B. Schenk de Regniers (ed.), *Sing a Song of Popcorn: Every Child's Book of Poems*. New York: Scholastic Books.

Cole, Jonathan. 1998. *About Face*. Cambridge, Mass.: MIT Press.

Cole, M. 1989. *Education for Equity*. London: Routledge.

Collins, Patricia Hill. 1991. *Black Feminist Thought*. New York: Routledge.

Connell, Robert. 1989. "Cool Guys, Swots and Wimps: The Interplay of Masculinity and Education." *Oxford Review of Education* 15(3): 291–303.

Cooke-MacGregor, Frances. 1974. *Transformation and Identity: The Face and Plastic Surgery*. New York: Quadrangle Press/New York Times Book Co.

Corrigan, Philip. 1991. "The Making of the Boy: Meditations on What Grammar School Did With, To, and For My Body." In H. Giroux (ed.), *Postmodernism, Feminism, and Cultural Politics: Redrawing Educational Boundaries*. New York: State University of New York Press.

Crichlow, Warren. 1999. "Role Models, Heroes and the Inconsolability of Teaching Education." Scandling Lecture, University of Rochester, New York, March.

Crites, S. 1986. "Storytime: Recollecting the Past and Projecting the Future." In T.R. Sarbin (ed.), *Narrative Psychology: The Storied Nature of Human Conduct*. New York: Praeger.

Cudmore, James. (2000). "Alberta bill bans same-sex marriages". In The National Post 2000-03-17. http://www.gaylifecanada.com/news/?view=4

Culley, Margo. 1985. "Anger and Authority in the Women's Studies Classroom." In M. Culley and C. Portugese (eds.), *Gendered Subjects: The Dynamics of Feminist Teaching*. Boston: Routledge and Kegan Paul.

Das Gupta, Tania. 1996. *Racism and Paid Work.* Toronto: Garamond.

Davison, Kevin. 1996. *Manly Expectations: Memories of Masculinities in School.* Unpublished master's thesis, Simon Fraser University, British Columbia.

Dion, Karen, and Ellen Berscheid. 1972. "What is Beautiful is Good." *Journal of Personality and Social Psychology* 24(3): 285–90.

Doxtator, D. 1988. "The Home of the Indian Culture and Other Stories in the Museums." *Muse* 6(3): 26–28.

Duval, M. 1984. "Psychosocial Metaphors of Physical Distress among Multiple Sclerosis Patients." *Social Science and Medicine* 19(6): 635–38.

EGALE (Equality for Gays and Lesbians Everywhere). 2000. Equality For Gays and Lesbians Everywhere. www.egale.ca/documentsC23submission.htm

———. 1999. {www.egale.ca/pressrel/990611e.htm}

Elkins, J. 1996. *The Object Stares Back: On the Nature of Seeing*. New York: Simon & Schuster.

Farmbry, Deidré R. 1993. "The Warriors, the Worrier, and the Word." In M. Cochran-Smith and S.L. Lytle (eds.), *Inside/Outside: Teacher Research and Knowledge*. New York: Teachers College Press.

Fels, L., and K. Meyer. 1997. "On the Edge of Chaos: Co-Evolving World(s) of Drama and Science." *Teaching Education* 19(1): 75–81.

Fine, M., and A. Asch. 1988. *Women with Disabilities: Essays in Psychology, Culture and Politics*. Philadelphia: Temple University Press.

Fiske, J. 1990. *Understanding Popular Culture*. New York: Routledge.

Fitznor, L. 1998. "The Circle of Life: Affirming Aboriginal Philosophies in Everyday Living." In D. McCance (ed.), *Life Ethics in World Religions*. Atlanta: Scholar's Press.

Flax, Jane. 1993. *Disputed Subjects: Essays on Psychoanalysis, Politics and Philosophy*. London: Routledge.

Flesche, Rudolf F. 1995. *Why Johnny Can't Read: What You Can Do About It.* New York: Harper & Row.

Francis, Daniel. 1997. *The Imaginary Indian: The Image of the Indian in Canada*. Fifth edition. Vancouver: Arsenal Pulp Press.

Frank, Blye. 1994. "Queer Selves/Queer in Schools: Young Men and Sexualities." In S. Prentice (ed.), *Sex in Schools: Canadian Education & Sexual Regulation*. Toronto: Our Schools/Our Selves Education Foundation.

———. 1993. "Straight/Strait Jackets for Masculinity: Educating for 'Real Men.'" *Atlantis* 18(1 & 2): 47–59.

———. 1992. "Hegemonic Heterosexual Masculinity: Sports, Looks and a Woman, That's What Every Guy Needs to be Masculine." *Institute of Social and Economic Research Papers* 3: 271–303.

Frankenberg, Ruth. 1997. "Introduction: Local Whitenesses, Localizing Whiteness." In R. Frankenberg (ed.), *Displacing Whiteness: Essays in Social and Cultural Criticism*. Durham, N.C.: Duke University Press.

Freire, Paulo. 1985. "Rethinking Critical Pedagogy: A Dialogue with Paulo Freire." In Henry A. Giroux (ed.), *The Politics of Education: Culture, Power and Liberation*. South Hadley, Mass.: Bergin and Garvey.

———. 1983. *Pedagogy in Process: The Letters to Guinea-Bissau*. New York: Continuum.

Frey, Darcy. 1994. *The Last Shot: City Streets, Basketball Dreams*. New York:

Houghton Mifflin.

Frye, Marilyn. 1992. *Willful Virgin: Essays in Feminism*. Freedom, CA.: Crossir Press.

———. 1983. *The Politics of Reality: Essays in Feminist Theory*. Freedom, CA.: Crossing Press

Gardner, Saundra. 1993. "What's a Nice Working-Class Girl Like You Doing in a Place Like This?" In M.M.Tokarczyk and E.A. Fay (eds.), *Working-Class Women in the Academy: Laborers in the Knowledge Factory*. Amherst, Mass.: University of Massachusetts Press.

Gillmor, Don. 1997. "Satellite City." *Toronto Life* (November):146–150.

Gilroy, Paul. 1993. *The Black Atlantic: Modernity and Double Consciousness*. Cambridge: Harvard University Press.

Gliedman, J., and W. Roth. 1980. *The Unexpected Minority: Handicapped Children in America.* New York: Harcourt Brace Jovanovich.

Graveline, Fyre Jean. 1998. *Circle Works: Transforming Eurocentric Consciousness.* Halifax: Fernwood.

———. 1994. "Lived Experiences of an Aboriginal Feminist Transforming the Curriculum." *Canadian Woman Studies* 14(2): 52–55.

Grayson, Paul, Tammy Chi and Darla Rhyne. 1994. *The Social Construction of "Visible Minority" for Students of Chinese Origin*. Toronto: Institute for Social Research, York University.

Grossberg, Lawrence. 1996. "Identity in Cultural Studies—Is That All There Is?" In S. Hall and P. du Gay (eds.), *Questions of Cultural Identity*. London: Sage.

Gunn Allen, Paula. 1986. *The Sacred Hoop: Recovering the Feminine in American Indian Traditions*. Boston: Beacon.

Gunn, J.V. 1981. *Autobiography: Toward a Poetics of Experience*. Philadelphia: University of Pennsylvania Press.

Haig-Brown, Celia. 1998. "Warrior Mothers: Lessons and Possibilities." *Journal for Just and Caring Education* 4(1): 96–109.

———. 1995. *Taking Control: Power and Contradiction in First Nations Adult Education.* Vancouver: University of British Columbia Press.

Haig-Brown, Roderick. 1950. *Measure of the Year*. Toronto: Collins.

Hall, Stuart. 1996. "Introduction: Who Needs 'Identity'?" In S. Hall and P. du Gay (eds.), *Questions of Cultural Identity*. London: Sage.

Halperin, D. 1995. *Saint Foucault: Towards a Gay Hagiography*. Oxford: Oxford University Press.

Harris, Cheryl L. 1993. "Whiteness as Property." *Harvard Law Review* 106.

Harris, Daniel. 1998. "The Selling of the Subculture." *Harvard Gay & Lesbian Review* (June).

———. 1996. "Transformations in Gay Male Porn." *Harvard Gay and Lesbian Review* 3(3).

Haug, F. 1987. *Female Sexualization: A Collective Work of Memory*. London: Verso Press.

Hayden, Gene. 1998. "Seeing Double" *Profiles: The York University Magazine for Alumni and Friends* (August): 13–14.

Hebb, D.O. 1954. "The Problem of Consciousness and Introspection." In E. Adriane et al. (eds.), *Brain Mechanics and Consciousness*. Oxford: Oxford University Press.

illyer, B. 1993. *Feminism and Disability*. Norman: University of Oklahoma Press.

offmeister, R. 1992. *Why* MCE *Won't Work:* ASL *Forms Inside Signed English*. Working paper 16. Boston: Boston University Center for the Study of Communication and Deafness.

hooks, bell. 1994. *Teaching to Transgress: Education as the Practice of Freedom*. New York: Routledge.

———. 1993. "Keeping Close to Home: Class and Education." In Michelle Tokarczyk and Elizabeth Fay (eds.), *Working Class Women in the Academy: Labourers in the Education Factory*. Amherst: University of Massachusetts Press.

———. 1992. *Black Looks: Race and Representation*. Toronto: Between the Lines.

———. 1990. *Yearning: Race, Gender, and Cultural Politics*. Boston: South End Press.

Jagose, A. 1996. *Queer Theory*. New York: State University of New York Press.

James, Audrey. 1999. "Growing Up Mixed Heritage: Encountering Difference Within and Without." M.Ed. research paper, York University, Toronto.

James, Carl E. 1999. *Seeing Ourselves: Exploring Race, Ethnicity, and Culture*. Toronto: Thompson Educational Publishing.

———. 1998. "'Up to No Good': Black on the Streets and Encountering Police." In V. Satzewich (ed.), *Racism and Social Inequity in Canada*. Toronto: Thompson Educational Publishing.

———. 1997a. "Contradictory Tensions in the Experiences of African Canadians in a Faculty of Education with an Access Program." *Canadian Journal of Education* 22(2): 158–74.

———. 1997b. "The Distorted Images of African Canadians: Impacts, Implications, and Responses." In C. Green (ed.), *Globalization and Survival in the Black Diaspora*. Albany, N.Y.: State University of New York Press.

———. 1996. "Race, Culture, and Identity." In C.E. James (ed.), *Perspectives on Racism and the Human Services Sector: A Case for Change*. Toronto: University of Toronto Press.

———. 1994. "I've never had a Black teacher before." In C.E. James and A. Shadd (eds.), *Talking about Difference: Encounters in Culture, Language and Identity*. Toronto: Between the Lines.

James, Carl E., and Adrienne Shadd (eds.). 1994. *Talking About Difference: Encounters in Culture, Language and Identity*. Toronto: Between the Lines.

Johnson, R., S. Liddell and C. Erting. 1989. "Unlocking the Curriculum: Principles for Achieving Access in Deaf Education." Working/occasional paper series, 89(3). Washington, D.C.: Gallaudet Research Institute.

Julien, Isaac, and Kobena Mercer. 1996. "De Margin and De Centre." In D. Morley and K-H. Chen (eds.), *Critical Dialogues in Cultural Studies*. New York: Routledge.

Kalia, Si. 1991. "Addressing Race in the Feminist Classroom." In J. Gaskell and A. McLaren (eds.), *Women and Education*. Calgary: Detselig.

Kelly, Ursula. 1997. *Schooling Desire: Literacy, Cultural Politics, and Pedagogy*. New York: Routledge.

Khayatt, Didi. 1997. "Sex and the Teacher: Should We Come Out in Class?" *Harvard Educational Review* 67(1): 126–43.

———. 1996. "Revealing Moments: The Voice of One Who Lives with Labels." In C.E. James and A. Shadd (eds.), *Talking About Difference: Encounters in Culture Language and Identity*. Toronto: Between the Lines.

Kinsman, Gary. 1996. *The Regulation of Desire: Homo and Hetero Sexualities*. Montreal: Black Rose Press.

Krashen, S. 1981. *Second Language Acquisition and Second Language Learning*. Oxford: Pergamon Press.

Laghi, B., and K. Makin. 1998. "Court Protects Gays." *Globe and Mail*, April 3, A1.

Lane, H. 1992. *The Mask of Benevolence: Disabling the Deaf Community*. New York: Knopf.

Lee, Stacey. 1996. *Unraveling the "Model Minority" Stereotype: Listening to Asian American Youth*. New York: Teachers College Press.

Leonard, Peter. 1990. "Fatalism and the Discourse of Power: An Introductory Essay." In L. Davies and E. Shragge (eds.), *Bureaucracy and Community*. Montreal: Black Rose.

Li, Peter S. 1988. *The Chinese in Canada*. Toronto: Oxford University Press.

Linton, S. 1998. *Claiming Disability*. New York: State University of New York Press.

Livingston, S. 1997. *Rethinking the Education of Deaf Students: Theory and Practice from a Teachers' Perspective*. Portsmouth, N.H.: Heinemann.

Lorde, Audre. 1984. *Sister Outsider.* Trumansburg, N.Y.: Crossing Press.

Loughran, John, and Jeff Northfield. 1996. *Opening the Classroom Door: Teacher, Researcher, Learner.* London: Falmer Press.

Lucas, C., and C. Valli. 1988. "Language Contact in the Deaf Community: Linguistic Change and Contact." Proceedings of the 16th Conference on New Ways of Analyzing Variation, Texas Language Forum 30, Department of Linguistics, University of Texas, Austin.

Mac an Ghaill, Máirtín. 1994. *The Making of Men: Masculinities, Sexualities and Schooling*. Buckingham: Open University Press.

Magee, B. 1995. *On Blindness: Letters between Bryan Magee and Martin Milligan.* Oxford: Oxford University Press.

Mahshie, S. 1995. *Educating Deaf Children Bilingually*. Washington, D.C.: Gallaudet University Press.

Martin, June Roland. 1994. "Methodological Essentialism, False Difference, and Other Dangerous Traps." *Signs* (Spring).

Mason, D. (forthcoming). "Mainstream Education and Deaf Students (Revised)." *ACEHI Journal*.

Mason, D., and C. Ewoldt. 1999. "Deaf Education, Blind Education: A Dialogue about Assumptions." *Perspectives in Education and Deafness* 17(3): 16–18.

Mather, S., and Mitchell, R. 1994. "Communication Abuse: A Sociolinguistic Perspective." In B. Snider (ed.), *Post-Milan ASL and English Literacy Issues, Trends, and Research*. Washington, D.C.: Gallaudet University College for Continuing Education.

McGibbon, E. 1999. *The Mental Health Experiences of Female Street Youth*. Unpublished master's thesis. Dalhousie University, Halifax, Nova Scotia.

———. 1998. "Racism and Health: Some Reflections." *Street Feat: The Voice of the Poor* 1(7).

McIntosh, Peggy. 1989. "White Privilege: Unpacking the Invisible Knapsack." *Peace and Freedom* (July / August): 10–12.

McKay, Sandra L., and Sau-Ling Cynthia Wong. 1996. "Multiple Discourses, Multiple Identities: Investment and Agency in Second-Language Learning among Chinese Adolescent Immigrant Students." *Harvard Education Review*

6(3): 577–608.
McLaren, Peter. 1991. "Schooling the Postmodern Body: Critical Pedagogy and the Politics of Enfleshment." In H. Giroux (ed.), *Postmodernism, Feminism, and Cultural Politics: Redrawing Educational Boundaries*. New York: State University of New York Press.
McVittie, Janet. 1998. E-mail correspondence. September 29.
Means, Russell. 1980. "Fighting Words on the Future of the Earth." *Mother Jones* (December): 22–28.
Mercredi, O., and M.E. Turpel. 1993. *In the Rapids: Navigating the Future of First Nations*. Toronto: Viking.
Meyer, K. 1998. "Reflections on Being Female in School Science: Toward a Praxis of Teaching Science." *Journal of Research in Science Teaching* 35(4): 463–71.
Milkman, Ruth. 1997. *Farewell to the Factory: Autoworkers in the Late Twentieth Century*. Berkeley: University of California Press.
Mohanty, Chandra Talpade. 1994. "On Race and Voice: Challenges for Liberal Education in the 1990's." In H. Giroux and P. McLaren (eds.), *Between Borders: Pedagogy and the Politics of Cultural Studies*. New York: Routledge.
Monbeck, M. 1973. *The Meaning of Blindness*. Bloomington, Ind.: Indiana University Press.
Monture-Angus, Patricia. 1996. *Thunder in My Soul: A Mohawk Woman Speaks.* Halifax: Fernwood.
Morrison, Toni. 1992. *Playing in the Dark: Whiteness and the Literary Imagination.* New York: Vintage.
Moschkovich, Judith. 1987. "—But I Know You, American Woman." In C. Moraga and G. Anzaldua (eds.), *This Bridge Called My Back: Writings by Radical Women of Color*. Watertown, Mass.: Persephone.
National Association of the Blind. n.d. Video: "That the Blind May Read." Baltimore: National Association of the Blind.
Neumann, E. 1954. *The Origins and History of Consciousness*. R.F.C. Hull (translator). Bollingen Series no. 42. New York: Pantheon.
Ng, Roxanna. 1994. "Sexism and Racism in the University: Analyzing a Personal Experience." *Canadian Woman Studies* 14(2).
Norquay, Naomi. 1993. "The Other Side of Difference: Memory-Work in the Mainstream." *Qualitative Studies in Education* 6(3): 241–51.
Oliver, M. 1990. *The Politics of Disablement*. London: MacMillan.
Padden, C., and T. Humphries. 1988. *Deaf in America: Voices from a Culture*. London: Harvard University Press.
Parker, David. 1995. *Through Different Eyes: The Cultural Identities of Young Chinese People in Britain.* Aldershot: Avebury.
Partridge, James. 1990. *Changing Faces.* London: Penguin.
Peshkin, Alan. 1988. "In Search of Subjectivity—One's Own." *Educational Researcher* (October): 17–21.
Petrone, Penny (ed.). 1983. *First People: First Voices.* Toronto: University of Toronto Press.
Pogrebin, Letty Cottin. 1991. *Deborah, Golda and Me: Being Female and Jewish in America*. New York: Crown.
Pon, M. 1996. "Like a Chinese Puzzle: The Construction of Chinese Masculinity in *Jack Canuck.*" In J. Parr (ed.), *Gender and History in Canada.* Toronto: Copp

Clark.

Porter, John. 1965. *The Vertical Mosaic*. Toronto: University of Toronto Press.

Prince, Althea. 1996. "Black History Month: A Multicultural Myth or 'Have-Blac History-Month-Kit-Will-Travel.'" In K.S. Brathwaite and C.E. James (eds. *Educating African Canadians*. Toronto: Our Schools/Our Selves, Jame Lorimer & Co.

Rachlis, M., and C. Kushner. 1994. *Strong Medicine: How to Save Canada's Healt Care System*. Toronto: Harper Collins.

Razack, Sherene H. 1998. *Looking White People in the Eye: Gender, Race and Culture in Courtrooms and Classrooms*. Toronto: University of Toronto Press.

Reagon, Bernice Johnson. 1983. "Coalition Politics: Turning the Century." In B. Smith (ed.), *Home Girls: A Black Feminist Anthology*. New York: Kitchen Table, Women of Color Press.

Renooy, Lorna. 1999. "Redefining Difference: An Interview with Ani Aubin." *Aboutface: A Support & Information Network Concerned with Facial Differences* 13(1): 1, 4.

Rofes, Eric. 1995. "Making Our Schools Safe for Sissies." In G. Unks (ed.), *The Gay Teen: Education, Practice and Theory for Lesbian, Gay and Bisexual Adolescents*. New York: Routledge.

Root, Maria. 1997. "Mixed-Race Women." In N. Zack (ed.), *Race/Sex: Their Sameness, Difference and Interplay*. New York: Routledge.

Roy, Arundhati. 1997. *The God of Small Things*. Toronto: Vintage Canada.

Rutherford, Jonathan. 1990. "A Place Called Home: Identity and the Cultural Politics of Difference." In J. Rutherford (ed.), *Identity: Community, Culture, Difference*. London: Lawrence and Wishart.

Salisbury, Jonathan, and D. Jackson. 1996. *Challenging Macho Values: Practical Ways of Working with Adolescent Boys*. London: Falmer.

Samis, S., and S. Goundry. 1998. "The First National Survey of Lesbians, Gay Men and Bisexuals in Canada." Ottawa: EGALE (Equality for Gays and Lesbians Everywhere).

Saul, R. 1993. *Voltaire's Bastards: The Dictatorship of Reason in the West*. Toronto: Penguin.

Schulz, P. 1980. *How does it feel to be blind? The Psychodynamics of Visual Impairment*. Los Angeles: Muse-Ed Company.

Schuster, Charles I., and William van Pelt (eds.). 1992, *Speculations: Readings in Culture, Identity and Values*. Englewood Cliffs, N.J.: Blair.

Scotch, R. 1988. "Disability as the Basis for a Social Movement: Advocacy and the Politics of Definition." *Journal of Social Issues* 44(1): 159–72.

Simon, Roger. 1992. *Teaching Against the Grain: Texts for a Pedagogy of Possibility*. Toronto: Ontario Institute for Studies in Education (OISE) Press.

Singleton, Sharon. 1994. "Faculty Personal Comfort and the Teaching of Content on Racial Oppression." *Journal of Multicultural Social Work* 3(1): 5–16.

Smith, George W. 1998. "The Ideology of 'Fag': The School Experience of Gay Students." *Sociology Quarterly* 39(2): 309–35.

Spelman, Elizabeth. 1988. *Inessential Woman: Problems of Exclusion in Feminist Thought*. Boston: Beacon.

Statistics Canada. 1996. Census. Ottawa: Supply and Services Canada.

Taliaferro, Martena B. 1991. "The Myth of Empowerment." *Journal of Negro Edu-*

cation 60(1): 1–2.
eeple, Gary. 1995. *Globalization and the Decline of Social Reform.* Toronto: Garamond.
izard, Barbara, and Ann Phoenix. 1993. *Black, White or Mixed Race? Race and Racism in the Lives of Young People of Mixed Parentage.* New York: Routledge.
Toronto Star. 1998. "How 28 bar exam failures became lawyers." Saturday, October 24, A1 and A25.
Tsang, Pui Yee Beryl. 1994. "There's a White Man in My Bed: Scenes from an Interracial Marriage." In C.E. James and A. Shadd (eds.), *Talking about Difference: Encounters in Culture, Language and Identity.* Toronto: Between the Lines.
Valaskakis, G. 1993. "Postcards of My Past: The Indian as Artefact." In V. Blundell, J. Shepherd and I. Taylor (eds.), *Relocating Cultural Studies: Developments in Theory and Research.* London: Routledge.
Vernon, M., and S. Koh. 1971. "Effects of Oral Preschool Compared to Early Manual Communication on Education and Communication in Deaf Children. *American Annals of the Deaf* 116: 569–74.
Vizenor, G. 1984. *The People Named the Chippewa: Narrative Histories.* Minneapolis: University of Minnesota Press.
———. 1972. *The Everlasting Sky: New Voices from the People Named the Chippewa.* New York: Crowell-Collier Press.
Weinstein, Gerald, and Donna Mellen. 1997. "Antisemitism Curriculum Design." In M. Adams, L.A. Bell and P. Griffin (eds.), *Teaching for Diversity and Social Justice.* New York: Routledge.
Weir, Lorna. 1991. "Anti-Racist Feminist Pedagogy, Self-Observed." *Resources for Feminist Research/Documentation sur la Recherche Feministe* 3/4: 19–26.
Wexler, Philip. 1992. *Becoming Somebody: Toward a Social Psychology of School.* London: Falmer.
Wienke, Chris. 1998. "Negotiating the Male Body: Men, Masculinity, and Cultural Ideas." *American Journal of Men's Studies* 6(2): 255–82.
Williams, Patricia. 1997. *Seeing a Color-Blind Future: The Paradox of Race.* New York: Noonday Press.
Willis, Paul. 1977. *Learning to Labor: How Working Class Kids Get Working Class Jobs.* New York: Columbia University Press.
Wilton, T. 1995. *Lesbian Studies: Setting an Agenda.* New York: Routledge.
Wong, Sau Ling Cynthia. 1993. *Reading Asian American Literature: From Necessity to Extravagance.* Princeton University Press.
Woon, Yuen-Fong. 1998. *The Excluded Wife.* Montreal: McGill-Queens University Press.
Wright, B. 1960. *Physical Disability: A Psychological Approach.* New York: Harper & Row.
Yee, May. 1993. "Finding the way home through issues of gender, race, and class." In Himani Bannerji (ed.), *Returning the Gaze: Essays on Racism, Feminism and Politics.* Toronto: Sister Vision Press.
Yúdice, George. 1995. "What's a Straight White Man to Do?" In M. Berger, B. Wallis and S. Watson (eds.), *Constructing Masculinity.* New York: Routledge.
Zack, Naomi. 1993. *Race and Mixed Race.* Philadelphia: Temple University Press.
Zack, Naomi. (ed). 1995. *American Mixed Race: The Culture of Microdiversity.* Lanham, MD: Roman & Littlefield.